W9-DFX-872

THE WORLD BOOK ENCYCLOPEDIA OF
PEOPLE AND PLACES

THE WORLD BOOK ENCYCLOPEDIA OF PEOPLE AND PLACES

4/M-R

WORLD BOOK, INC.
a Scott Fetzer company
CHICAGO

Acknowledgments:

Front cover
large photo, © PhotoDisc, Inc.
left inset, © Victor Englebert
center inset, © Corbis
right inset, © Neil Rabinowitz, Corbis

Back cover
© PhotoDisc, Inc.

For information on other World Book publications, visit our Web site at **http://www.worldbook.com** or call **1-800-WORLDBOOK (967-5325).** For information on sales to schools and libraries, call **1-800-975-3250 (United States); 1-800-837-5365 (Canada).**

THE WORLD BOOK ENCYCLOPEDIA OF PEOPLE AND PLACES

This edition published by
World Book, Inc.
233 N. Michigan Ave.
Chicago, IL 60601

The Library of Congress has cataloged a previous edition of this title as follows:

Library of Congress Cataloging-in-Publication Data

The World Book encyclopedia of people and places.
p. cm.
Includes index.
~~ISBN 0-7166-3750-2~~
1. Encyclopedias and dictionaries. [1. Geography—Encyclopedias.] I. World Book, Inc.

AE5 . W563 2001
031.02—dc21

~~2001023546~~

ISBN 0-7166-3754-5 (this edition)

Printed in the United States of America

15 16 05 04 03

Staff

Contents

Political World Map

The world has 193 independent countries and about 40 dependencies. An independent country controls its own affairs. Dependencies are controlled in some way by independent countries. In most cases, an independent country is responsible for the dependency's foreign relations and defense, and some of the dependency's local affairs. However, many dependencies have complete control of their local affairs.

By 2000, the world's population surpassed 6 billion, and the yearly rate of population growth was about 1.4 per cent. At that rate, the world's population would double in about 49 years. Almost all of the world's people live in independent countries. Only about 10 million people live in dependencies.

Some regions of the world, including Antarctica and certain desert areas, have no permanent population. The most densely populated regions of the world are in Europe and in southern and eastern Asia. The world's largest country in terms of population is China, which has more than a billion people. The independent country with the smallest population is Vatican City, with only about 1,000 people. The Vatican City, covering only 1/6 square mile (0.4 square kilometer), is also the smallest in terms of size. The world's largest nation in terms of area is Russia, which covers 6,592,850 square miles (17,075,400 square kilometers).

Every nation depends on other nations in some ways. The interdependence of the entire world and its peoples is called *globalism.* Nations trade with one another to earn money and to obtain manufactured goods or the natural resources that they lack. Nations with similar interests and political beliefs may pledge to support one another in case of war. Developed countries provide developing nations with financial aid and technical assistance. Such aid strengthens trade as well as defense ties.

Nations of the World

Name	Map key
Afghanistan	D 13
Albania	C 11
Algeria	D 10
Andorra	C 10‡
Angola	F 10
Antigua and Barbuda	E 6
Argentina	G 6
Armenia	C 12
Australia	G 16
Austria	C 10
Azerbaijan	C 12
Bahamas	D 6
Bahrain	D 12
Bangladesh	D 14
Barbados	E 7
Belarus	C 11
Belgium	C 10
Belize	E 5
Benin	E 10
Bhutan	D 14
Bolivia	F 6
Bosnia-Herzegovina	C 11
Botswana	G 11
Brazil	F 7
Brunei	E 15
Bulgaria	C 11
Burkina Faso	E 9
Burundi	F 11
Cambodia	E 15
Cameroon	E 10
Canada	C 4
Cape Verde	E 8
Central African Republic	E 10
Chad	E 10
Chile	G 6
China	D 14
Colombia	E 6
Comoros	F 12
Congo (Brazzaville)	F 10
Congo (Kinshasa)	F 11
Costa Rica	E 5
Côte d'Ivoire	E 9
Croatia	C 11
Cuba	D 5
Cyprus	D 11
Czech Republic	C 11
Denmark	C 10
Djibouti	E 12
Dominica	E 6
Dominican Republic	E 6
East Timor	F 16
Ecuador	F 6
Egypt	D 11
El Salvador	E 5
Equatorial Guinea	E 10
Eritrea	E 11
Estonia	E 11
Ethiopia	E 11
Federated States of Micronesia	E 18
Fiji	F 1
Finland	B 11
France	C 10
Gabon	F 10
Gambia	E 9
Georgia	C 12
Germany	C 10
Ghana	E 9
Great Britain	C 9
Greece	D 11
Grenada	E 6
Guatemala	E 5
Guinea	E 9
Guinea-Bissau	E 9

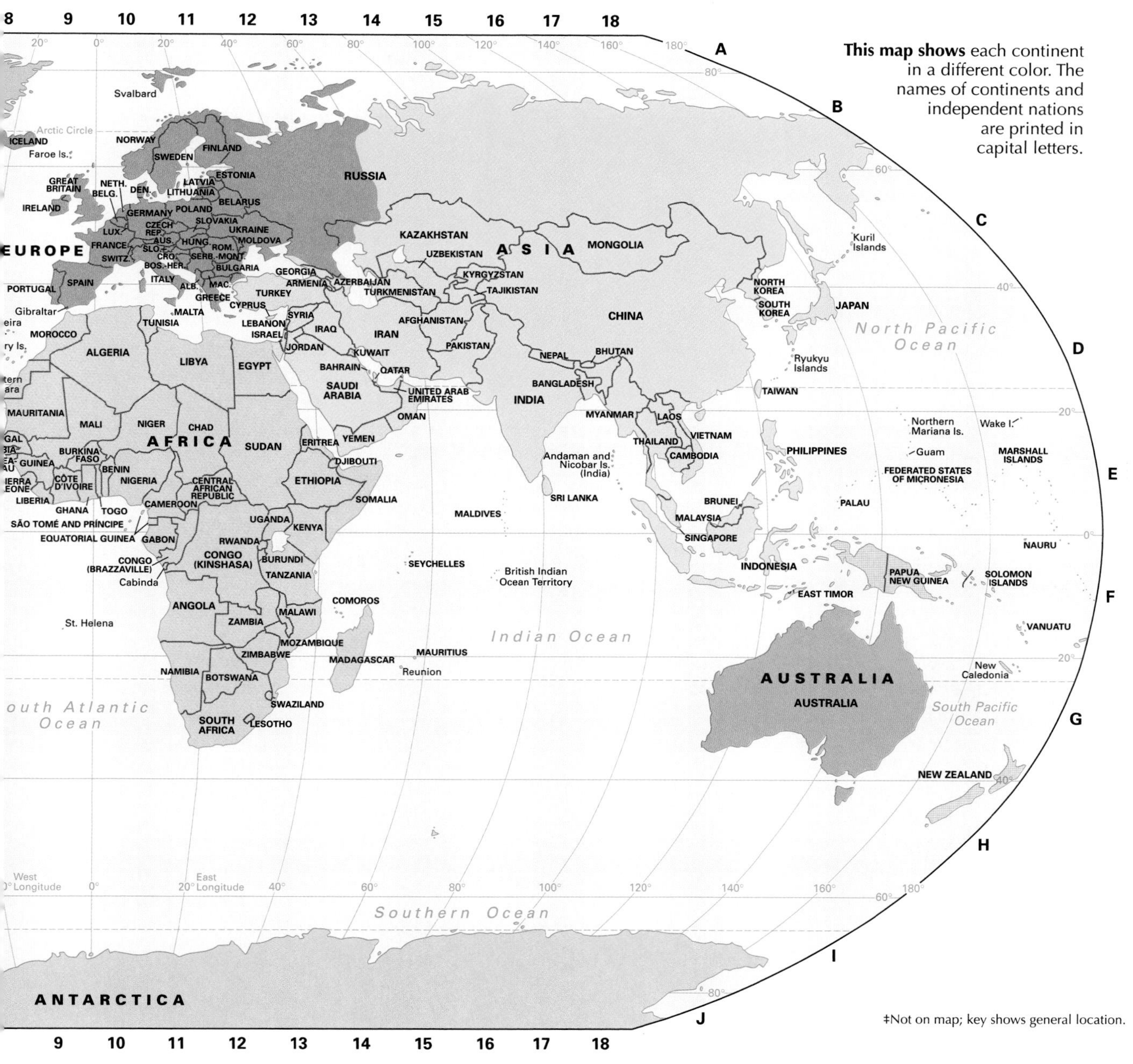

This map shows each continent in a different color. The names of continents and independent nations are printed in capital letters.

‡Not on map; key shows general location.

Name	Map key
Guyana	E 7
Haiti	E 6
Honduras	E 5
Hungary	C 10
Iceland	B 9
India	D 13
Indonesia	F 16
Iran	D 12
Iraq	D 12
Ireland	C 9
Israel	D 11
Italy	C 10
Jamaica	E 6
Japan	D 16
Jordan	D 11
Kazakhstan	C 13
Kenya	E 11
Kiribati	F 1
Korea, North	C 16
Korea, South	D 16
Kuwait	D 12
Kyrgyzstan	C 13
Laos	E 15
Latvia	C 11

Name	Map key
Lebanon	D 11
Lesotho	G 11
Liberia	E 9
Libya	D 10
Liechtenstein	C 10‡
Lithuania	C 11
Luxembourg	C 10
Macedonia	C 11
Madagascar	F 12
Malawi	F 11
Malaysia	E 15
Maldives	E 13
Mali	E 9
Malta	D 10
Marshall Islands	E 18
Mauritania	D 9
Mauritius	G 12
Mexico	D 4
Moldova	C 11
Monaco	C 10‡
Mongolia	C 15
Morocco	D 9
Mozambique	F 11
Myanmar	D 14

Name	Map key
Namibia	G 11
Nauru	F 18
Nepal	D 14
Netherlands	C 10
New Zealand	G 18
Nicaragua	E 5
Niger	E 10
Nigeria	E 10
Norway	B 10
Oman	E 12
Pakistan	D 13
Palau	E 16
Panama	E 5
Papua New Guinea	F 17
Paraguay	G 7
Peru	F 6
Philippines	E 16
Poland	C 10
Portugal	D 9
Qatar	D 12
Romania	C 11
Russia	C 13
Rwanda	F 11
St. Kitts and Nevis	E 6‡

Name	Map key
St. Lucia	E 6
St. Vincent and the Grenadines	E 6
Samoa	F 1
San Marino	C 10‡
São Tomé and Príncipe	E 10
Saudi Arabia	D 12
Senegal	E 9
Serbia and Montenegro	C 10
Seychelles	F 12
Sierra Leone	E 9
Singapore	E 15
Slovakia	C 11
Slovenia	C 11
Solomon Islands	F 18
Somalia	E 12
South Africa	G 11
Spain	C 9
Sri Lanka	E 14
Sudan	E 11
Suriname	E 7
Swaziland	G 11
Sweden	B 10
Switzerland	C 10
Syria	D 11

Name	Map key
Taiwan	D 16
Tajikistan	D 13
Tanzania	F 11
Thailand	E 15
Togo	E 9
Tonga	F 1
Trinidad and Tobago	E 6
Tunisia	D 10
Turkey	D 11
Turkmenistan	D 12
Tuvalu	F 1
Uganda	E 11
Ukraine	C 11
United Arab Emirates	D 12
United States	C 4
Uruguay	G 7
Uzbekistan	C 13
Vanuatu	F 18
Vatican City	C 10‡
Venezuela	E 6
Vietnam	E 15
Yemen	E 12
Zambia	F 11
Zimbabwe	G 11

Macedonia

Macedonia is a mountainous land in the Balkan Peninsula in southeastern Europe. Formerly one of the six republics of Yugoslavia, Macedonia withdrew from the federation and declared its independence in 1991.

About 67 per cent of the people in Macedonia belong to the Macedonian nationality group and speak their own Slavic language, which is similar to Bulgarian. Many of Macedonia's cultural traditions, including music, arts, and crafts, have remained free from outside influences. As a result, Macedonian songs, dances, embroidery, carpet weaving, and woodcarving have a style all their own. Even so, the Macedonians' claim to a separate, national identity has been challenged. From earliest times, various ethnic groups have laid claim to this mountainous region situated in the heart of the Balkan Peninsula.

The name *Macedonia* originally referred to a region that included parts of Greece and Bulgaria as well as present-day Macedonia. After about the 800's B.C., the Macedonians came under the influence of the Greeks. The son of King Philip II of Macedonia, Alexander the Great, conquered the Persian Empire in 331 B.C. and founded a vast empire on its ruins.

Macedonia was a Roman province from the 140's B.C. to A.D. 395, when the region became part of the Byzantine Empire. Macedonia was included in the first Bulgarian Empire in the 800's and in the Serbian Empire in the early 1300's. In 1371, the Ottoman Turks began their conquest of the region and ruled Macedonia for over 500 years.

Under Ottoman rule, various groups fought for dominance in Macedonia. The Greeks claimed the entire southern region, the Serbs claimed the northern region around Skopje, their ancient capital, and the Bulgarians claimed all of Macedonia except for the southern region.

The First Balkan War (1912–1913) freed Macedonia from the Ottomans. The area was finally divided between Greece, Serbia, and Bulgaria after the Second Balkan War in 1913. The peace treaties that followed World War I (1914–1918) divided Macedonia among three nations. The largest region became part of the new Kingdom of the Serbs, Croats, and Slovenes (which later changed its name to Yugoslavia). Smaller sections of Macedonia went to Greece and Bulgaria.

During World War II (1939–1945), Axis forces invaded and occupied Yugoslavia. Macedonia was partitioned between Bulgaria and Albania, both allies of the Axis powers. The section given to Albania became part of Greater Albania, a state created by Italian dictator Benito Mussolini.

After World War II, when Yugoslavia became a federal republic under Communist

COUNTRY

Official name: Republika Makedonija (The Former Yugoslav Republic of Macedonia)
Capital: Skopje
Terrain: Mountainous territory covered with deep basins and valleys; three large lakes, each divided by a frontier line; country bisected by the Vardar River
Area: 9,781 sq. mi. (25,333 km^2)
Climate: Warm, dry summers and autumns and relatively cold winters with heavy snowfall
Main river: Vardar
Highest elevation: Mount Korab (Golem Korab), 9,068 ft. (2,764 m)
Lowest elevation: Vardar River, 164 ft. (50 m)

GOVERNMENT

Form of government: Emerging democracy
Head of state: President
Head of government: Prime minister
Administrative areas: 34 opstini (counties)
Legislature: Sobranje (Assembly) with 120 members serving four-year terms
Court system: Constitutional Court, Judicial Court of the Republic
Armed forces: 16,000 troops

PEOPLE

Estimated 2002 population: 2,048,000
Population growth: 0.04%
Population density: 206 persons per sq. mi. (80 per km^2)
Population distribution: 59% urban, 41% rural
Life expectancy in years:
Male: 72
Female: 76
Doctors per 1,000 people: 2.2
Percentage of age-appropriate population enrolled in the following educational levels:
Primary: 103*
Secondary: 83
Further: 22

rule, the section of Macedonia in Yugoslavia became the Republic of Macedonia, one of six Yugoslav republics. Funding from Yugoslavia's government helped build new roads, the tourist trade, and heavy industry.

Many people still make their living as farmers, however, raising cotton, grapes, rice, tobacco, and vegetables. Extensive irrigation systems provide water for about 20 per cent of the farmland. The republic is also rich in mineral resources, including chrome, copper, gold, iron ore, lead, manganite, mercury, nickel, silver, and zinc.

In the 1990's, tension surrounded the newly independent Macedonia. Greece opposed recognition of the new country because it saw the use of the name *Macedonia* as a claim to some of its territory. Also, Macedonia feared it might be drawn into the conflict between other former Yugoslav states. The United Nations sent troops to protect the country in late 1992.

In 1993, Macedonia and Greece reached a compromise allowing Macedonia to join the United Nations under the temporary name of the Former Yugoslav Republic of Macedonia. Greece still objected to the name Macedonia and to its flag, so Greece applied a trade embargo to the country in 1994. Greece lifted the embargo in 1995 in exchange for Macedonia's pledge to change its flag and to make no claims to territory outside its borders.

The traditional costumes of Macedonia, *above,* which show an Oriental influence, are sometimes worn on special occasions.

Languages spoken:
Macedonian 70%
Albanian 21%
Turkish 3%
Serbo-Croatian 3%

Religions:
Macedonian Orthodox 67%
Muslim 30%

*Enrollment ratios compare the number of students enrolled to the population which, by age, should be enrolled. A ratio higher than 100 indicates that students older or younger than the typical age range are also enrolled.

TECHNOLOGY

Radios per 1,000 people: 205

Televisions per 1,000 people: 282

Computers per 1,000 people: N/A

ECONOMY

Currency: Macedonian denar

Gross national income (GNI) in 2000: $3.7 billion U.S.

Real annual growth rate (1999–2000): 4.3%

GNI per capita (2000): $1,820 U.S.

Balance of payments (2000): -$107 million U.S.

Goods exported: Food, beverages, tobacco; miscellaneous manufactures, iron and steel

Goods imported: Machinery and equipment, chemicals, fuels; food products

Trading partners: Germany, Serbia and Montenegro, United States, Slovenia

A country of towering mountains and broad plains, Macedonia is bordered by Serbia and Montenegro, Bulgaria, Greece, and Albania. Skopje is the capital and largest city.

Madagascar

The country of Madagascar is made up of one large island off the east coast of Africa and a number of small nearby islands. The large island, also called Madagascar, is the fourth largest island in the world.

Cool, temperate highlands make up much of the island of Madagascar. Central Madagascar consists of plateaus and hills that rise 2,000 to 4,000 feet (610 to 1,200 meters) and some mountains that are even higher. In the north, Maromokotro rises more than 9,000 feet (2,800 meters) above sea level.

Much of the highland region has been *deforested* (cleared of its trees), and therefore much of the soil has eroded. This region has the densest population, however, and the capital city of Antananarivo is located in the highlands. Because of its altitude, temperatures at Antananarivo range from 50° to 67° F. (13° to 19° C).

The mountains separate northern Madagascar, which has some of the country's richest soil, from the rest of the island. Southern Madagascar is mainly desert, and people of isolated southern tribes often wear little clothing in the hot, dry climate.

Western Madagascar has wide plains, some fertile river valleys, and a fairly sheltered coast. Eastern Madagascar, on the other hand, is a narrow plain, and offshore reefs and storms make the east coast dangerous for ships. Both coasts are warm and humid.

About 80 per cent of Madagascar's people make their living as farmers and herders. Rice is their chief food crop. Cassava, bananas and other fruits, and vegetables such as sweet potatoes are also grown for their own use. Cattle is the country's most important livestock, though meat is not eaten regularly.

Coffee is Madagascar's most valuable export crop, and the country is also the world's leading producer of natural vanilla and cloves. Other agricultural exports include sugar and *sisal,* which is used to make rope.

The country has a few valuable mineral resources. Chromite, graphite, and some semiprecious stones are mined.

Madagascar's few industries process the country's agricultural products—hides, meat, sisal, and sugar—for export. During the 1970's, military leaders took control of certain kinds of businesses. But since 1983, the government has reduced its role in the national economy.

Most of the roads that link the chief towns and cities of Madagascar are unpaved, and many are badly rutted and impassable during the rainy season. In the desert of southern Madagascar, people often use cattle, such as zebu, to haul heavy wooden carts loaded with goods.

Mahajanga on the west coast and Toamasina on the east coast are the leading seaports. Ships that need to sail along the dangerous east coast can use the Ampanalana Canal, which runs between Mahavelona and Farafangana.

A fisherman angles for his dinner in a peaceful Madagascar setting. Fish is an occasional dish for the islanders. But rice, vegetables, and fruit form the basis of the people's diet.

Tourism is not a major source of income in Madagascar, but the island has much to attract visitors. For example, Madagascar has distinctive plants and animals that are found nowhere else except on the nearby Comoros Islands. The island also offers travelers a fascinating glimpse of a unique culture. Local people practice traditional religions that include the worship of ancestors and spirits, cattle sacrifices, and ceremonies at the tombs of family members.

Grassy hills make up much of the highland landscape of central Madagascar. The highlands were once forested, but the trees were cut down, and the soil has eroded.

Goods are unloaded from a transport ship at a northern port in Madagascar. The country imports petroleum, machinery, and other products.

Balconied apartments, *center,* and a church crowd one another in a highland town. Many houses in the country are several stories high and built of brick, with tile or thatched roofs.

Woven mats are offered for sale at a street market. Market days are a popular part of life in Antananarivo, the capital city, and other Madagascar towns.

Madagascar Today

Madagascar's population is made up mostly of farmers or herders of either black African or Indonesian descent. More than 40 per cent of the people practice Christianity, and 7 per cent are Muslims. The rest worship ancestors and spirits according to traditional African religious beliefs. Madagascar has two official languages—French and Malagasy.

Government

In August 1992, Madagascar's voters approved a new Constitution. The Constitution provided for a two-tier legislature, made up of a National Assembly and a Senate. The National Assembly is elected under a system of proportional representation to serve four-year terms. The president is elected to a five-year term. The prime minister, the head of government, is elected by the National Assembly.

Historical background

Madagascar was settled by Indonesians who sailed across the Indian Ocean from the east—a migration that started before the time of Christ and continued until the A.D. 1400's. They settled in the central highlands of the

Crowds of shoppers throng a steep-staired, bustling thoroughfare in Antananarivo, *right,* the capital of Madagascar. Some of the signs recall the country's period of French rule.

Fact Box

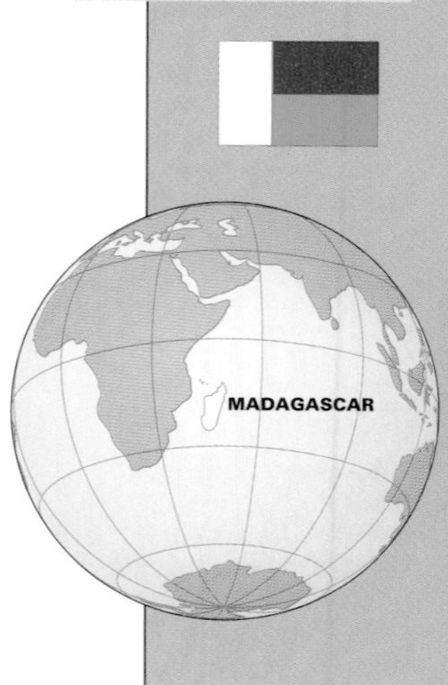

Country

Official name: Republique de Madagascar (Republic of Madagascar)
Capital: Antananarivo
Terrain: Narrow coastal plain, high plateau and mountains in center
Area: 226,657 sq. mi. (587,040 km^2)
Climate: Tropical along coast, temperate inland, arid in south
Main rivers: Betsiboka, Mangoky
Highest elevation: Maromokotro, 9,436 ft. (2,876 m)
Lowest elevation: Indian Ocean, sea level

Government

Form of government: Republic
Head of state: President
Head of government: Prime minister
Administrative areas: 6 faritany (provinces)
Legislature: Assemblee Nationale (National Assembly) with 150 members serving four-year terms
Court system: Cour Supreme (Supreme Court), Haute Cour Constitutionnelle (High Constitutional Court)
Armed forces: 21,000 troops

People

Estimated 2002 population: 16,811,000
Population growth: 3.02%
Population density: 74 persons per sq. mi. (29 per km^2)
Population distribution: 78% rural, 22% urban
Life expectancy in years:
Male: 53
Female: 57
Doctors per 1,000 people: 0.1
Percentage of age-appropriate population enrolled in the following educational levels:
Primary: 93
Secondary: 16
Further: 2

large island. Immigrants from the African mainland and the Arabian Peninsula settled along the coasts.

Madagascar was a favorite base for pirates in the 1600's and 1700's, including the notorious Scottish pirate known as Captain Kidd.

A number of kingdoms developed on what is now Madagascar, but in the early 1800's, the Merina kingdom, whose people were of Indonesian descent, gained control of most of the island. Radama I, who became the Merina king in 1810, outlawed the foreign slave trade, but kept many of his own people in slavery.

English and French traders and missionaries brought European influences to the island. After 1869, the French expanded their political influence on the island. Conflicts broke out between the French and the Merina. The French forces gained control, and France made all of Madagascar a French colony in 1896.

France granted the people of Madagascar some self-rule after World War II (1939–1945). Full independence was finally granted in 1960, but French influence remained strong in the new nation, called the Malagasy Republic.

In May 1972, demonstrations caused elected President Philibert Tsiranana to resign. A series of military rulers took over the government as well as important parts of the country's economy. In late 1975, the military government under Didier Ratsiraka changed the name of the nation to Madagascar.

In 1977, the nation became a republic again as the people elected a legislature. In 1982, they elected Ratsiraka president and reelected him in a one-party election in 1989. In 1991, protests against the government and general strikes led to the dissolution of the government. Although Ratsiraka remained in office, he was forced to share power with members of the opposition. In 1993, Albert Zafy, the leader of the opposition, was elected to replace Ratsiraka.

In 1996, Zafy resigned after the National Assembly impeached him on charges that he had engaged in unconstitutional acts. Ratsiraka was reelected president in a special election. After a violently disputed election that led to a vote recount, Marc Ravalomanana, former mayor of Antananarivo, succeeded Ratsiraka as president in 2002.

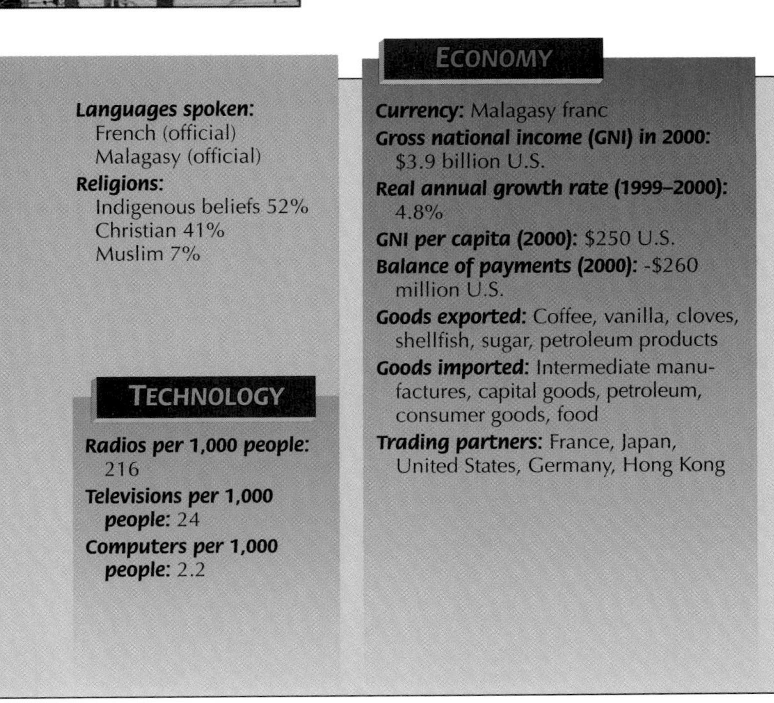

Languages spoken:
French (official)
Malagasy (official)

Religions:
Indigenous beliefs 52%
Christian 41%
Muslim 7%

Technology

Radios per 1,000 people: 216

Televisions per 1,000 people: 24

Computers per 1,000 people: 2.2

Economy

Currency: Malagasy franc

Gross national income (GNI) in 2000: $3.9 billion U.S.

Real annual growth rate (1999–2000): 4.8%

GNI per capita (2000): $250 U.S.

Balance of payments (2000): -$260 million U.S.

Goods exported: Coffee, vanilla, cloves, shellfish, sugar, petroleum products

Goods imported: Intermediate manufactures, capital goods, petroleum, consumer goods, food

Trading partners: France, Japan, United States, Germany, Hong Kong

Wildlife

The huge island of Madagascar is home to unusual wildlife. In fact, most of Madagascar's animals and plants are found nowhere else in the world except the nearby Comoros Islands. This makes the island a unique resource for biologists and other scientists. But Madagascar is also home to nearly 16 million people, and that number is expected to double between 2000 and 2024. As a result, much of this remarkable wildlife is at risk.

Madagascar was once part of the African mainland. About 125 million years ago, the piece of land that became Madagascar broke away and drifted north and east. The water that separates the island from the African mainland, now a passage 240 miles (386 kilometers) wide, prevented most mainland animals from spreading to Madagascar and most Madagascar animals from spreading to the mainland.

In the process of *evolution,* groups of animals change over time as they adapt to changes in their environment. The animals on Madagascar changed in isolation and developed in different ways from the animals on mainland Africa. For example, the absence of competition from monkeys and large predators allowed animals called *lemurs* to evolve from an animal that died out almost everywhere else.

The size of the island and the variety of weather conditions there permitted the development of numerous unique species of plants and animals. A listing of Madagascar's wildlife includes 1,000 species of orchids, almost all of them native only to Madagascar; 800 species of moths and butterflies; 50 of the world's 100 species of chameleons; and 22 species of lemurs.

Scientists classify lemurs as primates, together with monkeys, apes, and human beings. On Madagascar, lemurs range in size from the 2-ounce (56-gram) gray mouse lemur—the world's smallest primate—to the black-and-white indri, weighing about 20 pounds (9 kilograms).

All but the ring-tailed lemur travel in trees rather than on land. The indri and the sifaka can cover more than 30 feet in a single leap from one tree trunk to another. Some lemurs are nocturnal; others are *diurnal*—that is, active during the day.

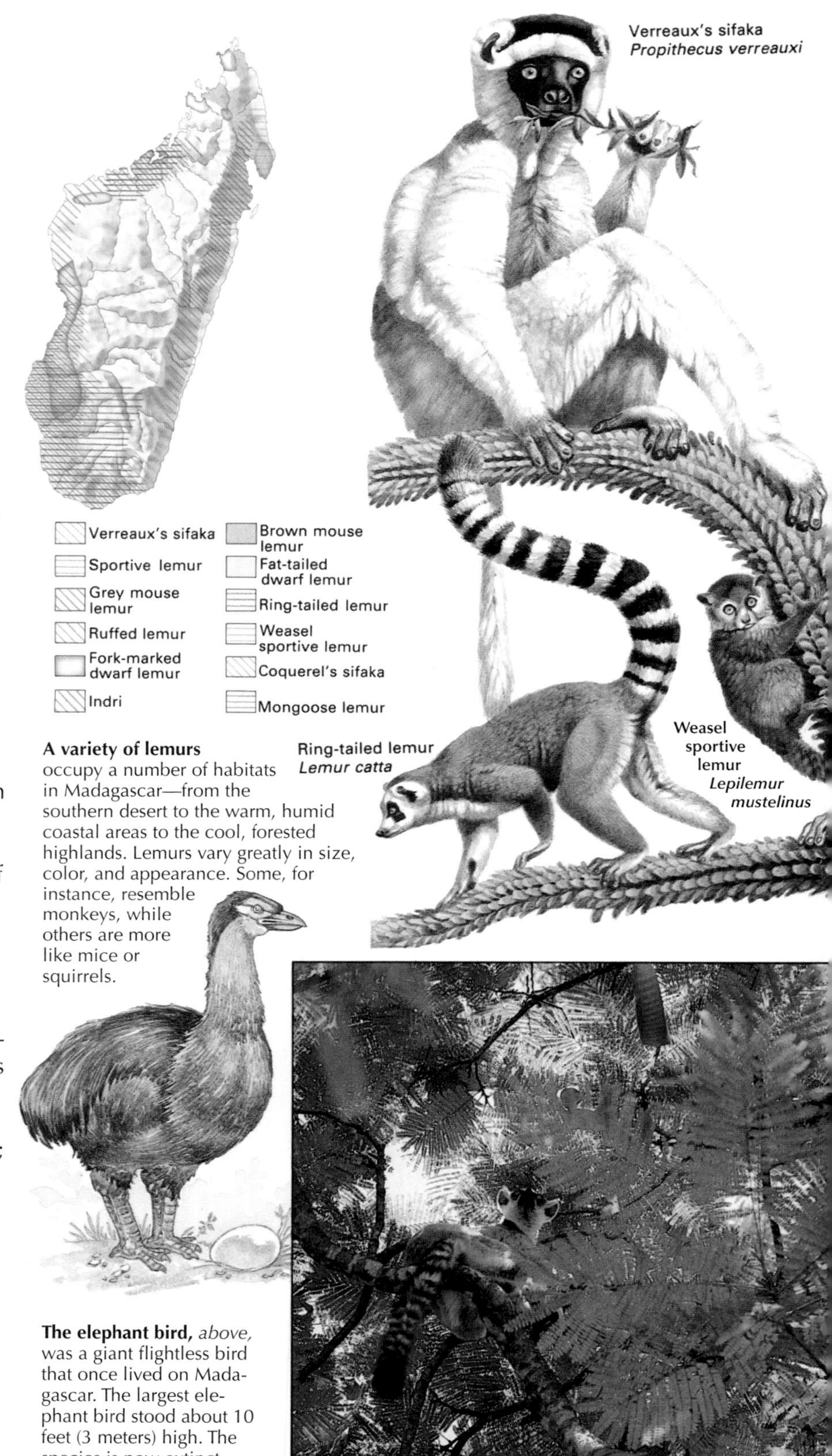

A variety of lemurs occupy a number of habitats in Madagascar—from the southern desert to the warm, humid coastal areas to the cool, forested highlands. Lemurs vary greatly in size, color, and appearance. Some, for instance, resemble monkeys, while others are more like mice or squirrels.

The elephant bird, *above,* was a giant flightless bird that once lived on Madagascar. The largest elephant bird stood about 10 feet (3 meters) high. The species is now extinct.

The ring-tailed lemur, *far left,* is one of the most common species of lemur.

The lesser mouse lemur, *left,* is the smallest existing primate, weighing about 2 ounces (60 grams).

The aye-aye, *below,* is a unique lemur that uses its long narrow middle fingers to draw insect larvae out of tree branches. The aye-aye is now considered an endangered species.

Some lemurs—such as the ring-tailed and ruffed lemurs—resemble monkeys. Others—for example, the lesser mouse lemur—are more like mice. The aye-aye lemur plays the ecological role that woodpeckers play elsewhere, eating insect larvae that it digs out of tree branches.

Madagascar's lemurs have few natural enemies because the island has few large predators. Today, however, many species are endangered, mainly because people have cut down so many trees to build villages, clear farmland, or harvest the timber. The rain forest on the east side of the island is shrinking. There and in other regions of Madagascar, the lemurs' habitat is disappearing.

Without its forest or grass cover, *erosion*—the wearing away of the fertile top layer of soil—is occurring rapidly. If this destruction of vegetation is left unchecked, not only lemur species but also a native eagle, two large tortoises, and other unique animals may become extinct.

Human destruction of animal habitats has already caused the extinction of several of Madagascar's animals, including a lemur the size of an orangutan, giant tortoises with shells 4 feet (1.2 meters) long, a pygmy hippopotamus, and the elephant bird.

The elephant bird was huge—up to 10 feet (3 meters) high and weighing about 1,000 pounds (450 kilograms). Old legends tell of a giant bird called a roc, and some people think that the legends were based on the elephant bird.

Seven species of the elephant bird were widespread on Madagascar when people first arrived about 2,000 years ago. The last of these birds were sighted in the 1600's.

The people and government of Madagascar have long recognized the importance of the island's wildlife both to science and to their own economy. The hunting of lemurs has been illegal since 1927, and the country has 34 wildlife preserves.

Since the 1980's, however, more attention has been given to the problem. In 1984, the government established a National Conservation Strategy. Its goals include educating the population about the need for conservation, restoring woodlands, eliminating soil erosion, and protecting endangered animals.

Malawi

Malawi, a small nation in southeastern Africa, is a poor country, but one that is rich in natural beauty. Several lakes, including deep blue Lake Nyasa, lie in the Great Rift Valley that runs the length of Malawi from north to south. West of Lake Nyasa, the land rises steeply to a plateau. Grasslands and *savannas* (grassy plains with scattered trees) cover much of the region, but hardwood forests stretch across the northwest.

The country's magnificent landscape is partly responsible for its poverty. Malawi's economy is based on agriculture, yet its mountains, forests, and infertile pastures cover so much of the land that only about one-third of the area can be farmed. Malawi has no important mineral deposits and very little industry. A few factories produce bricks, cement, cotton goods, and processed foods. The government has tried to encourage foreign investment and aid.

Although little of the land is farmed, Malawi has areas of rich volcanic soil—perfect for growing tea, the nation's most important export crop. The tea is grown on highland plantations owned by Europeans. Malawi farmers also grow a variety of other crops, including corn, sorghum, cotton, peanuts, sugar cane, and tobacco. Many farmers raise livestock too, and some people fish for a living.

Traditionally, Malawi women raised the food crops, while the men provided the family's meat and fish. Today, both men and women farm the land—women grow the food crops while men raise most of the crops grown for sale.

Women have a special position in Malawi society. In most Western traditions, the father is the head of the family, and descent is determined through him. But most people in Malawi determine descent through the mother. Couples often establish their households near the wife's family.

Most of Malawi's people are black Africans who belong to Bantu groups. The leading Bantu ethnic groups are the Chewa (Cewa), Lomwe, Nyanja, Yao, and Ngoni (Angoni). Chichewa and English are the official languages of the country, but most people in central and southern Malawi speak Nyanja and Yao. Tumbuka is spoken by most people in the north.

Bantu-speaking people began living in the region about 2,000 years ago, and some formed kingdoms—including the Kingdom of Malawi, which was established during the 1500's. In the 1830's, two other Bantu

Fishermen prepare to launch their canoes on Lake Chilwa, *far right*. Freshwater fishing on Malawi's lakes, especially Lake Nyasa, contributes to the diet of the people of this poor country, where only about a third of the land is suitable for farming. Fishing has also become an important industry in Malawi.

FACT BOX

MALAWI

COUNTRY

Official name: Republic of Malawi
Capital: Lilongwe
Terrain: Narrow elongated plateau with rolling plains, rounded hills, some mountains
Area: 45,745 sq. mi. (118,480 km^2)
Climate: Sub-tropical; rainy season (November to May); dry season (May to November)
Main rivers: Shire, Bua
Highest elevation: Sapitwa, 9,843 ft. (3,000 m)
Lowest elevation: Junction of the Shire River and international boundary with Mozambique, 121 ft. (37 m)

GOVERNMENT

Form of government: Republic
Head of state: President
Head of government: President
Administrative areas: 24 districts
Legislature: National Assembly with 193 members serving five-year terms
Court system: Supreme Court of Appeal, High Court, magistrate's courts
Armed forces: 5,000 troops

PEOPLE

Estimated 2002 population: 11,449,000
Population growth: 1.61%
Population density: 250 persons per sq. mi. (97 per km^2)
Population distribution: 80% rural, 20% urban
Life expectancy in years:
Male: 37
Female: 38
Doctors per 1,000 people: Less than 0.05
Percentage of age-appropriate population enrolled in the following educational levels:
Primary: 134*
Secondary: 17
Further: 1

groups, the Ngoni and the Yao, invaded the area. The Yao were slave traders who sold African slaves to the Arabs.

When the Scottish missionary David Livingstone reached the area in 1859, he found it torn by local wars and the suffering caused by the slave trade. To help bring peace, the Free Church of Scotland set up a mission in the area, and to replace the slave trade, Scottish businessmen tried to introduce businesses there. In 1889, the British made treaties with the local chiefs, and two years later Britain proclaimed the area the Protectorate of Nyasaland.

In 1958, an independence movement sprang up. In July 1964, the protectorate gained independence as the nation of Malawi. A new Constitution, adopted in 1966, made Malawi a republic.

In June 1993, leader Hastings Kamuzu Banda was forced to hold a referendum on one-party rule, and voters approved the legalization of all political parties. In May 1994, Banda conceded defeat in the country's first multiparty elections. Bakili Muluzi, leader of the United Democratic Front, became Malawi's new president.

Languages spoken:
- English (official)
- Chichewa (official)
- Regional languages

Religions:
- Protestant 55%
- Roman Catholic 20%
- Muslim 20%
- Indigenous beliefs

**Enrollment ratios compare the number of students enrolled to the population which, by age, should be enrolled. A ratio higher than 100 indicates that students older or younger than the typical age range are also enrolled.*

Technology

Radios per 1,000 people: 499

Televisions per 1,000 people: 3

Computers per 1,000 people: 1.2

Economy

Currency: Malawian kwacha

Gross national income (GNI) in 2000: $1.7 billion U.S.

Real annual growth rate (1997–1998): 1.5%

GNI per capita (2000): $170 U.S.

Balance of payments (2000): -$523 million U.S.

Goods exported: Tobacco, tea, sugar, cotton, coffee, peanuts, wood products

Goods imported: Food, petroleum products, semimanufactures, consumer goods, transportation equipment

Trading partners: South Africa, Zimbabwe, Germany, United States, Zambia

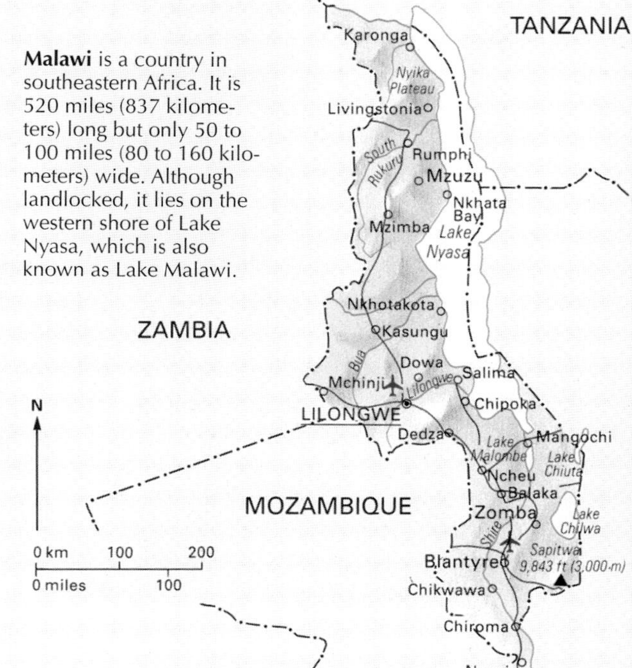

Malawi is a country in southeastern Africa. It is 520 miles (837 kilometers) long but only 50 to 100 miles (80 to 160 kilometers) wide. Although landlocked, it lies on the western shore of Lake Nyasa, which is also known as Lake Malawi.

Malaysia

Malaysia is a tropical land rich in natural resources. The world's largest producer of natural rubber, tin, and palm oil, Malaysia also has deposits of petroleum and natural gas, bauxite, copper, gold, and iron ore. Large amounts of timber come from the nation's dense rain forests. Because of its abundant resources, Malaysia has one of the strongest economies in Southeast Asia.

About 22 million people live in Malaysia. Of these people, about 50 per cent are Malays, about 35 per cent are Chinese, and about 10 per cent are Asian Indians.

Malaysia's ethnic groups speak different languages or dialects, and, in many areas, have different ways of life. Although Malays are the most powerful group in Malaysian politics, the Chinese control much of the nation's economy. Social, economic, and political differences between the Chinese and Malays have led to friction—and sometimes violence.

Malaysia consists of two regions about 400 miles (644 kilometers) apart, separated by the South China Sea. Peninsular Malaysia, the smaller region, lies on the southern part of the Malay Peninsula, while Sarawak and Sabah covers most of the northern part of Borneo. Peninsular Malaysia has many bustling cities, their narrow streets crowded with motor vehicles. The region also has large rural areas where people live in thatch-roofed houses built on stilts. Sarawak and Sabah is mainly rural.

Most Malays live in the rural areas of the peninsula in settlements called *kampongs* and work as farmers. Malays who live in cities usually have jobs in industry or in government.

Most of Malaysia's Chinese people live in the cities and work in stores, banks, or offices. Wealthy and middle-class Chinese live in high-rise apartments in downtown areas or in comfortable suburban homes.

The people of Sarawak and Sabah generally live in small rural settlements. Several families often live together in *long houses* along rivers. Many of these farmers are barely able to produce enough food for their families.

Malaysia has a good road system. Most people in Malaysia travel by bus or shared taxi. Railroads link Kuala Lumpur with Singapore and with Bangkok, Thailand. Kuala Lumpur, Kota Kinabalu, Kuching, and Pinang Island have international airports. Malaysian Air System (MAS) provides domestic and international air service.

Malaysia Today

Beginning in the 1500's, the area that is now Malaysia was controlled, in turn, by the Portuguese, the Dutch, and the British. These European nations wanted colonies in Southeast Asia—as in other parts of the world—for economic benefits. They hoped to expand their industry and trade by gaining sources of raw materials and markets for their goods. They also wanted strategic locations from which to control trade.

The road to independence

At the same time European powers struggled for economic control of the area, they

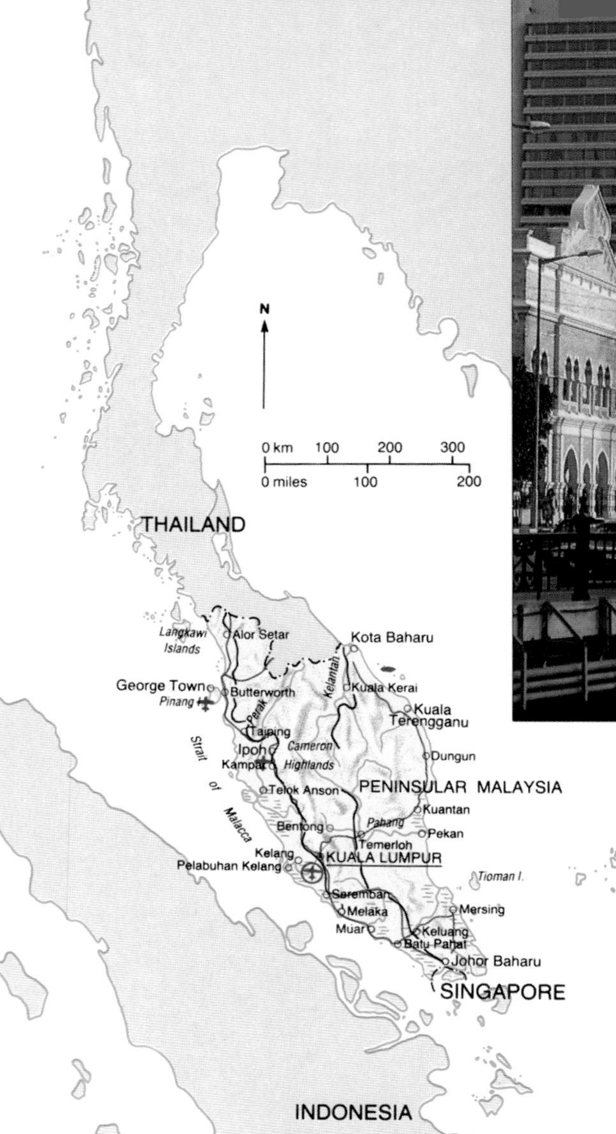

Malaysia is made up of two main regions separated by the South China Sea. Peninsular Malaysia, the southern part of the Southeast Asian mainland, has the smaller land area. Sarawak and Sabah, on the northwest coast of Borneo, is the larger part of Malaysia.

Fact Box

Country

Official name: Malaysia

Capital: Kuala Lumpur

Terrain: Coastal plains rising to hills and mountains

Area: 127,317 sq. mi. (329,750 km²)

Climate: Tropical; annual southwest (April to October) and northeast (October to February) monsoons

Main rivers: Kelantan, Perak, Pahang, Kinabatangan, Rajang

Highest elevation: Mt. Kinabalu, 13,431 ft. (4,094 m)

Lowest elevation: Indian Ocean, sea level

Government

Form of government: Constitutional monarchy

Head of state: King

Head of government: Prime minister

Administrative areas: 13 negeri-negeri (states), 2 wilayah-wilayah persekutuan (federal territories)

Legislature: Parlimen (Parliament) consisting of Dewan Negara (Senate) with 69 members serving three-year terms and the Dewan Rakyat (House of Representatives) with 193 members serving five-year terms

Court system: Supreme Court

Armed forces: 105,000 troops

People

Estimated 2002 population: 23,002,000

Population growth: 2.01%

Population density: 181 persons per sq. mi. (70 per km²)

Population distribution: 57% urban, 43% rural

Life expectancy in years:
Male: 68
Female: 74

Doctors per 1,000 people: 0.5

Percentage of age-appropriate population enrolled in the following educational levels:
Primary: 99
Secondary: 98
Further: N/A

Languages spoken:
Bahasa Melayu (official)
English
Chinese dialects

brought economic development by introducing Western agricultural, industrial, and medical techniques. For example, the first seedlings for rubber trees were brought from Great Britain in the 1870's; roads, railroads, hospitals, and schools were built toward the end of the 1800's; and efforts to conquer malaria began in the early 1900's. Still, after World War II (1939–1945) and the Japanese occupation of Malaysia, the people began to demand better economic and social conditions and started to work toward independence.

In 1948, the states on the Malay Peninsula, plus Pinang, united to form the Federation of Malaya, a partially independent territory under British protection. During the late 1940's and 1950's, rebel groups on the peninsula fought the British. The conflict ended when the Federation of Malaya gained complete independence in 1957.

In 1963, Malaya, Singapore, and what is now Sarawak and Sabah united and formed the new independent nation of Malaysia. Singapore, however, withdrew from Malaysia in 1965 to become an independent country.

Kuala Lumpur, *left,* the capital and largest city of Malaysia, lies along both banks of the Klang River on Peninsular Malaysia. Its mixture of Moorish architecture and modern high-rise buildings reflects the city's colorful history.

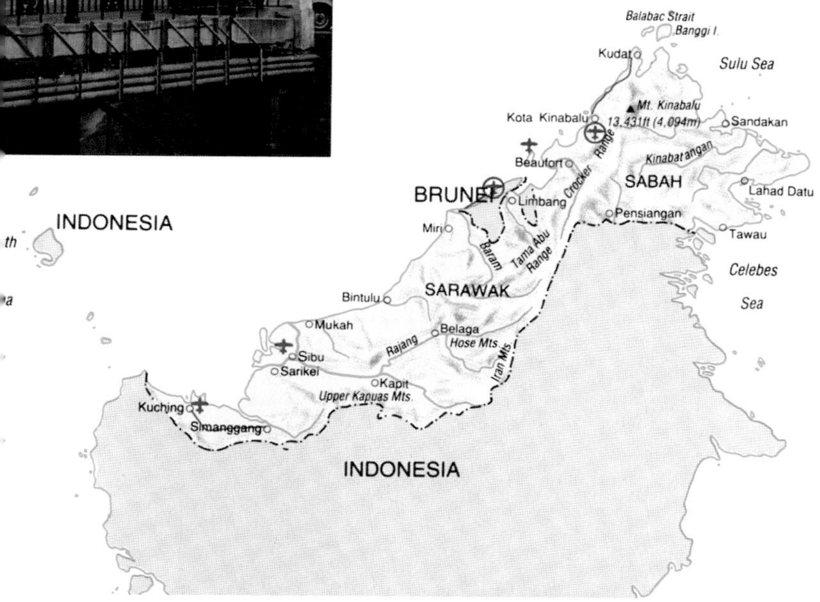

Tamil
indigenous and other languages

Religions:
Islam
Buddhism
Daoism
Hinduism
Christianity
Sikhism
Shamanism

Technology

Radios per 1,000 people: 420
Televisions per 1,000 people: 168
Computers per 1,000 people: 103.1

Economy

Currency: Ringgit
Gross national income (GNI) in 2000: $78.7 billion U.S.
Real annual growth rate (1999–2000): 8.3%
GNI per capita (2000): $3,380 U.S.
Balance of payments (2000): $12,606 million U.S.
Goods exported: Electronic equipment, petroleum and liquefied natural gas, chemicals, palm oil, wood and wood products, rubber, textiles
Goods imported: Machinery and equipment, chemicals, food, fuel, lubricants
Trading partners: United States, Japan, Singapore

King and Parliament

Today, Malaysia is a constitutional monarchy. A Parliament makes the country's laws, and a prime minister serves as the top government official and selects a Cabinet to help carry out the operations of the government. The king, called the *yang di-pertuan agong,* serves as head of state, but his duties are largely ceremonial. Each of the nation's 13 states and the 2 federal territories have their own local government.

Malaysia's Parliament is made up of a House of Representatives with 193 members elected to five-year terms and a Senate with 69 members who serve three-year terms. Each state legislature elects two Senate members, and the king appoints the other senators on the advice of the prime minister. The head of the political party with the most seats in the House serves as prime minister. Every five years, the rulers of nine of Malaysia's states elect a king from among their number.

Kuala Lumpur, the capital and largest city of Malaysia, attracts many tourists. The eastern part of the city has high-rise buildings, small shops, a busy outdoor market, and many beautiful *mosques* (Muslim houses of worship). Kuala Lumpur is also home to the Petronas Twin Towers, which was named the world's tallest building in 1996.

Environment

Malaysia's two main regions cover 127,317 square miles (329,749 square kilometers). Peninsular Malaysia, the smaller region, is bordered on the north by Thailand, on the west by the Strait of Malacca, and on the south by the island of Singapore. The region covers 50,806 square miles (131,588 kilometers).

Across the South China Sea to the east, Sarawak and Sabah covers 76,511 square miles (198,161 square kilometers) on the island of Borneo. Borneo is the third largest island in the world.

Malaysia holds a strategic position along the Strait of Malacca, a major commercial route between the Indian and Pacific oceans. Malaysia's location, which has shaped the country's cultural identity, economy, history, and religion for centuries, guarantees the nation a key role in the affairs of modern Southeast Asia.

Both parts of Malaysia have tropical climates. Coastal temperatures usually stay between 70° and 90° F. (21° and 32° C). About 100 inches (250 centimeters) of rain falls annually in Peninsular Malaysia, while Sarawak and Sabah gets about 150 inches (381 centimeters) each year.

Both parts of Malaysia have *monsoons*—winds that blow regularly in the same direction during definite seasons. Monsoons from the northeast pass through Southeast Asia from November to March, ushering in cooler weather. However, beginning in April, monsoons from the southwest bring extremely hot temperatures. From May to October, wet monsoons bring heavy rains from the south seas. Many of these monsoons cause floods, and some are so destructive that they ruin crops and livestock and disrupt the nation's economy.

A great variety of animals roams the Malaysian rain forests, including civets, deer, elephants, monkeys, tapirs, tigers, and wild oxen. The interior landscape includes lush groves of camphor, ebony, fig, mahogany, rubber, and sandalwood trees, while mangrove and palm trees line the swampy coastal area.

Graceful palm trees, *below,* sway above a traditional village on Peninsular Malaysia's swampy northeast coast. The wooden houses are built on stilts to protect them from flooding.

Tropical rain forests blanket Mount Kinabalu in Sabah, the highest peak in Malaysia at 13,431 feet (4,094 meters). From its peaks, climbers can see the Philippines across the South China Sea.

Peninsular Malaysia

Mountains covered with dense tropical rain forests run along the center of Peninsular Malaysia from north to south. Rugged limestone hills on both sides of the mountain range slope down to low, swampy plains on the coasts.

Most of Peninsular Malaysia's cities and major seaports, including George Town, Kuala Lumpur, and Melaka, are located along the Strait of Malacca. The lowland that covers parts of the region east of the mountains is only about 5 miles (8 kilometers) wide in some areas and flooded with swamps and lagoons in other areas, making it a difficult region to live in or to develop.

A Malaysian youngster, *above,* rides a bicycle through a tropical rain forest on the way to school. This low-lying region on Peninsular Malaysia's east coast also has swampy areas.

Tropical rain forests cover much of the area east of the mountains. Major rivers of Peninsular Malaysia include the Kelantan, Perak, and Pahang.

Sarawak and Sabah

This eastern region of Malaysia covers most of the northern part of Borneo. Much of the coastal area along the South China Sea is low and swampy, while inland areas are mountainous and covered with rain forests. Mount Kinabalu, the highest peak in Malaysia, rises 13,431 feet (4,094 meters) in the northeastern part of Sarawak and Sabah.

The area's extensive river systems include the Kinabatangan, the longest river in Sabah, and the Rajang. Shallow-draft vessels, such as rafts and scows, can travel up to 100 miles (160 kilometers) inland on these rivers. The entrances to many rivers and ports, however, are obstructed by deposits of soil, sand, or clay.

Cattle, *below,* are raised by some Malaysian farmers for meat. Farmers also use cattle to pull plows through rice fields.

This peaceful beach, *far left,* lies on the island of Kuah in the Langkawi island group. Malaysia holds a strategic position along the strait of Malacca, a major commercial route between the Indian and Pacific oceans.

Batu Caves, *left,* north of Kuala Lumpur, are formed out of limestone. One of these caves, known as the "cathedral," serves as the setting for an annual Hindu ceremony.

People

The Malays are the largest ethnic group in Malaysia. Most Malays speak Bahasa Malaysia, the country's official language. In addition, most are Muslims—followers of Islam, the country's official religion.

The great majority of the Malay people live in rural areas on the peninsula. Many Malay men and women, especially in rural areas, wear a *sarong,* a traditional length of cloth wrapped around the body as a skirt. Others, however, wear Western clothing.

The ancestors of the Malays migrated to Southeast Asia from southern China thousands of years ago. Malay people value social harmony, courtesy, and respect for authority. They are known as *bumiputras,* or sons of the soil, and their importance to the nation has been recognized in the Constitution. For example, only a Malay can become *yang dipertuan agong* (king and head of state) or prime minister.

The Chinese are Malaysia's second largest ethnic group. Chinese people began to arrive on the peninsula in large numbers in the 1850's to work in the tin mines. As their numbers grew, so did their need for services, and adventurous Chinese started businesses that catered to the needs of new arrivals. Gradually, they began to control the nation's economy. The Chinese also developed their own school system, focusing on traditional Chinese subjects. Today, most Chinese in Malaysia still use the Chinese language and follow Buddhism, Confucianism, or Taoism.

These critical differences between the Malays and the Chinese involving language, religion, race, and social position have caused racial tensions, which led to rioting in 1970 and 1987. The Malays resent the superior economic and social position of the Chinese, while the Chinese believe that the government favors the Malays.

The Asian Indians are the third major ethnic group. In Malaysia, the term *Indian* includes people from Pakistan and Sri Lanka, as well as those from India. Most Indians are employed on plantations, or work as merchants, money lenders, or white-collar workers. The Malays do not resent the Indians as they do the Chinese because the Indians have not attempted to gain political power.

Ceramic tiles, *above,* such as those that decorate the entrance to this house in Melaka, are a legacy of Dutch rule. The Dutch took Melaka from the Portuguese in 1641 but lost it to the British in the late 1700's.

An Iban, or Sea Dyak, holds the skull of an enemy killed by one of his ancestors. He stands outside a village long house in which many families live, each in a separate room.

Incense sticks line the shelves of this store near a Chinese temple in Melaka. The Chinese exercise a large degree of control over the nation's economy, causing tension with the Malays, the country's other main ethnic group.

A group of people called the *Dyaks* live mainly in Sarawak. The *Sea Dyaks,* or *Ibans,* who make up about 31 per cent of Sarawak's population, live along the seacoast and rivers. The *Land Dyaks*—about 9 per cent of the population—live inland and call themselves by the name of their village or locality. Most Dyaks are farmers or plantation workers, and their major crop is rice. A majority of the people in this group follow traditional religions, but some are Christians or Muslims.

Two Malay boys, *left,* cycle to a kite-flying contest on the east coast of Peninsular Malaysia. The bamboo-and-paper kites used in the contests can reach a height of more than 1,475 feet (450 meters).

Economy

From the mid-1970's to the mid-1990's, Malaysia had one of the strongest economies in Southeast Asia. The Malaysian economy slowed somewhat in the late 1990's. The Malaysian economy depends heavily on the production of petroleum, rubber, timber, and tin, but the country also produces a variety of farm crops and manufactured goods.

Vital markets

In the 1970's, Malaysia was primarily an exporter of raw commodities such as timber, rubber, tin, and palm oil. It still produces these goods, but they play a smaller role in Malaysia's economy. Much of the country's wealth now comes from manufacturing. The Malaysian electronics industry has been a major success, and Malaysia is a leading producer of integrated circuits and other semiconductor devices.

Malaysia still produces tin; *bauxite* (aluminum ore); copper; gold; iron ore; and *ilmenite,* an ore that contains a valuable metal called titanium. In addition, petroleum and natural gas production has increased in Malaysia since the 1970's, and petroleum is now the country's chief export.

The country's vast rain forests yield valuable timber, but worldwide concern about the destruction of these forests is starting to affect this important market. In 1987, for example, the World Bank gave Malaysia $9 million to halt the destruction of its forests. As a result, timber exports declined by 6.9 per cent in 1988.

Rice, the nation's chief food crop, is grown on small farms throughout Malaysia. However, even with the introduction of new varieties of high-yield rice and improvements in drainage and irrigation, Malaysia cannot grow enough rice to feed its people. The nation's small farms also produce cacao, coconuts, pepper, pineapples, and vegetables. Some farmers raise cattle or pigs for meat.

Economic planning

The continued prosperity of Malaysia's economy depends on its ability to strengthen its export markets. In recent years, Malaysia has greatly increased its manufacturing to lessen its economic reliance on agriculture and mining.

Malaysia belongs to the Association of Southeast Asian Nations (ASEAN), an organization made up of six Southeast Asian countries that promotes economic, cultural, and social cooperation among its members. The organization also works to reduce trade barriers. In 1976, the member nations of ASEAN agreed to share basic products during shortages and to gradually remove trade restrictions, especially taxes on imports.

Along with other members of ASEAN, Malaysia has tried to attract international bus-

Rubber

Rows of rubber trees grow on plantations all over Malaysia, *left.* The rubber is processed, *right,* in small factories. Latex from the tree is filtered and mixed with acid (1) to make it more solid. The rubber is separated into slabs (2). These are dried, first by rollers (3), and then by being passed through an air tunnel (4). The slabs are then packed for export (5).

inesses. Foreign businesses in Malaysia receive generous tax breaks, duty-free export zones, and a relatively cheap labor force.

In 1970, the government of Malaysia instituted its New Economic Policy (NEP), a 20-year program intended to increase the participation of the Malays in the economy. The program has been only partially successful because of shortages of money for investment.

In mid-1985, the Malaysian government announced a program to encourage long-term development of manufacturing. Shortly thereafter, Malaysia produced its first passenger cars, in a joint venture with a Japanese company. The country began exporting these automobiles to Great Britain in 1989.

Workers take a break in a timber yard, *left*. Much of Malaysia is still covered by rain forests, though these areas are now overdeveloped. Timber and timber products are among the country's most important exports.

A Chinese shop, *above,* in George Town on Pinang Island, displays a wide variety of goods. The Chinese operate most businesses in Malaysia and provide a large part of the labor force.

The powerful water buffalo makes large-scale rice farming possible in Sarawak and Sabah and other parts of Asia. Although new varieties of rice and improved irrigation techniques have been introduced, Malaysia still cannot produce all the rice it needs to feed its people.

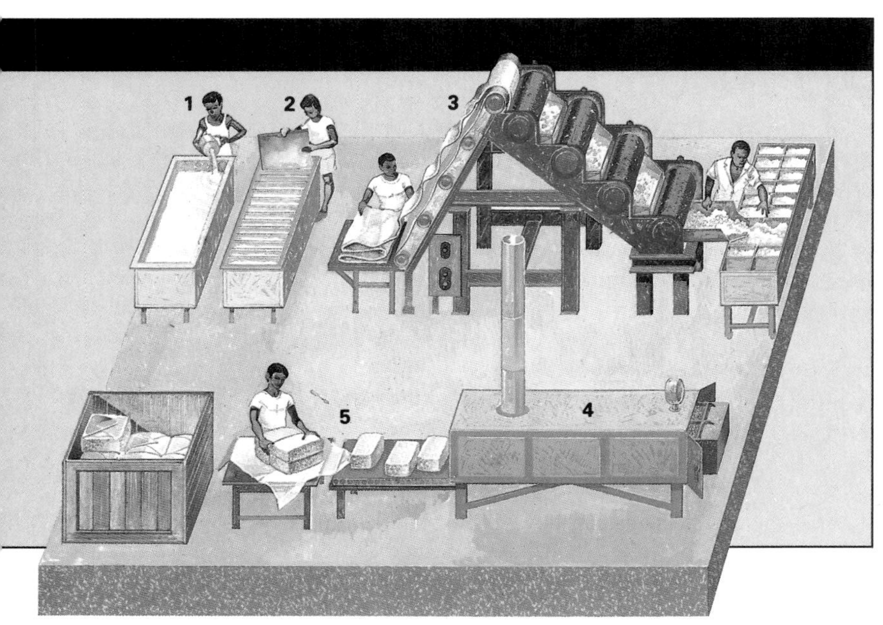

History

The community marketplace is one of Malaysia's great attractions—a meeting place for Chinese, Indians, and Malays, with elements of both the traditional and modern. Among the cans of paraffin and cheap plastic goods are many fine, traditional Malaysian products, such as the famous *batik* cloth printed with brilliant designs, elaborate metalwork, handcrafted bamboo items, and the marvelous kites that are flown in competitions. Adding color to the crowd are such exotic sights as snake charmers, dancing bears, and fortunetellers, as well as vendors of traditional Chinese folk medicines selling dried antler or preserved turtles.

The marketplace is a fitting introduction to a country whose history has been shaped by trade and by its location on the trade routes linking India and China. Chinese and Indian merchants used the peninsula as a stopping place for their ships 2,000 years ago. Here they found shelter from the monsoon winds and bought exotic goods ranging from gold and spices to aromatic woods and rhinoceros horn.

A Malay woman, *above,* puts the finishing touches on a *wau* kite. These kites play an important part in Malaysian traditions and are often flown at festivals.

The impact of trade

Trade brought wealth to the region, and settlements sprang up along the coast. Some became thriving commercial areas, including Melaka, which developed into a major trading center in the early 1400's. In 1409, Melaka was declared a kingdom by the emperor of China.

Melaka owed much of its importance to its location and its ideal port. Melaka's rulers controlled the trade through the Strait of Malacca, and its harbor provided a safe place for ships to anchor. Melaka's rulers wisely kept their toll and customs charges reasonable. The "golden age" of Melaka lasted only a century, but it provided cultural heroes and enduring standards of ideal behavior for the Malays.

By 1509, the strategic importance of Melaka had attracted the attention of Portugal, and in 1511 its forces captured the town. To withstand rival powers, the Portuguese built a massive fort called *A Famosa* ("The Famous One"), which withstood enemy assaults for 130 years. In 1641, however, the Dutch stormed the fort and took Melaka, which they held for more than 100 years.

In the late 1700's, traders from Great Britain began setting up trading posts on the peninsula and nearby islands. Soon, British forces captured Melaka from the Dutch. They bombed A Famosa, and today only its great carved gateway stands as a reminder of the city's historic past.

In 1826, the British formed the Colony of the Straits Settlements, which included Melaka, the island of Pinang, and the island of Singapore. During the 1800's and early 1900's, the British gained control of the Malay states on the peninsula, as well as what is now Sarawak and Sabah. Like the Dutch and Portuguese before them, the British were more interested in gaining a strategic trade location than in acquiring territory. Their presence had a lasting impact on the country's economy.

Cultural imports

The Indian traders who visited the area 2,000 years ago had a tremendous effect on Malaysian culture. They brought political ideas and practices, art forms, and popular legends. Indian traders also introduced Hinduism, Buddhism, and Islam.

Signs on the main street of Kuala Lumpur, Malaysia's capital, *above,* reflect the many cultures that make up the nation's identity. Modern Malaysia includes aspects of Islamic, Indian, European, and Chinese life styles.

Portuguese-style galleons, *far left,* sail into the harbor at Melaka to celebrate the feast day of St. Peter. The ships, with their brightly colored sails, are a reminder of the power and pageantry of Portuguese rule.

The annual Thaipusam ceremony has Hindu roots. The celebrations take place in Malaysia every year around the beginning of February. Batu Caves, north of Kuala Lumpur, are one of the most famous sites for the ceremony.

Everywhere in Malaysia today, there are reminders of other civilizations. Using Indian ideas of political organization, Southeast Asians in early trading communities began to organize settlements and villages into city-states and kingdoms. Over time, villagers who became citizens of these kingdoms and city-states were governed by rulers. These rulers claimed the profits of trade and justified the new arrangements by citing Hindu and Buddhist religious doctrines.

Islam, which was introduced by Indian traders, is now Malaysia's state religion. The country's many impressive mosques are everpresent reminders of these ancient seafarers.

Maldives

The Maldives is a small, independent country that consists of about 1,200 small coral islands off the southwest coast of India. The islands form a chain 475 miles (764 kilometers) long and 80 miles (129 kilometers) wide in the Indian Ocean. None of the islands is larger than 5 square miles (13 square kilometers), and some are little more than small platforms about 6 feet (1.8 meters) above sea level. The total land area of the Maldives is 115 square miles (298 square kilometers), making it the smallest independent country in Asia.

History

Little is known of the Maldives before the arrival of European traders in the 1500's. The Portuguese were the first to stake their claim on the islands, but the Dutch took control from 1656 to 1796. In 1887, the Maldives became a British protectorate. The Maldivians governed themselves, while the British conducted their foreign affairs.

The Maldives gained complete independence from the United Kingdom on July 26, 1965. In 1985, the Maldives and six other countries established the South Asian Association for Regional Cooperation (SAARC). This organization, which deals with social and economic issues, also helps the Maldives ensure their political neutrality.

Land and climate

The islands of the Maldives are grouped in clusters called *atolls*. Barrier reefs around the atolls protect the islands from the open sea. The climate is hot and humid. Daytime temperatures average about 80° F (27° C).

The islands are quite beautiful, with clear lagoons and white sand beaches. The land is covered with grasses and low-growing tropical plants. Coconut palms and fruit trees also grow on the islands. Tourists come from all

FACT BOX

COUNTRY

Official name: Dhivehi Raajjeyge Jumhooriyyaa (Republic of Maldives)
Capital: Male
Terrain: Flat, with white sandy beaches
Area: 115 sq. mi. (300 km²)
Climate: Tropical; hot, humid; dry, northeast monsoon (November to March); rainy, southwest monsoon (June to August)
Highest elevation: Unnamed location on Wilingili Island in the Addu Atoll, 7 ft. (2 m)
Lowest elevation: Indian Ocean, sea level

GOVERNMENT

Form of government: Republic
Head of state: President
Head of government: President
Administrative areas: 19 atholhu (atolls), 1 first-order administrative division
Legislature: Majlis (People's Council) with 50 members serving five-year terms
Court system: High Court
Armed forces: N/A

PEOPLE

Estimated 2002 population: 302,000
Population growth: 3.06%
Population density: 2,626 persons per sq. mi. (1,023 per km²)
Population distribution: 75% rural, 25% urban
Life expectancy in years: Male: 61; Female: 63
Doctors per 1,000 people: N/A
Percentage of age-appropriate population enrolled in the following educational levels: Primary: N/A; Secondary: N/A; Further: N/A

A view from the air shows the ring-shaped form of the Maldives' coral atolls. The bright white sand is a stunning contrast to the brilliant blue of the surrounding tropical waters. Scientists are now concerned about the possible rise in sea level caused by global warming. Some experts believe that the Maldives may be underwater early in the next century. Many low-lying nations share this problem.

over the world to see the coral and the dazzling fish that inhabit the islands' many reefs.

People

The Maldivians live on only about 210 of the country's 1,200 islands. Most are descendants of Sinhalese people who came from Sri Lanka. Others claim the people of southern India and Arab traders and sailors as their ancestors. Almost all of the Maldivians are Sunni Muslims.

Most of the Maldivian men make their living as fishermen. Each day, thousands of men go out to sea in boats made of coconut or other timber. They use rods and reels to catch bonito, tuna, and other fish.

At the end of the day, they bring their catch home to the women, who cook and smoke the fish over an open fire. Most of the fish is prepared for export. The people eat some fish as part of their diet, along with coconuts, papayas, pineapples, pomegranates, and sweet potatoes.

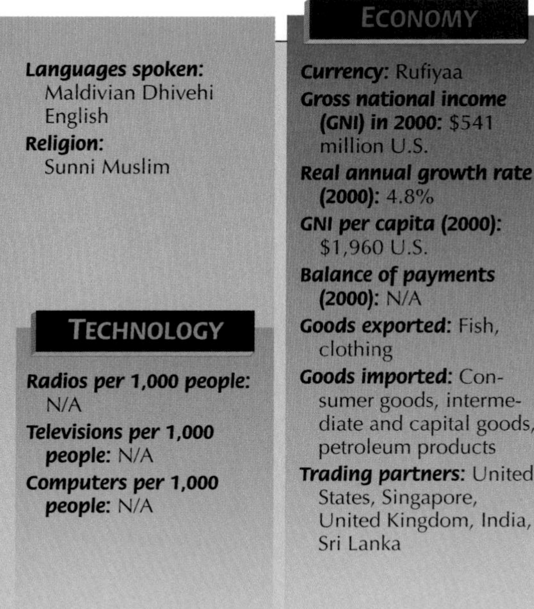

Languages spoken:
Maldivian Dhivehi
English

Religion:
Sunni Muslim

Technology

Radios per 1,000 people: N/A
Televisions per 1,000 people: N/A
Computers per 1,000 people: N/A

Economy

Currency: Rufiyaa
Gross national income (GNI) in 2000: $541 million U.S.
Real annual growth rate (2000): 4.8%
GNI per capita (2000): $1,960 U.S.
Balance of payments (2000): N/A
Goods exported: Fish, clothing
Goods imported: Consumer goods, intermediate and capital goods, petroleum products
Trading partners: United States, Singapore, United Kingdom, India, Sri Lanka

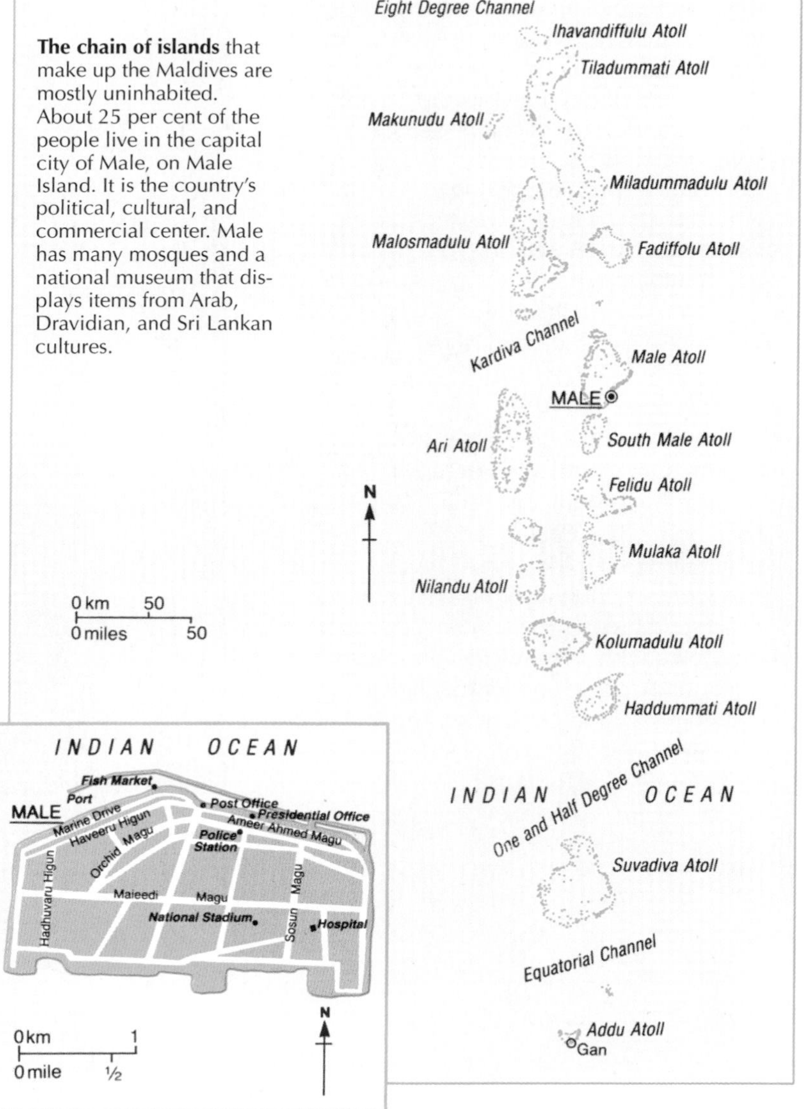

The chain of islands that make up the Maldives are mostly uninhabited. About 25 per cent of the people live in the capital city of Male, on Male Island. It is the country's political, cultural, and commercial center. Male has many mosques and a national museum that displays items from Arab, Dravidian, and Sri Lankan cultures.

Beneath the Maldives

Coral islands are formed by the shells of tiny marine animals. The tropical waters of the Indian Ocean are an ideal environment for the formation of coral islands. The Maldives include some of the world's largest coral atolls. The atolls are home to a great variety of plant and animal life, including more species of plants and animals than any habitat on earth except tropical rain forests.

How coral is formed

Coral is a limestone formation formed in the sea by millions of tiny animals. Individual coral animals are called *polyps*. They belong to the same animal group as hydras, jellyfish, and sea anemones. Most polyps have a cylinder-shaped body that is about 1 inch (2.5 centimeters) long. At one end is a mouth surrounded by small *tentacles* (feelers). The other end attaches to hard surfaces on the sea floor.

Most coral polyps live together in colonies. These formations can be seen in a variety of colors, including shades of tan, orange, yellow, purple, and green. When the animals die, they leave limestone "skeletons" that form the foundations of coral reefs. Sometimes these coral masses build up to the point where they rise above the water. They are then called coral islands.

An underwater paradise

Coral reefs look like lovely sea gardens, because many colorful and interesting sea creatures live among the coral. The reefs provide a home for sponges, sea fans, mussels, sea anemones, tube-dwelling worms, and a wide variety of brightly colored algae.

Each coral reef is a fascinating *ecosystem,* where a variety of organisms live together. Plankton provides food for much of the smaller marine life, such as shrimp and crab. These crustaceans and other small fish in turn become food for larger fish. This balance of nature provides enough food for every species.

In the underwater world of the Maldives, a diver, *right,* observes red sponges colonizing a group of dead coral. A sponge has *ostia* (pores) that allow water to enter its body. The water carries tiny plants and animals for the sponge to eat.

A flash photograph shows the natural colors of a *crinoid,* also known as a sea lily, as it perches on the leafy branches of a gorgonian coral, *far left.* Millions of years ago, the crinoid was a thriving species, but only a few survive today.

The clown fish, found mainly in the Indian Ocean, uses large sea anemones for shelter. The stinging tentacles of the sea anemone can be fatal to other fish, but the clown fish comes and goes unharmed.

A beautifully patterned starfish nestles on a coral formation, *above.* The starfish is a spiny sea animal with thick, armlike extensions on its body. Most species look like five-pointed stars but some have 40 "arms" or more.

The coral atolls of the Maldives provide a home for massive swarms of yellow-striped snappers. These fish, an important catch for local fishermen, live close to shore, usually among rocks and reefs.

Fighting for survival

In order to avoid being eaten by predators, living creatures constantly look for ways to improve their survival techniques. Many reef dwellers live a secret life, creeping around narrow cracks and crevices to avoid their enemies.

Some animals try to fool predators by changing their shape or color to blend in with the surroundings, or by developing bright colors and patterns. Still others form an alliance with another species. The clown fish, for example, finds safety among the sea anemone's stinging tentacles. Of course, their enemies also adapt themselves, thus keeping nature in balance.

The cracks, overhangs, and caves of the coral reef provide an ideal home for many kinds of fish. Some live by themselves, some live in pairs, and some live in large groups called *shoals*. Each group defends its territory against competitors for food—usually members of their own species.

Some fish are scavengers, cleaning food debris from the sea floor or attacking parasites attached to larger fish. Other species hide in cracks and openings until their prey comes too close. This technique is used by robber fish, moray eels, and many types of perch.

Larger fish with the open seas sometimes visit the coral reefs. Huge shoals of mackerel often appear, along with larger, more solitary fish like sharks and barracudas.

Mali

Mali is a large, landlocked country in western Africa. Today, it is a poor, thinly populated nation where droughts have killed many people and animals, but Mali was once the site of powerful African empires.

A former colony of France, Mali is now an independent republic. According to its Constitution, a president is elected by voters. The president appoints a Cabinet that helps run the government. The voters also elect the members of the National Assembly, the country's lawmaking body.

For many years, Mali had a one-party political system—only candidates from the Mali People's Democratic Union could run for office, and the military controlled the party. However, in 1992, a new Constitution allowing for multiparty elections was adopted. A civilian president, Alpha Oumar Konare, and a new National Assembly were elected.

Like other developing nations, Mali faces major problems. Many of its people are uneducated, and about 90 per cent of the adults cannot read and write. In addition, poor health conditions prevail in Mali, and only a few hundred doctors live there. Malaria is a major cause of death among Mali's children.

Although Mali is economically poor, it has a rich cultural heritage. In the past, three great black empires ruled parts of what is now Mali.

The Ghana Empire flourished from about the A.D. 300's to the mid-1000's. It was known as "the land of gold" because traders brought gold into the empire from the south to exchange for salt and other goods.

The Mali Empire, which lasted from about 1240 to 1500, was the wealthiest and most powerful state in western Africa, and Mali cities were centers of the caravan trade. At the invitation of King Mansa Musa, who ruled from 1312 to 1337, Islamic scholars came to the empire, and the city of Timbuktu became a center of Muslim learning.

The Songhai Empire began in the 700's and flourished alongside the Mali Empire. After about 1400, it began to conquer some of Mali's outlying areas, and by 1500 it controlled most of the Mali Empire. Under Songhai rulers, Timbuktu reached its peak as a center of wealth and learning.

After Songhai was overrun by Moroccan invaders in 1591, many small kingdoms ruled the region. About 300 years later, in 1895, France gained control of the area.

The French colony, called French Sudan, became part of French West Africa. In 1959, French Sudan and Senegal united to form the Federation of Mali, but Senegal dropped out of the federation in August 1960. On Sept. 22, 1960, the nation gained complete independence as the Republic of Mali.

Fact Box

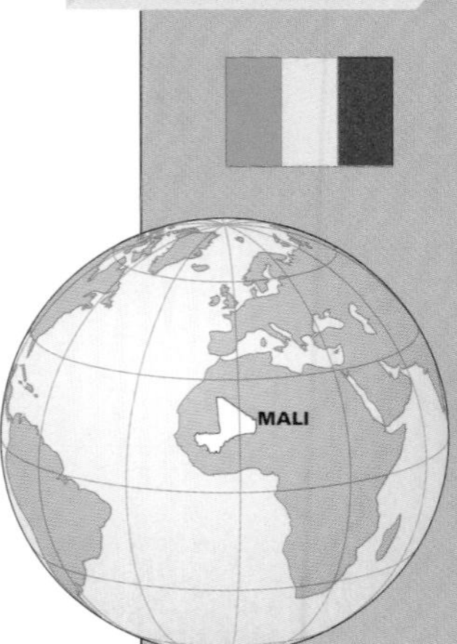

Country

Official name: Republique de Mali (Republic of Mali)
Capital: Bamako
Terrain: Mostly flat to rolling northern plains covered by sand; savanna in south, rugged hills in northeast
Area: 478,767 sq. mi. (1,240,000 km²)
Climate: Subtropical to arid; hot and dry February to June; rainy, humid, and mild June to November; cool and dry November to February
Main rivers: Sénégal, Niger
Highest elevation: Hombori Tondo, 3,789 ft. (1,155 m)
Lowest elevation: Senegal River, 75 ft. (23 m)

Government

Form of government: Republic
Head of state: President
Head of government: Prime minister
Administrative areas: 8 regions
Legislature: Assemblee Nationale (National Assembly) with 147 members serving five-year terms
Court system: Cour Supreme (Supreme Court)
Armed forces: 7,350 troops

People

Estimated 2002 population: 11,810,000
Population growth: 2.98%
Population density: 25 persons per sq. mi. (10 per km²)
Population distribution: 74% rural, 26% urban
Life expectancy in years: Male: 46 Female: 48
Doctors per 1,000 people: 0.1
Percentage of age-appropriate population enrolled in the following educational levels: Primary: 53 Secondary: 14 Further: 2

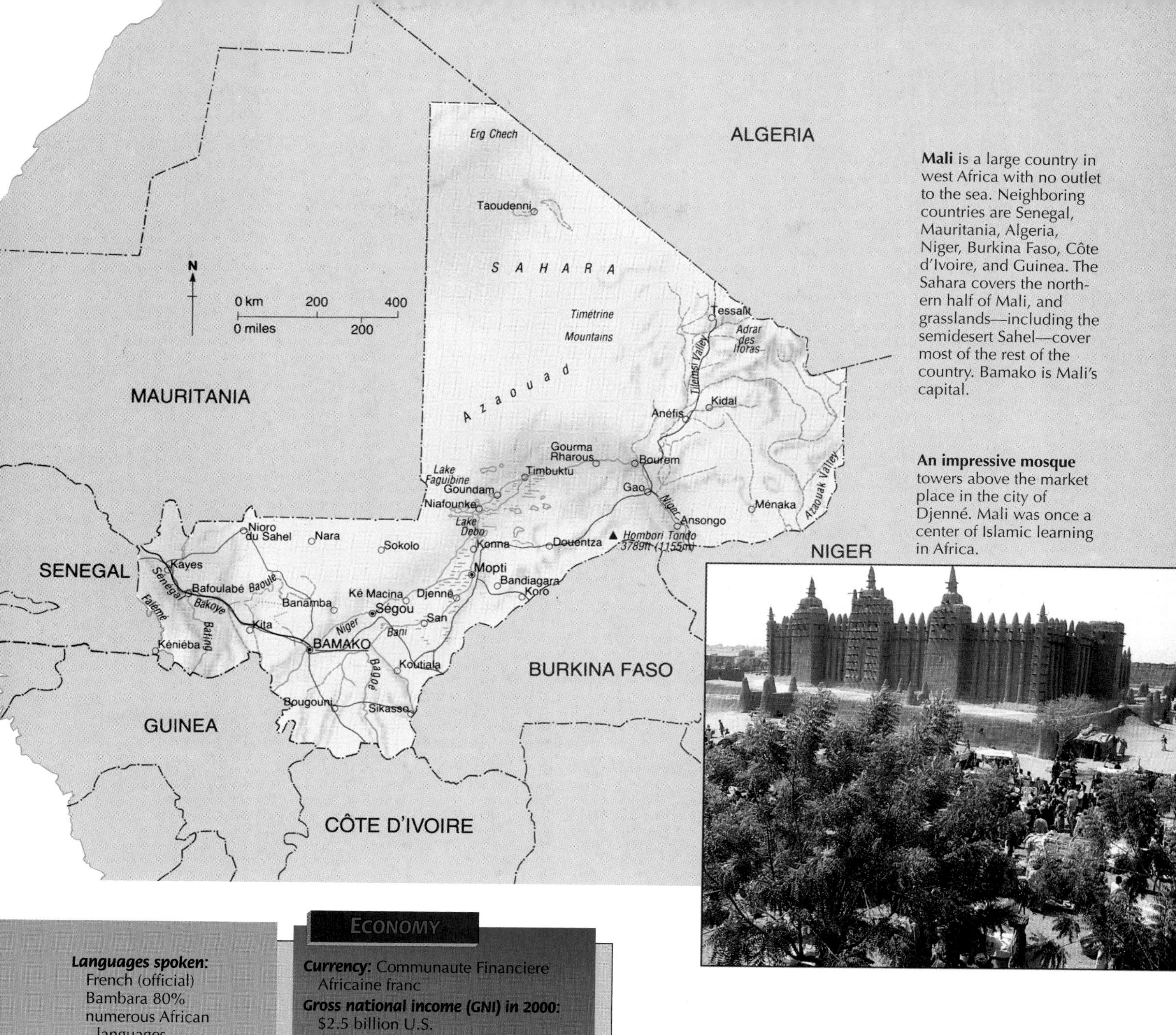

Mali is a large country in west Africa with no outlet to the sea. Neighboring countries are Senegal, Mauritania, Algeria, Niger, Burkina Faso, Côte d'Ivoire, and Guinea. The Sahara covers the northern half of Mali, and grasslands—including the semidesert Sahel—cover most of the rest of the country. Bamako is Mali's capital.

An impressive mosque towers above the market place in the city of Djenné. Mali was once a center of Islamic learning in Africa.

Languages spoken:
French (official)
Bambara 80%
numerous African languages

Religions:
Muslim 90%
indigenous beliefs 9%
Christian 1%

TECHNOLOGY

Radios per 1,000 people: 56

Televisions per 1,000 people: 14

Computers per 1,000 people: 1.2

ECONOMY

Currency: Communaute Financiere Africaine franc

Gross national income (GNI) in 2000: $2.5 billion U.S.

Real annual growth rate (1999–2000): 4.5%

GNI per capita (2000): $240 U.S.

Balance of payments (2000): N/A

Goods exported:
Mostly: cotton
Also: gold, livestock

Goods imported: Machinery and equipment, construction materials, petroleum, foodstuffs, textiles

Trading partners: Thailand, Italy, Côte d'Ivoire, France, China

Modibo Keita, Mali's first president, tried to develop the economy, partly by establishing close ties with Communist countries. But Mali went into debt, and in 1968, a group of military leaders overthrew Keita. One officer, Moussa Traore, took control and was later elected president. In March 1991, Traore was overthrown in a military coup, whose leaders later established a multiparty democracy. Traore was tried for his government's actions in killing opponents. In 1993, he was convicted and sentenced to death.

During the 1970's and early 1980's, severe droughts brought widespread famine to Mali, and thousands died.

People and Economy

Africa's great desert, the Sahara, covers the entire northern half of Mali. The Sahel, a semidesert grassland, lies south of the Sahara in central Mali.

The Sahel has been especially dry since 1968. The severe droughts of the 1970's and 1980's destroyed much of the region's plant and animal life, including crops and livestock. Thousands of people died of starvation, and thousands of others poured into Mali's urban areas, seeking water and food.

Mali's urban areas lie mainly in the southern portion of the country, a region of rolling grassland. Most of Mali's people live in villages and cities along the Sénégal and Niger rivers or their branches. The interior delta of the Niger is Mali's most fertile area.

The vast majority of Mali's people are black Africans, but they belong to different ethnic groups. The Fulani and Toucouleur—related peoples—make up the largest ethnic group. The Fulani have both black and white ancestors. The next largest group is the Mandingos—made up mainly of the Bambara, Malinke, and Soninke. Other black groups include the Dogon, Songhai, and Voltaic.

Most blacks live in small rural villages in southern Mali and farm for a living. Many of the Fulani live in dome-shaped, thatched huts. Those who herd cattle live in low huts made of straw mats or branches. Still other blacks live in houses made of mud bricks.

Most Mali farmers can raise only enough food for their own use. They usually work on village-owned plots, using old-fashioned hand tools. They grow cassava, corn, millet, rice, sorghum, and yams.

Whites make up about 5 per cent of the population, including Arabs, Europeans (mainly French), Moors (of Arab and Berber descent), and Tuareg (of Berber descent). Many of the Arabs and Moors and almost all the Tuareg people are nomads. They herd cattle, goats, sheep, camels, and donkeys across the Sahel and Sahara in search of water and pasture. The nomads travel in groups led by *marabouts* (holy men). They live in tents made of camel hair and eat mainly dates and millet.

Most of the Europeans live in modern houses in Bamako and other cities. Many own businesses or have jobs in government, the professions, stores, banks, or offices.

Mali is an agricultural country, and more than 75 per cent of its workers farm or herd for a living. Yet only about a fifth of the land is suitable for farming. The government has sometimes discouraged farming by keeping food prices low, and droughts have damaged crops and reduced the amount of pasture.

Some farmers raise cotton, peanuts, and sugar cane as cash crops. Cotton is Mali's chief export, but sharp drops in world cotton prices have hurt the country's economy. Fishing is an important industry in the south.

Mali has few mineral resources. Salt mining is the only major mining activity, though some gold is also produced. The rising cost of importing petroleum has also damaged Mali's economy.

Timbuktu rose up at the "meeting point of camel and canoe," about 8 miles (13 kilometers) from the Niger River, near the southern edge of the Sahara on one of the caravan routes. Parts of the old city now lie under desert sands.

The Niger River is Mali's lifeline, *right*. Its network of branches and lakes in southern Mali provides well-watered, fertile land, as well as a bountiful catch of carp, catfish, and perch for the country's fishing industry.

The government owns almost all the large factories in Mali, but it encourages private enterprise. Most of the largest factories were built with foreign aid. Only a small per cent of Mali's workers are employed in manufacturing. The main products are leather products, processed foods, and textiles.

The slow growth of industry and the nation's continuing dependence on agriculture have hurt Mali's development. Today, the people of Mali are working toward a more balanced economy that will lessen the hardship caused by droughts and other agricultural problems.

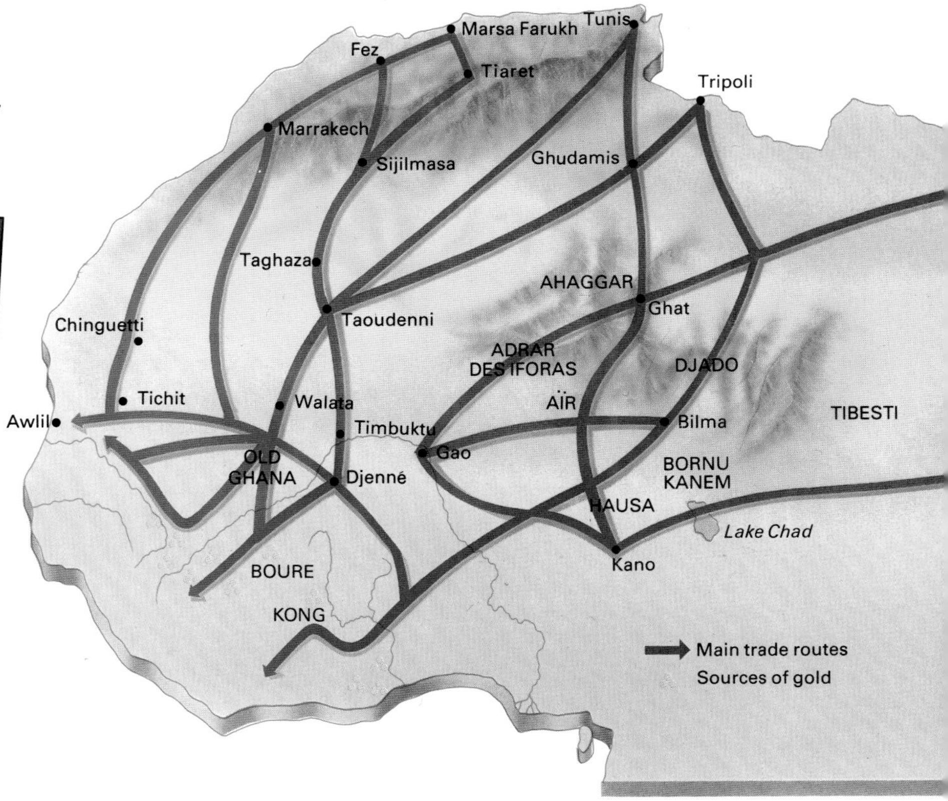

The main caravan routes across the Sahara were well established by A.D. 1000. Southbound caravans carried salt as well as cloth, glass beads, and other products. Northbound caravans carried gold, kola nuts, leather, pepper, and slaves. The great black empires that once ruled Mali became rich and powerful because they controlled important trade routes.

Bamako, *left,* the capital and largest city of Mali, has a population of about 400,000. Only about 20 per cent of Mali's people live in urban areas, including many Europeans.

A Mali woman waters an onion field as her ancestors did—using a gourd to carry the water. Mali women help plant, water, and harvest the crops.

Living African Arts

The arts have been highly developed in Africa for thousands of years. The oldest known African artwork—dating from before 5000 B.C.—is the prehistoric rock painting found in the Sahara and elsewhere. Today, art is part of the African's everyday life, as well as an essential element in African rituals.

Islamic designs are characteristic of the art of northern Africa. Because Islam forbids artists to create images of living things, Islamic artists developed an abstract, flat style of depicting people, animals, and birds that makes them look more like geometric symbols than lifelike pictures. Such designs decorate the walls of many magnificent mosques in the region, as well as the fine jewelry, metalware, pottery, rugs, and other handicrafts produced by North African artists.

Farther south, in western Africa, traditional African music, dance, and sculpture have their own distinctive beauty. But because many Africans south of the Sahara are Muslims as well, the Arab Islamic style has sometimes influenced their art. Arab religious chants and musical instruments used in northern Africa have also spread southward to influence the music of people in Mali, Senegal, Niger, and Chad.

Traditional black African music is part of almost every aspect of life in western Africa, especially religious ceremonies, festivals, and social rituals. Many Africans believe that music is a link with the spirit world.

The instrument most strongly identified with African music is the drum. Some drums are made of animal skins and played with the hands. Others are hollow logs played with sticks. The complex rhythms of African music are created by combining different patterns of drumbeats. Sometimes iron bells or handclaps are used to create rhythms.

Other instruments include harps, horns, flutes, lyres, zithers, and xylophones. In Senegal, stringed instruments called *kora* are made from huge gourds.

Songs are a part of religious ceremonies and celebrations as well as a means of telling stories or teaching. The *dweli* (singers) of the Malinke people in Mali pass along their tribal history in songs.

The complicated rhythms, choral singing, and flattened, or *blue,* notes heard in African-American blues songs and church music reflect African traditions. African music has also influenced Western popular music, jazz, West Indian calypso, and Latin-American dance music.

Dogon dancers perform the *dama,* a dance that embodies the beliefs and history of these Mali people. The dancers wear stilts because the Dogon believe that long ago they came from a land of long-legged herons.

Djenné Mosque in Mali, *right,* shows a blend of Islamic religious influence and an architectural style typical of the Sahara region. Many buildings in rural Africa are constructed of adobe, which keeps out the intense heat.

Because dancing developed in Africa as a part of village life, African dancing is nearly always a group activity. In most village dances, everyone joins in the dance—men, women, and children. Sometimes they form a circle, clap their hands, and call out to dancers within the circle. For important ceremonies, professional dancers may perform, using traditional symbolic movements.

One of the most famous African dances is the splendid *dama* performed by the Dogon people of Mali. The dance lasts for hours. The dancers wear elaborate masks that symbolize the Creator and the works of creation.

The home of the ancestors, a series of caves cut in rock, *below,* marks the starting place of the Dogon *dama* festival.

They dance to direct the spirits of the dead to join their ancestors and to show the link between humans and God. Every important event in African life—birth, death, marriage, coming of age, and the planting and harvesting of crops—includes dancing.

Traditional crafts such as sculpting are also involved with African rituals. Ethnic groups such as the Bambara and Dogon are noted for their wonderful carved masks and the striking figures of their ancestors. The antelope masks of the Bambara are worn in harvest ceremonies, and Dogon masks are worn at such ceremonies as the *dama* festival.

Few people outside Africa knew about African sculpture until the 1900's, but it has since become a major influence on Western artists.

Musicians play under the palm trees of Dakar, Senegal, *below*. Drums are the most important instrument in African music, which for many Africans is a link with the spirit world.

Malta

The republic of Malta consists of the inhabited Mediterranean islands of Malta, Gozo, and Comino, as well as the smaller, uninhabited islands of Cominotto and Filfla. Malta is located about 60 miles (97 kilometers) south of Sicily.

For centuries, the strategic location of the islands of Malta has made them a stopping place for sailors in the Mediterranean Sea. According to tradition, Saint Paul the Apostle was shipwrecked near Malta about A.D. 60 and converted the inhabitants to Christianity. As recently as World War II (1939–1945), Malta was used as a naval base by the Allied forces.

For almost 150 years, until it was granted independence in 1964, Malta was a British crown colony. Today, it is an independent republic within the British Commonwealth.

Malta is one of the most densely populated countries in the world. The population is concentrated on the northeast coast of the main island of Malta, around two natural harbors, Marsamxett and Grand Harbour.

Across the Grand Harbour stand the crowded buildings and ancient forts of Valletta, capital and major port of Malta.

People

With Italy to the north and Libya to the south, Malta is neither European nor African. Its people are determined to remain neutral in their political affairs and keep friendly ties with all their neighbors. Perhaps their tolerant spirit comes from their mixed ancestry and their blend of cultural heritages.

While the Maltese have the black hair, dark eyes, and medium height of most Mediterranean people, the Maltese language combines a West Arabic dialect with some Italian words. Although the Arabs held Malta for only 220 years, many of the region's place names and family names reflect the days of Arab rule. However, almost all the islanders are Roman Catholics.

Although about 50 per cent of the Maltese people are farmers, Malta imports most of its food. Many Maltese people work at the dockyards and in the building industry.

History

Malta's history goes back to prehistoric times. The small Cave of Ghar Dalam on the island of Malta contains the remains of settlements dating from 7,000 years ago. About 1000 B.C., the Phoenicians colonized the islands, and their temples, tombs, and other relics still stand on Malta.

Greek, Carthaginian, Roman, and Arab conquerors followed the Phoenicians into Malta. During the Middle Ages, control of Malta passed to the Norman kings of Sicily. Finally, in 1530, the Holy Roman Emperor

Fact Box

MALTA

Country

Official name: Repubblika ta' Malta (Republic of Malta)
Capital: Valletta
Terrain: Mostly low, rocky, flat to dissected plains; many coastal cliffs
Area: 122 sq. mi. (316 km²)
Climate: Mediterranean with mild, rainy winters and hot, dry summers
Highest elevation: Ta'Dmejrek, near Dingli, 830 ft. (253 m)
Lowest elevation: Mediterranean Sea, sea level

Government

Form of government: Parliamentary democracy
Head of state: President
Head of government: Prime minister
Administrative areas: None
Legislature: House of Representatives usually consisting of 65 members serving five-year terms
Court system: Constitutional Court, Court of Appeal
Armed forces: 1,900 troops

People

Estimated 2002 population: 394,000
Population growth: 0.74%
Population density: 3,230 persons per sq. mi. (1,247 per km²)
Population distribution: 89% urban, 11% rural
Life expectancy in years:
Male: 75
Female: 81
Doctors per 1,000 people: N/A
Percentage of age-appropriate population enrolled in the following educational levels:
Primary: N/A
Secondary: N/A
Further: N/A

The Republic of Malta, *map above,* an island country in the Mediterranean Sea, has a balmy climate and magnificent scenery that attract many visitors.

Brightly painted boats are moored in one of the many natural harbors that have made Malta a center for Mediterranean shipping since the island was colonized by the Phoenicians.

Balconies overlooking the streets of Valletta allow tenants of this old high-rise apartment building to enjoy some fresh air.

Languages spoken:
Maltese (official)
English (official)

Religion:
Roman Catholic 91%

TECHNOLOGY

Radios per 1,000 people: N/A

Televisions per 1,000 people: N/A

Computers per 1,000 people: N/A

ECONOMY

Currency: Maltese lira

Gross national income (GNI) in 2000: $3,559 million U.S.

Real annual growth rate (2000): 4.7%

GNI per capita (2000): $9,120 U.S.

Balance of payments (2000): N/A

Goods exported: Machinery and transport equipment, manufactures

Goods imported: Machinery and transport equipment, manufactured goods; food, drink, tobacco

Trading partners: France, United States, Italy, Germany, United Kingdom

Charles V gave Malta to the Knights of the Order of Saint John of Jerusalem (sometimes called the Hospitallers), and in 1565, the Knights fought off a Turkish invasion. Over the next 200 years, the Knights brought much wealth to Malta.

The rule of the Knights came to an end when Napoleon I seized the islands on his way to Egypt in 1798. In 1800, the British helped the Maltese drive out the French, and the Maltese then offered control of the islands to the British. The United Kingdom developed important military headquarters there, and British troops remained on the island until 1979.

Marshall Islands

The Marshall Islands are a group of low-lying islands and coral *atolls* in the central Pacific Ocean which became an independent country in 1986. Atolls are ring-shaped reefs that enclose a lagoon. The Marshall Islands lie east of the Caroline Islands and northwest of the Gilberts, in the part of the Pacific referred to as Micronesia.

Land

The Marshall Islands lie in two parallel chains about 130 miles (209 kilometers) apart. The eastern group is called the *Radak,* or *Sunrise Chain.* The western group is called the *Ralik,* or *Sunset Chain.* Each chain extends about 650 miles (1,050 kilometers) in a curve from northwest to southeast. About 1,150 islets lie along the reefs that form the atolls.

The climate is tropical, but ocean breezes cool the air. Rainfall is light on the northern islands, but heavier in the south. Only a few kinds of plants, such as coconut palms and banana and papaya plants, grow in the coral sand that covers the land.

People and history

The people of the Marshall Islands are Micronesians—a dark-skinned people with wavy or woolly hair. The Marshall Islanders are noted for their handicrafts. About 57,000 people live on this island group.

The islands were named for John Marshall, a British sea captain who explored them in 1788. Germany gained possession of the islands in 1885 and bought them from Spain along with the Mariana and Caroline islands in 1899. Japanese forces occupied the Marshalls during World War I (1914–1918), and Japan was allowed to rule the islands after the war under a mandate of the League of Nations. In 1933, however, Japan left the League and took over the Marshalls, closing the islands to Europeans and building war bases there.

During World War II (1939–1945), American forces took possession of the Marshalls. In 1947, the islands became part of the United Nations Trust Territory of the Pacific Islands, administered by the United States. In that year also, the U.S. government decided to test nuclear weapons on Enewetak, an isolated atoll in the Marshalls. It was already testing nuclear devices on the Bikini atoll. In both cases, the island's inhabitants were moved to other atolls. Tests were conducted until the late 1950's. Because of radiation contamination, the United States conducted cleanup operations, but Bikini and some islands of Enewetak will remain unfit for human habitation for hundreds of years. Inhabitants of Enewetak's southern islands were finally

FACT BOX

MARSHALL ISLANDS

COUNTRY

Official name: Republic of the Marshall Islands
Capital: Majuro
Terrain: Low coral limestone and sand islands
Area: 70 sq. mi. (181 km²)
Climate: Wet season from May to November; hot and humid; islands border typhoon belt
Highest elevation: Unnamed location on Likiep, 33 ft. (10 m)
Lowest elevation: Pacific Ocean, sea level

GOVERNMENT

Form of government: Constitutional government in free association with the United States
Head of state: President
Head of government: President
Administrative areas: 33 municipalities
Legislature: Nitijela (Parliament) with 33 members serving four-year terms
Court system: Supreme Court, High Court
Armed forces: The United States is responsible for the Marshall Islands' defense

PEOPLE

Estimated 2002 population: 68,000
Population growth: 3.88%
Population density: 971 persons per sq. mi. (376 per km²)
Life expectancy in years: Male: 66; Female: 69
Languages spoken: English (official); Marshallese dialects from the Malayo-Polynesian family; Japanese
Religion: Christian (mostly Protestant)

ECONOMY

Currency: United States dollar
Gross national income (GNI) in 2000: $102 million U.S.
Real annual growth rate (2000): 0.5%
GNI per capita (2000): $1,970 U.S.
Goods exported: Fish, coconut oil, trochus shells
Goods imported: Foodstuffs, machinery and equipment, fuels, beverages and tobacco
Trading partners: United States, Japan, Australia

No data are available for population distribution, doctors, education, technology, and balance of payments.

allowed to return in 1980. In 1985 all residents of Rongelap atoll were forced to relocate to Mejato atoll after tests showed high levels of radiation.

In 1986, the United States granted the Marshalls a form of self-government called *free association.* Under this system, the people control their internal and foreign affairs, and the United States is obligated to defend the islands in emergencies.

United States military concerns continue to dominate the Marshalls, as Kwajalein atoll serves as an essential element of the Pacific Barrier radar system and certain Kwajalein islands are used as targets for missiles test-fired from California.

In 1994, several members of the Marshalls' legislature demanded that the U.S. government release information on the effects of nuclear tests on the area. Lawmakers suggested that the information remains classified so that the United States does not have to pay adequate compensation to residents, who have the highest rate in the world for some cancers.

Coral atolls

The coral atolls and reefs that dot the Pacific are limestone formations composed of tiny sea animals and plants and their remains. They may grow around a volcanic island (1),

forming a ring in the warm, shallow water around the shoreline (2). With a rise in sea level or the movement of oceanic plates, the island may sink.

But the reef grows upward and forms a ringlike *barrier reef* (3). After the island has submerged, only a circular reef called an *atoll* remains. Often, soil lodges on the coral, and vegetation grows (4).

The Marshall Islands consist of coral atolls and islands that lie in two parallel chains about 130 miles (209 kilometers) apart.

Martinique

Martinique is the second largest island, after Trinidad, in the Lesser Antilles. It lies north of St. Lucia and south of Dominica in the Caribbean Sea. It is an overseas *department* (administrative district) of France. The oval-shaped island covers 425 square miles (1,102 square kilometers). Most islanders are descendants of African slaves, though some people are of mixed black and European origin.

In addition to its delightful French atmosphere, Martinique boasts beautiful mountains, tropical rain forests, scenic coasts, sunny beaches, and charming villages. The island attracts more than 200,000 tourists a year. About two-thirds of these visitors come from France, and many others come from the United States.

An island of mountains

Martinique has three volcanic, forest-covered mountain regions in the north, center, and south. The tallest mountain on the island is Mount Pelée, which rises to 4,583 feet (1,397 meters). Flatter areas in the south are covered by huge plantations where bananas, pineapples, and sugar cane are grown.

An unusual landscape called the *Savane des Petrifactions* (the Petrified Savanna) lies in the far south of the island, near the village of Ste.-Anne. The Petrified Savanna appears to be a forest of petrified wood, but it is actually a series of lava flows.

Martinique's coastal plains are narrow, and beautiful beaches—some consisting of white sand and some of black volcanic sand—face the Caribbean Sea. The eastern coast, which faces the Atlantic Ocean, has a wild, natural beauty with dramatic bays and rough seas.

History

Christopher Columbus reached Martinique in 1502, on his fourth voyage to the New World, but it was not until 1635 that the French began to colonize the island. French settlers established coffee and sugar-cane plantations and used slave labor to work them. Great Britain occupied the island for short periods before French rule was officially recognized in the early 1800's.

The French government made Martinique an overseas department in 1946. In 1958, Martinique chose to remain an overseas department. The island sends three deputies to the French National Assembly.

Through substantial financial aid, France has done much to develop Martinique and bring a modest level of prosperity to its people. France and Martinique maintain close ties, and about two-thirds of the island's trade is with France.

Fort-de-France

Fort-de-France, the capital and chief commercial and cultural center of Martinique, is also home to about one-third of the island's population. The city lies on a large bay on the west coast and also serves as a busy port of call for cruise ships.

Fort-de-France's central area has elegant colonial buildings that are similar to those in the old French Quarter of New Orleans. Large, handsome homes from the colonial era, set amid splendid gardens, reflect the wealth of the former plantation owners. La Savane square is a popular spot for a friendly chat while islanders are out for their evening stroll.

The cloud-covered peak of Mount Pelée rises high above the small town of St.-Pierre. This town was once a city known as *Little Paris of the West Indies*—the capital city of Martinique. The city was destroyed when Mount Pelée erupted in 1902, and about 38,000 people died. Only one person survived.

Villagers haul their fishing nets ashore on a sandy beach along Martinique's west coast, which faces the Caribbean Sea. The waters of the Caribbean are warm and relatively calm, but off the eastern coast, the waters of the Atlantic are often cold and rough.

Martinique, *above,* is a mountainous island in the Lesser Antilles. While sugar cane is the chief crop, bananas, cotton, pineapples, and tobacco are also grown. Rum distilling is the island's only important manufacturing activity.

A hardware store owner waits for customers. The sign above the store is written in French, Martinique's official language. Many people also speak Creole, a French *patois* (dialect).

Mauritania

Mauritania, a country on the western bulge of the African continent, was once a French colony. In French, its name is République Islamique de Mauritanie (Islamic Republic of Mauritania).

Mauritania is often described as a bridge linking North Africa and west Africa, and its flag, a yellow crescent and star on a green background, reflects this connection. The color green and the star and crescent stand for Mauritania's ties to Islamic North Africa. The color yellow stands for the country's ties to the black African nations south of the Sahara.

However, conflict between the two cultures has troubled Mauritania. The government has also been plagued by *desertification*—the nation's continuing loss of land to the growing Sahara, which now covers about two-thirds of Mauritania. Severe droughts and human activity along the edges of the desert have contributed to the expansion of the desert. In the 1980's, the Sahara was moving south at the alarming rate of almost 4 miles (6 kilometers) a year.

Military leaders controlled Mauritania between 1978 and 1992, when multiparty elections were held. Maawiya Ould Sid Ahmed Taya, who had served as president of the military government, was elected president. National Assembly elections also were held.

The growing desert and the clashing cultures have long played a role in Mauritania. Early black people farmed the region and lived alongside hunters, herders, and fishers. But as the climate became drier and the land turned to desert, these people began to move south. Beginning in the A.D. 200's, Berbers from the north forced more farmers to move south.

From the A.D. 300's until the 1500's, three great west African powers controlled parts of Mauritania—the Ghana, Mali, and Songhai empires. During this time, Arabs began their conquest of North Africa.

The Arabs—and Arab influence—slowly moved south toward Mauritania. The Berbers, driven farther and farther south, forced most of the black people to the Sénégal River. The Berbers were eventually dominated by the Arabs, and their descendants became known as Moors.

Major European contact began in the 1600's. For the next 200 years, France, Great Britain, and the Netherlands all competed for the valuable gum arabic trade in Mauritania. France made the region a protectorate in

FACT BOX

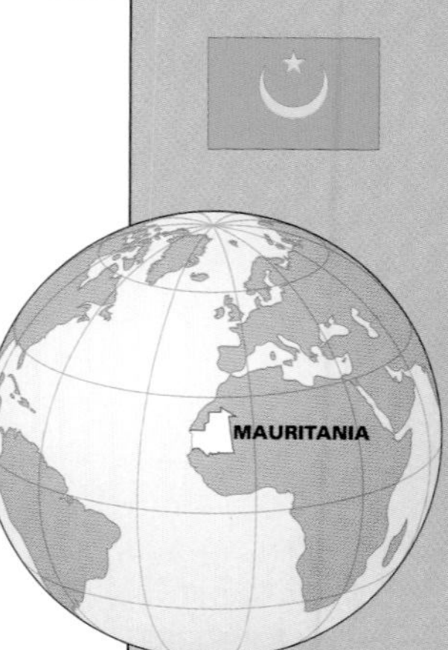

COUNTRY

Official name: Al Jumhuriyah al Islamiyah al Muritaniyah (Islamic Republic of Mauritania)
Capital: Nouakchott
Terrain: Mostly barren, flat plains of the Sahara; some central hills
Area: 397,955 sq. mi. (1,030,700 km²)
Climate: Desert; constantly hot, dry, dusty
Main river: Sénégal
Highest elevation: Kediet Ijill, 3,002 ft. (915 m)
Lowest elevation: Sebkha de Ndrhamcha, 10 ft. (3 m) below sea level

GOVERNMENT

Form of government: Republic
Head of state: President
Head of government: Prime minister
Administrative areas: 12 regions, 1 capital district
Legislature: Legislature consisting of the Majlis al-Shuyukh (Senate) with 56 members serving six-year terms and the Majlis al-Watani (National Assembly) with 79 members serving five-year terms
Court system: Cour Supreme (Supreme Court), court of appeals, lower courts
Armed forces: 15,650 troops

PEOPLE

Estimated 2002 population: 2,814,000
Population growth: 2.94%
Population density: 7 persons per sq. mi. (3 per km²)
Population distribution: 54% urban, 46% rural
Life expectancy in years:
Male: 49
Female: 53
Doctors per 1,000 people: 0.1
Percentage of age-appropriate population enrolled in the following educational levels:
Primary: 83
Secondary: 18
Further: 6

A typical suburb of Nouakchott, the capital and largest city of Mauritania, sprawls along the Atlantic coast. During the 1970's, severe droughts drove many rural people to the city, where they live in makeshift shantytowns.

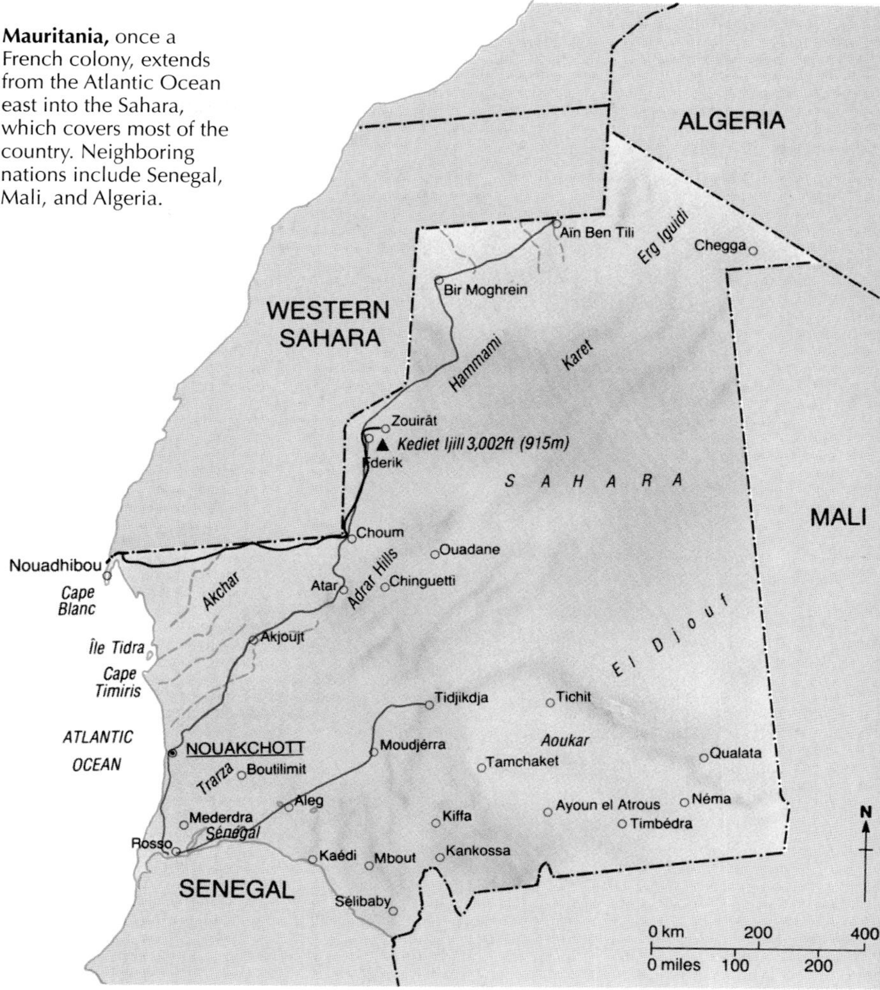

Mauritania, once a French colony, extends from the Atlantic Ocean east into the Sahara, which covers most of the country. Neighboring nations include Senegal, Mali, and Algeria.

Languages spoken:
- Hasaniya Arabic (official)
- Pular
- Soninke
- Wolof (official)
- French

Religion:
- Muslim 100%

Technology

Radios per 1,000 people: 149
Televisions per 1,000 people: 96
Computers per 1,000 people: 9.4

Economy

Currency: Ouguiya
Gross national income (GNI) in 2000: $1.0 billion U.S.
Real annual growth rate (1999–2000): 5.2%
GNI per capita (2000): $370 U.S.
Balance of payments (2000): $90 million U.S.
Goods exported: Fish and fish products, iron ore, gold
Goods imported: Machinery and equipment, petroleum products, capital goods, foodstuffs, consumer goods
Trading partners: France, Japan, Italy, Spain, Germany

1903, and Mauritania became a French colony in 1920.

In 1958, Mauritania became a self-governing republic in the French Community. Mokhtar Ould Daddah was elected prime minister in 1959. Ould Daddah favored independence. On Nov. 28, 1960, Mauritania became a free nation.

Mauritania has had many problems since independence. First, Morocco laid claim to the region. Then Mauritania fought a nationalist movement in Western Sahara for control of part of that area. In 1978, Ould Daddah was overthrown by military leaders, partly because he was unable to end the war with Western Sahara. In 1979, the military rulers gave up Mauritania's claim to Western Sahara. The military ruled until 1992, when a multiparty democracy was established.

People and Economy

One thing that almost all Mauritanians have in common is their religion—about 99 per cent of the people are Muslims. However, Islam is not enough to bring the two main ethnic groups in the country together. Each follows a different way of life.

The majority of the Mauritanian people are Moors, descendants of Arabs and Berbers. Although French is the nation's official language, most Moors speak Arabic. Some are nomads, who move through the desert with their animals in search of water and pasture. Others live in the cities or villages. Since severe droughts began in the 1960's, the Sahara has been spreading, and a growing number of nomads have flocked to the urban areas.

The Moors themselves are divided into classes. The highest classes are the warriors and the *marabout* (saintly) tribes. Before the French colonized Mauritania, the warriors were the nobility. They were served by other tribes, and they made slaves of many blacks. The warriors' chief occupation was fighting.

In contrast, the marabout tribes were peaceful people who raised livestock. Before French rule, marabout leaders were educated people who studied law and religion and advised the warriors.

Other Moor classes are the vassals—who still work for the nobles—craft workers, entertainers, and black slaves or former slaves. Slavery has been outlawed in Mauritania, but certain Mauritanian blacks still are treated as slaves.

The second major group of Mauritanians are black Africans. About one-third of the people belong to one of the five main black ethnic groups: the Toucouleur, the Fulbe, the Soninké, the Wolof, and the Bambara.

Most black Mauritanians are farmers who live along the Sénégal River in the south of the country. Their round, mud-brick huts stand along twisting village pathways.

The nation's educational system is poor. Less than half of Mauritania's children enter elementary school, and 15 per cent enter high school.

Fishing is an important source of export earnings in Mauritania, where the catch includes both ocean and freshwater fish.

Black Africans, like the woman and her child in the photo below, make up about one-third of Mauritania's population. Most of the rest are Moors, descended from Berbers and Arabs. Some Mauritanians have both Moorish and black ancestors.

A market in Nouakchott, *right,* is strewn with baskets of goods. A young city, the capital was founded in 1957 by the French as a colonial seat. Today, the city is a magnet for Mauritanians fleeing the drought-stricken interior.

Open-pit iron ore mines near Zouirât and Fdérik, *far right,* contain large, high-grade deposits of Mauritania's most important mineral resource. The ore is exported mainly to Germany, Great Britain, and Italy.

An underdeveloped economy

Incomes in Mauritania are low, and most workers make barely enough to support their families. The majority of the people are farmers and livestock herders. Farmers grow chiefly corn, dates, millet, red beans, and rice. Some food must be imported, but some livestock is exported.

Some of Mauritania's people make their living by fishing. The government has expanded the fishing industry, and it is now an important part of the economy.

Gum arabic, which comes from the sap of acacia trees, is exported for use in making perfumes, medicine, candies, and glue. Iron ore is another important export.

However, the government of Mauritania depends on economic aid from other coun-

tries, especially France, to balance its budget. Poor communications and transportation hurt the country's economic development.

Further problems

A severe drought in the early 1980's destroyed food crops and killed livestock in Mauritania. As the drought continued, cities became vastly overcrowded with rural refugees.

Blacks protested against the discrimination they suffered from the Moors, and a group of blacks reportedly attempted—but failed—to overthrow the government. Blacks also suspected that government land programs were designed to steal their valuable land along the Sénégal River. A dispute with the neighboring country of Senegal resulted in Mauritania forcing some blacks to move to Senegal, and Senegal forcing some Moors into Mauritania.

The growing desert and the long-standing conflict between Moors and blacks continued to cause problems for Mauritanians in 1990.

Mauritius

The island nation of Mauritius lies in the middle of the Indian Ocean, about 500 miles (800 kilometers) east of Madagascar and 2,450 miles (3,943 kilometers) southwest of India. Mauritius consists of one main island—also called Mauritius—and several other islands or island groups, including Rodrigues, Agalega, and the Cargados Carajos Shoals. Mauritius also claims the Chagos Archipelago, an island group about 1,300 miles (2,100 kilometers) northeast of the island of Mauritius that is controlled by the United Kingdom.

Mauritius was a constitutional monarchy from its independence in 1968 until 1992, when it became a republic. Voters elect most of the members of the National Assembly. To guarantee fair representation, an election commission also chooses four members from minority groups that are not adequately represented, and four members on the basis of their minority group and political party.

Mauritius was formed by volcanoes that left the land covered with rocks and a thick layer of lava. Coral reefs surround all but the southern part of the island. A misty plateau rises in the center of Mauritius, and black volcanic peaks tower above the sugar cane fields that cover about half the island.

More than a third of Mauritius' income comes from the sugar industry. About 90 per cent of its farmland is planted with sugar cane, and almost all its exports are sugar or sugar products. Sugar is processed in factories on the island. About one-third of all workers grow, harvest, or process sugar cane.

People grow vegetables for their own use in small gardens or between the rows of sugar cane. But most of their food must be imported.

Almost 70 per cent of the people of Mauritius are Asian Indians. Almost 30 per cent are *Creoles*—people of mixed European and African descent or mixed European and Indian descent. The rest of the people are Chinese or Europeans.

English is the official language, but French may be used by government officials, and most of the people speak Creole, a French dialect. Some Indians speak one or more of six Indian languages, and the Chinese speak one of two Chinese dialects.

More than 50 per cent of Mauritians are Hindus. Christians and Muslims make up most of the rest of the population. Dotting the island are Hindu temples, Christian churches, Muslim mosques, and Buddhist pagodas.

This mix of peoples, languages, and faiths reflects the history of Mauritius. The Dutch claimed the island in 1598 and named it after Prince Maurice of Nassau. France later ruled the island and founded Port Louis, now its

The country of Mauritius, *map right,* consists of the islands of Mauritius, Rodrigues, Agalega, and the Cargados Carajos Shoals. Rodrigues lies about 350 miles (563 kilometers) east of Mauritius Island, Agalega about 580 miles (933 kilometers) north, and the Cargados Carajos Shoals about 250 miles (402 kilometers) north.

Fact Box

MAURITIUS

Country

Official name: Republic of Mauritius
Capital: Port Louis
Terrain: Small coastal plain rising to discontinuous mountains encircling central plateau
Area: 718 sq. mi. (1,860 km²)
Climate: Tropical, modified by southeast trade winds; warm, dry winter (May to November); hot, wet, humid summer (November to May)
Main rivers: Black, Grand
Highest elevation: Piton de la Rivière Noire, 2,711 ft. (826 m)
Lowest elevation: Indian Ocean, sea level

Government

Form of government: Parliamentary democracy
Head of state: President
Head of government: Prime minister
Administrative areas: 9 districts, 3 dependencies
Legislature: National Assembly with 66 members serving five-year terms
Court system: Supreme Court
Armed forces: None

People

Estimated 2002 population: 1,177,000
Population growth: 0.89%
Population density: 1,494 persons per sq. mi. (577 per km²)
Population distribution: 57% rural, 43% urban
Life expectancy in years:
Male: 67
Female: 75
Doctors per 1,000 people: 0.9
Percentage of age-appropriate population enrolled in the following educational levels:
Primary: 108*
Secondary: 71
Further: 7
Languages spoken:
English (official)
Creole

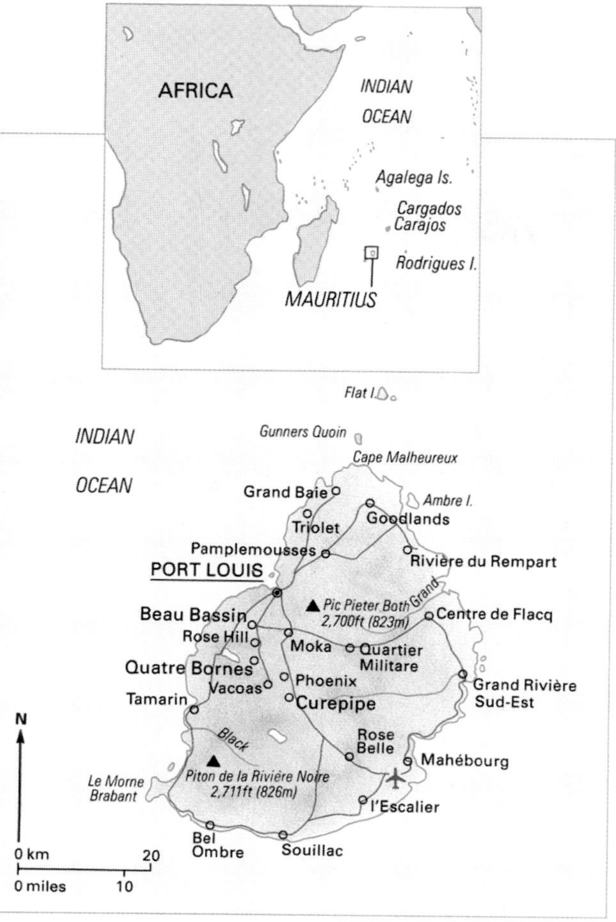

A spectacular display of sea shells from the Indian Ocean fills the craft of this Mauritian boatman, who hopes to sell them to tourists as souvenirs.

Port Louis, capital, largest city, and leading port of Mauritius, lies on the northwest coast of the island of Mauritius. The town was named for Louis XV, king of France.

French
Hindi
Urdu
Hakka
Bojpoori

Religions:
Hindu 52%
Roman Catholic 26%
Muslim 17%
Protestant 2%

*Enrollment ratios compare the number of students enrolled to the population which, by age, should be enrolled. A ratio higher than 100 indicates that students older or younger than the typical age range are also enrolled.

Technology

Radios per 1,000 people: 379

Televisions per 1,000 people: 268

Computers per 1,000 people: 100.5

Economy

Currency: Mauritian rupee

Gross national income (GNI) in 2000: $4.4 billion U.S.

Real annual growth rate (1999–2000): 8.0%

GNI per capita (2000): $3,750 U.S.

Balance of payments (2000): -$33 million U.S.

Goods exported: Clothing and textiles, sugar, cut flowers, molasses

Goods imported: Manufactured goods, capital equipment, foodstuffs, petroleum products, chemicals

Trading partners: France, United Kingdom, United States, South Africa, India

capital. Both the Dutch and the French brought African slaves.

The British took control in 1810 and freed the slaves 23 years later. Almost half a million Indian workers came to replace the slave laborers over the next 75 years. Chinese traders also settled on the island.

Mauritius became independent in 1968. The Labor Party controlled the government until 1982, when the leftist Mauritian Militant Movement (MMM) gained control through elections. In 1983, the Militant Socialist Movement won legislative elections. On March 12, 1992, Mauritius became a republic. An alliance of the Labour Party and the MMM won elections held in 1995, and Navinchandra Ramgoolam of the Labour Party became prime minister.

Mexico

The fascinating country of Mexico lies in the extreme north of Latin America—just south of the United States. The great majority of its people are *mestizos*—people of mixed European and Indian ancestry—and almost all of them speak Spanish. Mexico itself is an enchanting blend of Spanish and Indian cultures.

Mexico's cultural mix is a result of its long and colorful history. Hundreds of years ago, Mexico was the home of great Indian civilizations. They built cities and temples. They developed a calendar, a counting system, and a form of writing. But the last of these Indian empires fell to Spanish invaders in 1521. For the next 300 years, Mexico was a Spanish colony. The Spaniards introduced new agricultural methods and new forms of government. They also took Mexico's land and mineral riches, and the Indians were left poor, uneducated, and without political power. Mexico is now an independent nation, and its mestizo population takes great pride in its Indian ancestry.

The Rio Grande forms about two-thirds of the border between Mexico and the United States. In the Western Hemisphere, only the United States and Brazil have more people than Mexico. Only Canada, the United States, Brazil, and Argentina have more land.

Few other countries have landscapes and climates so varied and lying so close to one another. Mexico is a land of towering mountains, high plateaus, dry deserts, and coastal rain forests. Some mountain peaks in tropical southern Mexico are permanently snow-capped.

Only about an eighth of Mexico's land is farmed. The rest of the country is too dry, mountainous, or otherwise unsuitable. However, Mexico is a leading producer of coffee, corn, and cotton. It is also rich in minerals—silver, copper, and gold. Its petroleum industry is especially important to the country and to the energy-hungry world. Manufacturing is important too.

A social and economic revolution began in Mexico in 1910. The government took over huge, privately owned farms and divided them among millions of landless farmers. Since the 1940's, the government has encouraged manufacturing and petroleum production. But these changes have not kept up with the nation's rapid population growth. More than a third of the Mexican people live in poverty. Each year many leave the rural areas to seek work in the cities or in other countries, especially the United States. The population of Mexico City has swelled, making it the largest city in the world. For many Mexicans, it seems that the revolution that began in 1910 is still going on.

Mexico Today

Mexico's flag features three colored stripes: green for independence, white for religion, and red for union. The country is made up of 31 states and a Federal District.

Mexico's constitutional government

The Mexican government is based on the Constitution of 1917. The Constitution calls for three branches of government—executive, legislative, and judicial.

Most of the power is held by the executive branch, especially the president. Mexico has no vice president. If the president does not finish a term of office, the Congress chooses a temporary president. A president is normally elected to one 6-year term.

The Congress is composed of two houses. The Senate has 128 members—2 senators elected from each state and the Federal District and 64 allocated on the basis of each party's popular vote. The Chamber of Deputies has 500 members—300 elected from electoral districts, and 200 allocated on the basis of each party's popular vote. A member of Congress cannot serve two consecutive terms.

The highest court in the judicial branch is the Supreme Court of Justice. The president appoints the 21 justices for life, with approval of the Senate. The Supreme Court appoints the judges of the 21 Circuit Courts and the 68 District Courts to life terms.

Mexico's Constitution also sets up the state governments. Each state has an elected governor and legislature.

The Constitution gives the federal government great power over the economy, education, and affairs of state. The government has used its power to take privately owned estates and divide them among poor farmers. It has taken over some of the nation's key industries, such as railroads, banking, and the petroleum industry. The government has also established a national school system and built many hospitals.

Until recently, Mexico's major political party has been the *Partido Revolucionario Institucional* (Institutional Revolutionary Party), or PRI. Controversy engulfed PRI in the 1990's. In March 1994, a gunman killed a PRI presidential candidate. The government said that the gunman acted alone, but most Mexicans doubted this. In September 1994, a top PRI official was shot to death. His brother, Assistant Attorney General Ruíz Massieu, investigated the killing but resigned, claiming PRI officials were trying to hide the party's role in the crime. Ruíz himself was later arrested and accused of obstructing the probe. Despite the turmoil, in late 1994 PRI member Ernesto Zedillo Ponce de León was elected president.

In 1997, the PRI lost its majority in the Chamber of Deputies for the first time. In

Fact Box

Country

Official name: Estados Unidos Mexicanos (United Mexican States)
Capital: Mexico City
Terrain: High, rugged mountains; low coastal plains; high plateaus; desert
Area: 761,606 sq. mi. (1,972,550 km²)
Climate: Varies from tropical to desert
Main rivers: Balsas, Rio Grande, Yaqui
Highest elevation: Volcan Pico de Orizaba, 18,701 ft. (5,700 m)
Lowest elevation: Laguna Salada, 33 ft. (10 m) below sea level

Government

Form of government: Federal republic
Head of state: President
Head of government: President
Administrative areas: 31 estados (states), 1 distrito federal (federal district)
Legislature: Congreso de la Union (National Congress) consisting of the Camara de Senadores (Senate) with 128 members serving six-year terms and the Camara Federal de Diputados (Federal Chamber of Deputies) with 500 members serving three-year terms
Court system: Corte Suprema de Justicia (Supreme Court of Justice)
Armed forces: 178,770 troops

People

Estimated 2002 population: 101,709,000
Population growth: 1.53%
Population density: 135 persons per sq. mi. (52 per km²)
Population distribution: 75% urban, 25% rural
Life expectancy in years: Male: 68, Female: 75
Doctors per 1,000 people: 1.7
Percentage of age-appropriate population enrolled in the following educational levels: Primary: 114*, Secondary: 71, Further: 18

Mexico is made up of 31 states and the Federal District. Mexico shares its long northern border with the United States and extends 1,250 miles (2,012 kilometers) south to Central America. Airlines, highways, and railroads connect Mexico's major cities, but some farmers still carry goods to market on their heads or by burro.

Languages spoken:
Spanish
Mayan
Nahuatl
regional indigenous languages

Religions:
Roman Catholic 89%
Protestant 6%

**Enrollment ratios compare the number of students enrolled to the population which, by age, should be enrolled. A ratio higher than 100 indicates that students older or younger than the typical age range are also enrolled.*

Technology

Radios per 1,000 people: 330
Televisions per 1,000 people: 283
Computers per 1,000 people: 50.6

Economy

Currency: New Mexican peso
Gross national income (GNI) in 2000: $497 billion U.S.
Real annual growth rate (1999–2000): 6.9%
GNI per capita (2000): $5,070 U.S.
Balance of payments (2000): -$18,157 million U.S.
Goods exported: Manufactured goods, oil and oil products, silver, coffee, cotton
Goods imported: Metal-working machines, steel mill products, agricultural machinery, electrical equipment, car parts for assembly, repair parts for motor vehicles, aircraft, and aircraft parts
Trading partners: United States, Japan, Canada, Germany, Spain

2000, Vicente Fox Quesada was elected president of Mexico. He became the first non-PRI candidate to be elected to that office in 71 years.

Problems

The North American Free Trade Agreement (NAFTA) between Mexico, the United States, and Canada, ratified in 1993, was expected to improve Mexico's economy by lifting trade barriers. In January 1994, a rebel group called the Zapatista National Liberation Army seized four towns in the state of Chiapas. The rebels claimed the government discriminated against the region's Indian population and that NAFTA would help only the elite. A shaky peace held for most of 1994. In 1996 the Popular Revolutionary Army (known by the Spanish acronym EPR) staged another guerrilla uprising, when they attacked police and military posts in four states.

Land and Climate

Mexico has six main land regions. Within these regions are many smaller areas that differ greatly in altitude, climate, landforms, and plant life. The result is a land of constant variety.

The Plateau of Mexico is by far the largest of the land regions, covering most of the interior of the country. It also has the most varied landscape.

The Mesa Central, or Central Plateau, is the heart of Mexico. Averaging about 7,000 feet (2,100 meters) above sea level, this highland area gets enough rain to produce crops. The Aztec Indian capital of Tenochtitlán once stood at its southern edge, in the beautiful Valley of Mexico. Today, Mexico City rises on the same site.

The Volcanic Axis marks the southern edge of the Plateau of Mexico. This chain of volcanoes includes Orizaba, the highest point in Mexico at 18,701 feet (5,700 meters). Southeast of Mexico City, the volcanoes Ixtacihuatl and Popocatépetl soar more than 17,000 feet (5,180 meters).

Rimming the eastern and western edges of the Plateau of Mexico are two mountain ranges—the Sierra Madre Oriental and the Sierra Madre Occidental. The Sierra Madre Oriental is actually a series of ranges. The Sierra Madre Occidental is steep and rugged.

The Mesa del Norte, or Northern Plateau, stretches from the Mesa Central to the United States. As it extends north and east, it drops in altitude from 9,000 feet (2,700 meters) to less than 4,000 feet (1,200 meters). The low mountains that rise above its plains contain some of the richest silver deposits in the world.

The five other main land regions of Mexico lie along the coasts. The Pacific Northwest is generally dry. The Peninsula of Lower California, called Baja California, is mostly rolling or mountainous desert. Fertile river valleys lie along the mainland coast of the Gulf of California.

The Southern Uplands and Chiapas Highlands line Mexico's southern coast. A hot, dry valley lies along the Balsas River in the Southern Uplands. On the Oaxaca Plateau in the east, ancient Indians built a religious center, and the Aztecs once mined gold. The rugged Sierra Madre del Sur rises along the coast.

Lacandón Indians, *below,* pole through a marshy area in a rain forest in the Chiapas Highlands, where rivers have cut broad, deep valleys through the mountains. Indians farm on the high flatlands.

An aerial view of the Valley of Mexico, *right,* shows the mountains rising above Mexico City. In the foreground are the cones of extinct volcanoes. Some other volcanoes in Mexico are still active.

In the Chiapas Highlands, blocklike mountains tower more than 9,000 feet (2,700 meters). Indians who speak Maya and other ancient languages live on the high, flat tablelands.

The Gulf Coastal Plain and the Yucatán Peninsula lie along Mexico's eastern coast. The plain's dry northern section supports only low thorny bushes and trees, but rainfall increases toward the south, and the land there grows rich with rain forests and farmland. At the plain's southeastern edge, the Yucatán Peninsula begins. The Yucatán is a low limestone plateau with no rivers. Rainfall reaches the sea through underground channels dissolved through the limestone.

The climate of Mexico also varies greatly. The northern half of the country is generally dry, though the mountains receive more rainfall than other sections. Above 2,000 feet (610 meters), summers are hot and winters are mild. Nights are much cooler than days. The coastal lowlands are hot and humid.

In the southern, tropical half of Mexico, altitude has created three main climate zones. The *tierra caliente* (hot land), which rises up to 3,000 feet (910 meters) above sea level, has long, hot, humid summers and mild winters. The *tierra templada* (temperate land), which extends from the *tierra caliente* up to 6,000 feet (1,800 meters), has mild to warm temperatures. In the *tierra fria* (cold land), which lies above the *tierra templada*, the highest peaks are always snow-covered. In tropical Mexico, short but heavy afternoon showers are common in summer.

A cable bridge spans a river in the Sierra Madre, *below*. The Sierra Madre is divided into three ranges: Oriental (east), Occidental (west), and del Sur (south). They form a horseshoe shape around the Plateau of Mexico. Roads and railroads climb the Sierra Madre Oriental to the plateau. The Sierra Madre Occidental is so steep that such routes were not built until the 1900's.

A hunter sits outside the entrance to a cave in the state of Chihuahua, *far left,* a dry highland region in northern Mexico.

El Rosario National Park has been set aside to preserve the winter resting grounds of the monarch butterfly. Thousands of these butterflies migrate to Mexico from the United States and Canada in the fall.

Forces of Nature

Mexico is located on the eastern edge of the *Ring of Fire,* a belt circling the Pacific Ocean where many earthquakes and volcanoes occur. It also lies in the path of hurricanes that form in the warm, tropical air over the Atlantic Ocean. As a result, these natural disasters are painfully familiar to the Mexican people.

Floating plates make up the earth's crust. These plates collide, separate, and grind past one another. This motion causes earthquakes and volcanic activity.

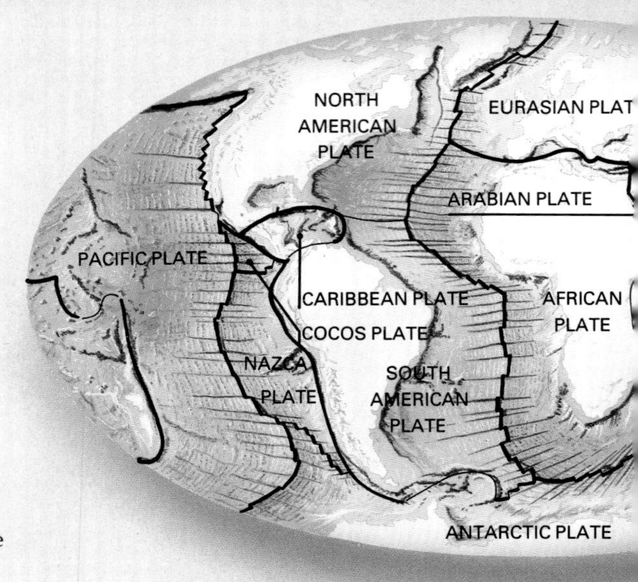

Earthquakes

On Sept. 19, 1985, the ground began to quake in Mexico City. For three minutes, the central area of the city shook violently, and dozens of high-rise buildings tumbled. By the time the earthquakes were over on Sept. 20, about 7,200 people had been killed.

Earthquakes occur mainly along the edges of rigid sections of the earth's crust called *plates*. Scientists believe that these plates slide slowly on a layer of puttylike hot rock beneath the plates. Pressure builds where the edges of these plates grind against each other. When the pressure grows too great, rocks break and the earth shifts, or quakes.

Mexico City is located near the border between two plates. The 1985 earthquake was particularly devastating because Mexico City was built on a dry lake bed, and the spongy ground beneath the city provides little support for structures.

Much of Mexico City lay in ruin after the 1985 earthquake, which measured 8.1 on the Richter scale. About 7,200 people died, and hundreds of buildings collapsed.

Volcanoes

The collision of two of the earth's plates can also force rock down, where it is melted by the earth's inner heat. The pressure on this melted rock is so great that it is sometimes forced up, escaping from the earth as *lava* and creating a volcano.

On Feb. 20, 1943, one such volcano, Paricutín, was born in Mexico. The most recent volcano to form in the Western Hemisphere started as a crack that appeared in a cornfield. Steam, smoke, and lava began to pour out of the opening. By the end of one week, the lava had formed a 450-foot (140-meter) high cone around the opening. Eventually, the volcano destroyed the nearby villages of Paricutín and San Juan Parangaricútiru.

Even more disastrous was the eruption of the volcano El Chichón in Mexico in 1982. This eruption killed 187 people and released a cloud of dust and sulfur dioxide gas high into the atmosphere.

Hurricanes

In September 1988, Hurricane Gilbert, the most powerful hurricane ever recorded in the Western Hemisphere, crossed the Caribbean Sea and slammed into Mexico. Hurricane Gilbert hit the tourist towns of Cancún and Cozumel along the Yucatán Peninsula.

Such storms develop over the warm waters of the North Atlantic or eastern Pacific in the summer and fall. The air over the warm water heats up, rises, and creates a low-pressure area. Winds begin to circle this area, increasing in speed. If their speed reaches 75 miles (120 kilometers) per hour or more, the storm is an official hurricane. The winds of Hurricane Gilbert reached a sustained speed on the ground of 137 miles (220 kilometers) per hour.

Earthquakes

The cause of the Mexico City earthquake was the motion of the North American Plate and the Cocos Plate. When the pressure on the rocks became too great, they cracked. A mighty shock wave shook the earth. Mexico City's location on a spongy, drained lake bed intensified the effect of the shock wave. Today, new buildings are constructed with special foundations that help keep them from sinking into the ground or toppling during a quake.

The Volcanic Axis is a series of volcanoes along the southern edge of the Plateau of Mexico. This axis is part of the *Ring of Fire*—the volcanic chain that runs around the rim of the Pacific Ocean. Movement of the earth's plates can put into motion a process that eventually forces lava to the surface. The volcanic eruption of El Chichón in 1982 sent millions of tons of ash into the air, possibly affecting the weather by blocking the sun's rays.

Seismic gaps, *below* (marked in yellow), along the west coast of Mexico and Central America, indicate areas of possible future earthquakes. Along this line, the Cocos Plate is being forced under the North American Plate. Scientists have learned that quakes are common where such pressure builds up.

Economy

In several important ways, the Mexican economy has changed greatly in the 1900's. Before the Mexican Revolution of 1910, the huge estates of wealthy landowners spread over many acres of the country. These estates, called *haciendas*, were owned by Spaniards or *creoles*, people of Spanish ancestry born in the New World.

Since 1910, the government has broken up most of the haciendas and given the land to the peasants. Since the 1940's, it has promoted manufacturing. Service industries, especially those involved in trade and tourism, now contribute much to the country's total production.

Manufacturing

The rapid expansion in Mexico's manufacturing industries since the 1940's has affected the nation's entire economy. Factories need raw materials to use in manufacturing, so the production of these materials increased. Banking and other services expanded to meet the needs of industry. The government spent heavily to construct housing around industrial centers. Power plants were built to provide energy for the new industries, and highways and railroads were constructed to carry their products.

Mexico City is the nation's leading manufacturing center. Its metropolitan area manufactures about half the country's products. Monterrey and Guadalajara are also important centers. Mexico's chief products include chemicals, clothing, iron and steel, petroleum, and processed foods. Before the 1960's, Mexican automobile factories assembled cars using imported parts. Today, they manufacture the parts as well.

Mexico has long been famous for the skill of its craft workers. Silver jewelry is made in Taxco, glassware and pottery in Guadalajara and Puebla, and handwoven blankets and baskets in Oaxaca and Toluca. Many of these handicrafts are sold to tourists.

Agriculture and forestry

Since the revolution, the government has distributed millions of acres of land to the peasants. About half of the total cropland is now managed under the traditional system of the *ejido*, in which farmland belongs to all the people of a community. On the ejidos,

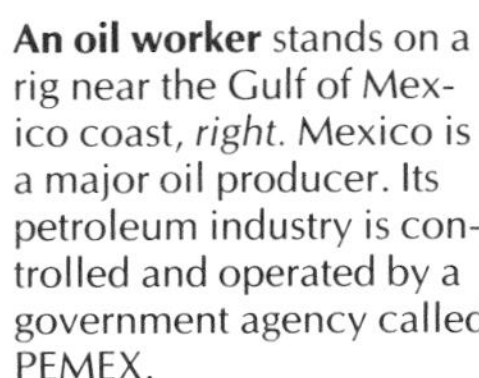

Coffee fields surround farm buildings on a plantation in the southern state of Chiapas. Most of the modern farming in this region takes place in deep, broad river valleys.

An oil worker stands on a rig near the Gulf of Mexico coast, *right.* Mexico is a major oil producer. Its petroleum industry is controlled and operated by a government agency called PEMEX.

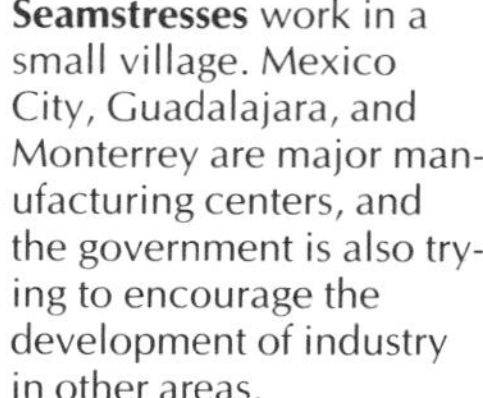

Seamstresses work in a small village. Mexico City, Guadalajara, and Monterrey are major manufacturing centers, and the government is also trying to encourage the development of industry in other areas.

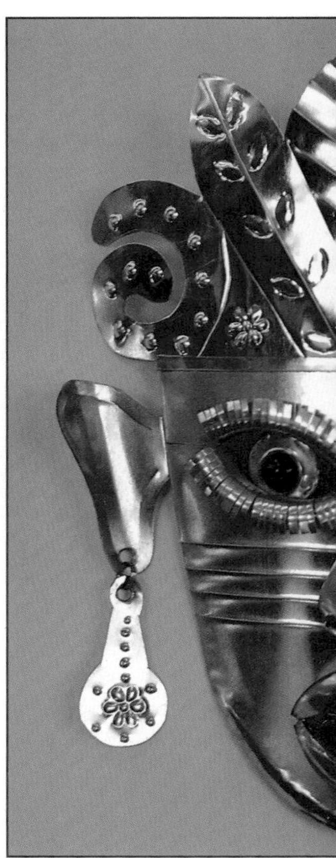

A silver mask, *right,* from Taxco shows the skill of Mexican craft workers. They use traditional Indian and Spanish colonial designs. Silver drew Spaniards to Mexico in the 1500's.

farmers either work on individual sections by themselves, or they work the whole area as a group. Today, most ejidos are farmed in individual sections. The rest of the nation's cropland consists of small family farms and the remaining haciendas.

Mexico's variety of climates leads to a variety of crops. Corn is Mexico's basic food, so more land is used for corn than for any other crop. Corn is used to make thin, round, flat bread called *tortillas*, which are eaten plain or made into tacos, enchiladas, or tostadas.

Other major crops include bananas, beans, coffee, cotton, oranges, sugar cane, and wheat. Mexican farmers also produce avocados, chili peppers, and tropical fruits and winter vegetables for export to the United States. Beef cattle are raised in the dry north, and dairy cattle graze in central Mexico.

Forests cover about a fifth of Mexico's land area. The forests provide hardwoods, such as ebony and mahogany for making furniture; pine trees for making wood pulp and paper; and sapodilla trees, which yield *chicle*—a juice used to make chewing gum.

A Maya Indian woman tends tomatoes and melons on the Yucatán Peninsula. The Mexican government promotes modern farming methods with education, financial aid, and irrigation and transportation systems. As a result, production has increased. However, primitive methods are still used in many areas, especially on the ejidos.

Mining

Gold and silver attracted Spaniards to Mexico in the 1500's. Silver mining has since been one of the nation's chief industries. Today, Mexico is the world's leading silver producer.

The country is also a major producer of petroleum, with an annual output of 900 million barrels. In the 1970's, major petroleum deposits were discovered on the east coast. The government used income from its oil to spur developing industry and also borrowed heavily for construction, expecting to repay the loans with oil profits. But the price of oil declined, and Mexico has had great difficulty paying its debts.

Also, Mexico now imports more products than it exports. Loans, foreign investment, and the tourist industry help make up the difference.

People

The Spaniards came to Mexico in the 1500's and conquered the Indians who lived there. In the Spanish colony of Mexico, a third group of people soon appeared. These people, who had both Indian and European parents, grandparents, or other ancestors, became known as *mestizos*.

Mexico still has some Indians and whites of unmixed ancestry, but today the great majority of Mexicans are mestizos. To be a mestizo is to be part of Mexico's history, and many mestizos are very proud of their Indian ancestors.

Almost all Mexicans speak Spanish, the official language of the country. Although most Indians speak Spanish as well as their own ancestral language, more than 5 million still use their Indian language in everyday life. Major Indian languages include Maya and Zapotec.

Being an Indian in Mexico does not depend on ancestry, but rather on a way of life and a point of view. A Mexican who speaks an Indian language, wears Indian clothes, and lives in a village where the people call themselves Indians is considered an Indian, even if the individual is a mestizo or a white person by ancestry.

Many Indian villages lie in the interior regions of Yucatán or in rugged areas of central and southern Mexico. There, the Indians still live much as their ancestors did. Government programs, however, are gradually bringing the Indian villagers into the mainstream of Mexican life.

Many Mexican farmers live near their fields in small villages, where houses stand along simple dirt roads or cobblestone streets. In most villages, a Roman Catholic church stands in the *plaza,* or public square, along with a few stores and government buildings. Almost every village has a market place.

Nearly 75 per cent of all Mexicans, however, live in cities or towns. Eight cities have populations of more than 500,000. Mexico City, one of the largest cities in the world, has more than 8 million people.

Many of Mexico's cities and towns began as Indian communities. Then the Spaniards made them more like Spanish towns, with central plazas and homes with patios. Today, in many ways, life in Mexico's larger cities is much like life in U.S. cities. Many city dwellers live in rows of homes built in the Spanish-colonial style, and suburbanites often live in modern apartment buildings and houses. The poorest Mexicans live in slum shacks or near-empty rooms. Many of these people came to the city to find jobs, but there is not enough work for the huge population.

The total population of Mexico is currently more than 100 million people. The population is increasing about 1.5 per cent each year. The rapid population growth is partly due to Mexico's traditionally high birth rate, and partly due to the sharply reduced death rate—a result of improved living conditions and better health care. Today, the government's chief problem may be providing jobs, housing, transportation, and schools for its growing population.

A Mexican teacher leads a class for refugees from Guatemala. Mexico has admitted a great number of refugees from Central America, where war and poverty affect many people.

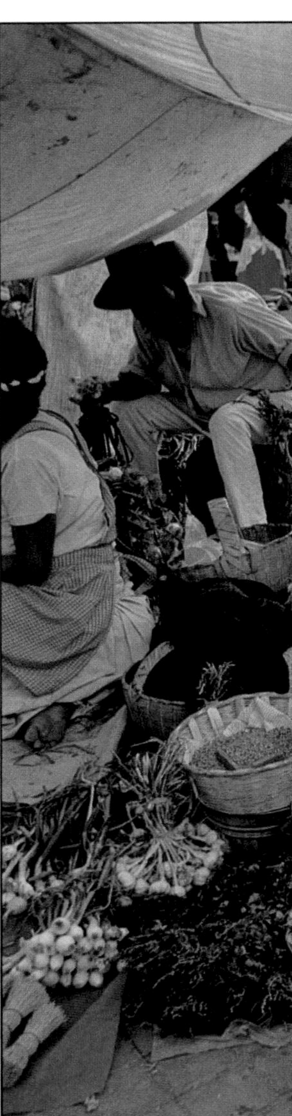

Mestizo girls, *right,* attend school in Taxco, near Mexico City. Many mestizos take pride in their mixed Indian and white ancestry. About 88 per cent of Mexican adults can read and write.

Campesinos wear local dress as they meet on the steps of a church in Chiapas. Many people in this area are descended from the Mayas.

At an outdoor market, *left,* an Indian woman sells herbs, spices, and vegetables. Going to market is an important activity for rural people. They spend the day chatting with friends and doing business.

The population of Mexico is increasing every year by 1.5 per cent. More than a third of the people still live in poverty. Many of the rural poor move to cities, hoping to find work.

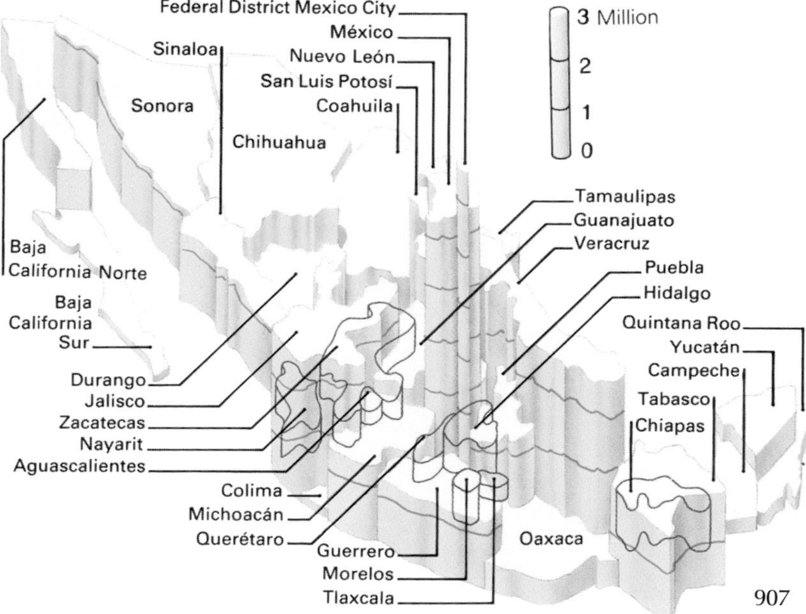

Mexico City

Mexico City is one of the largest cities in the world. About 23,000,000 people live in the city and in the surrounding area. The city is the capital of Mexico as well as its center of industry, education, transportation, and tourism.

Mexico City covers the same area as the Federal District of Mexico. But only the northern part of the Federal District is an urban area. The National Palace in the heart of the city houses the offices of Mexico's president and other officials.

The city's thousands of factories account for about half of the value of all the goods manufactured in Mexico. Important products include automobiles, chemicals, iron and steel, and textiles.

Mexico City has more than 4,000 schools. The country's oldest and largest university is the National Autonomous University of Mexico. It was founded in 1551, and in 1954 its new campus was completed in the capital. More than 300,000 students are enrolled in the university.

Almost all roads in Mexico lead to Mexico City. It is the center of the country's railroad network and of international air travel.

Tourists flock to Mexico City. The city is a fascinating contrast of old and new—of Indian, Spanish, and modern Mexican cultures. Aztec ruins still stand in some areas, along with beautiful palaces and houses of the Spanish colonial period. Modern skyscrapers and houses are sometimes decorated with brightly painted murals.

The city has more than 350 neighborhoods, many with parklike plazas. These public squares are centers of neighborhood life, where people gather to listen to band concerts and enjoy fiestas.

Constitution Plaza, called the Zócalo, is Mexico City's chief plaza, the site of the National Cathedral, National Palace, and Supreme Court of Justice. The heart of Mexico City extends west from the Zócalo to the Paseo de la Reforma, one of the most beautiful boulevards in the world. Nearby stands the majestic Palace of Fine Arts, with its theater and art galleries.

People have lived in what is now Mexico City for thousands of years. About the middle of the 1300's, the Aztec Indians founded their capital, Tenochtitlán, on this site, which was then an island in Lake Texcoco. The Aztecs built raised roads and elevated ramps to connect the city with the mainland.

Spanish invaders came to Tenochtitlán in 1519. Their leader, Hernando Cortés, destroyed the city almost completely in 1521 and built Mexico City, the capital of Spain's colony, on the ruins. After 30,000 people died in floodwaters in 1629, the Spaniards built a large canal to drain Lake Texcoco and carry off rain water. Mexico City remained under Spanish rule for 300 years, and became the largest city in the New World.

Although Mexico City has been a large, bustling city for a long time, new problems arose in the 1970's when its population increased by more than 70 per cent. Because of this phenomenal growth, the city faces many challenges today.

More jobs are needed for the many rural Mexicans who came seeking work. Housing is needed for the large numbers of poor people who live in slum shacks. And the city must deal with its traffic problems, as well as the serious air pollution caused by automobiles and factories.

Slum areas, the result of long-standing housing shortages, crowd the outskirts of Mexico City. In these areas, poor families live in wood or sheet-metal shacks that lack running water and electricity.

The "floating gardens" of Lake Xochimilco, *right*, are in the southeast part of the capital. Flower-bedecked boats glide along canals in this popular weekend spot.

Air pollution hangs over Mexico City, *far left.* The mountains that surround the city trap the pollution. They also keep water from draining naturally, causing flooding during heavy rains.

A street vendor, *left,* sells refreshments in busy Mexico City. Because of the country's economic problems, a growing number of urban Mexicans are forced to earn their living in such low-paying jobs.

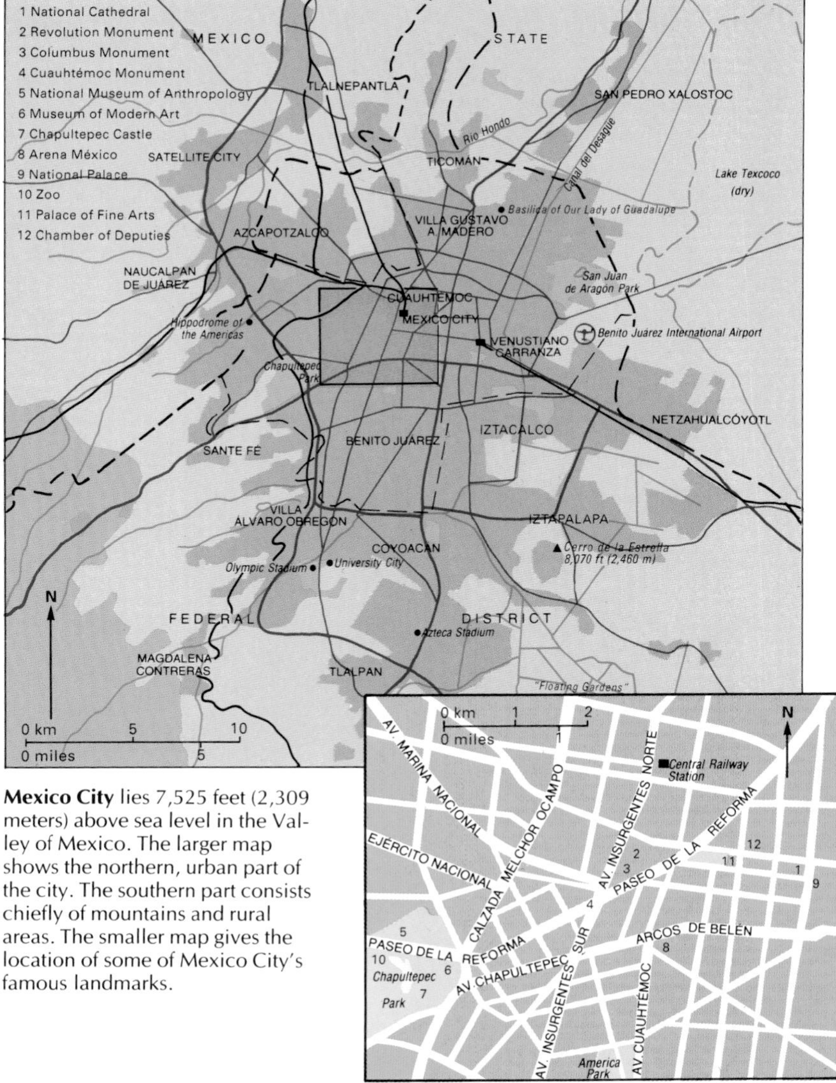

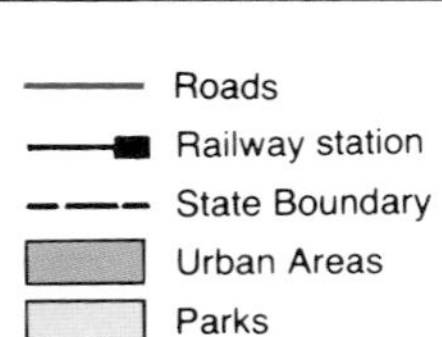

Mexico City lies 7,525 feet (2,309 meters) above sea level in the Valley of Mexico. The larger map shows the northern, urban part of the city. The southern part consists chiefly of mountains and rural areas. The smaller map gives the location of some of Mexico City's famous landmarks.

History

About 7000 B.C., the Indians in what is now the Puebla region of Mexico made a major discovery—they learned how to grow plants for food. Over time, the Indian hunters became farmers and settled in villages. Eventually, the villages grew into towns.

The years from A.D. 250 to 900, when great Indian civilizations thrived in Mexico, is called the Classic Period. During that time, the Mayas built huge pyramids and temples, developed mathematics, and studied astronomy. The Zapotec flattened a mountaintop and built a religious center there. They also made the first written records in the region.

The Aztecs built the last and the greatest Indian empire during the mid-1400's. Their capital, Tenochtitlán, stood on an island in Lake Texcoco. Here, in 1518, the Aztec Emperor Montezuma II heard reports of strangers on the coast. Because the strangers had guns and horses, which the Indians had never seen before, Montezuma thought they were gods. They were actually gold-hungry Spaniards exploring the "New World" they had discovered.

In February 1519, Hernando Cortés founded Veracruz, the first Spanish settlement in Mexico. He then marched toward Tenochtitlán and seized Montezuma for ransom. Cortés and his men had to flee when the Aztecs revolted, but he returned in 1521 and conquered the city. Cuauhtémoc, the last Aztec emperor, was tortured. He is now a Mexican hero.

For the next 300 years, Mexico was a Spanish colony. Europeans established haciendas and mined silver. They were mainly *creoles* (whites born in the New World). Mestizos labored in the cities. The Indians lived much as they always had, but sometimes they were forced to work on the haciendas. They also were made to accept the Roman Catholic religion, which they mixed with their traditional forms of worship.

In 1810, Miguel Hidalgo y Costilla, a creole priest, began Mexico's war for independence from Spain. Most of Hidalgo's followers were untrained mestizos and Indians, and almost all of them were captured or killed.

The king of Spain, annoyed by the uprising, began to tax the creoles, most of whom had not wanted independence. The king also

c. 7000 B.C. Farming develops.
c. 2000 B.C. Villages are established in the Valley of Mexico and in the south.
c. 1200 B.C. Olmec civilization arises.
c. A.D. 250-900 Great Indian civilizations thrive during the Classic Period.
c. 900-1200 Toltec empire flourishes.
mid-1300's Aztecs found Tenochtitlán (now Mexico City).
late 1400's Aztec empire reaches its peak.
1517 Spaniards discover Mexico.
1519-1521 Hernando Cortés conquers Aztec empire for Spain.
1810 Miguel Hidalgo y Costilla starts fight for independence.
1821 Mexico wins independence.
1824 Mexico becomes a republic.
1836 Texas wins independence from Mexico.
1846-1848 War with the United States. Defeated Mexico loses much land.
1855 Benito Juárez begins governmental and social reforms
1863 French troops occupy Mexico City.
1864 Maximilian of Austria becomes emperor of Mexico.
1867 Juárez returns to power.
1876-1880 and 1884-1911 Porfirio Diaz rules as dictator.
1910 Francisco I. Madero leads a revolution that overthrows Díaz.
1914 U.S. forces occupy Veracruz.
1917 Constitution is adopted.
1920's Period of economic and social reforms begins.
1934 President Cárdenas starts land distribution.
1938 Government takes foreign oil properties.
1942-1945 Mexico enters World War II on Allied side. Industries expand to supply war goods.
1953 Women receive right to vote in all elections.
1968 Summer Olympic Games held in Mexico City.
1970's Vast petroleum deposits discovered.
1985 Earthquakes in Mexico City kill thousands.
1994 The North American Free Trade Agreement (NAFTA) goes into effect.
2000 First non-PRI president in 71 years is elected.

Annexed by United States 1848
Purchased by United States 1853
Annexed by United States 1845
PACIFIC OCEAN

Hernando Cortés, *left,* conquered the Aztecs and won Mexico for Spain.

Lázaro Cárdenas, *far left,* oversaw major land reform during the 1930's.

Francisco "Pancho" Villa, a bandit chief, was a general in the Mexican Revolution of 1910.

The Building of the Dancers, constructed of stone blocks engraved with dancing figures like the one above, is part of Monte Albán, an ancient Zapotec religious center in what is now Oaxaca.

The ruins of Teotihuacán, near Mexico City, *left,* include the Avenue of the Dead and the Pyramid of the Moon. The city was built during Mexico's Classic Period (A.D. 250–900).

Spain's New World territories extended from Central America to what is now the U.S. Southwest. Its control began after it conquered the mighty Aztec empire in 1521. Mexico won independence in 1821 and later lost much land to the U.S.A.

The *Independence Mural* by Juan O'Gorman dramatizes Mexico's struggle for independence from Spain. This detail shows Miguel Hidalgo y Costilla, a creole priest, whose stirring speech, the "Grito de Dolores," encouraged Mexicans to revolt in 1810. The rebels won independence 11 years later.

organized a large army in Mexico. The creoles turned against the Spanish king and joined forces with an army officer, Agustín de Iturbide. By 1821, Mexico had won its independence.

Iturbide was named emperor, but was driven from power one year later. Although a republic was established in 1824, the mid-1800's were a time of great trouble in Mexico. Army generals often took control. One of them—Antonio López de Santa Anna—was president 11 times from 1833 to 1855. Santa Anna ruled as a dictator. During this time, Mexico fought wars with Texas and then with the United States. The United States took a vast area of land from Mexico.

Santa Anna seized power for the last time in 1853. Two years later, Benito Juárez, a Zapotec Indian, and other liberals took over and started reforms. They tried to break up the estates of the Roman Catholic Church and end its political power. A revolt followed, but Juárez remained in power.

France invaded Mexico and ruled for a time, but in 1867 Juárez again returned as president and ruled until his death in 1872. Next came the long reign of the dictator Porfirio Díaz. Mexico's economy improved under Díaz, but only his wealthy supporters benefited. Most Mexicans remained poor.

The Mexican Revolution of 1910 overthrew Díaz, aided by the U.S. seizure of Veracruz in 1914. Revolutionaries Francisco "Pancho" Villa and Emiliano Zapata turned against the new government because they wanted greater reform. A new Constitution, adopted in 1917, gave the government control over education, farm and oil properties, and the Roman Catholic Church. It also limited Mexico's president to one term and recognized labor unions.

In the 1900's, Mexico's presidents carried out the revolutionary programs to various degrees. Lázaro Cárdenas was especially successful in redistributing the land to the poor. He also took over the property of foreign oil companies. In the 1940's, during World War II, President Manuel Ávila Camacho encouraged industrial growth.

Despite the progress of the 1900's, many Mexicans still live in extreme poverty. A drop in oil prices in the 1980's led to government debt, unemployment, and rising prices.

Tourism

One industry that helps Mexico make up for its foreign trade imbalance is tourism. Every year, about 4 million foreign visitors come to Mexico to see the cultural treasures of the Indian ruins, the Spanish colonial architecture, and the modern performing and fine arts. They also come to enjoy Mexico's magnificent beaches, volcanic mountains, and desert landscapes.

Mexico City

Mexico City is the nation's center of tourism. In addition to the city's historic monuments and government buildings, tourists may visit the majestic Palace of Fine Arts. In this marble palace, the National Theater presents concerts, dance programs, operas, and plays.

North of Mexico City's downtown area is the Plaza of Three Cultures. In this single spot, tourists can see examples of the three cultures that combined to make Mexico. Ruins of ancient Aztec temples stand next to the remains of a colonial Spanish church built in 1524. Nearby, a huge government housing project reflects modern Mexican architecture.

The Basilica of Our Lady of Guadalupe is Mexico's most famous religious shrine, and pilgrims come to worship there throughout the year. The shrine stands in northern Mexico City at the foot of a hill where, according to Roman Catholic legend, the Virgin Mary appeared to a poor Indian man in 1531.

North of Mexico City are the handsome Spanish colonial churches of Acalmán and Tepoztlan. Also, many people visit the ancient Indian pyramids and temples at San Juan Teotihuacán, Tenayuca, and Tula.

The Yucatán Peninsula

Tourists interested in ancient Indian culture visit the Yucatán Peninsula to see the ruins of an ancient Mayan religious center at Chichen Itzá. Many visitors take day trips to the site from Cancún or Cozumel Island—two resorts on the Caribbean coast. These beach resorts, which sprang up in the 1970's when the government started to promote tourism, attract northerners seeking warmth and sunshine in the winter months.

Pacific coast resorts

Beautiful scenery and a warm, sunny climate make Acapulco one of the world's most popular vacation spots. This resort city lies on forested hills along a deep, natural harbor on Mexico's Pacific coast. Sunbathers, swimmers, boaters, deep-sea anglers, and water-skiers all come to Acapulco. The city has 20 beaches and more than 250 hotels and motels.

Visitors are thrilled to see daring divers plunge more than 120 feet (37 meters) from La Quebrada cliffs into the waters of a rocky cove. The water is too shallow except when large waves surge in, so the divers must time their dives carefully. People also enjoy Acapulco's fine restaurants and nightclubs.

Other beach resorts on the Pacific coast attract many tourists from the United States and Canada, especially during the winter months. These resorts include Ensenada, Manzanillo, Mazatlán, Puerto Vallarta, and Zihuatanejo.

Tijuana is on Mexico's far northwest coast just south of the U.S. border. A small village until about 1940, Tijuana began to grow rapidly thanks to its booming tourist trade. Today, it is a modern city with luxury hotels, nightclubs, gift shops, bullfights, and horse

Enterprising Mexicans carry colorful clothing for sale to tourists on an Acapulco beach. Many tourists come to Acapulco to enjoy water sports, sunbathing, and night life.

The ancient Maya city of Palenque, *right,* emerges from the tropical rain forest in Chiapas. This site, like the ancient religious center of Chichen Itzá in Yucatán, enchants tourists from all over the world.

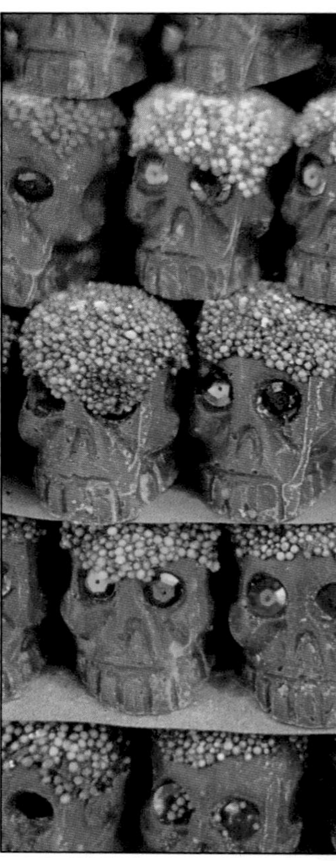

races. Tourists spend millions of dollars in Tijuana each year.

Fiestas

Tourists are attracted to the culture and life style of Mexico as well as to its spectacular ruins and sunny beaches. Mexicans celebrate many holidays with colorful festivals, known as *fiestas*. Most fiestas begin before daylight with a shower of rockets, exploding fireworks, and ringing bells.

During fiestas, people pray and burn candles to the saints in churches decorated with flowers and colored tissue paper. They also dance and hold parades. Festive crowds gather in the market places and public squares. Bullfights and carnival rides are popular, especially in the larger towns.

The Ballet Folklórico of Mexico has achieved international fame. The company performs many folk dances in an exciting spectacle of color and sound at the Palace of Fine Arts.

Children play with sea turtles on the resort island of Isla Mujeres, *below.* Along with Cancún and Cozumel Island, Isla Mujeres is part of the growing tourist area on the Yucatán Peninsula.

Sugar candy skulls, *left,* along with toy coffins and papier-mâché skeletons, are part of Mexico's All Souls' Day celebration. On November 2, the dead are honored with colorful celebrations, often held in graveyards.

Art and Culture

The arts have been important in Mexican life since the days of the ancient Indian cultures. The Mayas built beautiful limestone temples and painted colorful murals on their walls. The Aztecs composed music and poetry. Many Mexican artists today use the beautiful old Indian designs in their jewelry, pottery, blankets, and baskets.

Architecture

The ancient Indians devoted most of their architectural skills to religious construction. They built stone temples and flat-topped pyramids and decorated them with murals and sculptures. Symbols in their painting and sculpture often represented the feathered-serpent god Quetzalcóatl and other gods.

The early mission churches, built soon after the Spanish conquest, were simple in design. But the National Cathedral, built in 1573, started a more ornamental style. Churches built during the 1700's, such as the Church of Santa Prisca in Taxco, were even more highly decorated.

Today's Mexican architects combine ancient Indian designs with modern construction methods. Their work includes the beautiful buildings of the National Autonomous University and the National Museum of Anthropology in Mexico City.

Painting

During the Spanish colonial period, artists created murals in churches and painted portraits of government officials. But the most famous Mexican painting is the work that was done in the decades following the Mexican Revolution of 1910. Beginning in the 1920's, José Orozco, Diego Rivera, and David Siqueiros painted the story of the revolution on the walls of public buildings. Since the 1960's, however, many younger Mexican painters have turned away from revolutionary themes and followed styles from other countries.

Literature

Colonial writers in Mexico included Juan Ruiz de Alarcón, who wrote outstanding drama, and the poet Sor Juana Inés de la Cruz. Probably the first Latin-American novel was *The Itching Parrot,* published in 1816 by José Joaquin Fernández de Lizardi. As in art, revolutionary themes became important after 1910. Novelists of that time include Mariano Azuela and Martín Luis Guzmán. Contemporary writers include Carlos Fuentes, Mexico's best-known fiction writer, and Octavio Paz, a leading poet and essayist.

Music

Early Indians made music with drums, flutes, gourd rattles, and sea shells, and this ancient music is still heard in some parts of Mexico. Folk songs called *corridos* have also long been popular. They tell about such things as the Mexican Revolution and Mexican bandits and sheriffs. Modern Mexican composers such as Carlos Chávez and Silvestre Revueltas have used themes from Indian music or corridos in their own work.

Today, strolling musical groups called *mariachis* perform on the streets and in cafes. The music of *marimbas*—xylophonelike instruments—is also popular. Folk dances, especially the lively Mexican hat dance, are still much enjoyed.

A masked dancer performs in a folk dance. Folk dances are a colorful part of local fiestas and are also performed by the professional dance company Ballet Folklórico in Mexico City.

The marimba, *right,* is a popular instrument in Mexico, producing a rich, mellow sound. Some marimbas are so large that four or five musicians can play them at one time.

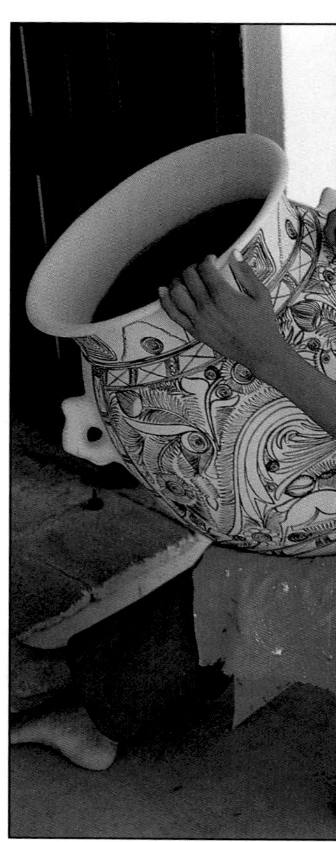

An Indian woman embroiders a beaded belt with traditional designs, *above*. These ancient designs include geometric shapes and stylized animals. Her dress is decorated in a similar style.

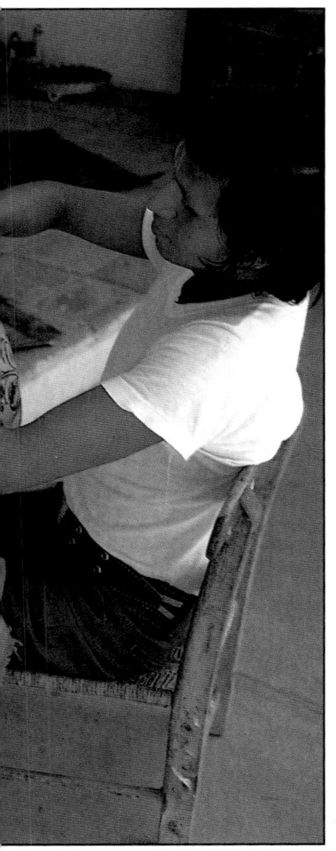

A Mexican craft worker paints swirling floral and animal decorations onto a large earthenware vessel, *far left*. Such pottery is prized by tourists.

Totonac Indians perform the Volador, *left,* one of the oldest Mexican dances. "Flying" Indians descend slowly on ropes wound around the top of a high pole. The dance's religious significance dates from Aztec times.

Moldova

Moldova shares its western border with Romania and its northern, southern, and eastern borders with Ukraine.

In 1991, Moldova (formerly Moldavia) declared itself an independent country and a member of the Commonwealth of Independent States (CIS). Moldova had been a union republic of the now-defunct Soviet Union since 1940. Moldova was called *Moldavia* until June 1990, when it changed its name to *Moldova*.

The history of Moldova is closely linked to that of the Moldavia district in northeastern Romania. These two regions, historically known together as Moldavia, had a long history of invasion and warfare, due to their strategic location between Asia and southern Europe. From the 900's to the 1100's, Moldavia was dominated by the Kievan state, and the Mongols took control in the 1200's and early 1300's. The main part of Moldavia was an independent principality from the middle 1300's until the early 1500's, when the Ottomans gained control of the region. In 1791, eastern Moldavia came under Russian rule, and Russia acquired more Moldavian territory in 1793. In 1812, the Russians received all of *Bessarabia*—the area of Moldavia between the Prut and Dnestr rivers. The Turks kept the rest of Moldavia, which later passed to Romania.

In 1918, Romania seized Bessarabia but was forced to surrender it to the Union of Soviet Socialist Republics (U.S.S.R.) in 1940, when most of Moldavia became a republic of the Soviet Union.

In the late 1980's, an independence movement developed in the Soviet republic. The nationalist Moldavian Popular Front gradually drove the Communist Party from power and, in 1990, the nationalists took over the government. The new government favored close cultural links with Romania, and they used their power to arrest minority groups who had

Fact Box

Country

Official name: Republica Moldova (Republic of Moldova)
Capital: Chisinau
Terrain: Rolling steppe, gradual slope south to Black Sea
Area: 13,067 sq. mi. (33,843 km^2)
Climate: Moderate winters, warm summers
Main rivers: Dnestr, Prut
Highest elevation: Dealul Balanesti, 1,411 ft. (430 m)
Lowest elevation: Nistru River, 7 ft. (2 m)

Government

Form of government: Republic
Head of state: President
Head of government: Prime minister
Administrative areas: 10 juletule, 1 municipality, 1 autonomous territorial unit
Legislature: Parlamentul (Parliament) with 101 members serving four-year terms
Court system: Supreme Court, Constitutional Court
Armed forces: 10,650 troops

People

Estimated 2002 population: 4,383,000
Population growth: 0%
Population density: 337 persons per sq. mi. (130 per km^2)
Population distribution: 54% rural, 46% urban
Life expectancy in years:
Male: 60
Female: 69
Doctors per 1,000 people: 3.5
Percentage of age-appropriate population enrolled in the following educational levels:
Primary: 97
Secondary: 81
Further: 27

rejected the 1989 change to Romanian as the republic's official language.

In the midst of political upheaval in the Soviet central government following an attempted coup in August 1991, Moldova declared its independence. Soon after, Moldova adopted a resolution outlawing Communist Party activities. When the Soviet Union was dissolved in December 1991, Moldova joined the newly established Commonwealth of Independent States. In 1994, Moldova held its first parliamentary elections.

Land and people

Moldova's gently rolling lowlands, fertile black soil, and mild climate make the region ideal for agriculture. Extensive irrigation systems supplement the moderate rainfall. Crop farmers grow barley, beets, corn, grapes, and sunflowers. Livestock farmers raise sheep and cattle.

Moldova has begun a transition to light industry linked to its traditional agricultural production. The new enterprises include food processing, meat packing, sugar refining, and textile and fertilizer production. The region's important woodworking industry uses timber from the wooded steppe of the northern region.

Spring blossoms forth in the Moldovan village of Tsbulyovka. The fertile black soil of the lowlands and the mild climate create excellent growing conditions for a variety of crops.

Languages spoken:
Moldovan (official)
Russian
Gagauz

Religions:
Eastern Orthodox 98%
Jewish 1%
Baptist

Technology

Radios per 1,000 people: 758

Televisions per 1,000 people: 297

Computers per 1,000 people: 14.5

Economy

Currency: Moldovan leu

Gross national income (GNI) in 2000: $1.4 billion U.S.

Real annual growth rate (1999–2000): 1.9%

GNI per capita (1998): $400 U.S.

Balance of payments (2000): -$121 million U.S.

Goods exported: Foodstuffs, wine, and tobacco; textiles and footwear, machinery

Goods imported: Mineral products and fuel, machinery and equipment, chemicals, textiles

Trading partners: Russia, Ukraine, Romania

About 66 per cent of the Moldovan people are ethnic Romanians. Immigrant Ukrainians and Russians make up most of the remainder.

In late 1991, Moldova became a battleground for violent ethnic conflict when ethnic Russians and Ukrainians in the Trans-Dnestr region declared their independence from Moldova. The separatists feared reunification of Moldova with Romania. By mid-1992, the Moldovan Parliament had voted to bring in a peacekeeping force created by the Commonwealth of Independent States to end the fighting. In September 1992, peace was restored when both sides agreed on certain conditions upon which a settlement could be reached.

In 1994, Moldova held its first parliamentary elections since declaring independence from the Soviet Union.

Monaco

Playground of the rich, jewel of the Riviera, Monaco is one of the wealthiest countries in Europe. It is also one of the smallest countries in the world, with a total area of only about 3/4 square mile (1.95 square kilometers). Nevertheless, Monaco enjoys a worldwide reputation for beauty, glamour, and sophistication. High on the cliffs overlooking the harbor, the royal palace stands guard over this independent principality, just as it has for more than 700 years.

The Monaco Grand Prix, an automobile race through the narrow, winding streets of the principality, is an annual highlight of the international motor-racing circuit.

Early history

Monaco has a long and colorful history, dating from the arrival of the Phoenicians in about 700 B.C. In the A.D. 1100's, the Genoese of northern Italy gained control of Monaco.

In 1308, the Genoese people granted governing rights over Monaco to the Grimaldi family, who were from the city of Genoa. At first, the Grimaldis allied themselves with France. Later, during the early 1500's to mid-1600's, they sought protection from Spain. During the French Revolution, France seized Monaco, but control was later returned to the Grimaldi family. France also seized some of Monaco's territory in 1848, but that too was later returned.

Before Prince Albert I approved a constitution in 1911, the princes of Monaco were

FACT BOX

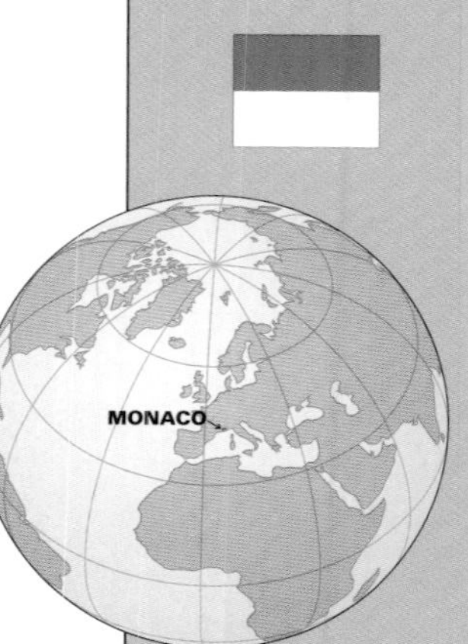

COUNTRY

Official name: Principaute de Monaco (Principality of Monaco)
Capital: Monaco
Terrain: Hilly, rugged, rocky
Area: 1 sq. mi. (2 km²)
Climate: Mediterranean with mild, wet winters and hot, dry summers
Highest elevation: Mont Agel, 459 ft. (140 m)
Lowest elevation: Mediterranean Sea, sea level

GOVERNMENT

Form of government: Constitutional monarchy
Head of state: Monarch
Head of government: Minister of State
Administrative areas: None
Legislature: Conseil National (National Council) with 18 members serving five-year terms
Court system: Tribunal Supreme (Supreme Court)
Armed forces: France is responsible for Monaco's defense

PEOPLE

Estimated 2002 population: 35,000
Population growth: 0.48%
Population density: 60,345 persons per sq. mi. (23,490 per km²)
Population distribution: 100% urban
Life expectancy in years:
Male: 75
Female: 83
Doctors per 1,000 people: N/A
Percentage of age-appropriate population enrolled in the following educational levels:
Primary: N/A
Secondary: N/A
Further: N/A

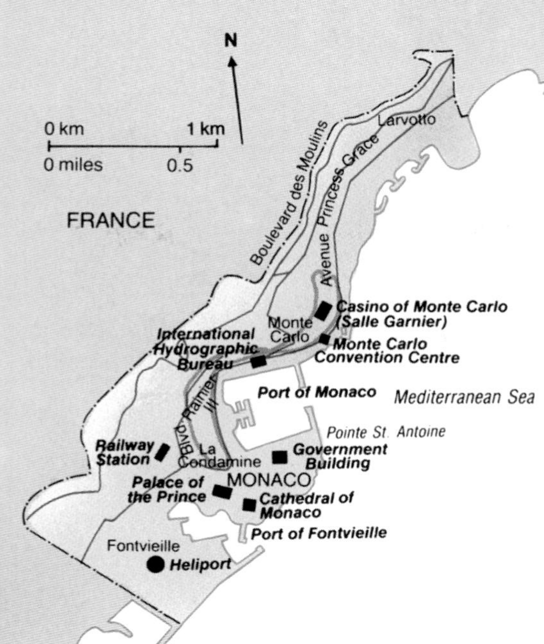

The town of Monaco, which stands on a rocky point high above the sea, is the site of the royal palace. Monte Carlo features the famous gambling casino, an opera house, hotels, and beaches. La Condamine, a port area, lies between the town of Monaco and Monte Carlo, while Fontvieille, the industrial zone, is west of the town of Monaco.

With its sunny beaches, glamorous casinos, and exciting nightlife, Monaco is best known as a popular tourist resort. But Monaco is also a major industrial and administrative center, producing cosmetics, electronics, and textiles. Monaco's colorful postage stamps are prized by collectors and represent an important source of income.

absolute monarchs. Today, an 18-member National Council shares the legislative powers with the prince. Under the terms of a treaty signed with France in 1918, Monaco will come under French control if the royal family produces no male heirs.

Land and economy

Monaco includes three towns and an industrial area. This small country lies at the foot of Mount Agel on the French Riviera, which borders the Mediterranean Sea. France borders Monaco on the other three sides.

Languages spoken:
French (official)
English
Italian
Monegasque
Religion:
Roman Catholic 90%

Technology

Radios per 1,000 people: N/A
Televisions per 1,000 people: N/A
Computers per 1,000 people: N/A

Economy

Currency: Euro
Gross domestic product (GDP) in 1999: $870 million U.S.
Real annual growth rate (1997–1998): N/A
GDP per capita (1999): $27,000 U.S.
Balance of payments (1998): N/A
Goods exported: N/A
Goods imported: N/A
Trading partners: France and other European Union countries

Across the entrance to the port of Monaco, *above left,* lies the town of Monte Carlo. The splendid, green-roofed gambling casino is one of Monaco's chief attractions. Monaco, *top,* lies on a rocky stretch of the Mediterranean coast, surrounded on three sides by France. The Palace of the Prince, *above right,* in the old town, is the residence of the Grimaldi family, rulers of Monaco since the 1300's. Part of the fortress was built in the 1200's.

Many foreign companies have headquarters in Monaco because of the low taxation there.

Many wealthy people from other countries make Monaco their home because the principality has no income tax. But since 1963, most French people living in Monaco have had to pay income tax at French rates.

Monaco is a center of learning and culture. The Grand Theater of Monte Carlo presents performances by some of the world's greatest singers and ballet dancers, and the Monaco government awards the Rainier III prize for literature each year to a writer in the French language. In addition, the study of marine life is the focus of Monaco's Oceanographic Museum and its world-famous aquarium.

Mongolia

Mongolia lies north of China in east-central Asia. Its official name is the Mongolian People's Republic. Mongolia is a rugged country covered mostly by plateaus and towering mountain ranges. The vast, bleak Gobi Desert blankets much of southeastern Mongolia. Temperatures in the country range from very hot to very cold, and rainfall is usually very light. Violent earthquakes sometimes rock the country.

Mongolia is the home of an Asian people called Mongols. Traditionally, the Mongols were nomadic herders who traveled from place to place with their animals. Today, some Mongols still follow their ancestors' nomadic life style, roaming the plains and living in collapsible felt tents called *ger* or *yurts*. Today, however, most Mongol people live on cooperative livestock farms set up by the government.

During the 1200's, the Mongols built the largest land empire in history. Led by Genghis Khan—the "lord of all the peoples dwelling in felt tents"—the Mongols conquered most of Asia and parts of eastern Europe.

The rise of the Mongol Empire

In the late 1100's, Temüjin, a Mongol chieftain who later became known as Genghis Khan, rose to power. He began to organize the Mongols and other scattered nomadic tribes and train them to be a superior fighting force.

Determined to build the Mongol Empire, Genghis Khan invaded China. First, he attacked and conquered the state of Xi Xia in northwestern China, and then he led his warriors across the Gobi Desert and seized North China in 1215. Before completing the conquest of China, Genghis Khan's armies turned westward and attacked Russia and Persia, almost reaching Constantinople (now Istanbul). The Mongols killed many people during their campaign and destroyed much of Islamic-Arabic civilization.

After Genghis Khan died in 1227, the Mongols pushed into Europe under Ogotai, a son of Genghis Khan, threatening western European civilization. However, Ogotai died during this campaign, forcing

the Mongols to return to Mongolia to elect a new khan. Kublai Khan, a grandson of Genghis Khan, was elected. He completed the conquest of China and founded the Yuan dynasty, which lasted from 1279 until 1368.

Decline of the empire

The Mongol Empire began to disintegrate shortly after it reached its peak in the late 1200's. In some areas, the Mongols had not succeeded in firmly establishing their rule, and corrupt government and incompetent administration resulted in revolts in different parts of the empire. The Mongols lost control of many of their conquered lands.

When Kublai Khan died in 1294, his empire broke up. The Yuan dynasty in China ended in the 1300's. In the late 1500's, Mongol princes reunited Mongolia and converted the people to Lamaism. In the early 1600's, the Manchu rulers of Manchuria divided Mongolia into Inner and Outer Mongolia and gained control of Inner Mongolia. The Manchus then conquered China in 1644 and seized Outer Mongolia in the 1680's. Mongolia, like China, had little contact with other nations during the 1700's and 1800's.

By 1911, the Manchu rulers had weakened, and the Mongolians drove the Chinese forces out of Outer Mongolia. They appointed a priest, called the *Living Buddha,* as king and appealed to Russia for support. However, in 1913, Outer Mongolia came under the control of Russia. In 1920, during Russia's civil war, anti-Communist Russian troops occupied Outer Mongolia and ruled it through the Living Buddha. Mongolian and Russian Communists gained control of Outer Mongolia in 1921, but though his authority was very limited, the Living Buddha retained his throne until his death in 1924. The Mongolian People's Republic was then established, and the new state supported the Soviet Union in the Soviet-Chinese dispute for leadership of the Communist world in the 1960's and 1970's.

Mongolia Today

After the Communists gained control of Mongolia in 1921, a Communist Party called the Mongol People's Revolutionary Party (MPRP) became Mongolia's only political party and had complete control of the government. In order to modernize the country's economy, the MPRP gradually replaced the Mongols' traditional nomadic way of life with a more settled lifestyle. The government set up about 300 livestock farms, and today about half of the Mongolian people have been placed on these farms.

The farms are like huge ranches with small towns in the center. The central buildings include houses, offices, shops, and medical clinics for the people and animals. The state has also settled nomadic farmers on agricultural cooperatives. As a result, agriculture has become important in Mongolia's economic production. In late 1993, snowfalls killed 3.8 million livestock, an economic loss that was Mongolia's worst in 50 years.

Advances in industry, which is also controlled by the state, have brought many

Mongolian citizens in Ulaanbaatar demonstrate for political freedom in 1990.

Fact Box

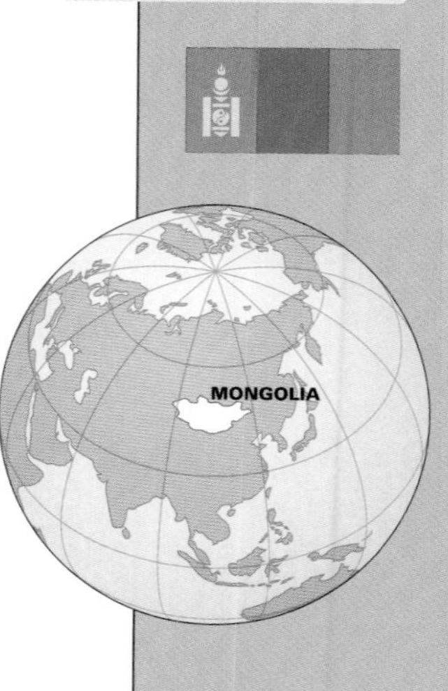

Country

Official name: Mongol Uls (Mongolia)
Capital: Ulaanbaatar
Terrain: Vast semidesert and desert plains; mountains in west and southwest; Gobi Desert in southeast
Area: 604,250 sq. mi. (1,565,000 km²)
Climate: Desert; continental (large daily and seasonal temperature ranges)
Main river: Selenge
Highest elevation: Nayramdal Uur, 14,350 ft. (4,374 m)
Lowest elevation: Hoh Nuur, 1,699 ft. (518 m)

Government

Form of government: Republic
Head of state: President
Head of government: Prime minister
Administrative areas: 18 aymguud (provinces), 3 hotuud (municipalities)
Legislature: State Great Hural with 76 members serving four-year terms
Court system: Supreme Court
Armed forces: 9,100 troops

People

Estimated 2002 population: 2,455,000
Population growth: 1.54%
Population density: 4 persons per sq. mi. (2 per km²)
Population distribution: 52% urban, 48% rural
Life expectancy in years:
Male: 65
Female: 70
Doctors per 1,000 people: 2.4
Percentage of age-appropriate population enrolled in the following educational levels:
Primary: 94
Secondary: N/A
Further: 25

Mongolia is governed by a one-body legislature, the State Great Hural.

people from the rural areas to Mongolia's cities. More than 20 per cent of the Mongolian people live in Ulaanbaatar, the country's capital and industrial center. Many of these people work in factories or government offices.

Progress has changed the Mongolian people's traditional way of life. Modern farming methods and livestock-breeding techniques have been adopted, and schools and medical care units have been established. The Mongols traditionally ate a great deal of meat, but today, they eat more grains, fruits, and vegetables. And many Mongols, particularly those in the cities, now wear Western-style clothing.

Progress continued in the late 1980's, when reforms that brought more freedom to the Soviet Union and eastern Europe influenced the Mongolian people. They held demonstrations in early 1990 to demand similar changes in their country. As a result, Mongolia's Communist Party gave up its monopoly on power, a multiparty system was adopted, and free elections were held in July 1990. Although Communists won a majority of the government positions, the opposition parties gained a large percentage of seats in Mongolia's two legislative houses.

In June 1992, new elections were held. The Communist Party had broken up, but a large majority of seats was won by the Mongolian People's Revolutionary Party (MPRP), largely made up of former Communist Party members. In June 1993, Punsalmaagiyn Ochirbat was reelected president in a political upset. Ochirbat had been elected in 1990 as a MPRP candidate, but criticized the party's refusal to make economic reforms. The party denied Ochirbat its presidential nomination, but he ran as the nominee of two other parties and won 60 per cent of the vote. In 1996, after 75 years of Communism, Mongolian voters ousted the MPRP.

Languages spoken:
Khalkha Mongolian 90%
Turkic
Russian

Religions:
Tibetan Buddhist
Muslim 4%

Technology

Radios per 1,000 people: 154
Televisions per 1,000 people: 65
Computers per 1,000 people: 12.6

Economy

Currency: Tughrik
Gross national income (GNI) in 2000: $0.9 billion U.S.
Real annual growth rate (1999–2000): 1.1%
GNI per capita (2000): $390 U.S.
Balance of payments (2000): -$52 million U.S.
Goods exported: Copper, livestock, animal products, cashmere, wool, hides, fluorspar, other nonferrous metals
Goods imported: Machinery and equipment, fuels, food products, industrial consumer goods, chemicals, building materials, sugar, tea
Trading partners: China, Russia, Switzerland, Japan

Land and People

Mongolia is a land of high mountains, plateaus, and barren desert. The Altai Mountains in western Mongolia, the highest mountains in the country, rise more than 14,000 feet (4,270 meters), and snow covers their peaks throughout the year. Farther east lie the Hangayn Mountains. North of these mountains lies a volcanic region, dotted with crater lakes and extinct volcanoes.

A high plateau lying between the Altai Mountains and the Hangayn Mountains in central Mongolia contains a number of large lakes. Uvs Lake, the largest, covers an area of about 1,300 square miles (3,370 square kilometers). Dense forests of spruce, pine, and fir trees cover the Hentiyn Mountains, northeast of Ulaanbaatar.

Most of the country's people live in eastern Mongolia, a lower plateau of grassland that includes Ulaanbaatar and other major population centers. The plateau is fed by numerous rivers, and many kinds of grass and flowers grow there.

The plateau becomes less fertile and drier as it nears the Gobi—a bleak desert area that stretches from southeastern Mongolia into Inner Mongolia in northern China. Much of the desert consists of dry, rocklike or sandy soil, but *steppes* (dry grassland areas) surround the central area of the Gobi.

The Gobi often has long heat waves in summer and cold waves in winter. The temperature averages 70° F. (21° C) in July and 10° F. (–12° C) in January. The rest of the country also experiences very hot summers and very cold winters. Temperatures ranging from –57° to 96° F. (–49° to 36° C) have been recorded in Ulaanbaatar. Heavy rains sometimes occur in July and August, but the entire country is normally very dry.

A growing population

Nearly all of the people of Mongolia are Mongols, though some Chinese, Kazakhs, and Russians also live in Mongolia. The country's official language is Mongolian, but most of the people speak Khalkha Mongolian, the official dialect. Mongolian is written in the letters of the Russian Cyrillic alphabet. However, there is a growing movement to replace the Cyrillic system with an old Mongolian alphabet.

Mongolia is very thinly populated, with an average density of only 4 people per square mile (2 per square kilometer). In the 1980's, the government introduced a program designed to encourage population growth by rewarding families with many children. Mongolia's population has grown as a result of this program, and today, almost half of the population is under 25.

A changing way of life

For centuries, nomads have roamed the Mongolian plains with herds of sheep, cattle, and goats in search of pasture for their animals. They lived in tents made of layers of felt covered with canvas or hide and traveled from place to place on horseback. Today, the government is gradually settling the nomads on farms, and few Mongolians follow this traditional way of life.

Nomadic herdsmen in the Gobi Desert stand guard while their camels drink at an oasis. Although camel caravans still cross the desert, their number continues to decline as the nomads give up their traditional way of life to settle on farms.

A camel and a pickup truck are both "parked" on the high plateau in central Mongolia in the shadow of the Altai Mountains. Today, the Mongolian people often use trucks rather than camels or horses for cross-country transportation.

A Mongol family living on a state-run livestock farm enjoys a meal of fried mutton. Radios and modern stoves have become common items in many Mongolian homes.

A Mongolian child heads for school. Schools and educational opportunities have increased as the Mongolian people settle in permanent homes.

Increasingly, the Mongolian people are moving to the cities. About half of the total population lives in Mongolia's towns and cities, including Ulaanbaatar and Darhan, a new industrial area. Many other Mongolians live on livestock and agricultural farms set up by the state. Modern conveniences such as radios, stoves, and television have become popular as the nomads give up their tents and settle in new apartments and houses.

Modernization has also changed some aspects of traditional family life in Mongolia. For example, parents have much less influence today in arranging their children's marriages, and elaborate marriage rituals have been replaced by more simple ceremonies. In addition, under the strict rule of the Mongol People's Revolutionary Party, traditional religious festivals were replaced by festivals celebrating the state, and the practice of Lamaism, Mongolia's chief religion, was discouraged. Today, however, Mongolia's democratic government permits greater religious expression.

Land of the Horse

Traditionally, the horse has been the most prized animal in Mongolia. For many centuries, it has been used in war, hunting, and traveling. According to a Mongol proverb, "the greatest misfortune is for one to lose his father while he is young or his horse during a journey." The Mongols also traditionally believed that the dead rode to heaven on a horse.

Mongol society has always been based on mobility. The early nomads learned to handle horses masterfully as they journeyed from place to place. They were accustomed to riding long distances, and they were also very accomplished with a bow and arrow, which they used for hunting and survival. The nomads frequently combined these skills and shot their prey while on horseback.

In the late 1100's, the Mongol chieftain Genghis Khan organized the nomadic tribes and trained them to be an extremely effective army. By taking advantage of the nomads' skills, Genghis Khan achieved a spectacular series of conquests. The horse was the fastest animal of the time that could be adapted for warfare, and the Mongols would fire their arrows at full gallop. The Mongol warriors were able to surprise their enemies, strike quickly and ruthlessly, and then speed to safety.

The enemies of the Mongols believed that Mongolian horses were much larger than other horses—probably because of the terror inspired by the warriors themselves. In fact, the Mongolian horse is generally small—though it does have a rather large head. Accustomed to finding its food on the cold plains, the Mongolian horse is tough and tireless in war or hunting campaigns. During the time of Genghis Khan, the Mongolian horse could carry a man for 100 miles (160 kilometers) a day. It could not carry a rider the following day, however, so the Mongol warriors traveled with plenty of fresh horses.

Mongolia is also home to Przewalski's horse, the only true wild horse that exists today. It is named for Russian explorer Nikolai M. Przewalski, who found the skin and skull of one of the wild horses in 1881. About 20 years later, 20 colts were collected. A small animal with a grayish-brown coat, Przewalski's horse resembles a donkey. Today, the horse is an endangered species. Only 20 to 30 survive in the wild, and more than 150 live in zoos. However, the Mongolian government has established a reserve for Przewalski's horse on the Gobi Desert in an effort to increase its numbers.

Although few Mongolians still follow the traditional way of life, some nomadic herders remain today. They travel from place to place on horseback with their yurts packed on camels or in oxcarts.

Some festivals also help preserve Mongolian culture. For example, traditional tournament games are conducted much as

The interior of a yurt is warm and comfortable. Rugs cover the wall and floor, providing insulation from the cold. Yurts are collapsible so that they can be easily transported.

they were in the past. Although today the games are played in large stadiums rather than on the open plain, the main events are still wrestling, archery, and horse racing.

Horse racing is an ancient Mongolian sport, and many competitions take place throughout the year. The jockeys, usually boys aged 15 years or younger, wear short, colorful jackets and no boots, and they ride bareback—without a saddle. As each boy approaches the finish line, he leans

over his horse's head and twirls a whip—an action that not only demonstrates the rider's ability, but also serves as a signal to the horse to go all out to complete the race.

The horse is still used for transportation in Mongolia, but less often than in the past, partly because of the changing Mongolian life style, and partly because of the cost. In cities like Ulaanbaatar, it is cheaper to run a motorbike than to keep a horse. It is also less expensive to travel across the country by truck than with a caravan of horses, camels, and livestock. As a result, buses, trucks, jeeps, and cars are gradually replacing the horse as Mongolia's main means of transportation.

Riding, *left,* is a favorite sport of the Mongolian people. Some competitions involve shooting with a bow and arrow while riding on horseback like the Mongol warriors of ancient times.

Music in Mongolia has been affected by the traditional nomadic life style. Because constant movement generally prevented the formation of orchestras, solo instruments came to dominate Mongolian music.

A herdsman, *left,* watches his sheep graze in a nomadic camp. When the sheep have eaten all of the grass, the nomads move on.

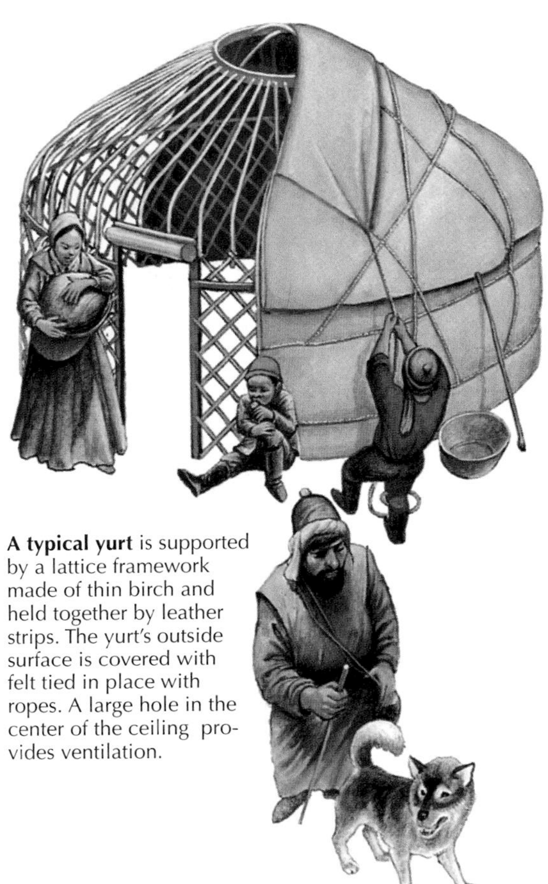

A typical yurt is supported by a lattice framework made of thin birch and held together by leather strips. The yurt's outside surface is covered with felt tied in place with ropes. A large hole in the center of the ceiling provides ventilation.

Morocco

The Kingdom of Morocco lies in the northwest corner of Africa. Because of its strategic location, many powers throughout history have tried to rule this region.

As early as 6000 B.C., farming people lived in what is now Morocco. By 1000 B.C., Berbers, who may have come from Europe, southwestern Asia, or northeastern Africa, migrated to the region. About A.D. 40, the area fell under the control of the Roman Empire. Then the Vandals, a barbarian tribe from northern Europe, took control, and later the region was conquered by the Byzantines of Constantinople.

During the 680's, Arab Muslims invaded Morocco, and the land became part of the Muslim Empire. Many Berbers adopted Islam, the religion of the Muslims, but they resented Arab control.

In the late 700's, an Arab leader named Idris ibn Abdallah created the first Moroccan state by uniting the region's Arabs and Berbers. The Idrisid *dynasty* (series of rulers from the same family) ruled Morocco for almost 200 years. Moroccan rulers came to be called *sultans*.

From about 1050 through the mid-1400's, three Islamic Berber dynasties governed Morocco. These sultans built empires that covered much of northern Africa as well as Spain and Portugal. But in the 1200's, European Christians began to drive the Muslims out of Spain and Portugal, and by 1500, when the last Muslims were forced to leave Spain, Spanish and Portuguese invaders had begun to seize land on Morocco's coast.

Muslims and Christians also fought naval battles on the Mediterranean Sea. Private warships commanded by Muslim *corsairs* (pirates) attacked the ships and coastal towns of Christian nations, and Christian corsairs attacked Muslim ships and bases.

In the mid-1500's, a family named the Saadians gained control of Morocco and ruled for about 100 years. The Saadians were *sharifs,* descendants of Muhammad, the founder of the Islamic religion. They were followed by the Alawis, a sharifian dynasty that has governed Morocco ever since.

By the early 1900's, though Moroccan sultans sat on the throne, Moroccans had actually lost control of their economy and politics to France and Spain. Through battles and treaties, the two European powers had estab-

lished separate zones of influence within Morocco. Spain controlled the north and a strip of land in the south, while France claimed the rest of the country.

Moroccans grew increasingly hostile toward the Europeans, and France sent troops into the country in 1907. In 1912, Sultan Abd al-Hafidh signed the Treaty of Fez, which officially gave control of Morocco to France. France in turn acknowledged Spain's control of its zone of influence.

In the 1920's, a rebel named Abd al-Krim led other Moroccans in a fight for independence. The French defeated the rebels in 1926, but the movement for independence continued until 1937, when its leaders were arrested or exiled.

An independence political party called the Istiqlal Party rose up in 1943. When Sultan Muhammad V supported the party, he was exiled. Moroccans reacted violently to their sultan's exile and formed a National Liberation Army to fight French troops. Two years later, France brought Sultan Muhammad V back and promised Moroccans their freedom. On March 2, 1956, Morocco became independent of France, and in April, Spain gave up nearly all its claims in northern Morocco.

Muhammad's great popularity with the Moroccan people allowed him to organize the government as he wished. In 1957, he changed his title from sultan to king as part of his plan to make Morocco a constitutional monarchy. When Muhammad died suddenly in 1961, his son, Hassan II, became king and prime minister. In 1965 and again in 1972, Hassan took control of the entire government.

In the 1970's, Hassan began to press Morocco's claim to the Spanish Sahara—the southern area still controlled by Spain. In 1976, Spain gave up the region, and its name was changed to Western Sahara. But an independence movement in Western Sahara called the Polisario Front challenged Morocco's claim. In 1991, the United Nations arranged a cease-fire between Morocco and the Polisario Front.

Morocco Today

The African country of Morocco is a kingdom lying on the continent's northwest corner. The Strait of Gibraltar, which connects the Atlantic Ocean to the Mediterranean Sea, separates Morocco from Spain by only 8 miles (13 kilometers).

Government

Morocco is a constitutional monarchy, but the Constitution gives the king broad powers. The king controls major government agencies and commands the armed forces, and the king's orders carry the full force of law.

The daily work of governing Morocco is carried out by a prime minister and a Cabinet of other ministers, all appointed by the king. A national legislature called the Chamber of Representatives makes the country's laws.

At the local level, Morocco is divided into 37 provinces and 2 wilayas. The capital city, Rabat, makes up one wilaya. Morocco's largest city, Casablanca, makes up the other. The king appoints a governor to head each province and wilaya.

Islam is the nation's official religion. About 99 per cent of its people are Muslims, or followers of Islam. The Istiqlal (Independence) Party promotes Arab culture and reforms based on Islamic teachings. The conservative Mouvement Populaire (Popular Movement) generally supports the king.

King Hassan II ruled Morocco from 1961, when his father died, until his own death in 1999. When unemployment and high inflation plagued Morocco in the 1960's, Hassan presented reforms to help the economy. When the legislature refused to accept the reforms, Hassan took control of the government for a time. After an attempt on his life in 1972, he again took control of the government.

Hassan's claim to Western Sahara, the area south of Morocco, created problems for the country. From the 1970's until 1991, Moroccan troops fought an independence organization in Western Sahara called the Polisario Front. Although most of Morocco's political parties supported the king's policy in Western Sahara, they resented his strong control of the government. The high cost of the war hurt Morocco's economy. The people of Western Sahara were to vote in 1994 on independence or unity with Morocco. Disagreements about voter eligibility pushed back the vote for several years. Ground rules for a referendum regarding Western Sahara's independence were worked out in 1997.

Hassan's son Sidi Muhammad succeeded him as King Muhammad VI.

Transportation, communication, and education

Few Moroccans own cars, but bus lines serve nearly all parts of the country. Highways and

COUNTRY

Official name: Al Mamlakah al Maghribiyah (Kingdom of Morocco)
Capital: Rabat
Terrain: Northern coast and interior are mountainous with large areas of bordering plateaus, intermontane valleys, and rich coastal plains
Area: 172,414 sq. mi. (446,550 km²)
Climate: Mediterranean, becoming more extreme in the interior
Main rivers: Tensift, Oum er Rbia, Moulouya, Sous
Highest elevation: Jebel Toubkal, 13,665 ft. (4,165 m)
Lowest elevation: Sebkha Tah, 180 ft. (55 m) below sea level

GOVERNMENT

Form of government: Constitutional monarchy
Head of state: Monarch
Head of government: Prime minister
Administrative areas: 37 provinces, 2 wilayas
Legislature: Parliament consisting of an upper house or Chamber of Counselors with 270 members serving nine-year terms and a lower house or Chamber of Representatives with 325 members serving five-year terms
Court system: Supreme Court
Armed forces: 196,300 troops

PEOPLE

Estimated 2002 population: 29,248,000
Population growth: 1.74%
Population density: 170 persons per sq. mi. (65 per km²)
Population distribution: 54% urban, 46% rural
Life expectancy in years:
Male: 67
Female: 71
Doctors per 1,000 people: 0.5
Percentage of age-appropriate population enrolled in the following educational levels:
Primary: 97
Secondary: 40
Further: 9

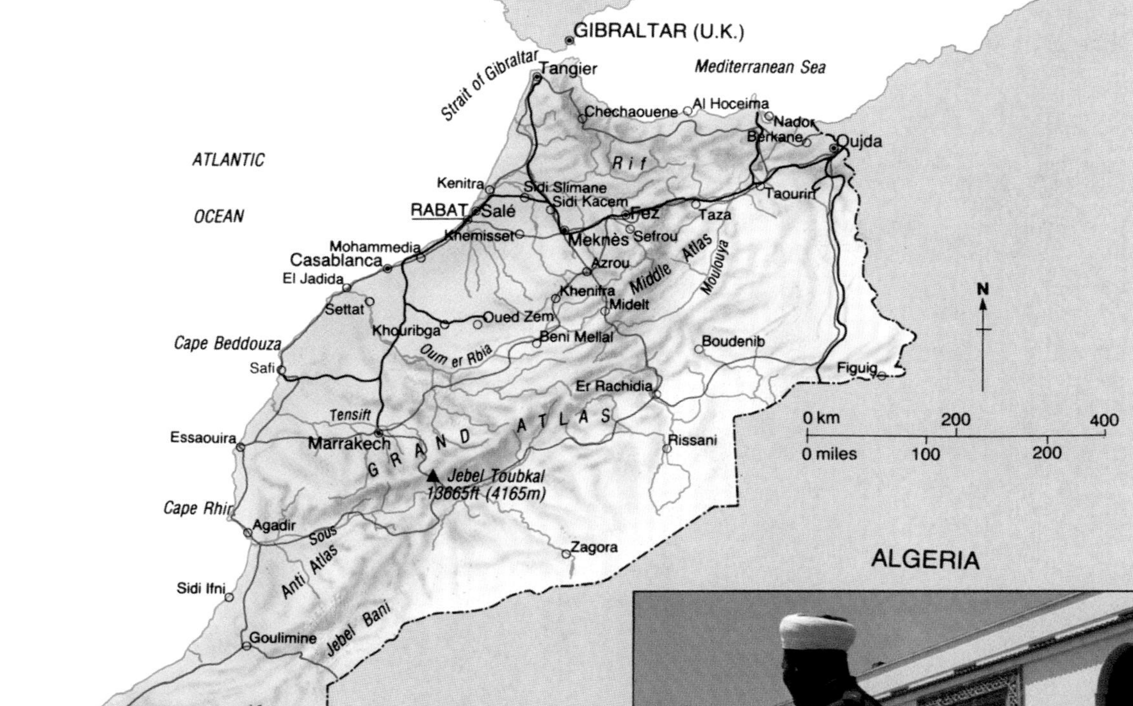

Morocco lies closer to Europe than any other African country, with Spain only 8 miles (13 kilometers) away across the Strait of Gibraltar. The Mediterranean Sea lies to the north; the Atlantic Ocean to the west; Algeria to the east; and Western Sahara to the south. Rabat is Morocco's capital, and Casablanca is its largest city.

Morocco's Royal Palace, which stands in the modern section of Rabat, was begun in 1774 by Muhammad III and expanded by Sultan Muhammad V and his son, King Hassan II. Hassan wrote Morocco's first Constitution, adopted in 1962. However, he twice took control of the government: in 1965, when the legislature blocked his economic program; and in 1972, when army officers tried to assassinate him.

Languages spoken:
- Arabic (official)
- Berber dialects
- French

Religions:
- Muslim 99%
- Christian
- Jewish

Technology

Radios per 1,000 people: 243

Televisions per 1,000 people: 166

Computers per 1,000 people: 12.3

Economy

Currency: Moroccan dirham

Gross national income (GNI) in 2000: $33.9 billion U.S.

Real annual growth rate (1999–2000): 0.9%

GNI per capita (2000): $1,180 U.S.

Balance of payments (2000): -$475 million U.S.

Goods exported: Phosphates and fertilizers, food and beverages, minerals

Goods imported: Semiprocessed goods, machinery and equipment, food and beverages, consumer goods, fuel

Trading partners: France, Spain, India, United States

government-owned railroads link the major cities as well as important mining and farm areas.

About 10 daily newspapers, printed in both Arabic and French, are published in Rabat and Casablanca. The government controls radio and television broadcasts, but few Moroccans own radios or television sets.

Elementary and secondary education is free in Morocco. Classes are taught in Arabic and French, and children from 7 to 13 are required to attend school. However, many children do not go to school, particularly in rural areas, due to a lack of schools and teachers, and only about 44 per cent of Moroccans above the age of 15 can read and write. The nation has 6 universities and about 25 colleges and technical schools.

Land and Economy

Morocco has three major land forms—lowlands, mountains, and desert. The fertile lowland plains along the coast have a mild and somewhat dry climate, but the rich farmland is irrigated by many shallow rivers. Most of Morocco's crops are grown on these lowlands.

Moving east from the Atlantic coast, the land gradually rises to form a plateau before it reaches the mountains. The Atlas Mountains cross the middle of Morocco from southwest to northeast. Three heavily forested ranges form this mountain chain: the Anti Atlas in the southwest; the Grand Atlas (sometimes called Haut Atlas or High Atlas) in the center of the chain; and the Middle Atlas (or Moyen Atlas) in the northwest. Peaks in the Grand Atlas rise more than 13,000 feet (4,000 meters). The Rif, a fourth mountain group that is sometimes included in the Atlas chain, rises in the far north.

The inland regions of Morocco are generally drier and warmer than the coast, but rainfall and temperatures vary greatly. Fertile valleys in the mountains provide farmland.

East and south of the mountains lies the Sahara, a vast and desolate desert region of sand dunes, rocks, and stones. Scattered throughout the desert are green oases.

Morocco is a developing country with an economy based on agriculture and mining. The government controls the mining industry and some manufacturing, but most farms and businesses are privately owned. King Hassan II has called the nation's economy a good blend of capitalism and socialism.

About 40 per cent of Morocco's workers farm or fish for a living. Most farmers own less than 10 acres (4 hectares) of land, but more than a third of the nation's farmland is owned by only 3 per cent of the farmers. These large farms produce about 85 per cent of all crops.

Moroccan farmers grow such cereals as barley, corn, and wheat as well as beans, citrus fruits, olives, potatoes, sugar beets, and tomatoes. Most cereal farmers use old-fashioned methods and grow their crops for their own use, while the large farms use modern methods to produce fruits and vegetables for export. Moroccan farmers also raise dairy cattle, goats, and sheep.

Fishing crews catch anchovies, mackerel, tuna, and sardines off the Moroccan coast.

A carpet woven in striking geometrical patterns forms a colorful backdrop for a Moroccan woman. Moroccans have long been known for producing fine rugs, and their beautiful carpets—along with other handicrafts—are valuable export items.

Carefully cultivated fields, *right,* lie at the foot of sparsely forested hills in central Morocco near the towering peaks of the Grand Atlas Mountains. The highest peak in Morocco, Jebel Toubkal, rises in this mountain chain.

Spices and vegetables tempt shoppers at an outdoor market in Tangier, an ancient port at the northwest tip of Morocco. Agriculture is extremely important to the Moroccan economy. When rainfall is adequate, Moroccan farmers can produce almost all the nation's food.

Fishing trawlers lie at anchor in the port of Essaouira on the Atlantic coast, *right.* The Portuguese built forts along the coast in the 1400's and 1500's. Today, Essaouira is a center for Morocco's fishing industry.

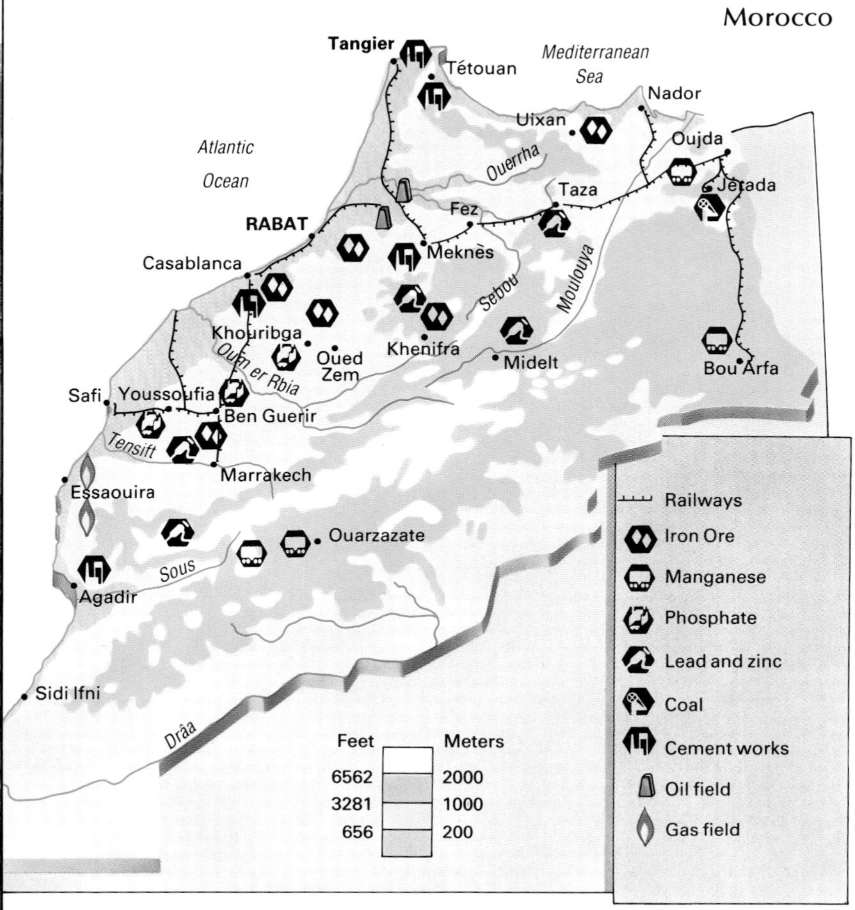

Morocco

Mining is an important economic activity in Morocco. The country has about two-thirds of the world's known reserves of phosphate rock, from which fertilizers and chemicals are made. Railroads connect many mines with major transportation centers.

Much of their catch is canned for export or processed as fertilizers or animal feed.

Another 40 per cent of the nation's workers are employed in service industries. Some work for the government or perform community service, and others have jobs in the tourist industry. Nearly 2 million tourists, mostly from Western Europe, come each year to enjoy Morocco's pleasant climate, white sandy beaches, and scenic mountains, and to visit the country's historic sites. Today, many Moroccans work in the hotels and restaurants that accommodate tourists.

Although mining does not create many jobs for Moroccans, it is extremely important to the nation's economy, bringing in more foreign money than any other activity. Morocco is the world's leading exporter of phosphate rock, which is used to produce fertilizers and other chemicals. Other minerals include coal, copper, iron ore, lead, natural gas, and zinc. However, Morocco imports oil to meet most of its energy needs.

Manufacturing provides jobs for less than 20 per cent of the work force. Small firms produce consumer goods, and most larger firms manufacture products for local use, including cement; chemicals; leather goods; metal, rubber, and plastic products; paper; processed foods; and textiles. Some large firms produce goods for export, especially fertilizers and petroleum products.

More people are employed in small workshops—making handicrafts and other goods—than work in large-scale manufacturing. Leather goods, rugs, and other handicrafts are valuable Moroccan exports.

People

Most of the people who live in Morocco reflect the history of the country in their mixed Berber and Arab ancestry. Berbers lived in the region as far back as 1000 B.C., and Arabs began to move into the area in the A.D. 600's.

Moroccans today are identified as Arabs or Berbers chiefly by their native language. Most Moroccans speak Arabic, but many speak Berber languages too. A large number of Moroccans also speak French or Spanish—a reminder of the days when France and Spain controlled parts of Morocco.

Over 30 million people live in Morocco. Arabs make up about 65 per cent of the population, and the rest are Berbers. Most Arabs live in the cities or on the Atlantic coast, and most Berbers live in rural mountain areas.

Almost all Moroccans—99 per cent—are *Muslims,* followers of Islam—the nation's official religion. Islamic teachings govern family and community life.

The traditional Moroccan household consists of a mother and father, their unmarried children, their married sons, and the wives and children of those sons. When the father dies, each married son establishes his own household. But in the cities, where there is not enough room for the whole family to live together, many households split up before the father's death.

Many urban Moroccans live in small houses that are attached to one another. Wealthier people live in modern apartments or large homes, while poor people live in slum shacks made of flattened tin cans. In rural areas, many people live in primitive houses made of dried mud bricks, wood, or stone. Many such homes have only one room, which serves as living room, kitchen, bedroom, and barn. In the desert, nomads live in tents.

The busy market place is the heart of a Moroccan city. In rural communities, people gather at a weekly outdoor market called a *souk* to buy and sell goods and chat with one another. Many people also enjoy meeting friends at neighborhood cafes.

Moroccans wear traditional clothing, but many city people wear Western clothes as well. Outside, men wear a loose-fitting hooded robe with long, full sleeves called a *jellaba.* Rural men wear a similar but heavier robe called a *burnoose.* Most men also wear a turban or a brimless cap. The *fez,* a red, flat-topped hat that many people identify with Morocco, was named for the Moroccan city of Fez, but nowadays it is usually worn only on formal occasions.

Moroccan women also wear jellabas outdoors. Indoors, they wear a long, beautiful robe called a *caftan.* Some older women and women in rural areas still follow Islamic tradition and cover their faces with veils in public.

In traditional Moroccan society, men and women live largely separate lives. Men dominate women in most areas of life, and fewer females attend school because parents place less value on education for girls than for boys. While many such practices continue,

Berber women wearing traditional dress add a drumbeat to the rejoicing at a feast. Moroccans enjoy many local and religious festivals throughout the year.

The tent, *far right,* is the home of nomadic Berbers in the Sahara, who move frequently in search of water and grazing land. Most Berbers live in the mountains and other rural areas of Morocco, where their homes are made of mud bricks, wood, or stone.

Berber warriors launch a thundering charge. In the past, such riders attacked communities, shooting from the backs of horses or camels. Today, they perform for visitors in a popular tourist attraction called the *fantasia.*

society is beginning to change. More girls now attend school, and more women work outside the home.

Moroccan Muslims fast during the month of Ramadan—eating nothing from sunrise to sunset—and, following Islamic custom, many Moroccans still stop to pray five times a day. However, some Moroccans, especially city office workers, no longer follow this practice.

Foods made of barley and wheat are the basis of the Moroccan diet. The national dish is *couscous,* steamed wheat served with vegetables, fish or meat, and a souplike sauce. The national drink is mint tea.

Berber shepherds watch their flocks in a remote mountain valley, *below.* Each is wrapped in the traditional hooded burnoose.

Royal Cities

Today, about half of all Moroccans live in cities. Many wealthy and middle-class people are urban dwellers, but sprawling slums called *bidonvilles* (tin-can towns) border the large cities. The bidonvilles got their name from the flattened bidons (tin cans) used to build these shacks. Severe overcrowding is also a problem in the *medinas,* or old sections, of the cities. Large urban areas grew around the medinas, which were the original city settlements.

The cities of Morocco were founded long ago, some as royal capitals. Morocco is part of an area once called the Maghreb. The name Maghreb included what are now Algeria, Tunisia, and part of Libya. The name *Maghreb* came from an Arabic word meaning *the place of the sunset—the west.* When Morocco was the heart of powerful empires that ruled the Maghreb as well as much of Spain, rulers called *sultans* established the cities as their royal capitals.

The simple but elegant interior of a mosque in Meknès features the graceful columns and geometric tilework found in many Muslim places of worship. Worshipers use the fountain for ceremonial washing before prayer.

Tourists crowd the central square of the *medina* (old section) of Marrakech, *right.* Founded in 1062, the city was the capital of a Berber empire until the 1400's, when Arab rulers replaced the Berbers and its importance declined.

Fez

The Moroccan ruler Sultan Idris II founded the city of Fez as the capital of his kingdom in A.D. 808. Fez was actually made up of two cities built near the site of the ancient Roman town of Volubilis—one Arab, the other Berber—and later enclosed within one wall. Fez became a major religious and cultural center of the Islamic world. The Mosque of Mulai Idris, a noted Muslim shrine, was built there, as was Karaouiyine University. Founded in A.D. 859, Karaouiyine is now one of the oldest universities in the world.

Marrakech

In 1062, the city of Marrakech was founded as the capital of a Berber dynasty, which, along with a second Berber dynasty, ruled a vast empire that included Spain. This empire produced the Moorish culture, renowned for its elegant and unique forms of art and architecture. Marrakech is now noted for its *mosques* (Muslim houses of worship) as well as its lovely parks, gardens, and pink clay buildings.

Rabat and Meknès

A third Berber dynasty founded a new capital at Rabat. Rabat was the site of an old settlement of the Roman Empire as well as a fort called Ribat al Fath (Camp of Victory). A huge wall was built along the coast to protect the city from enemy attack by sea.

Rabat remains Morocco's capital today. The royal palace stands in the city with the Hassan Tower—the *minaret* (prayer tower) of an incomplete mosque—rising above it on a bluff. Nearby is the tomb of Muhammad V, the first ruler of independent Morocco.

In the 1600's, an Arab sharifian tribe took control of Morocco. The sharifs were descended from Muhammad, founder of Islam. One of the sharifian rulers, Ismail, made Meknès his capital. There he built palaces like the Palace of Versailles in France. Ismail also had mosques erected, and ordered the construction of forts called *casbahs* (also spelled *kasbahs*) and deep dungeons for his prisoners.

Casablanca and Tangier

Casablanca was never a royal capital, but it is an important city and the largest in Morocco. Founded in 1575 by the Portuguese on the site of a small fishing village, Casablanca today is a dynamic industrial and

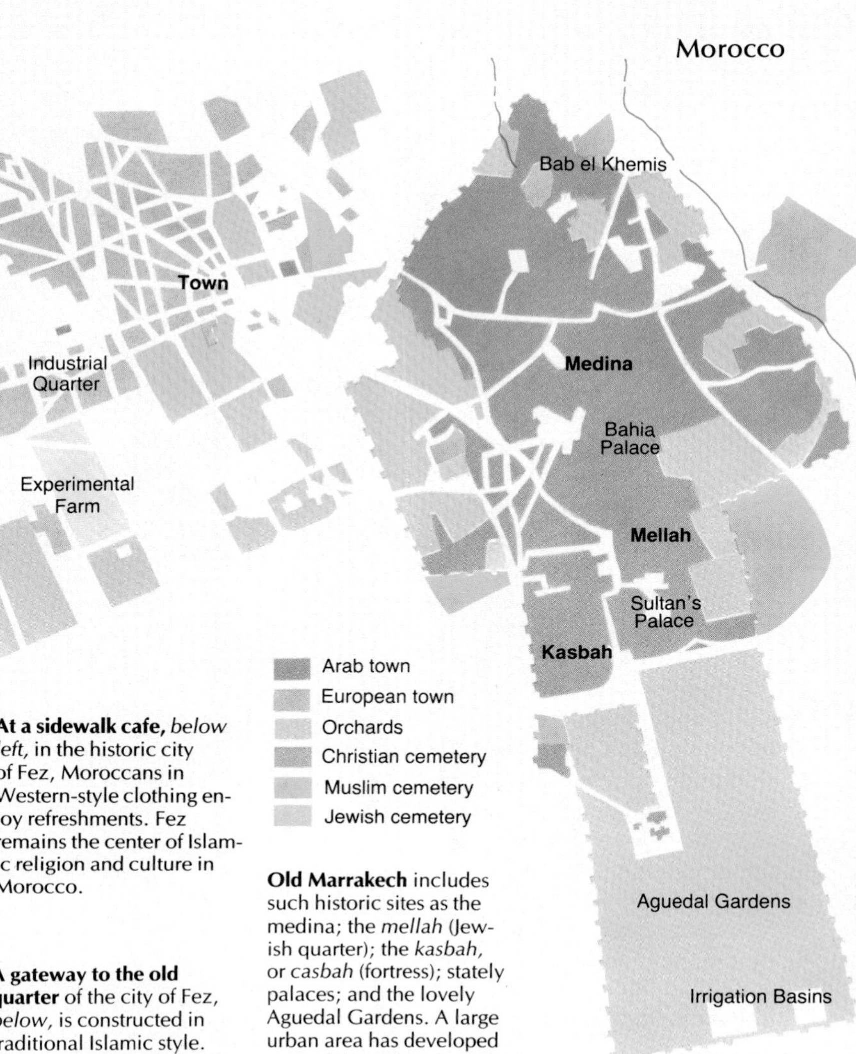

At a sidewalk cafe, *below left,* in the historic city of Fez, Moroccans in Western-style clothing enjoy refreshments. Fez remains the center of Islamic religion and culture in Morocco.

Old Marrakech includes such historic sites as the medina; the *mellah* (Jewish quarter); the *kasbah,* or *casbah* (fortress); stately palaces; and the lovely Aguedal Gardens. A large urban area has developed around this original royal capital.

A gateway to the old quarter of the city of Fez, *below,* is constructed in traditional Islamic style. The city was founded as a royal capital in 808. It declined during the 1600's, when a new capital was built at Meknès, but became the capital again from 1728 until 1912.

business center as well as a major port. Casablanca was also the site of a historic meeting in January 1943, when U.S. President Franklin D. Roosevelt and British Prime Minister Winston Churchill met in the city to plan the next phase of World War II (1939–1945).

Like Casablanca, Tangier was never a royal capital, but the city ranks second only to Casablanca among Moroccan seaports. Located near the northern tip of Morocco, Tangier came under Arab control in the 700's. Portugal, Spain, and England also held the city at various times. From 1923 to 1956, major European powers placed the city under international control. Today, Tangier is a center of shipping and tourism. From the sea, the city looks like an amphitheater, with rows of white houses lining its hills.

Tourism

Tourism is an important source of income for Morocco. Every year, almost 2 million tourists come to visit the nation's historic cities and enjoy its beach resorts, scenic mountains, and desert vistas.

The cities

Fez, Meknès, and Marrakech were once the capital cities of empires. Today, their royal palaces, graceful mosques, and colorful markets attract many tourists. In Marrakech, for example, a large square is the setting for busy *souks* (markets) that have taken place there every day for centuries. Water merchants pose for the tourists and sell a drink of water to the thirsty. Jugglers and storytellers entertain the crowds.

Some towns and cities draw tourists to their beautiful beach resorts. The southwest coastal town of Agadir, which was largely destroyed by an earthquake in 1960, was rebuilt and is now a popular seaside resort.

In addition to their many tourist attractions, the cities serve as starting points to the interior of Morocco. Roads link all major Moroccan cities, and bus lines reach almost every part of the country.

The mountains

The little town of Azrou, named for the huge rock bluff on which it stands, lies near the edge of Morocco's Middle Atlas Mountains. The town is surrounded by pine forests where monkeys leap from tree to tree, and some of the Middle Atlas range's most beautiful landscapes lie to the south of Azrou.

Pine and cedar forests line these mountain valleys, and tumbling cascades of water mark the source of the Oum er Rbia River. Nearby is a Berber village with ruins of a casbah built by Sultan Mulay Ismail. On the road from Azrou to Marrakech, a dramatic waterfall named Cascades d'Ouzoud plunges against a backdrop of dark red rocks. The Middle Atlas town of Midelt is famed for its carpet souk.

The Grand Atlas is Morocco's highest mountain range. These mountains act as a natural barrier between the coastal plains and towns to the northwest and the Sahara to the southeast. The main pass through the mountains is the Tichka Pass. The area was remote until the 20th century, and, even now, few tourists visit this area.

Hiking in the Atlas is popular among foreign tourists. The highest peaks in the Atlas include Jebel Toubkal, which soars 13,665 feet (4,165 meters) above sea level, and Irhil m'Goun, which rises 13,356 feet (4,071 meters). Hundreds of casbahs lie in the Grand Atlas valleys in the south near Ouarzazate.

The Atlas Mountains, which were a barrier to travel for centuries, are also a climate barrier, preventing ocean moisture from reaching the southeast. The western slopes receive rain and even snow in winter, but

A Berber woman goes to work with her small child strapped to her back.

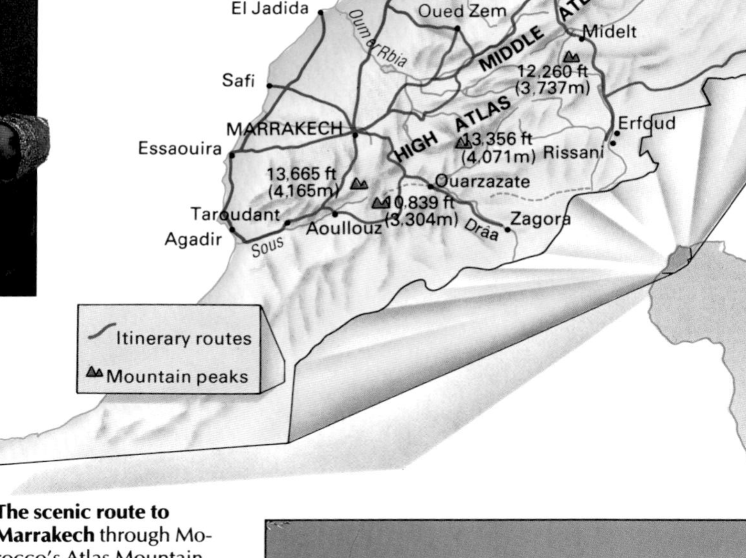

A river valley sprawls beneath the lofty Atlas Mountains, which guard the Sahara's northern approaches with their snow-capped peaks. For centuries, caravans passed this way on their long journeys across the region.

The scenic route to Marrakech through Morocco's Atlas Mountain region includes cascading waterfalls, areas of dense forests, ancient towns, and exotic markets.

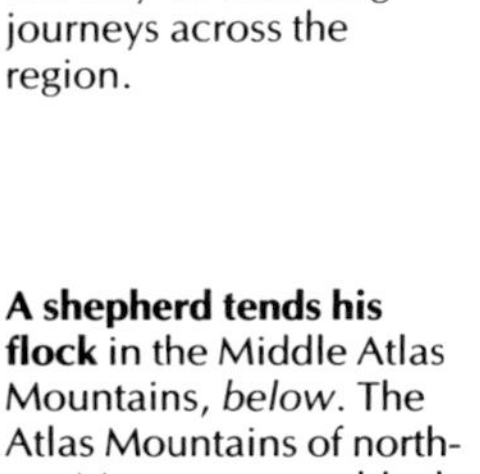

A shepherd tends his flock in the Middle Atlas Mountains, *below*. The Atlas Mountains of northern Morocco resemble the grassy mountains of Mediterranean Europe and have some heavily forested sections. But only scrubby vegetation grows on the Atlas slopes in the south.

A casbah, *right,* guards the road to the Middle Atlas city of Skoura. Great Moorish caravans, laden with gold, needed such protection on their dangerous journey to Moroccan cities through the Atlas Mountains.

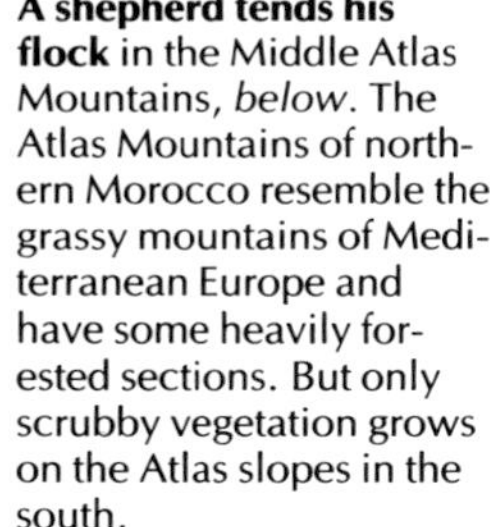

leave little moisture for the east and south. There, the mountain slopes descend gradually into the great Sahara.

The desert

From the eastern Grand Atlas slopes, the Sahara comes into view. River valleys lie green against the sand, and palm oases and mud villages are scattered throughout the desert.

Great Moorish caravans of traders and camels once crossed this region. Southbound caravans carried cloth, glass beads, salt, and other products, returning north with gold, slaves, leather, pepper, and kola nuts. Zagora was a stopping place for caravans en route to or from Timbuktu, a great trading center to the south in what is now Mali. Zagora has beautiful palm groves and several well-preserved *ksour* (fortified villages). From Zagora, travelers may journey out to Figuig near the Algerian border, one of the largest oases in North Africa.

Among the residents of the southern oases are the Harratines, a black people. Most Harratines work as farm laborers, and after choosing the Berber farmer they wish to work for, they sacrifice an animal at the Berber's door. This sacrifice involves a curse because any Berber who refuses to hire the Harratine is shamed in the eyes of God.

Mozambique

The nation of Mozambique lies along the southeastern coast of Africa. People have lived in this region since the 4000's B.C. Bantu-speaking people arrived and settled in the area before A.D. 100, and by the 800's Arabs were living in the region.

The first Europeans to visit what is now Mozambique were Portuguese explorers who arrived in 1497. They established a trading post in 1505 and eventually turned the region into a center for slave trading. Through the years, Portuguese control was threatened, but in 1885 Africa was divided among various European powers, and Mozambique was recognized as a Portuguese colony.

The Portuguese did little to develop Mozambique until the late 1800's, when towns and railroads were built. The colony's Portuguese population grew.

In the 1950's, many blacks became increasingly discontented with white Portuguese rule. A guerrilla group known as the Front for the Liberation of Mozambique, or Frelimo, was established in 1961. Frelimo began attacking the Portuguese in 1964 and eventually gained control of northern Mozambique. Fighting between Frelimo and Portuguese forces continued for 10 years, until Portugal finally agreed to give Mozambique its independence.

On June 25, 1975, the nation of Mozambique was born. Frelimo took control and created a *Marxist* government based on the Communist philosophies of Karl Marx and V. I. Lenin. The highest governmental power lay with the Frelimo party's Central Committee. The Frelimo government controlled education, health and legal services, housing, farmland, and major industries. Most of the Portuguese left Mozambique at that time.

In 1976, Mozambique closed its border with Rhodesia (now Zimbabwe) to protest that country's white minority government. Fighting broke out, but the problem was resolved when blacks gained control in Rhodesia in 1980.

Mozambique also aided guerrilla forces that were fighting the white minority government in South Africa. In turn, South Africa aided Renamo, a guerrilla group in Mozambique that was fighting the Frelimo government. In 1984, Mozambique and South Africa signed a treaty pledging to stop aiding the guerrillas.

But Renamo continued to fight in Mozambique, and the war became widespread and more vicious. Renamo attacked civilians, including women and children. Bridges and railroads were destroyed, and farming was disrupted. The violence caused some 1.5 mil-

Fact Box

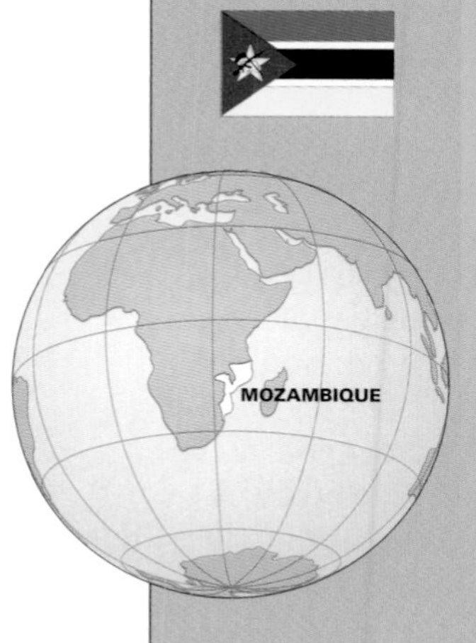

Country

Official name: Republica de Mocambique (Republic of Mozambique)
Capital: Maputo
Terrain: Mostly coastal lowlands, uplands in center, high plateaus in northwest, mountains in west
Area: 309,496 sq. mi. (801,590 km²)
Climate: Tropical to subtropical
Main rivers: Zambezi, Limpopo, Lugenda
Highest elevation: Monte Binga, 7,992 ft. (2,436 m)
Lowest elevation: Indian Ocean, sea level

Government

Form of government: Republic
Head of state: President
Head of government: Prime minister
Administrative areas: 10 provincias (provinces)
Legislature: Assembleia da Republica (Assembly of the Republic) with 250 members serving five-year terms
Court system: Supreme Court
Armed forces: 5,100 to 6,100 troops

People

Estimated 2002 population: 20,367,000
Population growth: 1.47%
Population density: 66 persons per sq. mi. (25 per km²)
Population distribution: 72% rural, 28% urban
Life expectancy in years: Male: 38 Female: 37
Doctors per 1,000 people: N/A
Percentage of age-appropriate population enrolled in the following educational levels: Primary: 71 Secondary: 9 Further: 1

lion people to flee the country. Droughts led to malnutrition and starvation for millions.

In 1989, the government ended its Marxist economic policies. A new constitution was adopted in 1990. In 1992, President Joaquim Chissano and the head of Renamo signed a peace treaty. Multiparty elections were held in October 1994. Frelimo won a majority of seats in the legislature, but Renamo won about 40 per cent.

In February 2000, Cyclone Eline and heavy rains struck Mozambique. The storms caused widespread flooding that produced power outages and washed away roads and bridges. Officials said that at least 70 people died as a result of the flooding, and more than 200,000 were left homeless.

Maputo, capital of Mozambique, lies on the shore of the Indian Ocean. Founded by the Portuguese in 1780, the town was called Lourenço Marques until 1976.

Mozambique, *map right,* once known as Portuguese East Africa, became independent in 1975. Civil war and droughts have badly hurt the country since that time.

Languages spoken:
Portuguese (official)
indigenous dialects

Religions:
indigenous beliefs 50%
Christian 30%
Muslim 20%

Technology

Radios per 1,000 people: 44

Televisions per 1,000 people: 5

Computers per 1,000 people: 3.0

Economy

Currency: Metical

Gross national income (GNI) in 2000: $3.7 billion U.S.

Real annual growth rate (1999–2000): 1.6%

GNI per capita (2000): $210 U.S.

Balance of payments (2000): -$764 million U.S.

Goods exported: Prawns, cashews, cotton, sugar, copra, citrus, coconuts, timber

Goods imported: Food, clothing, farm equipment, petroleum, transport equipment

Trading partners: South Africa, Spain, Portugal, Zimbabwe, Saudi Arabia

Economy and People

Mozambique stretches for about 1,500 miles (2,500 kilometers) along Africa's southeastern coast, and its shoreline has many fine harbors. The country's port facilities are used by neighboring countries, and payments by South Africa, Zimbabwe, Swaziland, and Malawi for the use of its railroads and ports are important to Mozambique's economy.

Behind the sand dunes and swamps that lie along the coastal region, a flat plain extends inland from the coast and covers almost half of Mozambique. Beyond the plain, the land rises steadily, and high plateaus and mountains run along much of the western border. The plain and highlands are covered mainly by grasslands and tropical forests. Crocodiles, elephants, lions, zebras, and other wildlife roam through Mozambique.

Many sizable rivers flow east through Mozambique into the Indian Ocean, creating river basins with extremely fertile soil. Agriculture is the people's leading economic activity. Cashew trees and coconut palms grow throughout the country, and both cashews and coconuts are important farm products. Other crops include cassava, cotton, and sugar cane.

While some Mozambicans use fairly modern techniques, most farming methods are extremely simple. Some farmers use the

Farmers carry sacks of produce to riverboats that will transport them down the Zambezi River.

Freight trains, *right,* carrying the products of neighboring southeast African countries to Mozambique's ports are subject to fees for the use of Mozambique's facilities. This money is important to Mozambique's economy.

Simple hand tools are used by farmers to prepare the ground for planting. The Marxist government's policy of setting up large collective farms was a failure. Today, small farms are encouraged in Mozambique.

Rural villagers, like these women with their children, make up about 75 per cent of Mozambique's population. Most are black Africans who speak Bantu languages.

ancient *slash-and-burn* method of farming, which involves cutting and burning forest trees to clear the land for planting. Ashes from the burned vegetation fertilize the soil, and the farmers can grow crops there for a year or two. When the soil loses its fertility, the farmers move on to a new plot of ground, where they repeat the process.

The Marxist government tried to create Communist-style cooperative farms after Mozambique became independent, but these were not successful. In the early 1980's, the government shifted to family-run farms.

The government also decided to allow private business to increase, and began helping some Mozambicans to start their own businesses. Industrial development has been slow, however, and limited mainly to food processing and oil refining. The nation's mining industry consists mainly of coal mining in central Mozambique.

While most Mozambicans are farmers, some people catch fish or shrimp in the Indian Ocean for a living. Many also go to South Africa in search of work.

Nearly three-quarters of the people live in rural areas. The rest live in urban centers, mainly along the coast.

Almost all Mozambicans are black Africans, and most belong to groups of Bantu-speaking peoples. The largest of these ethnic groups, called the Makua-Lomwe, makes up about 40 per cent of the population. Small groups of Arabs, Europeans, and Pakistanis, making up less than 1 per cent of the people, also live in Mozambique. Portuguese is the country's official language, but few black Mozambicans speak it. Some speak English when conducting business.

About half the people practice traditional African religions. Many of these people are *animists,* who believe that everything in nature has a soul, while others worship the spirits of their ancestors. Less than one-third of the people are Christians, mostly Roman Catholics. About one-fifth of the people are Muslims.

Only about 40 per cent of adult Mozambicans can read and write, but the government has started programs to educate the people. A university was established in Maputo in 1962.

For many years, the people of Mozambique did not vote for their government officials. Frelimo was the country's only political party, and it controlled the government.

Under a 1992 peace pact between Frelimo and the rebel group Renamo, other political parties were legalized. Multiparty elections were held on Oct. 27, 1994. Afonso Dhlakama, the leader of Renamo, charged election fraud and threatened to withdraw his name. He changed his mind, however, and the elections proceeded peacefully. Frelimo won a majority of seats, but Renamo won about 40 per cent of the seats.

Myanmar

Myanmar, formerly called Burma, is the largest nation on the Southeast Asian peninsula. Lying along the Bay of Bengal, Myanmar is bordered by mountains on the west, north, and east, enclosing the Irrawaddy River Valley. The Irrawaddy River empties into the Bay of Bengal through many mouths, forming a delta. Myanmar's capital and largest city, Yangon, lies on the Irrawaddy Delta. Yangon, also spelled Rangoon, is also the country's chief port and industrial center. It is the site of the golden-domed Shwe Dagon pagoda, the most famous Buddhist temple in Myanmar.

Most of the people of Myanmar live in villages on the Irrawaddy Delta and in the Irrawaddy Valley. The land in these areas is farmed by Burmans, an ethnic group that makes up about two-thirds of the population.

Smaller ethnic groups in Myanmar include the Karen, Shan, Arakanese, Chin, Kachin, Mon, Naga, and Wa. Most of these groups live in the hills and mountains that separate Myanmar from India, China, Laos, and Thailand. Each of these so-called *hill peoples* preserves its own culture, and some have fought to obtain more rights or to gain independence from the government of Myanmar.

Although today the Burmans greatly outnumber the Mon, the first known settlers in what is now Myanmar were Mon people who moved into the region as early as 3000 B.C. Many other ethnic groups, including the Burmans, came during the A.D. 800's. In 1044, a Burman ruler named Anawrahta united the region and founded a kingdom that lasted nearly 250 years. The kingdom's magnificent capital city of Pagan, which stood on the Irrawaddy River in central Myanmar, was destroyed by Mongol invaders led by Kublai Khan in 1287.

A one-party state

After the country, then known as Burma, gained its independence from Great Britain in 1948, its central government was plagued with uprisings by the hill peoples

and challenges by Communist forces. In 1962, the Socialists succeeded in taking control of the country and establishing a one-party state.

The new government imposed strict policies of economic self-sufficiency and cultural isolation on Burma. As a result, farm production fell, and consumer goods disappeared into the *black market,* which deals in the unlawful trading of goods. Student strikes in protest against the government were put down violently, and revolts by some of the hill peoples flared openly.

The government's policies had a devastating effect on Burma's economy. For example, in the early 1950's, the country was one of the world's leading exporters of rice, but by the 1970's Burma was barely able to feed its own people.

In 1989, the military government announced that it had changed the official name of the country from the Union of Burma to the Union of Myanmar. Some people, especially those who oppose the military regime, still refer to the country as Burma. Today, Myanmar is still ruled by one political party. Although the country's military rulers appeared ready to yield power in 1990, repression continues, and Myanmar's political and economic stability is still uncertain.

Natural resources

Despite Myanmar's political and economic woes, its potential for economic growth remains strong because of the country's wealth of natural resources. Rice, Myanmar's chief crop, is grown in the fertile Irrawaddy River Valley, where there is plenty of water and rainfall.

The forests that cover about half of Myanmar's land area have about 80 per cent of the world's teakwood. Unfortunately, much of this valuable forestland has been cut down for export to Thailand.

Myanmar also has a wealth of minerals, including zinc, lead, tin, tungsten, and silver, and the mountains in the north and east are rich in jade, rubies, and sapphires. However, the nation's mineral wealth remains undeveloped.

Myanmar Today

Myanmar, then called Burma, won full independence from the United Kingdom on Jan. 4, 1948, but the new government's conflict with Communist rebels and various ethnic groups led to civil war. In March 1962, General Ne Win seized control, and his Revolutionary Council set up a Socialist government in Burma that remained in power until 1988.

The government was organized under the banner of the Burma Socialist Programme Party (BSPP), the only political party allowed in Burma, with military officers in all the key posts. The BSPP cut Burma's ties with foreign countries—both cultural and economic—and restricted visits by foreign reporters and tourists. The government closed schools, took over newspapers, and established strict control over all the nation's industry and agriculture.

This rigid economic and political system had disastrous consequences. Farmers were paid so little for their crops that they grew no more than was absolutely necessary. And because many of the raw materials needed to run the nation's industries were no longer imported, production also decreased.

On March 2, 1974, a new Constitution officially created the Socialist Republic of the Union of Burma, with Ne Win as president. Although the new Constitution reestablished elections, the BSPP still held all power.

Free elections

In 1988, Burmese students rose up against the government, calling for an end to the country's one-party rule. As a result, Ne Win resigned as head of the BSPP in July, and over the next two months two other party leaders came to power.

A military coup in September 1988 finally overthrew the unstable government, replacing it with the newly established State Law and Order Restoration Council (SLORC). The new regime, led by General Saw Maung, killed hundreds of people in the protest demonstrations that followed the coup. General Saw Maung, a political ally of Ne Win, renamed the BSPP the National Unity Party. In 1989, the SLORC announced that it had changed the country's official name to the Union of Myanmar.

The main opposition party, the National League for Democracy, won a landslide victory in that election, but the party's leader—a woman named Aung San Suu Kyi—was in prison. Held on charges of inciting a pro-democracy uprising in 1989, she had also been banned from participating in the election.

Fact Box

Country

Official name: Pyidaungzu Myanma Naingngandaw (Union of Myanmar)
Capital: Yangon
Terrain: Central lowlands ringed by steep, rugged highlands
Area: 261,970 sq. mi. (678,500 km²)
Climate: Tropical monsoon; cloudy, rainy, hot, humid summers (southwest monsoon, June to September); less cloudy, scant rainfall, mild temperatures, lower humidity during winter (northeast monsoon, December to April)
Main rivers: Irrawaddy, Sittang, Salween
Highest elevation: Hkakabo Razi, 19,296 ft. (5,881 m)
Lowest elevation: Andaman Sea, sea level

Government

Form of government: Military regime
Head of state: Prime minister
Head of government: Prime minister
Administrative areas: 7 yin-mya (divisions), 7 pyine-mya (states)
Legislature: Pyithu Hluttaw (People's Assembly) with 485 members serving four-year terms
Court system: limited
Armed forces: 429,000 troops

People

Estimated 2002 population: 46,648,000
Population growth: 0.64%
Population density: 179 persons per sq. mi. (69 per km²)
Population distribution: 74% rural, 26% urban
Life expectancy in years: Male: 54; Female: 56
Doctors per 1,000 people: 0.3
Percentage of age-appropriate population enrolled in the following educational levels: Primary: 114*; Secondary: 36; Further: N/A

Visitors to Yangon's Shwe Dagon pagoda, Myanmar's most famous Buddhist temple, find shelter from the rain beneath their umbrellas. Nearly 90 per cent of the people of Myanmar are followers of Buddhism.

Myanmar, *map below,* has remained uninvolved in the conflicts that have devastated other Southeast Asian countries, but the Myanmar army continued to fight rebel groups until cease-fire agreements were reached with most of them in the mid-1990's.

Myanmar's military leaders violently put down any opposition to their power. Aung San Suu Kyi won the 1991 Nobel Peace Prize. In 1994, military leaders held talks with Aung San Suu Kyi, but the talks did not lead to immediate changes. Many countries had ostracized Myanmar, but in March 1994 Singapore's prime minister visited Myanmar. Later that year, foreign leaders agreed on a policy of "constructive engagement" with Myanmar.

Economy

Currency: Kyat

Gross domestic product (GDP) in 2000: $63 billion U.S.

Real annual growth rate (2001): 2.3%

GDP per capita (2001): $1,500 U.S.

Balance of payments (2000): -$651 million U.S.

Goods exported: Pulses and beans, prawns, fish, rice; teak, opiates

Goods imported: Machinery, transport equipment, construction materials, food products

Trading partners: Singapore, China, Thailand, India, Japan

Languages spoken:
- Burmese
- minority ethnic groups have their own languages

Religions:
- Buddhist 89%
- Muslim 4%
- Baptist 3%
- animist 1%
- Roman Catholic 1%

Enrollment ratios compare the number of students enrolled to the population which, by age, should be enrolled. A ratio higher than 100 indicates that students older or younger than the typical age range are also enrolled.

Technology

Radios per 1,000 people: 66

Televisions per 1,000 people: 7

Computers per 1,000 people: 1.1

History

The earliest inhabitants of what is now Myanmar were the Mon people, who moved into the region around 3000 B.C. They came from what is now southwestern China and settled near the mouths of the Salween and Sittang rivers, where they grew rice. In time, the Mon came to be greatly influenced by nearby India, and around 200 B.C., some members of the Mon group began to adopt Theravada Buddhism, which was founded in India.

The Pyu arrived in the A.D. 600's, followed, during the 800's, by the Burmans, Chin, Kachin, Karen, and Shan. Like the Mon, these later arrivals migrated from an area in central Asia that is now southwestern China. In general, these peoples lived apart from one another and kept their own cultures. The largest group—the Burmans—obtained the most fertile lands in the region.

In 1044, Burman ruler Anawrahta united the region under one kingdom. In order to keep peace with the Mon people, the Burmans adopted some features of the Mon and Pyu cultures, including Theravada Buddhism. Art and architecture flourished in the kingdom, and hundreds of beautiful Buddhist shrines and pagodas were built in the capital city of Pagan.

Foreign invaders

The rich kingdom was shattered by Mongol invaders led by Kublai Khan, who captured Pagan in 1287. The once-unified ethnic groups split apart and formed separate states.

Another Burman kingdom was established at Toungoo during the 1500's and lasted until 1752, when it was brought down by a Mon rebellion. By this time, European traders had become well established in Burma, and the Dutch and British East India Companies aided the Mon rebellion.

The last Burman kingdom was founded by Alaungpaya, a Burman leader, after the Mon rebellion. However, three wars with the British—triggered by resistance to Great Britain's commercial and territorial ambitions—led to the collapse of the last kingdom. By 1885, British forces had conquered all of the country then known as Burma.

British rule

Burma became a province of India, which was also under British rule, and its population and economy grew. However, many Burmese demanded separation from India and full independence. Although Britain allowed the Burmese to set up a legislature in the 1920's, unrest continued.

In the early 1930's, university students called the Thakins worked for independence. In 1936, led by Aung San and U Nu, the Thakins organized a student strike that forced Britain to separate Burma from India and grant the Burmese partial self-government. However, the Burmese still were denied full independence.

During World War II (1939-1945), the Thakins helped the Japanese drive the British out of Burma. The Japanese declared Burma's independence in 1943, but the Japanese actually controlled the government. Disliking Japanese rule even more than British rule, the Burmese then fought

Karen guerrillas proclaim their defiance of the Burmese government. The Karen people and many other ethnic groups fought the central government until the government reached cease-fire agreements with most of them.

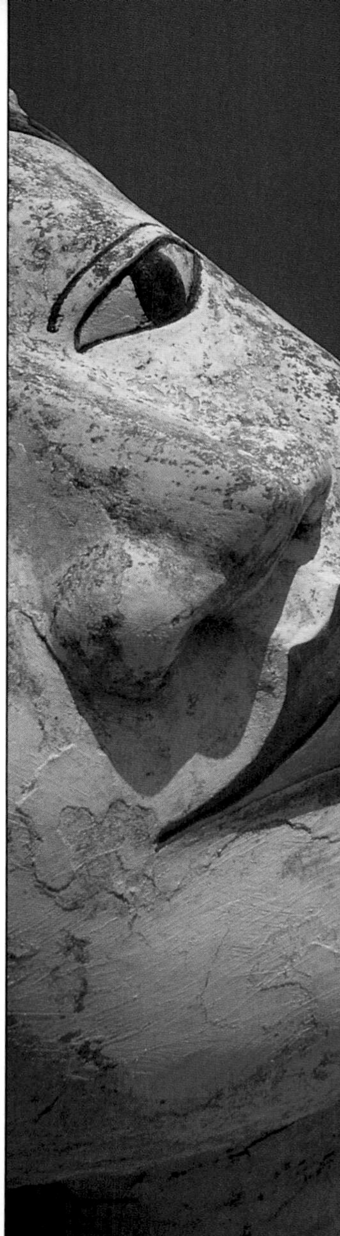

The Royal Palace at Mandalay, *right,* was renamed Fort Dufferin in 1885 after Great Britain occupied the city. Today, only the moat and parts of the walls remain. Most of the palace was destroyed during World War II.

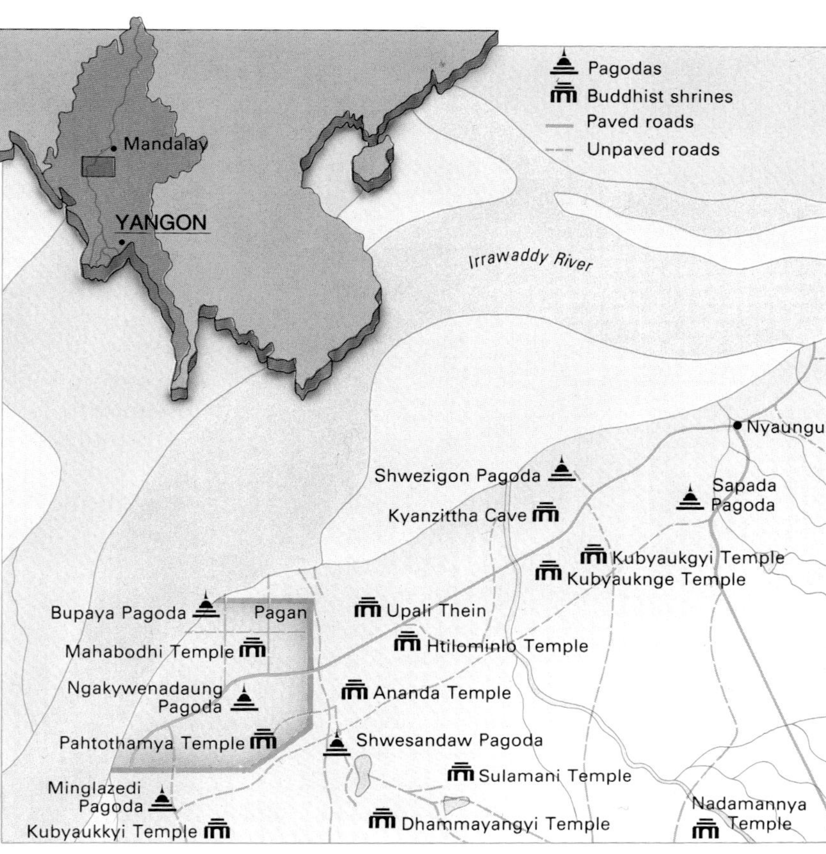

In Pagan, *above,* near what is now Mandalay, the cultures of the Mon, Pyu, and Burman peoples were united in a unique city of gilded Buddhist shrines and shimmering pagodas.

Statues of Buddha are found all over Myanmar. Buddhism, adopted by the Mon around the 200's B.C., was founded in India about 500 B.C. by a teacher called Buddha. Buddhism has been a dominant force in most of Asia for many centuries and has about 300 million followers today.

A young student of Buddhism, dressed in white to symbolize purity, reflects the continuity of the Buddhist tradition.

against Japan and formed the Anti-Fascist People's Freedom League (AFPFL), led by General Aung San, the former Thakin leader. The AFPFL helped Britain and other Allied powers regain control of Burma in 1945.

In the meantime, the AFPFL had become a powerful political party under the leadership of its president, Aung San, and the party resisted British rule. In the face of this challenge, Britain named Aung San prime minister of Burma in 1947. However, Aung San was assassinated before independence came, so the British appointed AFPFL Vice President U Nu as prime minister. Burma finally won full independence on Jan. 4, 1948.

Namibia

Namibia is a former territory in southwest Africa. When Namibia gained its independence in 1990, a new nation came into being, and 400 years of European colonial rule on the African continent ended.

Traditional Herero dress includes a headdress like the one worn by the woman above, a blouse, and hooped skirt.

South African rule

Most of Namibia's people are blacks, but the region had been controlled by Europeans since the 1800's. Beginning in 1868, Germans colonized the Namibian coastal area, which they called South-West Africa. They brutally put down a revolt that lasted from 1904 to 1907 by killing about 65,000 black Africans, but they lost the area to South African troops during World War I (1914–1918).

For many years, the white-minority government of South Africa ruled Namibia as if it were a province of its own country, despite protests from other nations. In 1966, the United Nations (UN) took steps to try to bring Namibia under UN control, and in 1971 the International Court of Justice declared South Africa's control of Namibia illegal.

Eleven years earlier, in 1960, black Namibians had formed a group called the South West African People's Organization (SWAPO). At first SWAPO tried to persuade South Africa to grant Namibia independence, but beginning in the mid-1960's, it began a guerrilla war. SWAPO and South African forces fought each other until 1989.

In 1988, South Africa finally agreed to grant Namibia independence. SWAPO candidates won elections held in November 1989, and Namibia officially became an independent nation in April 1990. In December 1994, SWAPO won 70 per cent of the popular vote in a peaceful election.

Fact Box

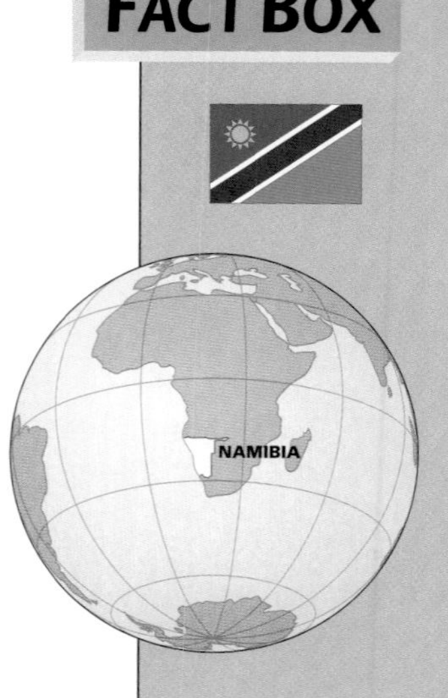

Country

Official name: Republic of Namibia

Capital: Windhoek

Terrain: Mostly high plateau; Namib Desert along coast; Kalahari Desert in east

Area: 318,696 sq. mi. (825,418 km²)

Climate: Desert; hot, dry; rainfall sparse and erratic

Main rivers: Kunene, Okavango, Kwando, Zambezi, Orange

Highest elevation: Brandberg, 8,465 ft. (2,580 m)

Lowest elevation: Atlantic Ocean, sea level

Government

Form of government: Republic

Head of state: President

Head of government: President

Administrative areas: 13 regions

Legislature: Legislature consisting of the National Council with 26 members serving six-year terms and the National Assembly with 72 members serving five-year terms

Court system: Supreme Court

Armed forces: 9,000 troops

People

Estimated 2002 population: 1,768,000

Population growth: 1.57%

Population density: 6 persons per sq. mi. (2 per km²)

Population distribution: 73% rural, 27% urban

Life expectancy in years:
Male: 44
Female: 41

Doctors per 1,000 people: 0.3

Percentage of age-appropriate population enrolled in the following educational levels:
Primary: 126*
Secondary: 59
Further: 7

Languages spoken:
English 7% (official)
Afrikaans (spoken by most of the population)

Fortresslike rock formations shaped by thousands of years of wind erosion rise up from the inland plateau near Khorixas, on the edge of the Namib Desert.

Namibia, *above right,* once called South-West Africa, is situated on Africa's west coast. Major rivers form its northern and southern borders, but inland Namibia is dry.

The people and their work

The black Africans who are now in control of Namibia make up 90 per cent of its population. They belong to several different ethnic groups, including the Ovambo, who make up more than half of all Namibians. The Ovambo live in the north, as do the Kavango and the Caprivians. The Damara and the Herero occupy central Namibia, and the San (Bushmen) and Tswana people live in the east. Two groups of mixed ancestry—the Basters and the Nama—live in central and southern Namibia.

Whites account for about 7 per cent of Namibia's population and include South Africans of Dutch, English, and German descent. People of mixed ancestry, called Coloreds, also live in Namibia.

Most of the whites and Coloreds live in urban areas. Many of Namibia's whites hold administrative jobs and generally have higher incomes and access to better medical services and schools than do blacks.

Most rural blacks in Namibia fish, grow crops, or raise livestock for a living. Their food crops include corn, millet, and vegetables. Cattle and sheep are the most important livestock. But since the late 1970's, drought and other problems have troubled farmers and herders. Most farmers grow barely enough food for their own use, and overfishing has reduced the catch of anchovies, mackerel, and sardines in the Atlantic Ocean.

Although much of Namibia's land is dry and infertile, the country is rich in minerals, including diamonds and uranium. Many Ovambo and Kavango men work in copper mines at Tsumeb or in southern diamond mines. Lead, tin, and zinc also help make mining Namibia's most important economic activity.

German 32%
Oshivambo
Herero
Nama

Religions:
Christian 80% to 90% (Lutheran 50% at least)
indigenous beliefs 10% to 20%

*Enrollment ratios compare the number of students enrolled to the population which, by age, should be enrolled. A ratio higher than 100 indicates that students older or younger than the typical age range are also enrolled.

Technology

Radios per 1,000 people: 141
Televisions per 1,000 people: 38
Computers per 1,000 people: 34.2

Economy

Currency: Namibian dollar
Gross national income (GNI) in 2000: $3.6 billion U.S.
Real annual growth rate (1999–2000): 3.9%
GNI per capita (2000): $2,030 U.S.
Balance of payments (2002): $204 million U.S.
Goods exported: Diamonds, copper, gold, zinc, lead, uranium, cattle, processed fish, karakul skins
Goods imported: Foodstuffs; petroleum products and fuel, machinery and equipment, chemicals
Trading partners: South Africa, United Kingdom, Spain, Germany, United States

Nauru

The republic of Nauru, a small island country in the central Pacific Ocean, is the third smallest country in the world, after Vatican City and Monaco. Nauru is rich in *phosphates*—valuable chemical compounds used in making fertilizers—and phosphate exports are important to Nauru's economy.

Land and people

Nauru is an oval-shaped coral island about 40 miles (65 kilometers) south of the equator, with an area of only 8 square miles (21 square kilometers). Most of the island consists of a plateau, 200 feet (61 meters) high, that contains deposits of phosphates. A small area of fertile land surrounds a lagoon near the center of the plateau, and another belt of fertile land extends around the coast. Nauru has a tropical climate, cooled by trade winds. Temperatures range from 76° to 93° F. (24° to 34° C), and the island has an annual rainfall of about 80 inches (200 centimeters).

About half of Nauru's population of 12,000 are Nauruans—people of mixed Polynesian, Micronesian, and Melanesian ancestry. They follow the Christian religion, and most speak both the Nauruan language and English. The rest of Nauru's people are temporary residents from the Pacific Island groups of Kiribati and Tuvalu, and from Hong Kong and

Fact Box

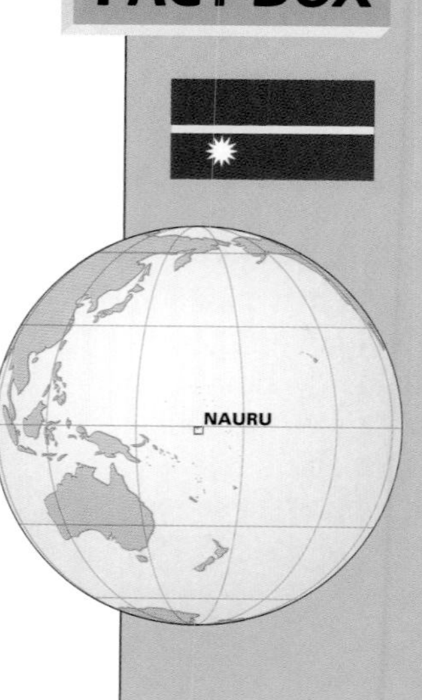

Country

Official name: Republic of Nauru
Capital: None
Terrain: Sandy beach rises to fertile ring around raised coral reefs with phosphate plateau in center
Area: 8 sq. mi. (21 km²)
Climate: Tropical; monsoonal; rainy season (November to February)
Highest elevation: Unnamed location along plateau rim, 229 ft. (70 m)
Lowest elevation: Pacific Ocean, sea level

Government

Form of government: Republic
Head of state: President
Head of government: President
Administrative areas: 14 districts
Legislature: Parliament with 18 members serving three-year terms
Court system: Supreme Court
Armed forces: Australia is responsible for Nauru's defense

People

Estimated 2002 population: 12,000
Population growth: 2.05%
Population density: 1,481 persons per sq. mi. (564 per km²)
Population distribution: N/A
Life expectancy in years:
Male: 57
Female: 65
Doctors per 1,000 people: N/A
Percentage of age-appropriate population enrolled in the following educational levels:
Primary: N/A
Secondary: N/A
Further: N/A

Australia. These people come to Nauru for limited periods to work in the phosphate industry. Most of the island's people live along the 12-mile (19-kilometer) coastline. In the past, the islanders raised their own food, but most food and other products are now imported.

History and government

In 1798, an English explorer named John Fearn became the first European to visit Nauru. Germany took over the island in 1888 and administered it until 1914, when Australia took control. After World War I (1914–1918), Australia began to administer the island under a League of Nations mandate held also by the United Kingdom, Australia, and New Zealand.

Japan seized Nauru during World War II (1939–1945). Australia retook the island in 1945, later gaining control of the area under a trusteeship with the United Kingdom and New Zealand. The United Nations granted Nauru independence in 1968. In 1970, the Nauruan government gained control of its phosphate industry.

Nauru is now a republic and a member of the Commonwealth of Nations. An 18-member Parliament makes its laws. The people elect Parliament members who, in turn, elect a president—all to three-year terms. The president selects a Cabinet, and together they carry out the government's operations. Nauru has no capital. The main government offices are on the southwestern part of the island.

The government provides Nauruans with free medical care and modern homes at low rents. Children between the ages of 6 and 17 attend school. The government pays the expenses of students who go to college in other countries.

The government has used revenue from phosphate exports to provide these services, but the phosphate deposits on the island are being used up rapidly. When they are gone, the people will have to find other ways to support themselves. Still, the government has saved revenue from phosphate exports to help the people after all the phosphates have been mined.

Ancient and modern vessels reflect the contrasting cultures in Nauru, *top.* Outrigger canoes sail near a dock where a freighter loads phosphates.

Sea birds on Nauru deposit droppings that are rich in phosphate—a valuable fertilizer. The nation's economy depends on phosphate exports.

Native Nauruans, *above left,* are of mixed Polynesian, Micronesian, and Melanesian ancestry. Today, about half the people on the island come from other countries to work in the phosphate industry.

Languages spoken:
Nauruan (official)
English

Religion:
Protestant 67%
Roman Catholic 33%

Technology

Radios per 1,000 people: N/A
Televisions per 1,000 people: N/A
Computers per 1,000 people: N/A

Economy

Currency: Australian dollar
Gross domestic product (GDP) in 2001: $60 million U.S.
Real annual growth rate (2001): N/A
GDP per capita (2001): N/A
Balance of payments (2001): N/A
Goods exported: Phosphates
Goods imported: Food, fuel, manufactures, building materials, machinery
Trading partners: Australia, New Zealand, United Kingdom

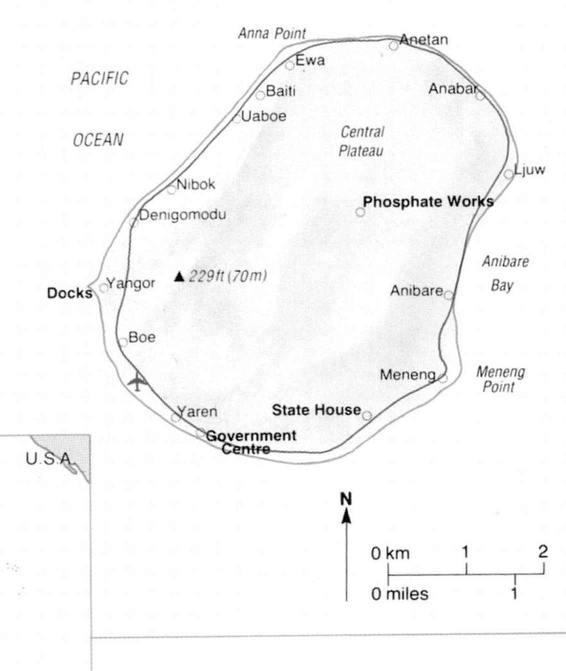

The republic of Nauru in the central Pacific is the third smallest country in the world. Most of the island is a plateau that contains deposits of phosphates.

Nepal

Nepal is a mountain kingdom located along the southern range of the Himalaya between China and India. Although it is a small country, Nepal has the widest variation in altitude on earth—ranging from the world's highest mountain, Mount Everest, at 29,035 feet (8,850 meters) to 150 feet (46 meters) above sea level.

An exotic land

Until the 1950's, Nepal was isolated from the rest of the world. Untouched by new developments and technologies, the Nepalese way of life had changed little through the centuries.

In recent years, the government has opened the country to tourists, and thousands of people now come each year to visit this enchanting land. From the crowded streets of Kathmandu to the remote mountain villages, Nepal appears to have escaped the passage of time. It is as exotic and mysterious today as it was centuries ago.

Nepal's extraordinary scenery also attracts visitors. Mountaineers come to scale the peaks of the Himalaya, and trekkers hike along the trails that link the villages and settlements.

The magnificent landscape of Nepal attracts thousands of trekkers each year. Travel agencies in Kathmandu provide transportation to mountain sites. The growing tourist industry is important to the country's economy.

Terracing, *right,* allows Nepalese farmers to use steep hillsides for growing crops. Terraces retain rain water and prevent soil from washing down the hillside. However, terracing can also weaken the stability of the slopes if they are not well designed and maintained.

Mountains, valleys, farmland, and jungles

Nepal can be divided into three land regions: (1) high mountains made up of the Himalaya, (2) the hills and valleys, and (3) low plains called the Tarai (or Terai). Because these regions are located at different altitudes, their climate, plants, and animals vary greatly.

The Himalaya make up much of the whole northern territory of Nepal. Up to an altitude of about 12,000 feet (3,660 meters), dense forests blanket the mountain slopes. At higher altitudes, permanent snow and ice cover the peaks that tower above the steep river valleys carved by the *glaciers* (huge rivers of ice).

Only grasses, moss, and *lichens* (mosslike plants) grow at elevations above 12,000 feet (3,660 meters). Birds and mammals are seen occasionally. The snow leopard, for example, may use one of the high mountain passes to get from one valley to another.

South of the Himalaya lie the hills and valleys. Corn, rice, millet, and wheat thrive in the cool, rainy climate on hillside terraces and in the valleys. A wide variety of trees and bamboo grasses are found in the dense forests of this region. Timber from the sal, sissoo, pine, oak, poplar, and walnut trees is an important natural resource for the Nepalese.

The valleys of this region are home to Nepal's historic cities—Kathmandu, Patan, Bhaktapur, Gurkha, and Pokhara. Kathmandu, Nepal's capital and largest city, is the center of the country's expanding tourist industry. Kathmandu is known the world over for its many Hindu and Buddhist temples.

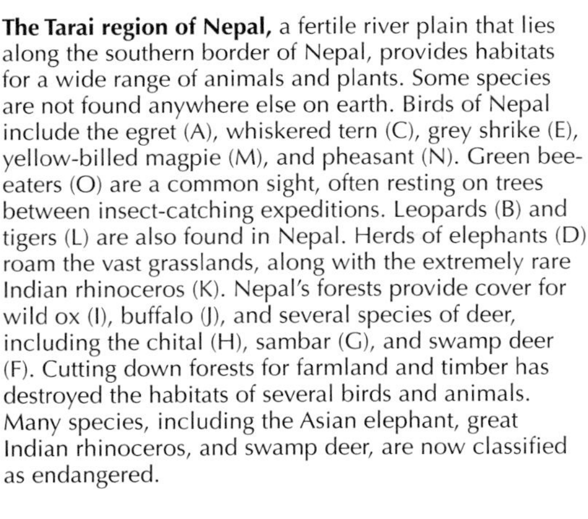

The Tarai region of Nepal, a fertile river plain that lies along the southern border of Nepal, provides habitats for a wide range of animals and plants. Some species are not found anywhere else on earth. Birds of Nepal include the egret (A), whiskered tern (C), grey shrike (E), yellow-billed magpie (M), and pheasant (N). Green bee-eaters (O) are a common sight, often resting on trees between insect-catching expeditions. Leopards (B) and tigers (L) are also found in Nepal. Herds of elephants (D) roam the vast grasslands, along with the extremely rare Indian rhinoceros (K). Nepal's forests provide cover for wild ox (I), buffalo (J), and several species of deer, including the chital (H), sambar (G), and swamp deer (F). Cutting down forests for farmland and timber has destroyed the habitats of several birds and animals. Many species, including the Asian elephant, great Indian rhinoceros, and swamp deer, are now classified as endangered.

A dye factory in the cloth-weaving town of Kirtipur, *above,* is one of the small industries that support many Nepalese people.

The Tarai is a flat, fertile river plain along Nepal's border with India. Its tropical climate and rich farmland make this region ideal for growing corn, jute, millet, mustard, rice, sugar cane, and tobacco. Tarai farmers also raise cattle and water buffalo.

Wildlife in the jungles of the Tarai includes crocodiles, elephants, deer, leopards, rhinoceroses, and tigers. The Tarai's Chitwan National Park is one of the greatest wildlife reserves in Asia.

Nepal Today

Until the late 1700's, Nepal consisted of many small, independent kingdoms located throughout the central valleys of the country.

In the mid-1700's, Prithwi Narayan Shah, king of the small kingdom of Gorkha, began a series of military campaigns to unite Nepal. By 1775, his army had conquered most of the other kingdoms.

During the early 1800's, the ruling dynasty tried to extend Nepal's territory into Kashmir, Sikkim, Bhutan, and Tibet. When the Nepalese attempted to invade northern India, they were met by British soldiers, who were at that time protecting the East India Company's territory. The United Kingdom declared war on Nepal in 1814 after Nepalese troops attacked a British outpost. Two years later, the British defeated the Nepalese.

Political struggles

In 1846, a political leader named Jung Bahadur seized control of Nepal's government. He took the name of *Rana*. Rana and his descendants ruled Nepal for more than 100 years. The Ranas were harsh leaders. They imprisoned and even murdered their political enemies. The Ranas also kept Nepal isolated from the rest of the world.

During the 1930's and 1940's, many Nepalese began to oppose Rana rule, and in 1950 a revolution overthrew the Rana government. In 1951, Nepal's monarchy was restored under King Tribhuwan Shah.

The modern monarchy

When Tribhuwan died in 1955, his son, Mahendra, became king. King Mahendra was so disturbed by fighting between political groups that in 1960 he banned all political parties and dissolved the elected government. In 1962, he established a *panchayat* (council) system, in which the king holds most of the power. King Mahendra died in 1972, and his son, Birendra, became king.

Many Nepalese objected to the panchayat system. In 1979, they staged violent demonstrations and demanded a more democratic government. In response, King Birendra gave the people permission to hold a national vote on the issue. By a very narrow margin, Nepalese voters chose to continue the panchayat system. But pressure for political change continued. In 1990, a new Constitution established a constitutional monarchy, and in 1991, multiparty elections were held. In November 1994, elections brought a coalition of the Nepal Communist Party-United Marxist Leninist (UML) to power. King Birendra named the chairman of the UML prime minister and head of a minority government. However, the Supreme Court ruled

Fact Box

Country

Official name: Kingdom of Nepal
Capital: Kathmandu
Terrain: Terai or flat river plain of the Ganges in south, central hill region, rugged Himalayas in north
Area: 54,363 sq. mi. (140,800 km²)
Climate: Varies from cool summers and severe winters in north to subtropical summers and mild winters in south
Main rivers: Seti, Karnali, Bheri, Sun Kosi, Arun, Tamur
Highest elevation: Mount Everest, 29,035 ft. (8,850 m)
Lowest elevation: Kanchan Kalan, 230 ft. (70 m)

Government

Form of government: Parliamentary democracy
Head of state: Monarch
Head of government: Prime minister
Administrative areas: 14 anchal (zones)
Legislature: Parliament consisting of the National Council with 60 members serving six-year terms and the House of Representatives with 205 members serving five-year terms
Court system: Sarbochha Adalat (Supreme Court)
Armed forces: 46,000 troops

People

Estimated 2002 population: 25,009,000
Population growth: 2.34%
Population density: 440 persons per sq. mi. (170 per km²)
Population distribution: 89% rural, 11% urban
Life expectancy in years:
Male: 58
Female: 57
Doctors per 1,000 people: Less than 0.05
Percentage of age-appropriate population enrolled in the following educational levels:
Primary: 114*
Secondary: 48
Further: 3

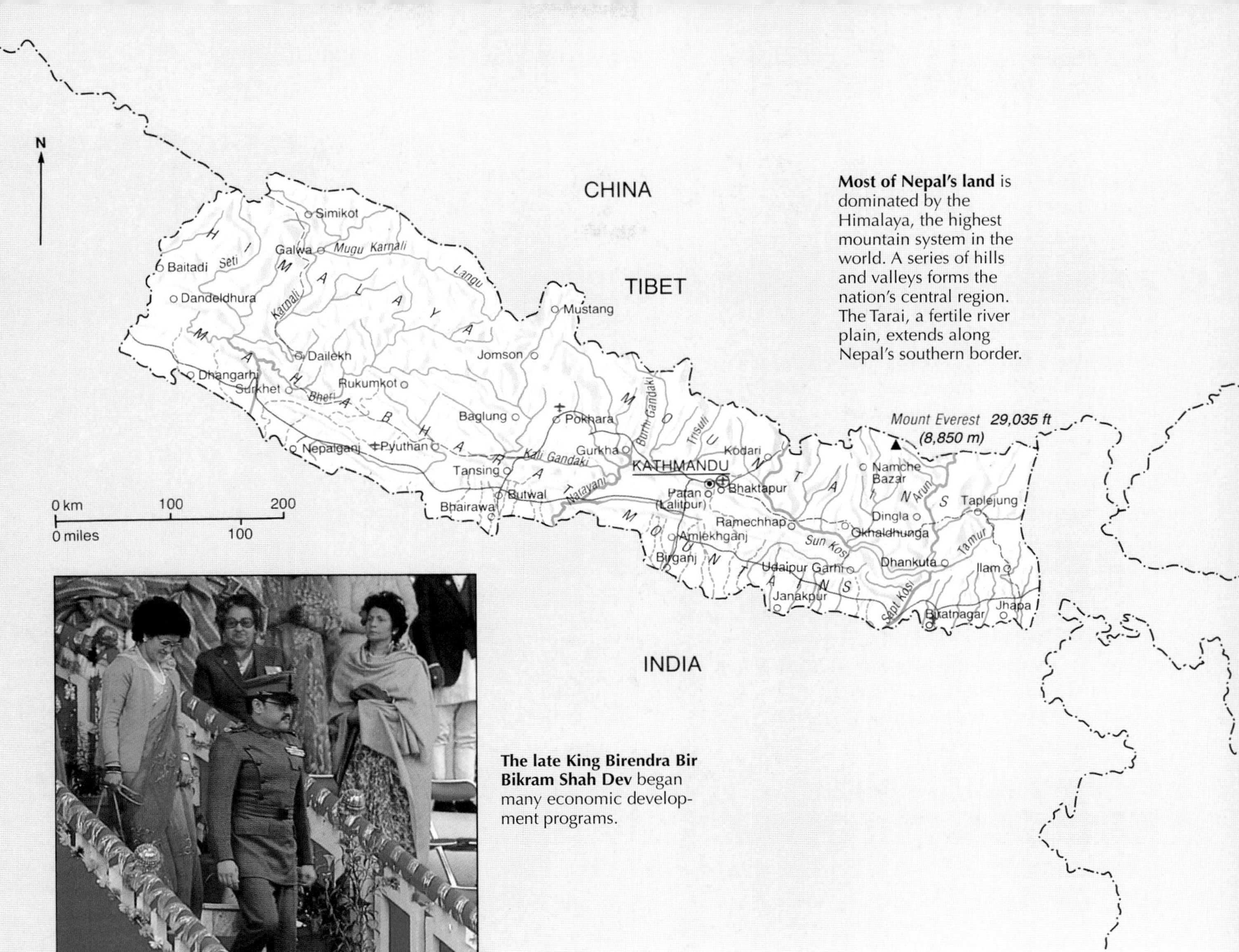

Most of Nepal's land is dominated by the Himalaya, the highest mountain system in the world. A series of hills and valleys forms the nation's central region. The Tarai, a fertile river plain, extends along Nepal's southern border.

The late King Birendra Bir Bikram Shah Dev began many economic development programs.

Languages spoken:
Nepali (official)
over 20 other languages divided into numerous dialects

Religions:
Hindu 90%
Buddhist 5%
Muslim 3%

Enrollment ratios compare the number of students enrolled to the population which, by age, should be enrolled. A ratio higher than 100 indicates that students older or younger than the typical age range are also enrolled.

Technology

Radios per 1,000 people: 39

Televisions per 1,000 people: 7

Computers per 1,000 people: 3.0

Economy

Currency: Nepalese rupee

Gross national income (GNI) in 2000: $5.6 billion U.S.

Real annual growth rate (1999–2000): 6.5%

GNI per capita (2000): $240 U.S.

Balance of payments (2000): -$239 million U.S.

Goods exported: Carpets, clothing, leather goods, jute goods, grain

Goods imported: Gold, machinery and equipment, petroleum products, fertilizer

Trading partners: India, United States, Germany, China, Singapore

the King's actions unconstitutional. Parliament reconvened, ousted the UML, and returned the Nepali congress party to power.

In June 2001, King Birendra's son Prince Dipendra killed the king and most of the royal family, then killed himself. The king's brother Gyanendra assumed the throne. Shortly after the royal massacre, the Communist rebels and the government began peace negotiations. However, talks broke down in late 2001, and violence resumed. Since then, thousands of people have been killed by both the rebels and the Nepalese army, and the country's economy has suffered greatly. In October 2002, King Gyanendra dismissed Nepal's elected prime minister and appointed an interim government to run the country. In January 2003, the rebels declared a cease-fire.

People

The earliest settlers in what is now Nepal were probably Mongoloid peoples from central Asia and Tibet. Later, Aryan immigrants from northern India entered the country. Eventually, the Aryans made up the majority of Nepal's people. By about A.D. 300, Hindu dynasties had established their rule over Nepal.

Today, the Nepalese population is made up of several ethnic groups. Each has its own language and its own cultural and religious practices.

The Sherpas are a Himalayan people who live in the mountainous northern and eastern regions of Nepal. The Sherpas are known for their mountaineering skills.

Sherpa men and women are able to carry heavy loads up to high altitudes and often serve as guides and porters for mountain-climbing expeditions from all over the world. In 1953, a Sherpa named Tenzing Norgay and Sir Edmund Hillary of New Zealand became the first people to climb to the top of Mount Everest.

The Gurkhas are Nepalese soldiers serving in the British or Indian army. The salaries and pensions paid to Gurkha soldiers are a significant contribution to Nepal's economy.

Way of life

The Nepalese people live a simple, rural life in small villages. Their homes are usually two-story houses made of stone or mud brick.

About 90 per cent of the people earn their living by farming and related work, though most Nepalese farmers can barely grow enough food for their own families. Any surplus crops are traded for such items as kerosene and salt.

Some Nepalese make their living as craft workers, including blacksmiths, goldsmiths, shoemakers, and tailors. Others are merchants and government workers. Today, many Nepalese work in the country's growing tourist industry.

Brightly colored prayer banners decorate a shrine during a Buddhist ceremony performed by Nepalese monks. Nepal is the birthplace of Siddhartha Gautama, the Buddha, who founded the Buddhism religion about 500 B.C.

The Swayambhunath Temple towers over the rooftops of Kathmandu from a hillside west of the city. The temple houses a long-established monastery as well as a resident troop of monkeys, who are cared for by the monks.

Nepal's century of isolation under the Rana dynasty held back the nation's social development. In the 1950's, only about 5 per cent of Nepalese over 15 years old could read and write. With the help of government programs, that percentage is now up to about 20 per cent.

Malnutrition, contaminated water, and poor sanitation have caused many health problems for the Nepalese people, and epidemics are a constant threat. Recently, however, government programs have helped control malaria, leprosy, and tuberculosis.

Poor communication and transportation systems have slowed further progress in raising educational and health levels. The wide, deep gorges across the Nepal landscape form natural barriers between the villages and settlements. In recent years, foreign aid has helped the Nepalese build roads for year-round traffic.

A poultry farmer, *below,* stands outside his home in Nepal's heartland, the Kathmandu Valley. Modern poultry farms are operated mostly by Newars, the original settlers of the valley. Newar towns include Thimi, Bode, and Chapagaon.

Nepalese mothers bring their babies everywhere they go. The government's development projects have helped many Nepalese villagers raise their standard of living. Improved health care and sanitation have reduced the infant death rate.

Language and religion

The official language, Nepali, has its origins in Sanskrit, the classic Hindu language. More than 50 other languages and dialects are spoken in Nepal.

Hinduism has long been Nepal's official religion, and some Nepalese worship the king as the Hindu god Vishnu reborn on earth. Nepalese Hinduism has been influenced by Buddhism, and both religious groups live in harmony. Buddhist temples are given as much respect as Hindu temples.

The Himalaya

According to an ancient Hindu proverb, "One hundred lives of the gods would not be long enough to describe all the wonders of the Himalaya." The world's highest mountain system, the Himalaya has some of the most spectacular scenery on earth.

The Himalaya is not a single mountain chain, but a system of parallel mountain ranges. It extends in a 1,500-mile (2,410-kilometer) curve across southern Asia. Beginning with the Pamirs, west of the great bend of the Indus River, the Himalaya sweeps eastward to the great bend of the Brahmaputra River near the border of Myanmar. The Karakoram range is the northwestern extension of the Himalaya.

Known as "the roof of the world," the Himalaya contains the five tallest mountains on earth. They are Mount Everest (29,035 feet or 8,850 meters), K2 (28,250 feet or 8,611 meters), Mount Kanchenjunga (28,208 feet or 8,598 meters), Mount Makalu (27,824 feet or 8,481 meters), and Annapurna (26,504 feet or 8,078 meters).

A biological wonderland

The Himalaya came into being less than 25 million years ago, which is fairly recent in geological terms. Its major river systems—the Indus, Sutlej, Kali Gandaki, Tista, and Brahmaputra—were in place before the mountains were pushed upward.

The great difference in altitude in many parts of the Himalaya has resulted in a variety of plant and animal life. Tropical heat and arctic cold can be found in a span only 40 miles (64 kilometers) wide in the Himalaya of Sikkim and Bhutan.

At the 20,000-foot (6,000-meter) *aeolian,* or highest zone, life is limited to bacteria, fungi, insects, and crustaceans that live on airborne food particles blown up by the wind. Moving down in altitude between the snow line and the timber line, the alpine meadows support such plants as stonecrops, rock jasmines, primroses, and edelweiss. Lynx, wolves, and brown bears are found in this zone.

Langtang-Lirung 23,750 ft (7,246m)
Gosainthan 26,150 ft (8,013m)
Gauri-Shankar 23,442 ft (7,145m)
Melungtse 23,560 ft (7,181m)

Khunjerab Pass 16,187 ft (4,934m)
Mount Godwin Austen (K2) 28,250 ft (8,611m)
Karakoram Pass 18,290 ft (5,575m)
Gilgit
KARAKORAM RANGE
Nanga Parbat 26,660 ft (8,126m)
LADAKH RANGE
Leh
Vale of Kashmir
Srinagar
KASHMIR
ISLAMABAD
Indus
ZASKAR MOUNTAINS
H I M A L A Y A
Kamet 25,447 ft (7,756m)
Simla
Nanda Devi 25,645 ft (7,817m)
MAHABHARAT MOUNTAINS

Myth and legend

The Himalaya has been the subject of myth and legend for centuries. The *Abominable Snowman,* a legendary beast that reportedly has a large apelike body and a face that looks human, is said to live on Mount Everest and other Himalayan peaks. There is no direct evidence that the Abominable Snowman exists, but sightings of the creature have been reported by travelers since the 1890's, when mountaineering first became popular.

Mount Everest was first scaled in 1953 by members of a British expedition. Avalanches, crevasses, and strong winds combine with extreme steepness and thin air to make climbing the mountain extremely difficult.

Wild goats, known as *tahr,* roam the crags of Sagarmatha National Park, a conservation area.

Below the timber line, about 15,000 feet (4,600 meters), a forest belt abounds in deodar cedar, Himalayan fir, blue pine, cypress, hemlock, and spruce trees. The Himalaya is famous for the variety of rhododendrons that flourish in this zone. Animal life ranges from wild goats, such as the serow, goral, and tahr, to macaque monkeys and rodents.

Tropical forests blanket the hills bordering the lowlands of the eastern and central Himalaya. Many hardwood trees grow in this zone, including bauhinia, teak, sal, horse chestnut, and walnut. At about 4,500 feet (1,400 meters), the tropical forests give way to the subtropical forest, where chital deer, tigers, water buffaloes, and hog deer roam.

A cross section of Nepal, covering just 100 miles (161 kilometers), includes many of the world's highest peaks. The Himalaya forms a huge arc that separates India from the Tibetan Plateau in China.

People of the Himalaya

Tucked in the foothills, valleys, and highland basins are settlements of strong, hardy, and religious Himalayan people. For centuries, they have lived and worked in the shadow of the highest mountains in the world. Some live in such fertile, sheltered areas as the Vale of Kashmir, the Kathmandu Valley, and the Tarai plain of southern Nepal. Others spend their lives in the remote highlands, almost completely cut off from the rest of the world.

A challenging way of life

Life in the Himalaya is difficult. The mountain people live mainly in small agricultural communities at altitudes between 3,000 feet (1,000 meters) and 12,000 feet (3,500 meters).

The harsh climate and poor soil of the mountain slopes make farming difficult. Farmers are able to grow only enough food to live on, and little more. A few mountain tribes consist of seminomadic farmers, who move from plot to plot, and herdsmen who lead their flocks through the mountains.

The Himalayan people are made up of many different ethnic and cultural groups, but they all share two important characteristics: physical strength and spiritual faith.

The Sherpas of Nepal, for example, take great pride in being able to carry a load equal to their own body weight up to a height of about 10,000 feet (3,050 meters). Most people could not carry such a load, even at ground level. This ability has allowed some Himalayan people to make their living as guides and porters for mountaineers and trekkers.

A deeply religious people

Religion plays a major part in the lives of the Himalayan people. Most follow one of the region's three great religions—Hinduism, Buddhism, or Islam. A few worship gods connected with plants, animals, or the forces of nature. Their beliefs are often combined with a deep respect for the beauty and mystery of their mountains.

To Himalayan people, the mountains are known as "the seat of the gods." Even their local names for various peaks carry religious symbolism. The Tibetans call Mount Everest *Chomolungma (Mother Goddess of the World),* while Annapurna means *Goddess of the Harvest,* and Kanchenjunga is described as *Treasure of the Eternal Snows.*

Mount Kailas, which rises 22,028 feet (6,714 meters), is sacred to the Hindus. They believe it is the secret home of their powerful god Shiva, and his wife, Parvati. It is also the source of four important rivers: the Brahmaputra, Indus, Sutlej, and the sacred Ganges.

Today, pilgrims from all parts of central Asia and India come to Nepal to climb the mountain. The journey takes them from tropical jungles to freezing heights. Below the peak, at an elevation of 14,950 feet (4,557

The charming village of Pangeboche, Nepal, *above,* is perched on a mountain slope. The well-constructed houses of the Sherpas are generally built of stone and timber, with a roof made of wooden slats.

A Nepalese citizen pays his respects, *above left,* at an entrance to the Royal Palace in Kathmandu, Nepal. The entrance to the palace bears the name *Hanuman Dhoka* in honor of the Hindu monkey god, one of the heroes of the epic *Ramayana.*

The market place in Thimphu, the capital of Bhutan, is a busy trading center. It also serves as a gathering place for social activities. Festivals that include dancing, eating, and entertainment provide welcome relief from the hard life of the Himalayan people.

meters), lies the holy Lake Mansarowar. The lake is worshiped by some who believe it is the home of the spirit of the god Brahma, creator of the universe who was born from a golden egg. Many religious ceremonies are held along the 54-mile (87-kilometer) path that surrounds the sacred lake.

Religion is at the heart of many political conflicts in the Himalaya region. India, a Hindu nation, controls the territory of Jammu and Kashmir, but the mostly Muslim inhabitants would like to be part of Pakistan. The Buddhist majority in Kashmir's eastern province of Ladakh would like to be more independent. At the same time, China claims Ladakh because its people belong to the Tibetan ethnic group and practice Tibetan Buddhism.

Nature Under Threat

The Himalaya is one of the world's most endangered environments. Although its terrain is mighty and rugged, its ecological balance is quite delicate. Many of the problems in the Himalaya occurred because people ignored this vital balance of nature.

Increasing population density

Many Himalayan areas have seen a rapid growth in population. The population of Nepal in particular has more than doubled in only 30 years. All these people need food and shelter.

Because the steep terrain of the Himalaya makes trade and industry difficult, most Nepalese make their living as farmers. As the population grows, they need more and more land to develop for agriculture. Forests are cleared to make room for farmland, and the trees that are cut down supply wood used in building, cooking, and domestic heating.

But clearing forests upsets the balance of nature. Forests keep water from running off the land by allowing it to filter into the ground. The water then flows through underground channels and refills lakes and streams. But when forests are cleared, the earth's plant cover is removed and this natural process is interrupted.

Soil erosion is another result of clearing the forests. The topsoil, which contains important nutrients and organic matter, is washed away by the monsoon rains. This leaves poor soil that is unable to absorb water.

Meanwhile, the topsoil washes down to the plains, where the muddy waters silt up the rivers. Even such large rivers as the Ganges, Brahmaputra, and Indus cannot absorb the huge quantity of muddy water. As a result, the rivers overflow and cause major flooding in Pakistan, India, and Bangladesh.

Clearing forests also destroys the natural habitat of the animals who live there. There is much less land where wild animals can nest, breed, and feed. Many species are threatened with extinction because they no longer have a place to live.

Another threat to the Himalayan environment is overgrazing of land. At higher

The environmental problems of the Himalaya affect huge numbers of people. The delicate balance of nature is disturbed when an increasing population makes greater demands on the environment. The clearing of forests causes soil erosion and destroys the natural habitats of wildlife. Overgrazing also upsets the balance of nature. Among the more serious problems are the ditches created by running water, *inset below,* and flooding in the lower plains, *inset below right.*

altitudes, where rainfall is scarce, the land is not suitable for growing crops. Instead, Himalayan herders tend flocks of sheep and goats. When too many animals graze an area, or when animals stay in one place too long, the land becomes overgrazed. The grasses die and are replaced by weeds and poisonous plants.

The threat of tourism

Tourism is a major source of revenue for Himalayan countries. Mountaineering and trekking are becoming very popular. However, trekkers in particular have become dangerous to the Himalayan environment

Soil erosion not only destroys the areas where the soil is washed away, it affects areas all the way down the watercourse. Droughts and floods occur when forests, which absorb water, are cleared for use in agriculture. Sediment chokes dams, silts up riverbeds, and destroys coastal fisheries because fish cannot survive in the muddy waters. In the Bay of Bengal, deposits of silt have formed an underwater delta so large that it may soon be visible above the surface of the water.

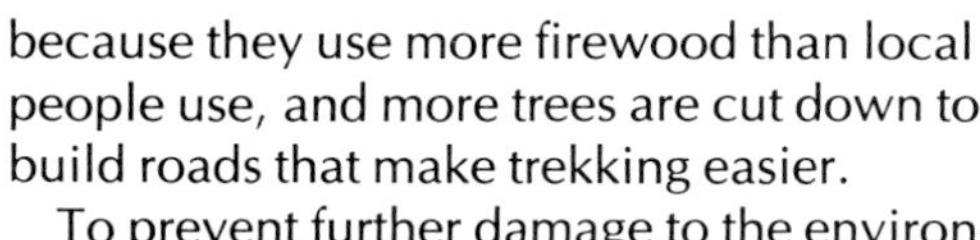

because they use more firewood than local people use, and more trees are cut down to build roads that make trekking easier.

To prevent further damage to the environment, Nepal has begun to restrict the movements of tourists in certain areas. India has severely restricted the hunting of wild game. The Indian government has also established a number of national parks and game reserves in the southern Himalaya. In mid-1989, the Himalayan countries announced the first steps in a united campaign to protect their mountains.

Many great Himalayan forests, *above,* fall victim to the woodcutter's ax, leaving the hillsides bare.

Supplies from a mountaineering expedition, *left,* litter the base camp on Mount Everest in Nepal. Pollution of the natural environment is threatening the future of the Himalaya.

Pakistan's magnificent Karakoram Highway, *below,* opened in 1978. It runs through the steep Hunza Valley to the Chinese border.

Trekking

The vast, almost unearthly landscape of the Himalaya has attracted thousands of adventurous tourists. In the past, most of those visitors were hardy mountaineers armed with ice axes, oxygen tanks, and *crampons* (metal spikes on boots that prevent slipping on hard ice or snow). They braved the harsh climate and terrain of the Himalaya's highest altitudes to see the most glorious scenery in the world.

Today, there is an easier way to experience the wonder and mystery of the soaring Himalaya. During the last 10 years, trekking—hiking through the mountain passes—has became one of the Himalaya's most popular attractions.

Trekking at elevations between 1,350 feet (500 meters) and 8,300 feet (2,500 meters) does not require unusual equipment, experience, or physical strength. Trekkers can enjoy all the magic and mystery of the Himalaya without the danger and hardship of climbing at higher altitudes.

Walking the mountain trails

People have traveled through the passes of the Himalaya for hundreds of years. Some were merchants and traders, whose caravans brought salt, tea, textiles, grains, spices, and other goods to Europe from the Far East. Others were political diplomats and pilgrims. Traders can still be seen along the Himalayan trails, carrying goods in homespun woolen bundles on the backs of sheep and goats.

Modern trekkers journey on foot over these same well-used trails, which vary from wide, stone-paved routes to winding paths and narrow ledges. Most trekking is done in the mild Himalayan summer, which lasts from May to October. A trek may range from a few days of backpacking along the trails to a three-week—or longer!—expedition from Kathmandu Valley to the base camp of Mount Everest.

Most trekkers travel in small groups with a porter as a guide. Larger groups often include a *sirdar* (foreman) with a crew of porters who make camp for the travelers at night and cook their meals. About five or six hours of hiking a day between 4,900 feet (1,500 meters) and 6,600 feet (2,000 meters) is typical. A long meal stop is usually made in the middle of the day. Meals are eaten either at camp or at a village tea shop.

Trekkers traveling in small groups often sleep in *bhattis* (wayside inns) or in village homes. There, an evening meal may include such local favorites as *dal bhatu* (rice with lentil paste) or curried potatoes washed down Tibetan-style with buttered and salted tea.

Preparing for a trek

Although trekking does not require unusual skills or equipment, a certain amount of advance preparation is necessary. All would-be trekkers must have the proper visas, immunizations, and trekking permits. Comfortable,

Because of Nepal's rugged terrain and limited medical facilities, experienced backpackers travel in small groups to assure a safe, enjoyable trek. Most groups hire a porter, who guides the travelers and helps carry food and equipment.

A trekking party, *right,* crosses a mountain stream in a Nepalese valley. A vast network of trails through the mountain passes connects remote Himalayan villages. Some of these trails include footbridges.

This simple dwelling is home to a Sherpa family. Because of their physical strength and mountaineering skills, Sherpas have been used as guides through the mountains and passes since the 1950's.

Nepalese porters, *below left,* prepare a campsite in a valley near Pokhara. Annapurna, the eleventh highest mountain in the world, rises in the distance. The Nepalese call it *Goddess of the Harvest* because they believe it watches over the farms below.

durable clothing is a must, along with a sleeping bag, cooking equipment, and a tent.

A serious health danger facing the inexperienced trekker is *altitude sickness.* This condition is caused by climbing too fast for the body to adjust to the change in altitude. The result is a decrease in the amount of oxygen in the blood, which causes headaches, weakness, sleeplessness, mild nausea, and loss of appetite. To prevent altitude sickness, careful trekkers sleep at an altitude that is lower than the highest point reached during the day.

Careful planning is important, but nothing can prepare a trekker for the magnificent scenery to be encountered on the Himalayan trails. From a view of snow-capped mountains to a walk through an alpine meadow or a forest of blooming rhododendrons, the Himalaya offers a new and wondrous sight with every footstep.

The Netherlands

The Netherlands is a small, densely populated, and highly industrialized country on the North Sea in northwestern Europe. The Netherlands is often called *Holland,* though this name actually refers to only one part of the country. The people call themselves *Hollanders* or *Nederlanders,* but in English-speaking countries, they are known as the *Dutch.*

The word *Netherlands* means "Low Countries,"—an appropriate name for a nation where more than 40 per cent of the land was once covered by sea, lakes, or swamps. The Dutch "created" this land by pumping out the water, and today these drained areas, called *polders,* support the richest farmlands and largest cities of the Netherlands. Amsterdam, the Dutch capital and largest city, is on a polder.

In 1986, the massive Delta Project was completed, to help control flooding. Nearly 30 years under construction, the Delta Project consists of a series of huge dams with floodgates that can be closed during storms. However, recovering land and protecting it from flooding is a constant battle in the Netherlands. Because most of the polders are below sea level, they have no natural drainage, so water must be continually pumped into a series of canals that flow into the North Sea.

In February 1995, the Netherlands suffered the worst floods since 1953. More than 250,000 people were moved from their homes, the largest evacuation in Dutch history. Authorities feared that the country's dikes would give way, flooding towns with up to 16 feet (4.8 meters) of water. The dikes held, however, and the floodwaters retreated. After the flood, the reinforcement of the dikes became a priority.

In addition to draining the low-lying Dutch land, the canals also serve as waterways, forming an extensive transportation network with the country's major rivers. When the winters are harsh enough to freeze the canals, they are also used for ice skating, an extremely popular sport. Schools sometimes close to let the children skate. The Dutch also enjoy watching the *Elfstedentocht,* an ice-skating race held on the canals of the northern province of Friesland.

In the Netherlands, where most of the countryside is flat, cycling is a good way to get around. Most Dutch own a bicycle; there are nearly as many bicycles as people in the country.

The Netherlands attracts many tourists throughout the year. In the spring, colorful fields of tulips, daffodils, and hyacinths attract thousands of visitors. In the summer, people flock to seaside resorts on the North Sea coast, especially those at Scheveningen, Noordwijk, Zandvoort, and Egmond aan Zee.

The Netherlands Today

The Netherlands is one of the most densely populated countries in the world today, but the Dutch keep their fields, towns, and cities so neat and clean that few areas ever seem crowded. The Netherlanders' particular style of good fellowship, called *gezelligheid,* also helps make life pleasant in their heavily populated country. This combination of order and tolerance is reflected in the Dutch society, which blends tradition with modern innovation.

Although the capital of the Netherlands is Amsterdam, the country's national government meets in The Hague, which is 34 miles (55 kilometers) away. Invading French troops captured Amsterdam in 1795 and made it the capital. The Dutch restored their government in The Hague in 1814.

The Netherlands is part of the Kingdom of the Netherlands, which includes the Netherlands Antilles and Aruba—islands in the Caribbean Sea.

Government

The Netherlands maintains its traditions even in its government. Although the country has a democratic government based on its Constitution, the Netherlands is officially a constitutional monarchy. The country's Constitution identifies the king or queen as the head of state, but gives the monarch little real power. The monarch names all appointed government officials on the advice of various government bodies and signs all laws passed by the parliament. A queen has served as the monarch of the Netherlands since 1890. Queen Beatrix became the Dutch head of state in 1980.

Town and country

The Netherlands is a highly industrialized and technically advanced nation. The country's key position at the mouth of the Rhine River has made it a gateway between the inland capitals of Europe and the North Sea. Vast urban centers have grown up in the area that includes Amsterdam, Rotterdam, and The Hague. This region of concentrated urban centers is called the *Randstad Holland.*

However, the Dutch balance the spread of urban centers by protecting their countryside and wildlife. In the Hoge Veluwe—a national park in the province of Gelderland—wild pigs and deer roam freely. Many of the coun-

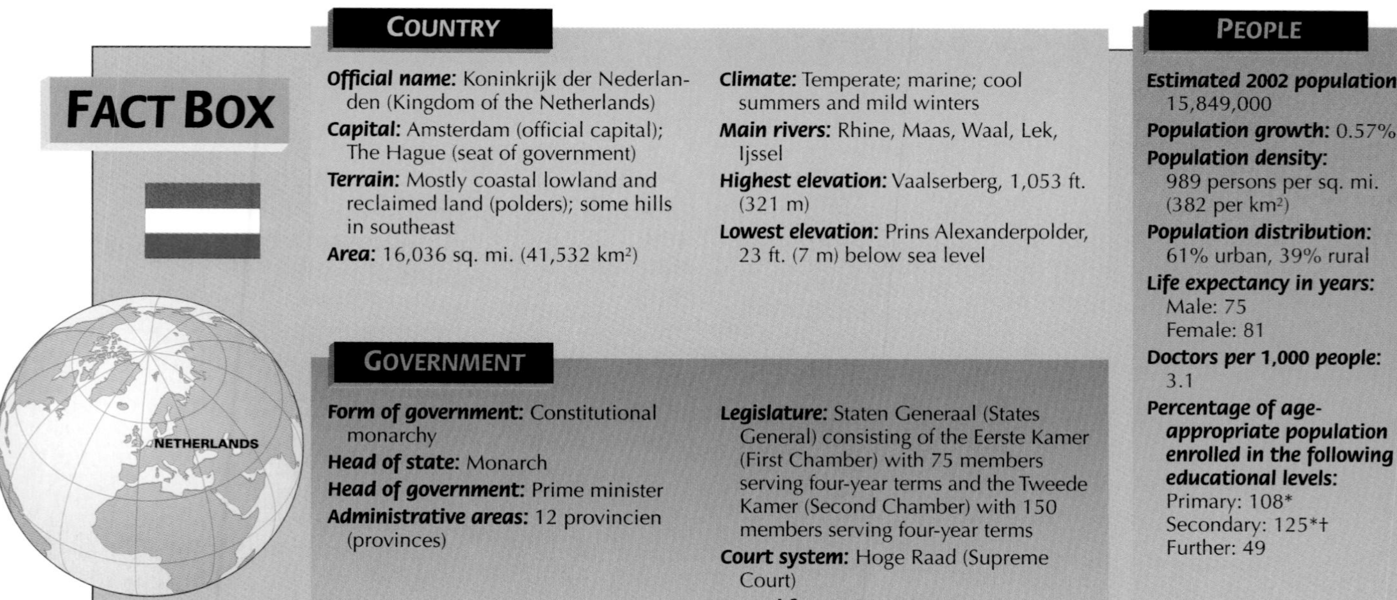
FACT BOX

COUNTRY

Official name: Koninkrijk der Nederlanden (Kingdom of the Netherlands)
Capital: Amsterdam (official capital); The Hague (seat of government)
Terrain: Mostly coastal lowland and reclaimed land (polders); some hills in southeast
Area: 16,036 sq. mi. (41,532 km²)
Climate: Temperate; marine; cool summers and mild winters
Main rivers: Rhine, Maas, Waal, Lek, Ijssel
Highest elevation: Vaalserberg, 1,053 ft. (321 m)
Lowest elevation: Prins Alexanderpolder, 23 ft. (7 m) below sea level

GOVERNMENT

Form of government: Constitutional monarchy
Head of state: Monarch
Head of government: Prime minister
Administrative areas: 12 provincien (provinces)
Legislature: Staten Generaal (States General) consisting of the Eerste Kamer (First Chamber) with 75 members serving four-year terms and the Tweede Kamer (Second Chamber) with 150 members serving four-year terms
Court system: Hoge Raad (Supreme Court)
Armed forces: 56,380 troops

PEOPLE

Estimated 2002 population: 15,849,000
Population growth: 0.57%
Population density: 989 persons per sq. mi. (382 per km²)
Population distribution: 61% urban, 39% rural
Life expectancy in years:
Male: 75
Female: 81
Doctors per 1,000 people: 3.1
Percentage of age-appropriate population enrolled in the following educational levels:
Primary: 108*
Secondary: 125*†
Further: 49

The former Royal Palace in The Hague, *left,* first built in 1533 and rebuilt in 1640, was the residence of the Dutch monarchs until invading French troops moved the capital to Amsterdam.

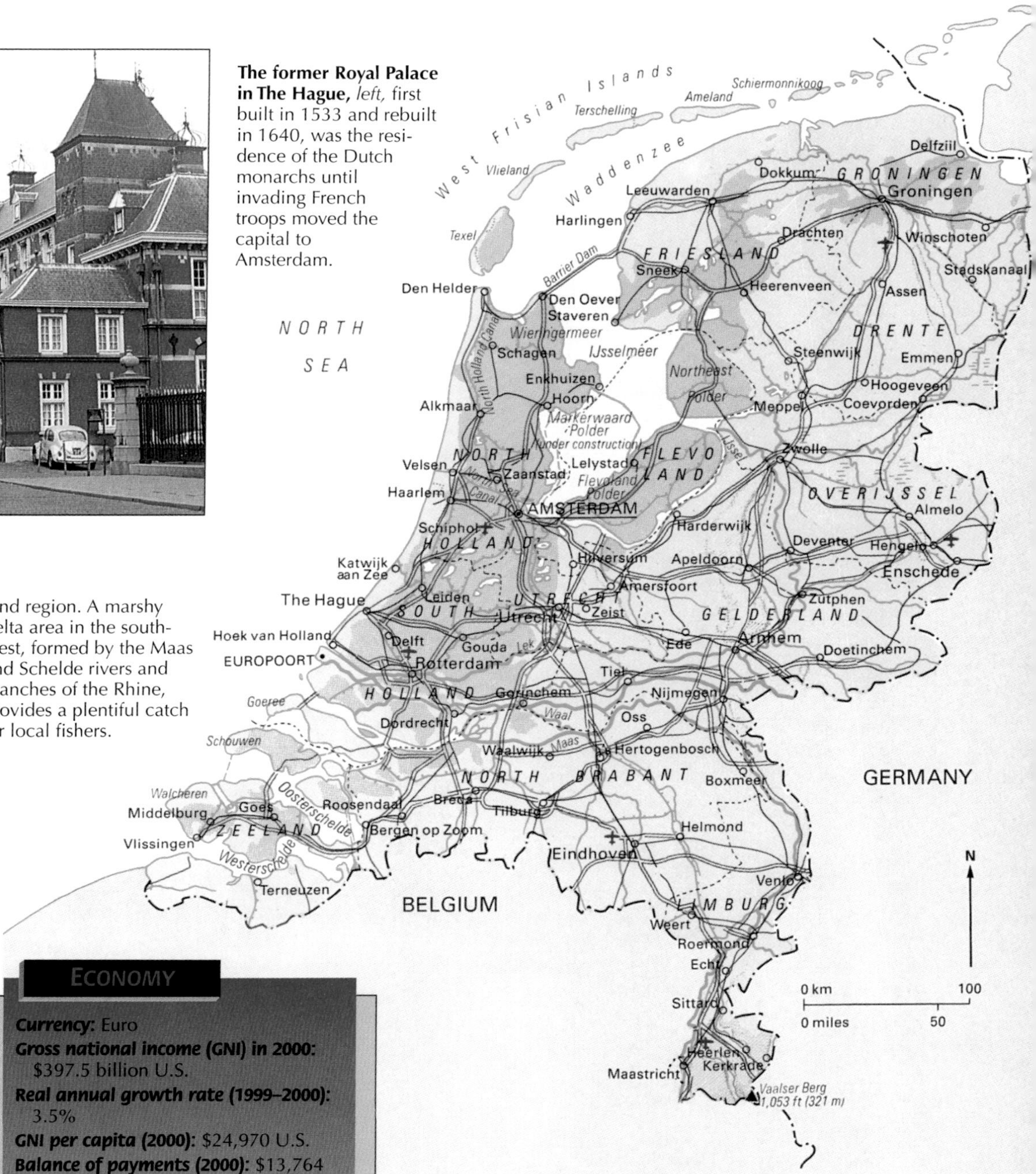

The Netherlands is a small country located in northwestern Europe. Its four main land regions include the sandy and infertile Dunes that line the North Sea coast; the flat, fertile recovered land regions of the Polders; the low, sandy ridges of the eastern Sand Plains; and the Southern Uplands, which form the highest land region. A marshy delta area in the southwest, formed by the Maas and Schelde rivers and branches of the Rhine, provides a plentiful catch for local fishers.

Language spoken:
Dutch

Religions:
Roman Catholic 34%
Protestant 25%
Muslim 3%
unaffiliated 36%

**Enrollment ratios compare the number of students enrolled to the population which, by age, should be enrolled. A ratio higher than 100 indicates that students older or younger than the typical age range are also enrolled.*

†Includes training for the unemployed.

Technology

Radios per 1,000 people: 980

Televisions per 1,000 people: 538

Computers per 1,000 people: 394.1

Economy

Currency: Euro

Gross national income (GNI) in 2000: $397.5 billion U.S.

Real annual growth rate (1999–2000): 3.5%

GNI per capita (2000): $24,970 U.S.

Balance of payments (2000): $13,764 million U.S.

Goods exported: Machinery and equipment, chemicals, fuels; foodstuffs

Goods imported: Machinery and transport equipment, chemicals, fuels; foodstuffs, clothing

Trading partners: European Union, United States, Central and Eastern Europe

try's coastal areas have also been preserved. Some of the people in these areas, particularly in the fishing communities, wear the Dutch national costume. Traditional clothing includes caps and full trousers for the men, lace caps and full skirts for the women, and wooden shoes for everyone.

People

The Dutch people are descended from several different Germanic tribes. The Frisians occupied the northern coastal area about 2,000 years ago, while the Saxons lived in the Rhine Delta. During the A.D. 400's, the Franks drove the Romans out of northern Europe and established their kingdom in the Low Countries, which included what are now the Netherlands, Belgium, and Luxembourg.

The Dutch language was influenced primarily by the many dialects of Old Low German spoken by the Franks. However, the Frisian language has survived and is still spoken in the northern province of Friesland. The Dutch language did not achieve its final written form until the 1600's, the Golden Age of the Netherlands.

In the 1600's, the country became the leading sea power and developed a profitable and far-flung colonial empire. Dutch trade gave the country the world's highest standard of living. Art also flourished during this period, when such artists as Rembrandt, Frans Hals, and Jan Vermeer produced some of the world's greatest paintings.

Traditional clothing is still worn by some Dutch people, particularly in fishing and farming areas. Wooden clogs, which protect the feet from mud, are left outside the doors of the spotless Dutch houses.

Rich farmland, much of it reclaimed from the sea, *right,* covers about two-thirds of the total land area in the Netherlands. The canals both drain the land (with the aid of pumps) and provide transportation.

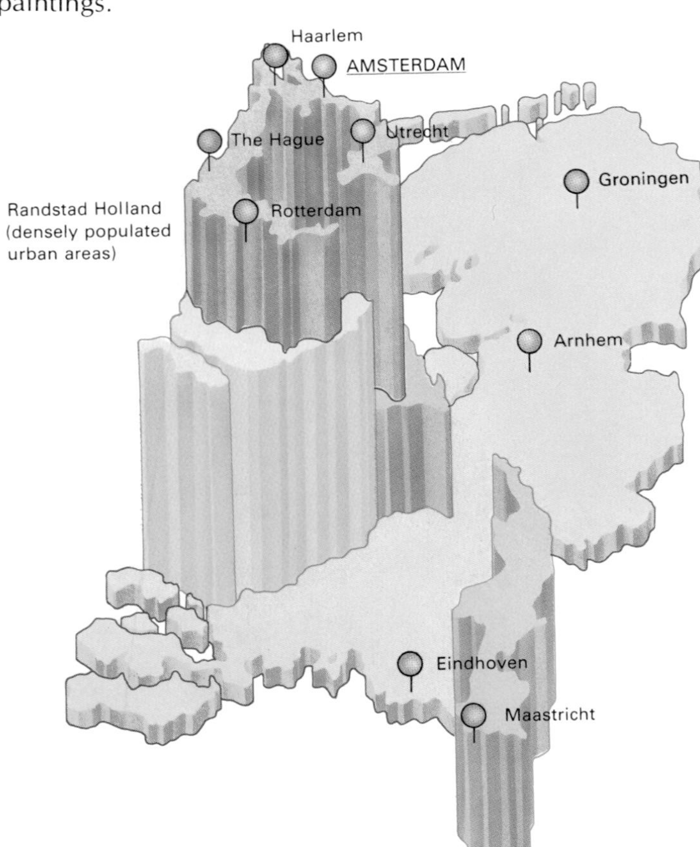

The Netherlands ranks among the most densely populated nations in the world. The majority of its people live in the cities and towns of the western part of the country known as *Randstad Holland.*

Superb seagoing ships, like this man-of-war, *above,* enabled the Netherlands to build a maritime empire during the 1600's. Dutch trading companies set up colonies in southern Africa, Indonesia, and the Americas.

Many people from the former Dutch colony of Indonesia, *above,* immigrated to the Netherlands during the 1960's and 1970's. The country has an excellent record in race relations.

The Dutch use their canals for ice skating when winter frosts cause the water to freeze, *below.* Some people skate to and from work.

Religious differences

During the 1600's, the Dutch gained their independence from Spain following a series of religious wars. In the 1500's, the Reformation spread through the Low Countries (what are now the Netherlands, Belgium, and Luxembourg). Protestantism became stronger in the northern provinces (now the Netherlands). During the 1560's, the northern provinces rebelled against rule by predominantly Roman Catholic Spain, and in 1581, they declared their independence. The new Dutch Republic—the Netherlands—finally gained its freedom in 1648. However, the country was still divided by religious differences. The southern provinces of the Netherlands had remained mostly Catholic, while the northern provinces had converted to Protestantism.

Today, although the geographical boundaries are not so clear-cut, these religious divisions still exist. Roman Catholics and Protestants each make up about 35 per cent of the Dutch population. And both religions have traditionally remained as separate as possible—each with its own schools, newspapers, and political parties. Since the 1950's, however, a new trend of tolerance has broken down this voluntary segregation, particularly among young people.

Population changes

During the 1960's and 1970's, the Dutch policy of tolerance extended to the hundreds of thousands of immigrants who swelled the country's population. People from former Dutch colonies, especially Indonesia and Suriname, and from Mediterranean countries moved to the Netherlands, attracted by its booming economy. These immigrants account for nearly 5 per cent of the population.

Today, the Netherlands has a population of almost 15 million. About 40 per cent of the people live in two coastal provinces—Noord-Holland (North Holland) and Zuid-Holland (South Holland). The three largest Dutch cities—Amsterdam, Rotterdam, and The Hague—are located in these provinces, along with much of Randstad Holland, a strip of densely populated urban centers.

Cities of the Netherlands

The cities of the Netherlands first began to achieve importance in the 1100's, when trade and industry with France and Germany expanded rapidly. The country's position at the mouth of the Rhine River made it a major trading center, and fishing, shipbuilding, shipping, and textile manufacturing became especially important. Commercial centers developed in the cities of Delft, Leiden, Gouda, and Haarlem, while cities such as Amsterdam, Edam, and Rotterdam, which are located at the mouths of rivers, became international ports.

By the 1600's, Dutch shipbuilders provided nearly half the world's shipping needs. The great Dutch artists of this period glorified the rich trading cities in paintings. Many of the buildings in these paintings are still standing today, in settings that are almost unchanged.

The Hague

The Hague was originally a hunting lodge belonging to the count of Holland. In 1250, it became his residence. The Hague's official name, *'s Gravenhage,* which means *the count's hedge,* is a reference to the city's origins.

Today, although Amsterdam is the Dutch capital city, The Hague is the Netherlands' seat of government and the official residence of the monarch. Also, the city's magnificent Peace Palace, built in the early 1900's, serves as headquarters for the Permanent Court of Arbitration and the International Court of Justice. When the Peace Palace was built, many people were hoping that The Hague would become an international neutral center where disputes among nations could be resolved peacefully.

The Hague is a handsome city with many stately old buildings and elegant residences that reflect its role as a center of government. In the heart of The Hague's old section stand the parliament buildings, called the Binnenhof. Next to the Binnenhof is the Mauritshuis, a famous art museum that contains the largest collection of Rembrandt paintings in the world. Nearby

Amsterdam's Leidseplein, *above,* attracts visitors with its modern nightclubs and cafes, but many local people prefer to get together in the city's little "brown cafes," *inset.*

Alkmaar's famous cheese market, *below,* is held on Fridays from spring to fall. Porters wearing colorful hats carry hundreds of delicious cheeses to the market on special racks.

The **delft porcelain of the Netherlands** has been famous since the mid-1700's. Craftspeople continue the tradition today.

is the *Huis ten Bosch,* or House in the Woods, the residence of Queen Beatrix, the country's monarch.

Utrecht

Utrecht, the capital of Utrecht province, lies along the Rhine River. A fortified Roman city in A.D. 48, Utrecht is one of the oldest cities in the Netherlands. In 696, it became a bishopric—a church district. Many medieval churches still stand in Utrecht, among them Saint Martin Cathedral, a beautiful Gothic structure that boasts the tallest church tower in the Netherlands. The tower, called the *Domtoren,* is 367 feet (112 meters) high and offers splendid views across the IJsselmeer. The University of Utrecht, one of the largest universities in the country, stands nearby.

Delft

In the Middle Ages, Delft was a flourishing commercial center. However, it was not until the mid-1700's that the city reached the height of its prosperity with the manufacture of its famous blue porcelain. Craftspeople continue to produce the traditional designs of Dutch delft pottery today.

Its cobbled streets, delicately curved bridges, and picturesque canals make Delft one of the most beautiful cities in the Netherlands. Many of the city's famous buildings have been preserved, including the Nieuwe Kerk (New Church), which was built in the 1400's. The church contains the tomb of William I, prince of Orange, who led a revolt against Spain in 1568. He was assassinated in the Prinsenhof, now a museum, in 1584. Other fine old buildings include the Town Hall, built during the Renaissance, and the Oude Kerk (Old Church), built from the 1200's to the 1500's.

Scheveningen, a large seaside resort near The Hague, *left,* attracts tourists with its fine beaches. Its picturesque pier has shops and restaurants as well as sun terraces and a huge aquarium.

Amsterdam

Amsterdam, the capital and largest city of the Netherlands, is situated at the mouth of the Amstel River. The word *Amsterdam,* which means *dam of the Amstel,* refers to a dam built there in the 1200's.

The city of Amsterdam lies on marshy land slightly below sea level. Most of its houses are built on wooden piles, or posts, driven into the soggy ground. More than 100 canals crisscross the city and help drain the land.

Amsterdam's historic center

The old section of Amsterdam lies at the heart of the city. Damrak, the city's main street, leads to Dam Square—the site of the Royal Palace and the Nieuwe Kerk (New Church). The palace was built in the mid-1600's, and the church, where the nation's monarchs are inaugurated, was built in the 1400's. Nearby stands one of the world's oldest exchanges, the Amsterdam Stock Exchange, built in 1612.

Damrak continues toward Munt Plein, or Mint Square, amid streets lined with shops and restaurants. Nearby Leidseplein, the center of Amsterdam's nightlife, has most of the city's cinemas, its municipal theater, and numerous nightclubs. South of this area lies the Museumplein, which houses many of Amsterdam's art museums, including the Rijksmuseum and the Van Gogh Museum. Down the street from the Rijksmuseum stands the Concertgebouw, home of the world-famous Concertgebouw Orchestra.

Transportation

Amsterdam's bright yellow trams crisscross the city, but many of its citizens prefer to travel by bicycle. They wind their way through the traffic, often transporting children or carrying the day's shopping in their baskets.

Boating on the canals is another popular means of transportation. Three canals—the Herengracht, the Keizersgracht, and the Prinsengracht—border the city's old section on the east, south, and west. A boat ride offers an excellent view of the impressive mansions, dating from the 1600's, that line the canals. Many of these mansions are now banks or office buildings.

But perhaps the best way to explore Amsterdam's narrow streets—many of which are closed to traffic—is on foot. The buildings that line the streets appear narrow on the outside but some are actually quite roomy. This is apparent in the house where Anne Frank and her family, German Jews, were concealed from the Nazis for two years (1942-1944) during World War II by Dutch friends. The family hid in a secret annex behind the office of Anne's father's business until they were betrayed, arrested, and sent to concentration camps, where the 16-year-old Anne died. Her diary, which her father published after the war, gives a vivid account of a life of hiding in the annex. Merchants in the 1600's built these secret rooms in their homes and offices to avoid paying extra taxes on their property.

Everyday life

Most of Amsterdam's nearly 700,000 citizens live in tall, narrow apartment buildings set very close together. The city has had a housing shortage since the end of World War II.

Many inhabitants enjoy getting together in Amsterdam's bars and cafes. When the weather is fine, a table at an outdoor cafe is a good spot from which to view the city—or listen to its sounds. Bells pealing from the many churches blend with the clanging of the trams and the music of street organs.

Amsterdam's many street markets include the Albert Cuypmarkt, where vendors sell a variety of food and clothing. Specialties from Suriname and Indonesia recall the country's days as a colonial empire, and Turkish and Moroccan goods draw Amsterdam's many *gastarbeideren,* or guest workers.

Waterlooplein, in Amsterdam's old Jewish quarter, was once the largest market in Europe. Jews made up about 10 per cent of Amsterdam's population before World War II, but the city's Jewish community was almost entirely wiped out in Nazi concentration camps during the war.

Amsterdam's many canals, *far left,* drain the city's marshy foundations. The city has more than 62 miles (100 kilometers) of canals and nearly 3,000 licensed houseboats.

Haircuts are given in Vondel Park on April 30, the queen's official birthday. In the summer months, Vondel Park is the setting for many open-air concerts, festivals, and plays.

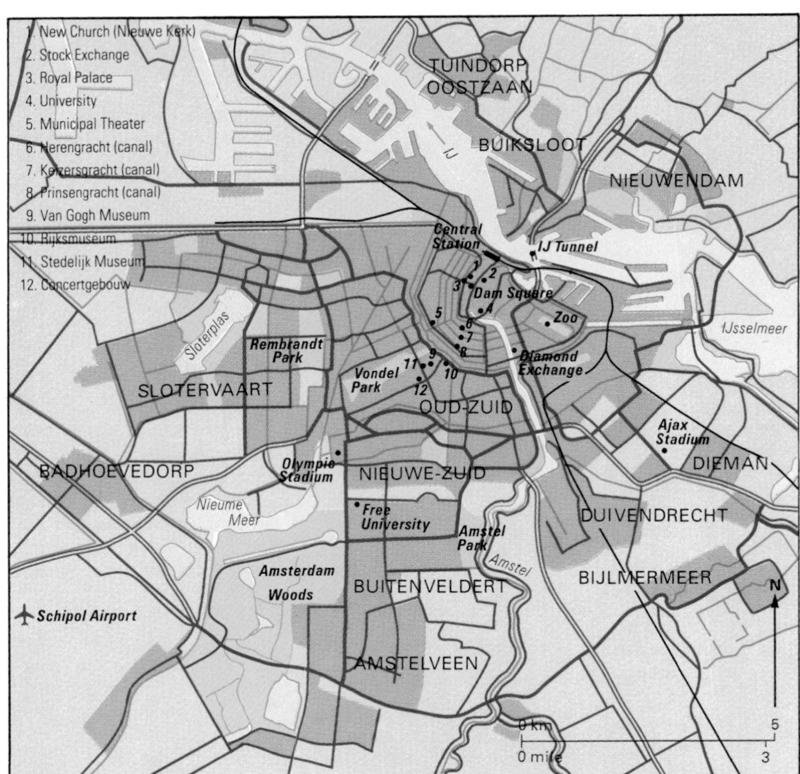

Amsterdam's city center resembles the wheel of a bicycle. Canals are shown as blue lines. The larger canals are arranged in circles around the city center, while the smaller canals branch out from its center like spokes. The Netherlands' capital boasts a sophisticated economy, but tourists flock to Amsterdam to visit major cultural attractions such as the Rijksmuseum, the Stedelijk Museum, and the Van Gogh Museum.

Bicycles outnumber cars in Amsterdam, and sometimes provide transportation for the whole family.

A wooden drawbridge called the Magerebrug, or "skinny" bridge, *far left,* spans the Amstel River.

Battle with the Sea

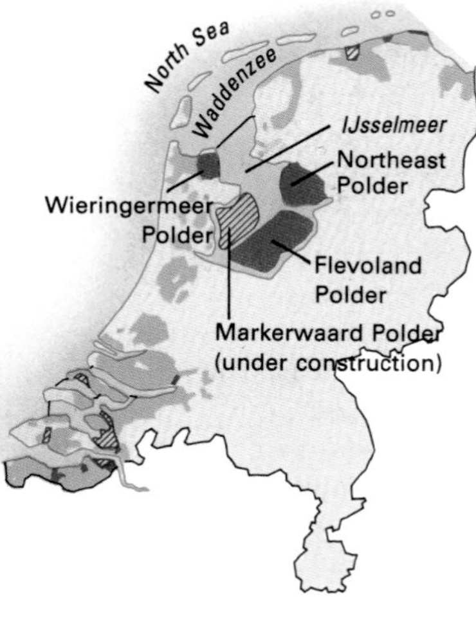

Reclaimed areas:
- 1300s to 1800s
- 1900s
- In progress

Their battles against the sea have won much rich farmland for the Dutch.

According to an old Dutch saying, "God created the world, but the Dutch created Holland." Almost half of the Netherlands has been "created" by pumping the water out of areas that were once swamps, marshes, and shallow river estuaries. Generations of Dutch farmers and engineers have turned these areas—called *polders*—into rich farmland.

The Polders region was drained by a network of canals, ditches, and dikes. However, pumping must be continued after the polders are built, because most of them are below sea level and have no natural drainage.

To make a polder, the Dutch build a dike around the area that is to be drained of water. The water is then pumped into a series of canals that flow into the North Sea. Windmills were originally used to power the pumps, but electric pumping stations now handle the job.

The sandy Dunes region, which lies along much of the coastline, does not provide adequate protection against the powerful storms, tides, and currents of the

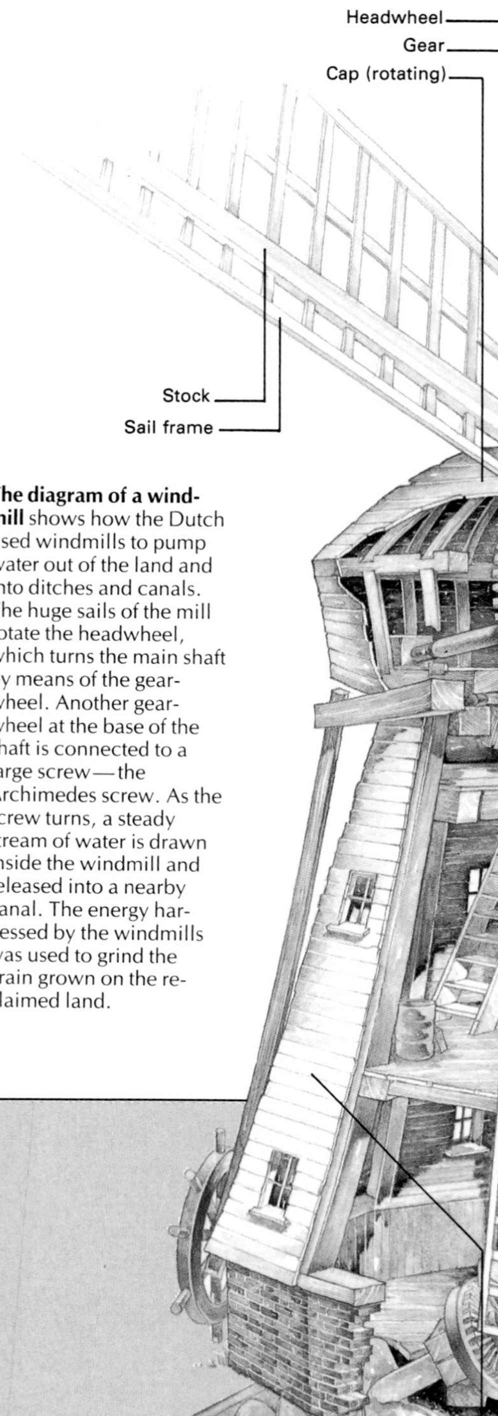

The diagram of a windmill shows how the Dutch used windmills to pump water out of the land and into ditches and canals. The huge sails of the mill rotate the headwheel, which turns the main shaft by means of the gearwheel. Another gearwheel at the base of the shaft is connected to a large screw—the Archimedes screw. As the screw turns, a steady stream of water is drawn inside the windmill and released into a nearby canal. The energy harnessed by the windmills was used to grind the grain grown on the reclaimed land.

The Oosterschelde surge barrier is one of the Delta Project's principal dams. Enormous floodgates in the dam allow salt water and natural tides to enter, thus protecting the fish, birds, and other wildlife in the area. During storms, the floodgates can be closed to keep out the dangerous high waters.

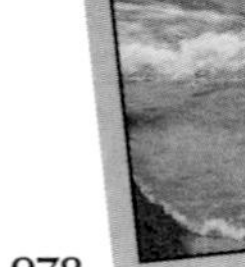

In 1953, the sea flooded the southwest delta region, killing hundreds of people and destroying much of the farmland.

North Sea. Therefore, all along the coast, the Dutch have strengthened these natural defenses with barricades and piers.

Battles won

The Dutch began their battle with the sea many centuries ago. In the 1300's, the sea level rose dramatically, and the Zuider Zee, which had been a river estuary, widened into a huge bay. To prevent their fragile coastline from further destruction, the people built dams to control the rivers, and barricades to protect the land from the tides. The dam on the Amstel River, for which the city of Amsterdam is named, was built in the 1200's.

By the 1200's, people in the Netherlands were using windmills to pump water from submerged areas and keep land dry. In the 1500's and 1600's, a new type of windmill that could pump more water made the construction of stronger defenses against the sea possible.

Over the next 300 years, the Dutch continued to "create" land from the sea. In 1932, the Zuider Zee was cut off from the North Sea by a dike 20 miles (32 kilometers) long. This project changed the Zuider Zee into a vast freshwater lake called the IJsselmeer. Since then, much of the lake has been drained, adding 710 square miles (1,838 square kilometers) of new land.

Battles lost

In spite of their skill at holding back the sea, the Netherlands suffered terrible floods in 1953. Storms broke the dikes in the southwestern delta area, and the sea flooded the land. More than 1,800 people drowned, and some 375,000 acres (151,800 hectares) of land were submerged.

In 1958, work began on the Delta Project to prevent a similar disaster. The project, completed in 1986, includes a series of massive dams and floodgates that have greatly reduced the risk of flooding. In February 1995, however, the country was hit by the worst floods since 1953. More than 250,000 people were evacuated from their homes, and several died.

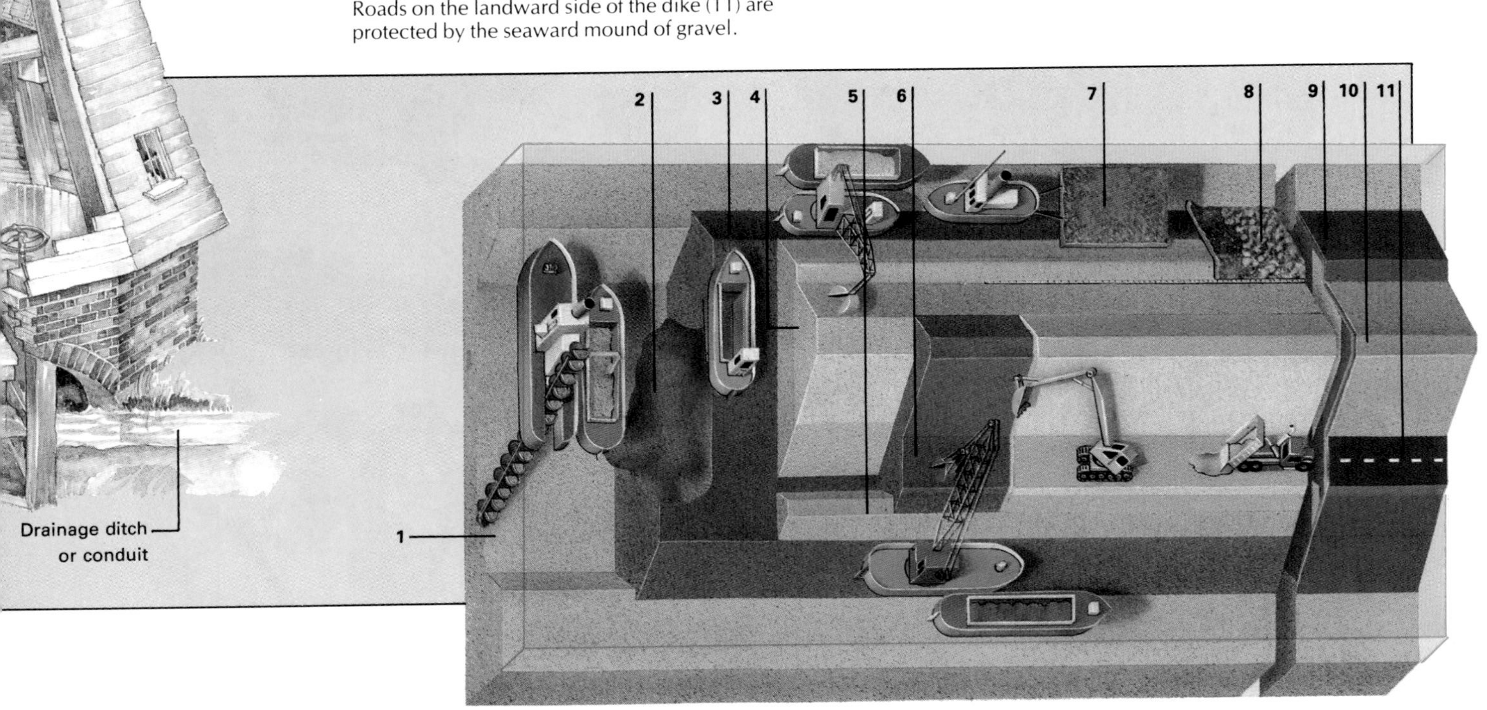

The modern method of constructing a sea dike, *below,* begins with digging a trench in the seabed parallel with the shore (1). Clay, which does not allow the seawater to seep through, is dumped into the trench (2) and built up to form a low mound (3). Gravel is then piled on top of the clay—a large mound on the seaward side (4), and a smaller mound on the landward side (5). The hollow center is filled with clay (6). On the seaward side, synthetic matting is used to cover the gravel mound (7), and is held in place with large boulders (8). Then the whole seaward side of the dike is topped with a layer of brick (9), the outermost defense against the sea. The top of the structure is covered with topsoil and planted with grass seed (10). Roads on the landward side of the dike (11) are protected by the seaward mound of gravel.

The Netherlands Antilles

The Netherlands Antilles, also called the Dutch West Indies, consists of two groups of islands. The southern group, made up of Bonaire and Curaçao, is located about 50 miles (80 kilometers) north of Venezuela.

The southern group also included Aruba until 1986, when that island separated from the Netherlands Antilles. Aruba is now self-governing, but the Netherlands is responsible for its defense and foreign affairs.

The northern group consists of Saba and St. Eustatius islands, and Sint Maarten, which is the southern part of St. Martin. These islands are located about 500 miles (800 kilometers) northeast of Bonaire and Curaçao.

The delicate pastel colors and red tile roofs of the Dutch colonial buildings in Willemstad, Curaçao, *above,* add an Old World charm to the city. Islanders speak Dutch, English, Spanish, and a mixture of all three called *Papiamento.*

History

Europeans first sighted the islands off Venezuela in 1499. Spaniards who arrived in Curaçao in 1527 killed the American Indians who lived there and used the islands as a base from which to conquer South America. The Dutch, however, were interested in the large salt deposits on the islands and captured the Antilles area in 1634.

Today, the Netherlands Antilles is an equal partner with the Netherlands in the Kingdom of the Netherlands. The islands are self-governing, and their governor is appointed by the Dutch monarch.

The economy of the Netherlands Antilles is based on oil refining and tourism. Crude oil is shipped from Venezuela to refineries on Curaçao. The islands' warm weather, lovely beaches, and picturesque cities and towns also draw thousands of tourists a year.

Curaçao and Bonaire

Famous for creating a touch of the Netherlands in the Caribbean, Curaçao and Bonaire are low-lying, rocky islands surrounded by coral reefs. Curaçao, the largest island in the Netherlands Antilles, is generally flat, with some low hills in the northwest. The island is so rocky that little farming is possible, and most food must be imported.

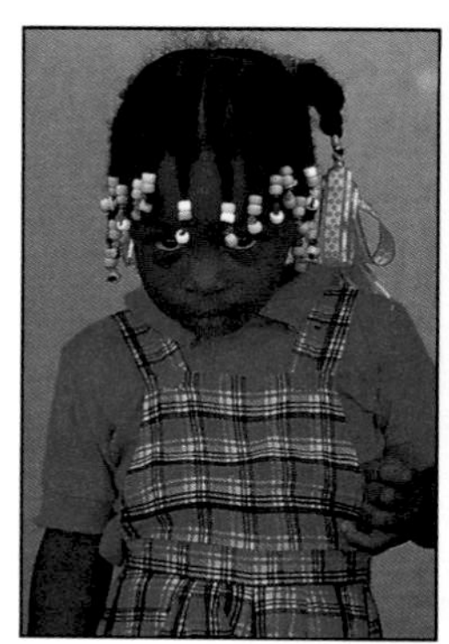

A young girl of African descent displays her elaborately braided hair. Most of Curaçao's people are blacks or have mixed black and white ancestry.

Aruba is a hilly, rocky island. Although its land supports little agriculture, the island's coral reefs, sandy beaches, and warm, dry climate attract many tourists. Curaçao, the largest island in the Netherlands Antilles, covers 171 square miles (443 square kilometers). It is a dry, nearly flat island with warm weather year-round. Bonaire lies east of Curaçao. Its capital city is Kralendijk. It is an arid, rocky island with salt mines, textile factories, and a busy tourist trade.

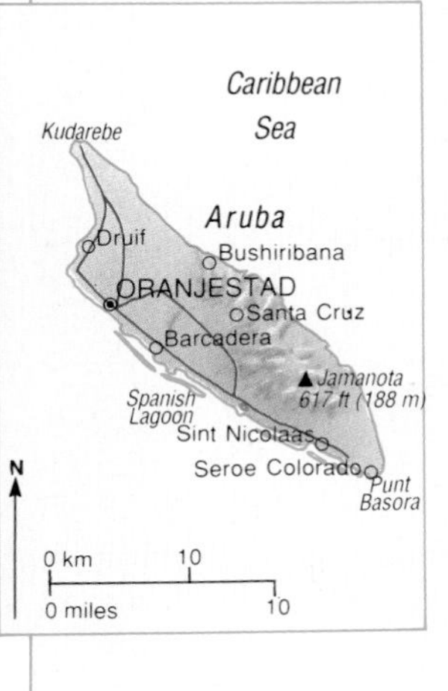

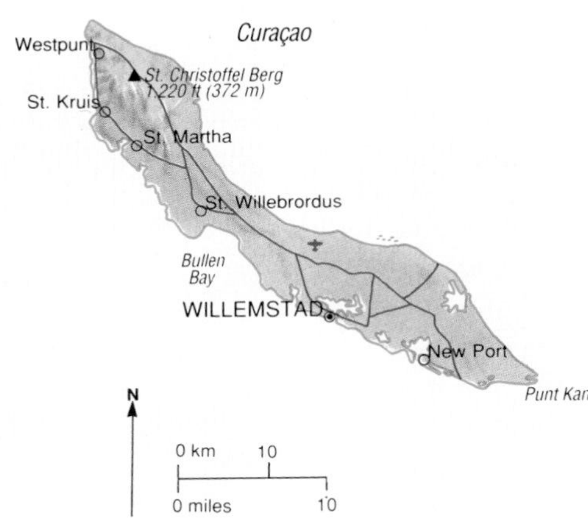

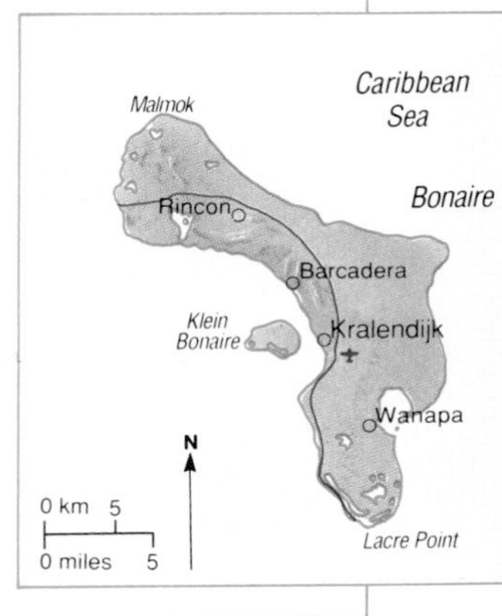

Imported fruits are displayed at a dockside market in Willemstad, Curaçao, *left*. The city, originally founded as a Dutch trading center in the 1600's, is built around the entrance to St. Anna's Bay, and its fine harbor makes Willemstad an important center for shipping and trading.

Palm trees shade the entrance to a colonial-style building on Bonaire. The island's abundant bird life includes its famous flamingo colonies, and the fascinating marine life of its coastal waters attracts divers from all over the world.

Willemstad, the capital of the Netherlands Antilles and a major oil-refining center, lies on the southwest coast of Curaçao. Willemstad has one of the Caribbean's finest harbors, and it is also noted for the traditional Dutch style of its pastel-colored houses.

The city contains two of the oldest Jewish landmarks in the Western Hemisphere—a cemetery established in 1659 and a temple built in 1732. Jews had fled to Curaçao during colonial times to escape religious persecution.

Bonaire is less developed than Curaçao. Plant life is scarce on this arid island, whose soil, like that of Curaçao, has been damaged by overgrazing, but many species of birds thrive. Bonaire also has some of the world's finest coral reefs.

New Caledonia

New Caledonia, an overseas territory of France, lies in the South Pacific Ocean about 1,100 nautical miles (2,000 kilometers) northeast of Sydney, Australia. The territory consists of one main island called New Caledonia, the Loyalty Islands, the Bélep Islands, the Isle of Pines, and a few uninhabited islands. The mountainous main island covers 6,467 square miles (16,749 square kilometers). The rest of the islands have a total area of only 899 square miles (2,330 square kilometers).

The main island is geologically similar to larger land masses, while some of the other islands are coral formations. New Caledonia's climate is subtropical, with higher temperatures in the rainy season, which lasts from December to March. Annual rainfall in the wettest region averages around 80 inches (205 centimeters). Such conditions encourage vegetation, and the islands have both tropical rain forests and grasslands.

History

Melanesians, probably from New Guinea, reached New Caledonia at least 4,000 years ago. In 1774, James Cook, the British navigator, became the first European to land on the main island. He called it New Caledonia because it resembled Scotland (*Caledonia* in Latin). France took possession of New Caledonia in 1853 in order to set up coconut palm, cocoa, and coffee plantations. The United States had a large military base on the main island from 1942 to 1945.

In 1946, New Caledonia was incorporated into the French republic as an overseas territory, and certain categories of its people became French citizens. The people gained civil rights in stages.

In the 1980's, many Melanesians demanded independence for New Caledonia, but most other New Caledonians favored continued French control. Riots between the opposing groups broke out on a number of occasions, but in a referendum held in 1987, New Caledonians voted to continue French control.

The result of the referendum was controversial, however, because voters who favored independence had boycotted the voting. This group continued to demand independence, and violence erupted in 1988 between some Melanesians and French officials. Later that year, voters approved a peace agreement that provided for a referendum on independence in 1998.

Way of life

New Caledonia has a population of about 165,000. Melanesians, the largest group of people, make up about 40 per cent of the population. Europeans form the second largest population group. Other groups include Indonesians, Polynesians, and Vietnamese. Nouméa, on the main island, is the capital and New Caledonia's only city.

Nickel mining and smelting are the leading industries of the territory, and New Caledonia ranks among the world's leading producers of nickel. The territory's economy boomed in the 1940's and 1950's due to the growth of its nickel industry, and Nouméa's

Île Ouen, *above,* also known as Turtle Isle, lies off the southeast tip of New Caledonia. A long barrier reef that encircles the main island is the second longest in the Pacific. Only Australia's Great Barrier Reef is longer.

Largely cleared of vegetation, a mountain on New Caledonia, *above left,* shows the effects of mining activity. The territory is a major mineral producer, with large deposits of nickel, chromite, and cobalt.

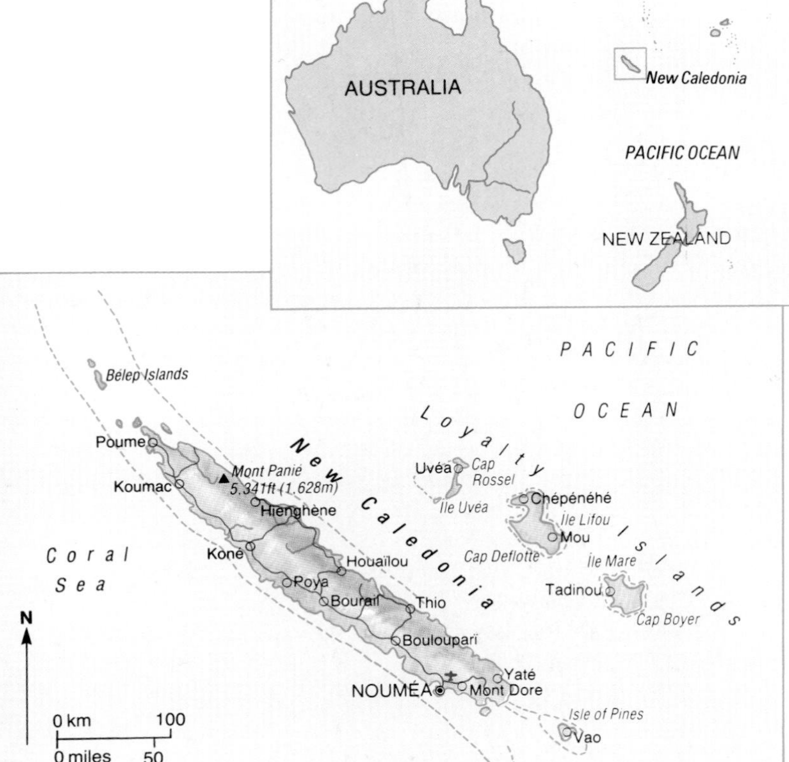

New Caledonia consists of one large island and a number of smaller ones in southern Melanesia. It is an overseas territory of France, which took possession of the islands in 1853. Nouméa is its capital and only city.

A New Caledonian fisherman removes a nautilus from a trap. The nautilus, a type of shellfish related to the squid and octopus, lives at depths of 20 to 1,000 feet (6 to 300 meters) in the South Pacific and Indian oceans.

A crowd of demonstrators shows its support for independence from France in the 1980's. At times, supporters of the independence movement clashed with those who favor French control. A referendum on this issue is scheduled for 1998.

standard of living increased, along with the population. However, mining has scarred vast areas of the countryside with ugly, open mines, and interest in farming and other traditional occupations has declined. Today, farmers raise their own food and sell small amounts of coffee and copra for export.

A French official appointed by the French government heads New Caledonia's government, presiding over a locally elected congress of New Caledonians who share in the government. New Caledonia is considered part of France. The people vote for the president of France and send representatives to both houses of the French Parliament.

New Zealand

The lovely island country of New Zealand lies about 1,000 miles (1,600 kilometers) southeast of Australia in the Southwest Pacific Ocean. New Zealand belongs to a large island group called *Polynesia* and is the country farthest south of all the Pacific nations. Unlike the rest of the countries of Polynesia, New Zealand is a highly developed nation with a modern economy.

The country consists of two main islands—the North Island and the South Island—and several dozen much smaller islands. The North and South islands extend in a curve more than 1,000 miles long. Most of the smaller islands are hundreds of miles from the main ones. Once part of the British Empire, New Zealand is now an independent member of the Commonwealth of Nations, an association of countries that once lived under British law and government.

New Zealand has a mild, moist climate like that of the Pacific Northwest Coast of the United States, but since New Zealand lies south of the equator, its seasons are opposite those of the Northern Hemisphere. Snow-capped mountains, green lowlands, sandy beaches, and many lakes and waterfalls grace the landscape throughout New Zealand. The Mount Cook region, on the South Island, has some of the country's most spectacular scenery. Glaciers cover the mountain slopes above the dense, green forests, and sparkling lakes nestle in the valleys.

The first people to live in New Zealand were a brown-skinned people called Maoris who came from Polynesian islands northeast of New Zealand. Today, only about 12 per cent of the people are Maoris. Most New Zealanders are descendants of Europeans who began to settle there in the 1800's.

New Zealand's standard of living ranks among the highest in the world. The country's economy, which depended largely on agriculture for many years, now also includes important manufacturing and service industries.

The New Zealand way of life combines an easy informality with a British and Polynesian sense of politeness. Since the arrival of British settlers around 1800, many New Zealanders have kept close cultural and emotional ties to Britain, and many New Zealand customs resemble British customs. But New Zealand has developed a feeling of national identity as a Pacific nation of both British and Polynesian heritage.

New Zealand Today

About 85 per cent of New Zealand's nearly 4 million people are descendants of British settlers who came to the country during the 1800's. About three-fourths of all New Zealanders live on the North Island, and more than five-sixths of the country's people live in urban areas.

Children must attend school from the age of 6 through 15, but most youngsters start school at 5. Education is free to all students up to the age of 19. New Zealand has six universities, and the government pays all or part of the expenses for about two-thirds of the nation's university students.

New Zealand is a constitutional monarchy. It recognizes the British monarch as its head of state, but this person has little real power. The British monarch appoints a governor general to represent the Crown in New Zealand. The legislature, prime minister, and Cabinet run the national government.

The United Kingdom gave New Zealand a constitution in 1852, when it was a British colony, but the New Zealand legislature has changed almost all its provisions through the years. For all practical purposes, the nation today has no written constitution.

However, New Zealand has thus far managed to limit or reduce many of the problems that face other countries, such as environmental pollution, poverty, racial conflict, and urban overcrowding. Today, New Zealand's top goals include environmental conservation, creating new job opportunities for women, and helping more Maoris obtain positions of leadership in industry and the professions.

At present, New Zealand is also concerned with finding new overseas markets for its dairy and meat products. The United Kingdom was the country's chief trading partner until 1973, when the United Kingdom joined the European Economic Community. This organization of European nations has no tariffs on trade among its members, but there is a common tariff on goods imported from other countries. Because goods from New Zealand carry this tariff, the country is now at a disadvantage in trading with the United Kingdom. New Zealand has since increased the variety of its exports and found some new markets for its new products.

In 1952, Australia, New Zealand, and the United States formed a collective defense treaty, called ANZUS. Each pledged to "meet the common danger in accordance with its constitutional processes" if any member faced an armed attack in the Pacific area.

In 1984, however, New Zealand adopted a policy that excluded nuclear weapons and

Fact Box

NEW ZEALAND

Country

Official name: New Zealand
Capital: Wellington
Terrain: Predominately mountainous with some large coastal plains
Area: 103,738 sq. mi. (268,680 km²)
Climate: Temperate with sharp regional contrasts
Main rivers: Waikato, Clutha
Highest elevation: Mount Cook, 12,349 ft. (3,764 m)
Lowest elevation: Pacific Ocean, sea level

Government

Form of government: Constitutional monarchy
Head of state: British monarch, represented by governor general
Head of government: Prime minister
Administrative areas: 93 counties, 9 districts, 3 town districts
Legislature: House of Representatives, commonly called Parliament, with 120 members serving three-year terms
Court system: High Court, Court of Appeal
Armed forces: 9,530 troops

People

Estimated 2002 population: 3,930,000
Population growth: 1.17%
Population density: 38 persons per sq. mi. (15 per km²)
Population distribution: 85% urban, 15% rural
Life expectancy in years: Male: 75 Female: 81
Doctors per 1,000 people: 2.3
Percentage of age-appropriate population enrolled in the following educational levels: Primary: 101* Secondary: 113* Further: 63
Languages spoken: English (official) Maori

The "Beehive," the circular building in which New Zealand's government ministers have their offices, stands next to the building in which the legislature meets in Wellington. New Zealand's legislature consists of a House of Representatives, also called Parliament.

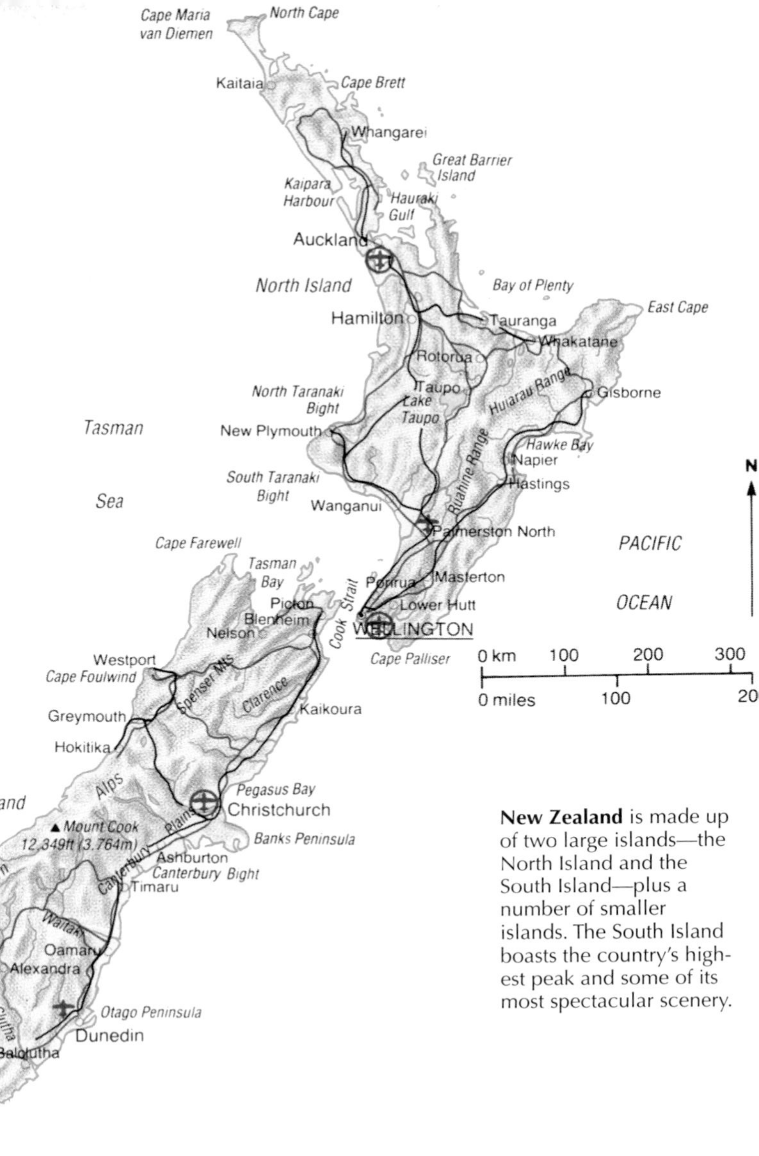

New Zealand is made up of two large islands—the North Island and the South Island—plus a number of smaller islands. The South Island boasts the country's highest peak and some of its most spectacular scenery.

Religions:
- Anglican 24%
- Presbyterian 18%
- Roman Catholic 15%
- Methodist 5%
- Baptist 2%
- other Protestant 3%
- unspecified or none 33%

*Enrollment ratios compare the number of students enrolled to the population which, by age, should be enrolled. A ratio higher than 100 indicates that students older or younger than the typical age range are also enrolled.

TECHNOLOGY

Radios per 1,000 people: 997

Televisions per 1,000 people: 522

Computers per 1,000 people: 360.2

ECONOMY

Currency: New Zealand dollar

Gross national income (GNI) in 2000: $49.8 billion U.S.

Real annual growth rate (1999–2000): 2.5%

GNI per capita (2000): $12,990 U.S.

Balance of payments (2000): -$2,734 million U.S.

Goods exported: Dairy products, meat, fish, wool, forestry products, manufactures

Goods imported: Machinery and equipment, vehicles and aircraft, petroleum, consumer goods, plastics

Trading partners: Australia, United States, Japan

ships powered by nuclear fuel from its ports and territorial waters. In 1985, a U.S. destroyer was denied access to a New Zealand port after U.S. officials refused to give assurance that the ship carried no nuclear weapons. In 1986, in response to this policy, the U.S. government announced that it would no longer guarantee New Zealand's security under the ANZUS treaty. Australia has continued to cooperate with New Zealand under separate arrangements. In December 1994, the United States agreed to honor New Zealand's ban against carrying nuclear weapons into its territory.

Economy

New Zealand has lots of sheep and cattle—about 25 times as many farm animals as people. No other country has so many farm animals in relation to its population. Sheep are so numerous that a distant hillside may resemble a field of cotton because so many fluffy white sheep are grazing there.

The economy of New Zealand has long depended on farming and foreign trade. Exports of butter, cheese, meat, and wool still provide much of the nation's income. But manufacturing has been increasing rapidly, and about twice as many New Zealanders now work in factories as on farms. Tourism has also become an important source of income.

New Zealand's economy depends heavily on trade. The country's chief trading partners are Australia, Japan, and the United States. Butter, cheese, dried milk products, lamb, and wool make up about half the value of New Zealand's exports. Exports of increasing importance, however, include manufactured goods, fish products, and forest products. The country's chief imports include iron and steel, machinery, motor vehicles, petroleum, scientific instruments, and telecommunication equipment.

Sheep raising is New Zealand's most important agricultural activity, and traveling down a rural highway often means giving the right of way to a passing flock, *right.*

Shearing, *above,* is the first step in the production of wool, one of New Zealand's principal exports.

Agriculture and mining

New Zealand's greatest natural resource is its land. About 55 per cent of the land consists of cropland and pastureland, and about 25 per cent is covered with forests that provide valuable timber as well as protection from land erosion. The remaining 20 per cent of the country is made up of lakes, rivers, and mountain areas.

The country has few minerals. The most important include coal, gold, iron ore, limestone, and natural gas. Water power provides about 65 per cent of the nation's electricity. Underground steam in the volcanic area of the North Island is becoming an increasingly important source of power.

New Zealand produces enough meat and dairy products to feed millions of people in other countries as well as its own people, thanks to the country's mild climate, modern machinery, and scientific farming methods. Sheep, bred for both meat and wool, are raised on both the North Island and the South Island. New Zealand farmers raise dairy cattle and beef cattle, mainly on the North Island. Milk and milk products account for an important share of the nation's income.

The chief crops include barley, potatoes, and wheat. New Zealand is the world's largest producer of kiwi fruit, and farmers also raise apples, grapes, onions, peas, and pears. Avocados, citrus fruits, and a wide variety of other subtropical fruits are grown in northern areas of the North Island.

Manufacturing

Processed foods rank as New Zealand's most valuable manufactured goods. Milk is made into butter, cheese, and dried milk, while

Wellington's fine harbor makes the city one of New Zealand's busiest ports. The city is also a hub for airline, shipping, and highway routes.

Skiers at Round Hill Ski Field near Lake Tekapo can enjoy the spectacular scenery of the South Island.

The Wairakei geothermal power station, *below,* the second geothermal station in the world, opened in 1958 on the North Island. This power station uses high-pressure steam from a vast underground hot-water system.

lamb and beef are frozen for export. Factories also process wool and weave woolen carpets. Other manufactured items include aluminum, chemicals, iron and steel, machinery, metal products, motor vehicles, paper, petroleum products, textiles, and wood products. Large-scale projects in the 1980's developed wider uses for local resources, including the use of *ironsand* (sand containing iron ore) in steel manufacture and the use of wood from plantation forests in pulp, paper, and packaging enterprises.

Auckland, New Zealand's most populous city, is its largest manufacturing center, with some 3,350 factories employing nearly 120,000 workers. About a third of New Zealand's manufacturing industries have their headquarters in Wellington, the country's capital and its second largest city.

Geothermal energy

Geothermal energy, which supplies nearly 7 per cent of New Zealand's electricity, is generated when water comes into contact with heated underground rocks and turns into steam. The layer of solid bedrock overlying the earth's mantle (1) conducts heat to porous rock layers (2), where water is heated to temperatures of 482° to 662° F. (250° to 350° C). Forced upward, the steam is trapped under layers of solid cap rock (3), where its pressure increases. The steam escapes to the surface through cracks and fissures (4), forming geysers or hot springs. Power companies drill into areas where underground steam is trapped and direct it into the blades of steam turbines. Geothermal power plants do not burn anything, so there is no smoke to pollute the air.

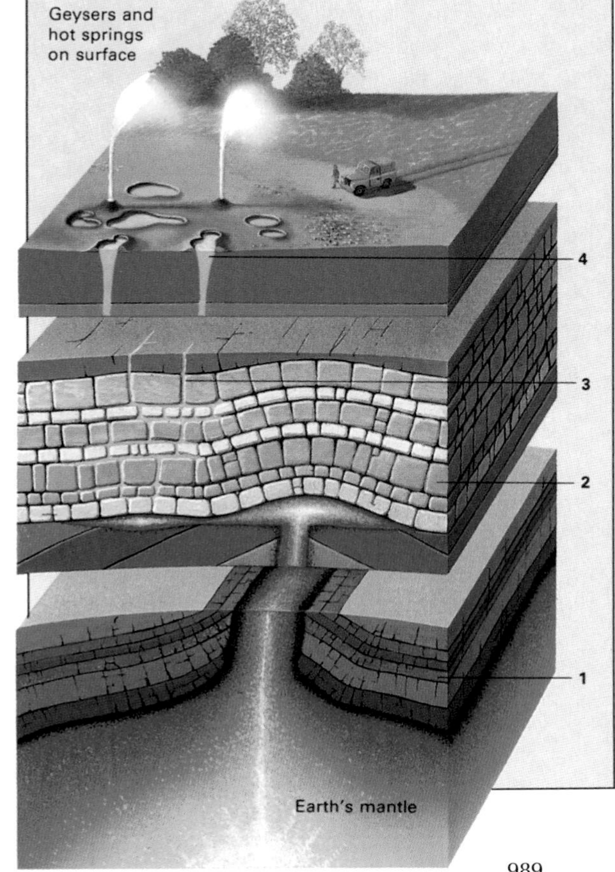

People

Most of New Zealand's nearly 4 million people are descendants of British settlers. Immigrants still come to New Zealand, chiefly from the United Kingdom, Australia, and other English-speaking countries.

About 290,000 Maoris live in New Zealand—the country's largest minority group. The Maoris are a Polynesian people whose ancestors came to New Zealand about 1,000 years ago. Through the years, many Maoris have intermarried with people of European ancestry. As a result, large numbers of New Zealanders of mixed parentage share the physical characteristics of both Europeans and Maoris. Of the 120 seats in the New Zealand House of Representatives, 5 are reserved for Maoris, who are voted on by Maoris only. Maoris who prefer to vote in the 115 general *electorates* (voting districts) may do so.

English, the official language of New Zealand, is spoken throughout the country. Many Maoris speak their own language, Maori, in addition to English.

The people of New Zealand have a high standard of living—they have long been among the best-fed people in the world. The nation also has a tradition of equal rights and benefits for all its citizens. In 1893, New Zealand became the first nation in the world to give women the vote. In addition, New Zealand was among the first countries to provide social security benefits and old-age benefits for its people. Today, the nation has one of the world's finest public health programs.

To protect the rights of citizens, Parliament selects an official called an *ombudsman*. The ombudsman investigates complaints by New Zealand citizens against government departments and sends an opinion to the department involved. If the department does not take the action that the ombudsman believes is needed, the findings may be reported to Parliament.

The law requires children from 6 through 15 to attend school, and New Zealand offers a free education to all students up to the age of 19. The government provides school bus service, particularly in rural areas, for children who live beyond walking distance from school.

About 70 per cent of New Zealand's families own their own homes, usually a single-family house, and almost every family has a

The All Blacks, New Zealand's famous national Rugby Union team, play in black jerseys, shorts, and socks, *above*. British settlers introduced the game in New Zealand about 1870, but some of the greatest players in the game's history have been Maoris.

Christchurch, where quaint Cathedral Square, *right,* and uniformed students, *above,* reflect New Zealand's British heritage, was founded in the 1850's. It is the South Island's largest city.

Shoppers at an outdoor market reflect New Zealand's mixture of British and Polynesian people. Many New Zealand customs resemble British customs, but the country has developed its own national identity as a Pacific nation.

car. Almost all New Zealanders have refrigerators, washing machines, and other modern electrical appliances.

Although most people live in urban areas, New Zealand's cities are relatively uncrowded, with few traffic problems even in downtown areas. The cities have theaters, concert halls, and other entertainment. In rural New Zealand, good roads link some settlements, but some ranchers in rugged country may live in near isolation.

New Zealanders enjoy outdoor activities and sports, and mild climate allows camping, hiking, hunting, and mountain climbing the year around. Ski areas attract large numbers of people, and many New Zealanders enjoy swimming and tennis, as well as such team sports as *cricket,* which somewhat resembles baseball, and *rugby,* a form of football.

Revelers crowd the streets, joining a parade in Dunedin, the southernmost of New Zealand's major cities. Many of Dunedin's people are of Scottish descent.

The Maoris

The first people to live in New Zealand were Maoris who probably came to the country by canoe during the A.D. 900's from the Polynesian islands northeast of New Zealand. Historians have disagreed about whether the Maoris arrived by accident or by planned migration. However, recent successful voyages between Polynesia and New Zealand—made without navigational instruments in replicas of the old Maori double canoes—tend to suggest that the voyages were planned.

Traditional Maori culture

The first Maoris lived in isolated villages, mainly by fishing and hunting. They have been called the *moa hunters* because their chief prey was the now-extinct *moas,* a group of large, wingless birds. Later, they also became farmers. The Maoris were skilled woodcarvers, and they decorated war canoes and communal houses with complicated designs. Their religion was based on *taboos* (prohibitions on certain objects, people, and places).

All the inhabitants of a village were related to one another and bore the name of their common ancestor. Villages were made up of tribes and subtribes. Each subtribe had a number of family groups, and each group had a leader who reached decisions by discussions with other leaders and with the people.

The people moved with the seasons to various parts of the tribal lands to hunt specific animals. In late summer, for example, they might travel to the sea to catch and dry sharks for winter food supplies.

Maoris and pakehas

Today, most New Zealanders are descendants of early European settlers. Only about 12 per cent of the people are Maoris. A New

Kiri te Kanawa, *right,* descended from Maori chiefs, enjoys international fame as an opera singer.

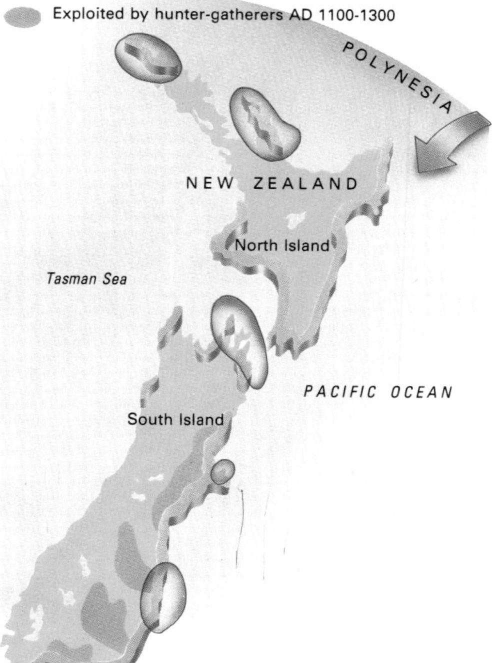

Maori migration from Polynesia occurred about 1,000 years ago. Most Maoris settled around the northern coast of the North Island where the soil was good and the climate was warm.

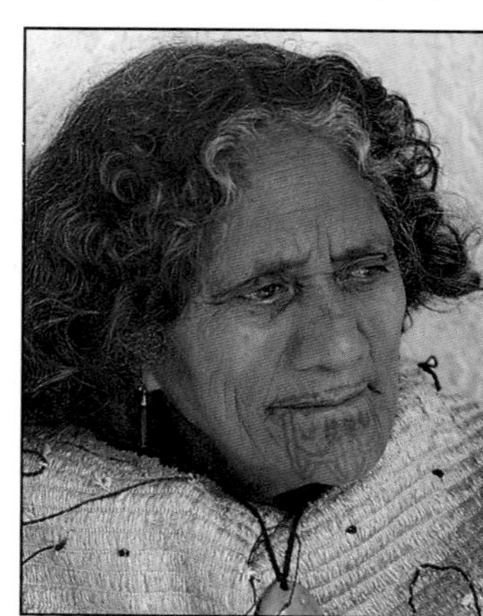

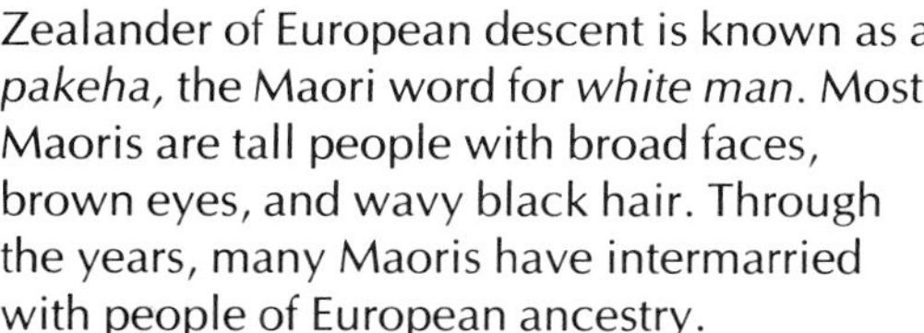

A Maori meeting house, *far left,* now the setting for ceremonial events, formed the center of tribal life during the 1800's. Parts of the building often symbolized the parts of an ancestor's body, with the face at the peak.

Maori woodcarving, *left,* developed into a major art form in New Zealand, where softwood timber and tough rock called *greenstone* for chisels were plentiful. With these materials, Maoris developed carving skills superior to any found elsewhere in Polynesia.

Maori "warriors," *below,* open the 1990 Commonwealth Games in Auckland, New Zealand. The Maori tribal history is a tale of conflict and warfare, but Maoris today live much like other New Zealanders.

Zealander of European descent is known as a *pakeha,* the Maori word for *white man.* Most Maoris are tall people with broad faces, brown eyes, and wavy black hair. Through the years, many Maoris have intermarried with people of European ancestry.

The arrival of the Europeans brought great suffering to the Maoris. The pakehas brought firearms, which intensified warfare among the Maori tribes. The newcomers also brought diseases against which the Maoris had no resistance. By 1840, warfare and disease had reduced the Maori population from about 200,000 to a little more than 100,000. Disputes over land ownership led to the New Zealand Wars, which lasted off and on from 1845 to 1872. In the 1890's, the Maori population dropped to its lowest level of only about 40,000.

Until World War II (1939–1945), the great majority of Maoris lived in rural districts. During the war, however, educational and job opportunities drew many Maoris into the cities. Today, the nation's Maoris and pakehas live in an atmosphere of common trust, and Maori political leaders and professional people play important roles. However, some Maori leaders see a need for better housing, employment opportunities, and education for their people, and they believe that Maoris should play a greater role in the government of New Zealand.

Maoris point out that subjects taught in New Zealand schools are almost entirely related to pakeha culture, and television and radio stations almost always broadcast in the English language. Many young Maoris feel that they have lost their cultural heritage, and they want to relearn the Maori language as well as Maori customs and traditions. Above all, they wish to regain ownership of Maori lands.

Tattooed designs adorn the lips and chin of an elderly Maori woman, *bottom left.* In traditional Maori culture, tattooing was a sign of rank. Tattoos sometimes covered warriors from waist to knees.

Wildlife

Most of New Zealand's land animals were introduced from other countries. European settlers brought deer and rabbits, as well as cattle, pigs, and sheep; *wallabies* (small kangaroos) and brush-tailed possums were brought from Australia. Two species of bats are the only native land mammals. The lizardlike tuatara, a native reptile unchanged since prehistoric times, still lives in New Zealand, and the lakes and rivers are well stocked with salmon and trout brought from other countries.

Most of New Zealand's trees are evergreens and tree ferns. In the country's luxuriant rain forests, where they stand close together, the trees grow very tall and straight. Moss, lichens, and ferns cover their trunks. The country's pulp and paper industry depends mainly on the fast-growing radiata pine imported from California, one of the many foreign trees introduced since 1900.

Animals

Birds are New Zealand's dominant *vertebrates* (animals with backbones). Native birds include such flightless species as the kakapo parrot, kiwi, takahe, and weka. The kiwi may be the best known, though it is a shy, nocturnal bird and usually runs away and hides when anyone comes near. The kiwi is the only bird that has nostrils at the tip of its bill.

During the last 100 years, nine species of birds from Australia have arrived and bred in New Zealand, suggesting that all New Zealand's native birds may have originally migrated from Australia. Birds such as the wekas and takahes must have lost their power of flight in New Zealand because related birds elsewhere can fly.

New Zealand once had many ostrichlike moas, but they have become extinct. Moas could not fly, and some grew to be 10 feet (3 meters) tall. These birds lived in New Zealand when the Maoris arrived there about 1,000 years ago. Hunting and the destruction of their lowland forest habitat probably led to the bird's extinction several hundred years later.

New Zealand has no snakes. Scientists believe that this may be due to the fact that New Zealand broke away from the large combined southern continent of Australia and Antarctica millions of years ago, before the region had snakes.

Plants

Volcanic eruptions in prehistoric times destroyed large areas of forest in the central plateau of the North Island. As a result, small shrubs, such as the manuka, now cover much of the region. Manukas, the most common shrub in New Zealand, have papery bark and masses of pink or white flowers.

Forests of pinelike kauri trees once thrived on the Northern Peninsula, but the early European settlers almost destroyed the kauri forests. However, some kauris still flourish on both the large islands. These huge trees, which live to a great age, are the most impressive of the many types of pine trees in New Zealand, growing up to 100 feet (30 meters) tall and towering above other trees in the forests. Great stands of kauris form a vaulted roof of branches.

The beech is one of the loveliest of New Zealand's trees. These trees belong to the oak family and grow up to 100 feet (30 meters)

A coastal highway offers a scenic route along the Bay of Plenty, on the central northern coast of the North Island. A volcanic plateau with geysers, hot springs, and boiling mud pools rises from the lowlands bordering the bay.

Mount Cook, *right,* the highest peak in New Zealand, towers over the Southern Alps of the South Island, attracting many mountain climbers. The Maori name for the mountain is *Aorangi,* which means *cloud piercer.*

high on the plains, on alpine slopes, and even on the sea coast. Beech forests grow on the cooler uplands of both islands.

Since 1900, many foreign trees have been introduced into New Zealand. The fast-growing radiata pine, an import from California, now supports the country's pulp and paper industry.

Cropland and pastureland occupy about 55 percent of New Zealand's land.

The green, rolling pastureland of the Wairarapa region makes it an important cattle- and sheep-raising area. The Wairarapa lies in the southeastern part of New Zealand's North Island, at the southern edge of a belt of farmland running from East Cape of Cook Strait. Farmers there also raise fruits and vegetables along the coast. Masterton, with a population of about 20,000, is the chief town of the region.

Several flightless birds were native to New Zealand, including the moa and the prehistoric Euryapteryx. The moas lived in lowland forests of New Zealand when the Maoris arrived about 1,000 years ago and became extinct several hundred years later. Some moas were as small as a turkey, while others grew to be 10 feet (3 meters) tall. The takahe, another flightless bird, is extremely rare, while the abundant kiwi is found in all the forest areas of New Zealand.

Nicaragua

Nicaragua, the largest Central American country in size, was named for an Indian chief and his people—both named Nicarao—who lived in the area when the Spaniards arrived in the 1500's. Today, Nicaragua is troubled by severe economic problems and other effects of the civil war that raged from the late 1970's through the 1980's.

Economy

Farming is the leading economic activity in Nicaragua. Cotton and coffee are the most important cash crops. Sugar cane, bananas, and rice are also exported. Corn, beans, and rice are the country's main food crops.

Nicaragua's leading service industry is wholesale and retail trade. The marketing of farm products is the most important sector of that industry.

The manufacturing industry produces mainly processed foods and beverages, clothing, and textiles. Other products are cement, cigarettes, leather goods, petroleum, and wood.

History

In 1502, Columbus landed in what is now Nicaragua and claimed the land for Spain. Settlements were built near the Indians so that they could work on the Spaniards' farms and in their mines.

The Caribbean Region, however, went largely unsettled and became a hideout for English, French, and Dutch pirates. In the 1700's, the English gained control over the Miskito, or Mosquito, Indians who lived there. However, the United Kingdom gave up its claim to the region in the mid-1800's.

On Sept. 15, 1821, Nicaragua and other Central American states declared their independence from Spain. They became part of Mexico, but in 1823 formed the United Provinces of Central America—a union with liberal political and economic policies. The union established civil rights and tried to curb the power of the rich landowners and the Roman Catholic Church.

However, Nicaragua left the union in 1838. By then, a dispute had started between liberal people in the city of León and conservative people in the city of Granada. The two cities fought for control of the country.

The liberals of León asked an American soldier and adventurer, William Walker, to help them. In 1855, Walker and his followers captured Granada in a surprise attack, but he then seized control of the government. In 1857, the liberals and conservatives joined forces and drove Walker out of the country.

In the late 1800's, the United States was planning to build a canal in Nicaragua that would link the Atlantic and Pacific oceans. In 1901, however, Nicaraguan President José Santos Zelaya began to argue with the United States over the agreement. When a revolt

Market stalls in Managua, *above,* display a colorful array of food. The Nicaraguan economy depends heavily on agriculture.

Nicaragua's canal

A canal through Central America was a dream as far back as the 1500's. Throughout most of the 1800's, Nicaragua was the focus of efforts to build such a canal. The engineers planned to follow the course of the San Juan River to Lake Nicaragua. From there, the canal would have cut across the 12 miles (19.3 kilometers) of land that separates Lake Nicaragua from the Pacific Ocean. But Nicaraguan President José Santos Zelaya wanted to limit U.S. rights in the proposed canal zone. Then a French company that hoped to sell its Panama rights and property persuaded the United States that earthquakes in Nicaragua would threaten the canal. In 1902, the United States shifted its interest to Panama.

A mass rally to celebrate May Day—the workers' holiday in socialist countries—was staged in Managua under the Sandinistas. National heroes such as Augusto Sandino were honored with large portraits.

Sandinista guards patrolled the border, *below,* during the 1980's, when contras operating from Honduran bases launched attacks on Nicaragua.

broke out against Zelaya's harsh rule in 1909, the United States sided with the rebels, and Zelaya was driven out.

In 1911, U.S. banks began to lend money to Nicaragua under agreements that gave them control over the country's finances until the debts were paid. Some Nicaraguans objected to this control. In 1912, U.S. Marines landed in Nicaragua to put down the protests and remained in the country.

When rebels led by General Augusto César Sandino tried to make U.S. forces leave, the United States trained a new Nicaraguan army, called the National Guard, to help the U.S. Marines. Anastasio Somoza Garcia headed the National Guard. When the U.S. Marines left in 1933, the National Guard, under orders from Somoza, killed Sandino.

Somoza then took control of the government and ruled as dictator. He established great political and economic power for himself and his family. Somoza was assassinated in 1956, and first one son and then another succeeded him. From 1937 to 1979, a Somoza was either the president of Nicaragua or the real power behind the president.

Widespread protests against Anastasio Somoza Debayle began in the mid-1970's. By 1978, the conflict had become a civil war. Many of the rebels were Sandinistas, members of a group named for the slain rebel leader Sandino.

In 1979, the Sandinistas drove Somoza from the country and took control of Nicaragua. The Sandinistas were *leftists* who favored increased governmental control over the economy. The Sandinistas took over agricultural exports, banking, insurance, and mining. The government also formed state farms and owned about a third of the nation's manufacturing companies.

In spite of these measures, manufacturing declined during the 1980's. In addition, war with antigovernment forces called *contras* drained the Nicaraguan budget. The United States began a trade embargo against Nicaragua in 1985, and the economy was damaged further. In 1990, the people voted the Sandinistas out of office, electing Violeta Barrios de Chamorro to the presidency. After the election of Chamorro, the United States ended its trade embargo against Nicaragua.

Nicaragua Today

Nicaragua stretches from the Pacific Ocean to the Caribbean Sea on the Central American land bridge. About three-fifths of the people live on the Pacific side, in one of the country's three main land regions.

The land and climate

The Pacific Region lies from north to south along the western coast. Lake Managua is in the center of this hot, humid region, and Lake Nicaragua takes up much of its southern portion. Volcanoes—both active and inactive—rise up out of this low area, while mountains up to 3,000 feet (910 meters) high rim the Pacific coast.

The Central Highlands are Nicaragua's highest and coolest region. The Cordillera Isabella mountain range rises to 8,000 feet (2,438 meters), the highest point in the country. Forests cover the mountain slopes, and deep valleys nestle between their peaks.

The Caribbean Region is mainly a long, flat plain stretching down the Caribbean coast. In the west, the land slopes up toward the highlands, and many rivers that rise in the Central Highlands flow through the plain. The region's only areas of fertile farmland line the riverbanks. Some grasslands and palm and pine forests lie in the north, but rain forests cover most of the Caribbean Region. Temperatures average 80° F. (27° C), and easterly trade winds drench the region with about 165 inches (419 centimeters) of rain each year. This hot, wet area is known as the Mosquito Coast.

In 1998, a hurricane struck Nicaragua, producing floods and landslides. The storm killed about 3,000 people and caused more than $1 billion in damage.

The people and their government

Nicaragua has nearly 5 million people. The great majority of them are *mestizos,* people with both Indian and European ancestors. They follow a Spanish American way of life, much as other Central American mestizos do. They speak Spanish and belong to the Roman Catholic Church.

The only Indian groups who still follow traditional Indian ways of life live in the Caribbean Region. This region also has several communities of black people or people with both black and Indian ancestors who speak Indian languages and generally follow Indian customs and traditions.

About a third of Nicaraguans are farmers. The majority live in the Pacific Region. Some peasants in this region work on their own

FACT BOX

NICARAGUA

COUNTRY

Official name: Republica de Nicaragua (Republic of Nicaragua)
Capital: Managua
Terrain: Extensive Atlantic coastal plains rising to central interior mountains; narrow Pacific coastal plain interrupted by volcanoes
Area: 49,998 sq. mi. (129,494 km²)
Climate: Tropical in lowlands, cooler in highlands
Main rivers: Río Tuma, Río Grande, Río Escondido, Río San Juan, Río Coco
Highest elevation: Cerro Mogotón, 6,712 ft. (2,107 m)
Lowest elevation: Pacific Ocean, sea level

GOVERNMENT

Form of government: Republic
Head of state: President
Head of government: President
Administrative areas: 15 departamentos (departments), 2 regiones autonomistas (autonomous regions)
Legislature: Asamblea Nacional (National Assembly) with 93 members serving five-year terms
Court system: Corte Suprema (Supreme Court)
Armed forces: 16,000 troops

PEOPLE

Estimated 2002 population: 5,350,000
Population growth: 2.2%
Population density: 107 persons per sq. mi. (41 per km²)
Population distribution: 63% urban, 37% rural
Life expectancy in years:
Male: 67
Female: 71
Doctors per 1,000 people: 0.9
Percentage of age-appropriate population enrolled in the following educational levels:
Primary: 102*
Secondary: 55
Further: 12
Languages spoken:
Spanish (official)
English
indigenous languages

Lake Nicaragua, *below,* lies in southwestern Nicaragua. Several large islands rise from the lake's waters, including Ometepe, the biggest, which has several small communities and two volcanoes.

Nicaragua straddles the Central American land bridge. Honduras lies to the north, Costa Rica to the south. All eight major Nicaraguan cities lie on the Pacific side of the country.

Religions:
Roman Catholic 85%
Protestant

*Enrollment ratios compare the number of students enrolled to the population which, by age, should be enrolled. A ratio higher than 100 indicates that students older or younger than the typical age range are also enrolled.

Technology

Radios per 1,000 people: 270
Televisions per 1,000 people: 69
Computers per 1,000 people: 8.9

Economy

Currency: Gold cordoba
Gross national income (GNI) in 2000: $2.1 billion U.S.
Real annual growth rate (1999–2000): 4.3%
GNI per capita (2000): $400 U.S.
Balance of payments (2000): -$493 million U.S.
Goods exported: Coffee, shrimp and lobster, cotton, tobacco, beef, sugar, bananas; gold
Goods imported: Machinery and equipment, raw materials, petroleum products, consumer goods
Trading partners: United States, Germany, Costa Rica, El Salvador, Guatemala

farms, some work on cooperatives or state farms, and some have jobs on large private farms. In the warmer areas, farmworkers live in houses with palm-leaf or metal roofs. In the colder areas of the Central Highlands, farmers live in adobe houses with tile roofs. Most of the Indians and blacks in the thinly populated Caribbean region live by farming small plots or by fishing, lumbering, or mining.

Nicaragua has eight cities with populations of more than 20,000. They all lie in the Pacific Region. Managua is the capital and largest city.

Nicaraguans elect a president and a legislature called the National Assembly. The president appoints a Cabinet to help run the government. However, the country has a history of political unrest and dictatorship.

Coping with Crisis

The history of Nicaragua is marked by natural, social, and political crises. In 1972, for example, an earthquake killed about 5,000 people and destroyed so much of Managua that the city had to be rebuilt. Poverty and lack of education affect much of the population. Political revolts have shaken the country.

From 1979 to 1984, the revolutionary Sandinista group controlled Nicaragua, largely through a three-member *junta,* or ruling council. In 1984, the Sandinista candidate Daniel Ortega was elected president. During the 1980's, the Sandinista government tried to correct some of the country's economic and social problems.

The Sandinistas took over key parts of the economy, including agricultural exports, banking, insurance, and mining. The government adopted programs to help the poor and tried to improve the economy, which had been damaged during the civil war of the 1970's.

The Sandinistas also spent a great deal of money on health and education. Before 1980, only about half the country's children went to school, and many rural areas had no schools at all. The Sandinista government built hundreds of rural schools and also established a successful literacy program, headed mainly by young volunteer teachers.

Under Ortega, however, the government also restricted civil rights, especially those of its political opponents. Press censorship was increased. Partially as a result of these measures, opposition to the Sandinistas developed in the early 1980's. In 1981, the United States charged that the Sandinistas were providing weapons to rebels in other countries and cut off all aid to Nicaragua. That same year, contras stepped up their attacks on Nicaragua from bases over the border in Honduras. Many contras were soldiers who had belonged to the National Guard under Anastasio Somoza Debayle, the president who was overthrown by the Sandinistas.

In response to contra attacks, the Nicaraguan government built up its military forces. In 1983, several thousand contras invaded northeastern Nicaragua, and fighting between government troops and contras began to take many lives.

Sandinista soldiers were everpresent in Nicaragua in the 1980's, even in the market places. The government built up its military forces to fight the contras.

A shantytown, *center,* shows the poverty of Nicaragua. The Sandinistas tried to mix socialism with private business, but economic problems plagued the nation during their rule.

Horse-drawn carriages provide the chief means of transportation for some people in Nicaragua. A widespread shortage of machinery and spare parts means that many Nicaraguans must make do without automobiles and other modern conveniences.

Coffee pickers in this mural display the blue identity cards of the Nicaraguan national militia. The coffee industry became a prime target for the contras in their war against the Sandinista government in the 1980's.

The Soviet Union, Cuba, and Western European nations aided the Nicaraguan government during the fight. The U.S. government under President Ronald Reagan gave financial aid to the contras. In 1983 and 1984, the United States also helped the contras place mines in Nicaraguan harbors. In 1985, Reagan ordered an embargo on trade with Nicaragua on the grounds that the government was a Communist dictatorship.

Some of the Indians in the Caribbean Region also helped the contras. The government moved these Indians from their homes near the border to the interior of the country.

The fighting continued until March 1988, when a cease-fire was negotiated. No peace agreement was ever reached, however, and a low level of fighting resumed. In February 1990, Daniel Ortega was defeated in a presidential election by Violeta Chamorro, and the Sandinistas lost control of the Nicaraguan government.

Economic recovery from the civil war in the 1970's was never completely achieved. The cost of war against the contras, the U.S. trade embargo, and the high government spending on health and education added to the country's economic problems. Life continues to be very difficult for many Nicaraguans.

Niger

Niger is a large, landlocked country in western Africa. It is an extremely poor country with few natural resources. Only 3 per cent of its land is used to grow crops, and years of drought have destroyed crops and livestock, forcing many of Niger's nomads into urban areas. About 11 million people live in Niger, and only about 14 per cent of them can read and write. "Tent schools" serve some of the nomad groups in the north—when a group moves, the school moves with it. Some areas have *Quranic* schools, which concentrate on the teachings of Islam. The government of Niger offers free public education, but many areas have no schools.

Government

Niger has only one political party, the National Movement of the Development Society. The country is governed by a Supreme Council made up of civilians and military officers and a National Assembly. To help the council run the government, the president of the council appoints a prime minister and heads of government agencies. Most of the people appointed are civilians. The president also names a *prefect,* or governor, to manage each of the nation's seven local regions, called *departments.*

History

During its history, Niger has been part of two great African empires. About A.D. 1000, Berber nomads called the Tuareg began moving south from the middle of the Sahara into what is now Niger. They eventually controlled the wealthy caravan routes that crossed the desert. By the 1400's, the Tuareg had created an empire around the city of Agadez.

The powerful Songhai Empire, based in neighboring Mali, conquered the Tuareg during the 1500's. Central and western Niger fell under Songhai control, but the empire collapsed under Moroccan invaders in 1591.

European explorers arrived in the Niger region in the early 1800's. France, which had gained control of most of Niger by 1900, overcame the fierce resistance of the Tuareg in 1906. Niger became part of French West Africa in 1922.

Niger won independence from France in 1960, and Hamani Diori—the leader of the Niger Progressive Party (*Parti Progressiste Nigérien,* or PPN) was elected Niger's first president. But in the late 1960's and early 1970's, a severe drought struck the country, causing food shortages and other problems.

In 1974, Diori was overthrown by a group of army officers led by Seyni Kountché.

Fact Box

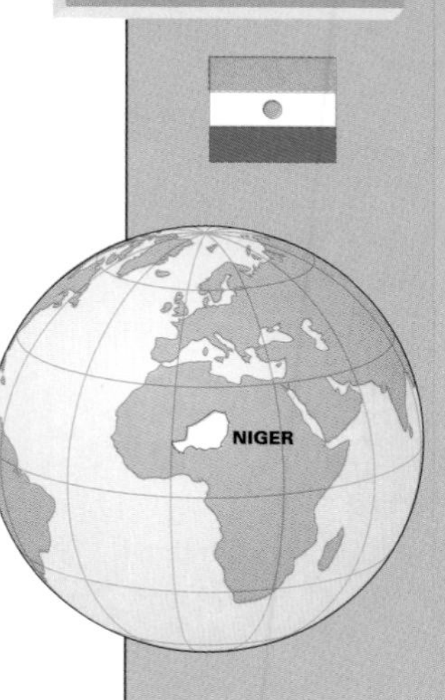

Country

Official name: Republique du Niger (Republic of Niger)
Capital: Niamey
Terrain: Predominately desert plains and sand dunes; flat to rolling plains in south; hills in north
Area: 489,191 sq. mi. (1,267,000 km²)
Climate: Desert; mostly hot, dry, dusty; tropical in extreme south
Main river: Niger
Highest elevation: Mont Greboun, 6,378 ft. (1,944 m)
Lowest elevation: Niger River, 656 ft. (200 m)

Government

Form of government: Republic
Head of state: President
Head of government: President
Administrative areas: 7 departements (departments), 1 capitale district (capital district)
Legislature: National Assembly with 83 members serving five-year terms
Court system: Cour d'Etat (State Court), Cour d'Appel (Court of Appeal)
Armed forces: 5,300 troops

People

Estimated 2002 population: 11,395,000
Population growth: 2.75%
Population density: 23 persons per sq. mi. (9 per km²)
Population distribution: 83% rural, 17% urban
Life expectancy in years: Male: 41, Female: 41
Doctors per 1,000 people: Less than 0.05
Percentage of age-appropriate population enrolled in the following educational levels: Primary: 31, Secondary: 7, Further: N/A

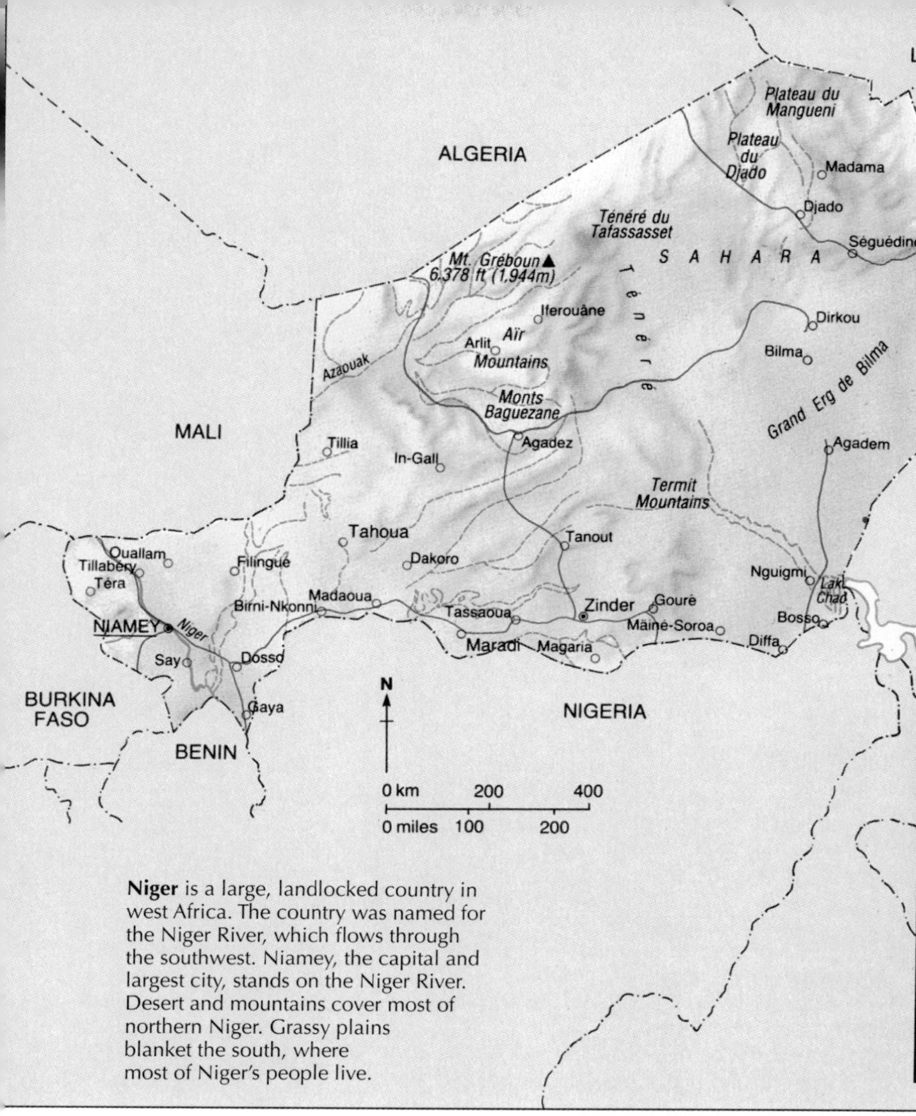

Niger is a large, landlocked country in west Africa. The country was named for the Niger River, which flows through the southwest. Niamey, the capital and largest city, stands on the Niger River. Desert and mountains cover most of northern Niger. Grassy plains blanket the south, where most of Niger's people live.

Tuareg nomads and their camel caravan, *below,* take shelter from an approaching sandstorm in the Sahara. The Tuareg established an empire in what is now Niger in the 1400's. Today's Tuareg live in the northern desert in the rainy season and move south in the dry months.

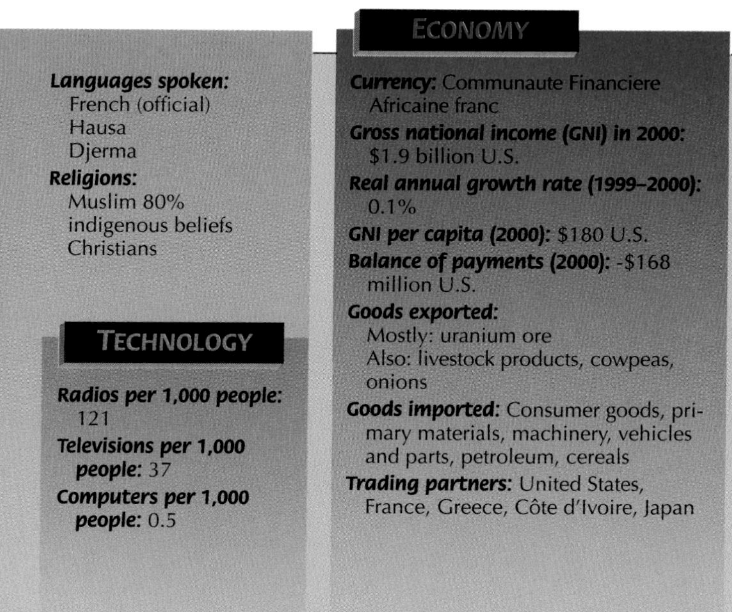

Languages spoken:
French (official)
Hausa
Djerma

Religions:
Muslim 80%
indigenous beliefs
Christians

Technology

Radios per 1,000 people: 121

Televisions per 1,000 people: 37

Computers per 1,000 people: 0.5

Economy

Currency: Communaute Financiere Africaine franc

Gross national income (GNI) in 2000: $1.9 billion U.S.

Real annual growth rate (1999–2000): 0.1%

GNI per capita (2000): $180 U.S.

Balance of payments (2000): -$168 million U.S.

Goods exported:
Mostly: uranium ore
Also: livestock products, cowpeas, onions

Goods imported: Consumer goods, primary materials, machinery, vehicles and parts, petroleum, cereals

Trading partners: United States, France, Greece, Côte d'Ivoire, Japan

Kountché outlawed the PPN, suspended the Constitution, and dissolved the national legislature. He then became president of the Supreme Council, which holds all power in the country. When Kountché died in 1987, the council chose Colonel Ali Saibou as president. However, the price of Niger's most important export—uranium—dropped, and Niger's economy continued to suffer. In September 1989, Niger adopted a new Constitution. In December 1989, Niger held a presidential election in which Saibou ran unopposed.

In 1992, Niger adopted a multiparty system. Mahamane Ousmane of the Alliance of the Forces of Change, a coalition of parties, was elected president in 1993. Ousmane was ousted in a coup d'état in January 1996. He was replaced by army officer Ibrahim Bare Mainassara. In April 1999, Mainassara was assassinated, and military leaders took control of the government. In November, Niger held elections to restore civilian rule.

Land and People

Niger is a large country. But the Sahara, with its sandy plateaus and central highland region called the Aïr Mountains, covers the northern two-thirds of the nation. A grassy, thinly wooded plain called a *savanna* stretches from the Niger River in the southwest to Lake Chad in the southeast.

The Niger savanna—home to such large animals as elephants, giraffes, and baboons—is one of the hottest places in the world, with average daily temperatures of 95° to 100° F. (35° to 38° C). Most of Niger's people also live on the savanna, where water and farmland are available. The area receives most of Niger's rain, and the seasonal floods of the Niger River provide water for irrigating crops.

About 98 per cent of the people of Niger are black Africans. Minority groups include the light-skinned Tuareg, whites from other countries, and Asians. Citizens of the country are called *Nigeriens.*

Even though almost all Nigeriens are black, they belong to different ethnic groups. About half the people are Hausa, who farm for a living, mainly in the south. They live in houses of sun-dried mud bricks in crowded villages and towns.

From 20 to 25 per cent of Nigeriens are Djerma-Songhai people, who farm along the Niger River in the southwest. About 5 per cent of the people are Kanuri, who farm the rich land in southeast Niger.

The farmers of Niger raise and sell cotton, livestock, and peanuts. They also raise camels, cattle, goats, and oxen for transport as well as food. Farmers also grow beans, cassava, millet, peas, rice, and sorghum as food crops. The basic foods of Nigeriens are grains and dairy products, and they enjoy dishes made with millet and sorghum, which are often cooked in a porridge and served with sauce.

Many Fulani, a fourth black ethnic group, are nomads like the Tuareg. They move across the desert with their herds of camels, cattle, goats, and sheep, searching for water and pasture. The nomads live mainly on milk products from their herds and trade these products with farmers for grains and vegetables.

Nigeriens "mine" salt at Bilma by pouring salty earth into pools of water. As the water evaporates in the desert heat, the salt rises to the surface. Niger's other mineral resources include iron ore, phosphate, tin, and uranium.

A camel caravan, *right,* crosses the bleak Saharan landscape in northern Niger. Such caravans once carried precious salt southward through the desert, where temperatures reach 122° F. (50° C).

A plane delivers disaster relief supplies to waiting Nigeriens. During the devastating drought of the late 1960's and early 1970's, many countries sent aid to Niger and other stricken countries in the African Sahel.

During the rainy season, the nomads travel through the northern desert, and during the dry season they move south. The Tuareg live in tents made of mats or animal skins. The Fulani have houses of straw and branches, so they must build new homes every time they move.

The savanna in Niger is part of a larger region called the Sahel. Since the late 1960's, severe droughts in the Sahel region have killed millions of livestock. As a result, many nomads have been forced to become farmers or move to urban areas.

Only about one-fifth of all Nigeriens live in cities or towns. Most urban workers have jobs with the government or other service industries, or in businesses. The government has built low-cost single-family homes for urban dwellers in the largest city, Niamey.

Niger's ethnic groups have long produced distinctive crafts, music, dance, and art. Craft workers make gold and silver jewelry, pottery, cloth, leatherwork, and woodcarvings.

Sahara

The expansion of the Sahara since the 1600's is dramatic—and continuing. Human populations along the edges of the desert are increasing, and the people cut down trees and shrubs for firewood and building material and allow their herds to overgraze. Removing the ground cover in this way robs the soil of its structure and fertility, allowing desert sands to take over. Some Sahel inhabitants can remember when grasslands covered areas that are now desert.

The Niger River gives Niger its name as well as valuable water to irrigate farmland. Some Nigeriens make a living by fishing in its waters. The Niger is the third longest river in Africa. Only the Nile and the Congo are longer, and only the Congo carries more water. The Niger River flows through Guinea, Mali, Benin, and Nigeria, in addition to Niger, before it empties into the Atlantic.

Most Nigerien women wear long wraparound skirts, topped with short blouses. The men wear pants or knee-length shorts with loose shirts or robes. The Fulani and Tuareg, however, wear long, loose robes to protect them from the desert sun. Tuareg men also wear turbans with veils over their faces as a shield against the blowing sand.

Because of Niger's colonial history, French is the official language of the country. But most Nigeriens speak the language of their ethnic group. Hausa is the language generally used in trade, and the Djerma-Songhai language is the second most widely spoken tongue.

Nigeria

The west African nation of Nigeria is a land of great variety in both its scenery and its people. Nigeria's landscape ranges from hot, rainy swamps and forests to dry, sandy reaches, grassy plains, and rocky mountains. More than 123 million people live in Nigeria, more than in any other African country, and they belong to more than 250 different ethnic groups.

Early history

Beginning about A.D. 1000, various kingdoms ruled different parts of what is now Nigeria, and the northern and southern regions developed independently of each other. The Kanem-Bornu kingdom, an Islamic trading kingdom, was centered in the northeast. The Hausa people developed a number of city-states in the region west of Bornu (now called Borno) that became important trade centers.

Throughout much of the 1500's, the Hausa city-states were under the control of the Songhai Empire, a powerful west African realm. The states later regained their independence and prospered during the 1600's and 1700's in the gold and slave trade.

Then in the early 1800's, local Fulani Muslims led by Usuman dan Fodio joined forces with Muslim Hausa rebels and overthrew the traditional leaders of the city-states. They formed a Hausa-Fulani empire that remained largely self-governing until the early 1900's.

Meanwhile in the south, the Yoruba people had established an important cultural center at Ife about A.D. 1000. Yorubas from Ife later moved into surrounding territories and founded other states. The kingdom of Benin developed in the area between Lagos and the Niger Delta and flourished as a prosperous trade center from the 1400's to the 1600's.

The Portuguese were the first Europeans to reach Nigeria. As early as the 1400's, they had established a trading post near Benin and developed a slave trade with African chiefs. The British, the Dutch, and other Europeans soon followed to compete with the Portuguese for control of the slave trade, and by the 1700's the British were the leading slave traders on the Nigerian coast.

Then in 1807, the United Kingdom not only outlawed the slave trade but began warring against slave ships of other nations and freeing their slaves. British traders then turned to dealing in palm oil and other Nigerian agricultural products. In 1851, the British seized the port of Lagos to increase their influence over the area, and in 1861 Lagos was named a British colony.

Parts of southern Nigeria became British protectorates late in the 1800's, and in 1900 most of northern Nigeria was also made into a protectorate. In 1906, these regions were combined into one large colony and protectorate. Nigerians resisted British rule, especially in the north, but they were unsuccessful. In 1914, the United Kingdom joined the northern and southern regions into one political unit called the Colony and Protectorate of Nigeria.

Ethnic conflict

Nigerians began demanding a say in their government during the 1920's, but the various ethnic groups also fought among themselves. In 1946, the United Kingdom divided Nigeria into three regions—each with an assembly made up of both Nigerian and British members that advised the central government in Lagos. In 1954, Nigeria became a federation of these three regions. Sir Abubakar Tafawa Balewa, a northerner, became the federation's first prime minister in 1957 and remained in that position when Nigeria gained full independence on Oct. 1, 1960.

Ethnic groups within the regions of the Nigerian federation continued to compete for power, while at the same time different groups fought for control of the federal government. Southern Nigerians, especially the Igbo people, resented the power of the Hausa in the north. Such ethnic rivalries would lead to assassinations, military revolts, and civil war in the years following independence.

Nigeria Today

Today, Nigeria has a civilian government, but many times in its history, Nigeria has had military rule. The current civilian government came into being when a new constitution was adopted in 1999.

The National Assembly is Nigeria's legislature. The Assembly consists of the 360-member House of Representatives and the 109-member Senate. Nigeria's people elect the representatives and senators to four-year terms. All Nigerian citizens who are 18 years of age or older may vote.

The previous military government was the result of one of the many military revolts that have taken place since Nigeria became independent. Much of the political turmoil in the country is due to differences between ethnic groups, especially between those in the south and those in the north.

Northerners controlled the new nation's federal government just after independence in 1960 because the north had more people than other regions. However, when censuses taken in 1962 and 1963 showed that the north had even more people than expected, people in the south protested that the censuses were not accurate, and some Nigerians also charged that a federal election in 1964 and a regional election in 1965 were dishonest. Violent riots followed.

In January 1966, a group of army officers—mainly Igbo people from the south—overthrew the federal and regional governments, and murdered Prime Minister Balewa and two regional officials. General Johnson Aguiyi-Ironsi, an Igbo army commander, then took control.

Aguiyi-Ironsi set up a strong central government and appointed many Igbo people as advisers, but riots broke out in the north, and thousands of Igbo were killed. Aguiyi-Ironsi's rule lasted only until July 1966, when he was assassinated by northern army officers.

Yakubu Gowon, the army chief of staff, then became head of the new military government. But the governor of Nigeria's Eastern Region, Colonel Odumegwu Ojukwu, refused to recognize Gowon as head of state. In 1967, when Gowon tried to divide the Eastern Region into three smaller states, Ojukwu declared the Eastern Region an independent republic named *Biafra*. A bloody civil war broke out and lasted for 2-1/2 years. In January 1970, Biafra surrendered.

The war caused widespread death and destruction in southeastern Nigeria. Gowon's government established relief programs to help the people.

A civilian government replaced military rule in 1979, but in 1983 military officers

FACT BOX

NIGERIA

COUNTRY

Official name: Federal Republic of Nigeria

Capital: Abuja

Terrain: Southern lowlands merge into central hills and plateaus; mountains in southeast, plains in north

Area: 356,669 sq. mi. (923,768 km²)

Climate: Varies; equatorial in south, tropical in center, arid in north

Main rivers: Niger, Benue

Highest elevation: Dimlang Peak, 6,699 ft. (2,042 m)

Lowest elevation: Atlantic Ocean, sea level

GOVERNMENT

Form of government: Republic transitioning from military to civilian rule

Head of state: President

Head of government: President

Administrative areas: 36 states, 1 territory

Legislature: National Assembly consisting of Senate with 109 members serving four-year terms and House of Representatives with 360 members serving four-year terms

Court system: Supreme Court, Federal Court of Appeal

Armed forces: 94,000 troops

PEOPLE

Estimated 2002 population: 128,886,000

Population growth: 2.67%

Population density: 361 persons per sq. mi. (140 per km²)

Population distribution: 64% rural, 36% urban

Life expectancy in years:
Male: 52
Female: 52

Doctors per 1,000 people: 0.2

Percentage of age-appropriate population enrolled in the following educational levels:
Primary: 98
Secondary: 33
Further: 4

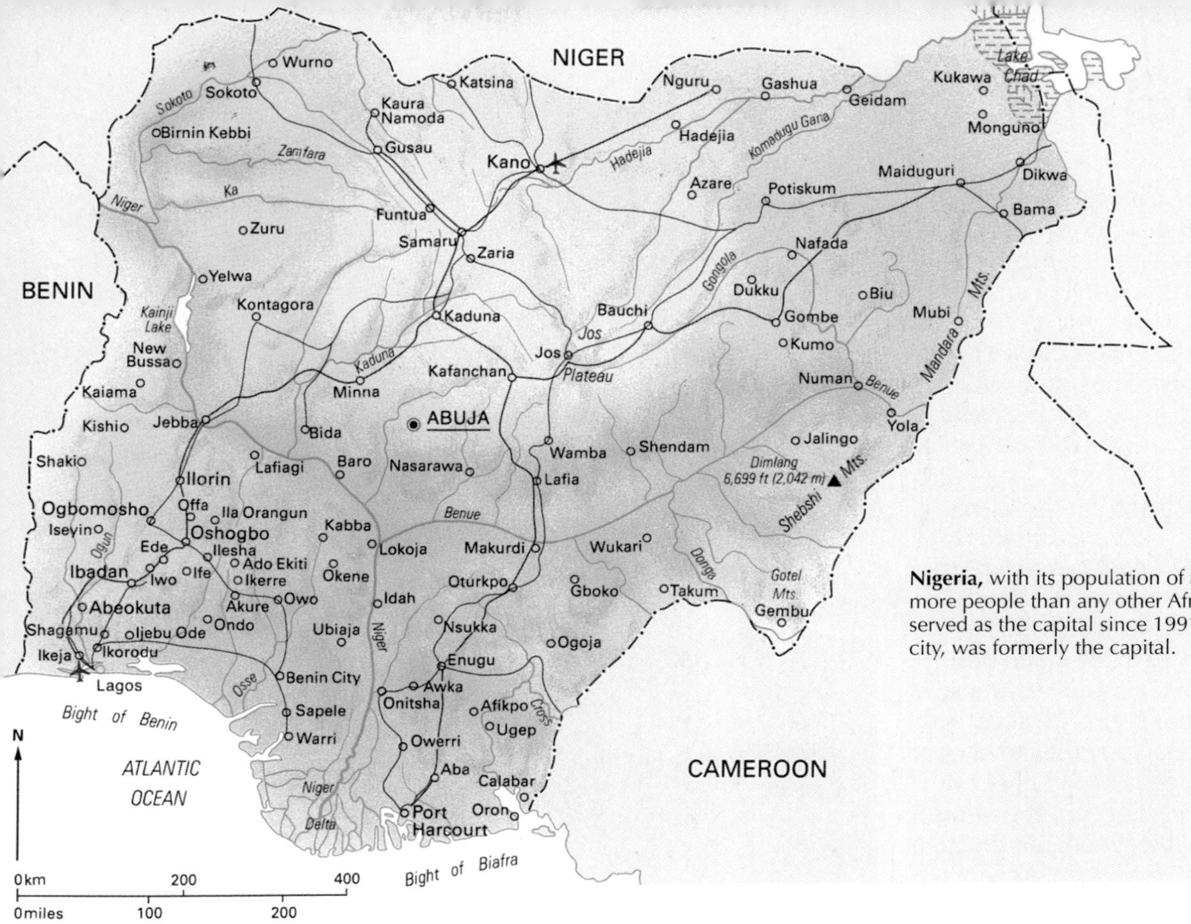

Nigeria, with its population of about 128 million, has more people than any other African nation. Abuja has served as the capital since 1991. Lagos, Nigeria's largest city, was formerly the capital.

overthrew the civilian government and placed Major General Mohammed Buhari in power. In 1985, Buhari in turn was overthrown by Major General Ibrahim Badamosi Babangida.

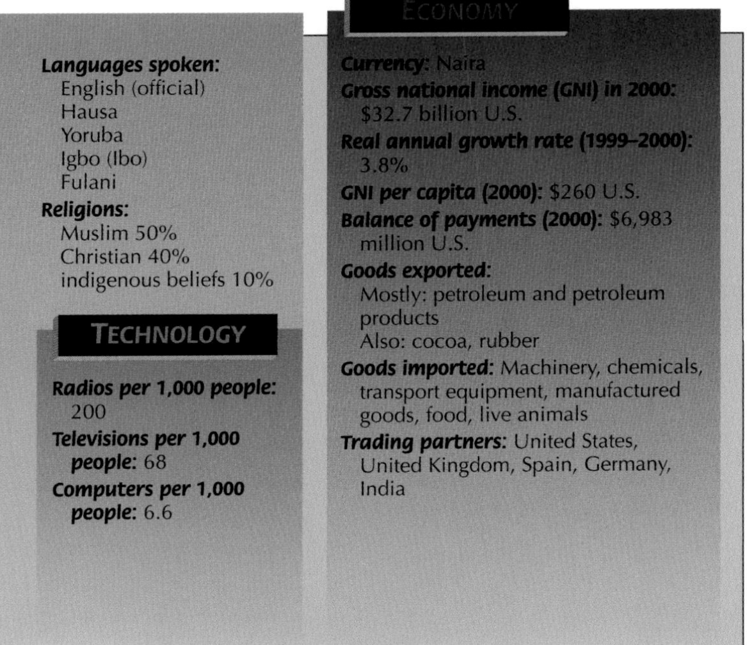

Languages spoken:
English (official)
Hausa
Yoruba
Igbo (Ibo)
Fulani

Religions:
Muslim 50%
Christian 40%
indigenous beliefs 10%

Technology

Radios per 1,000 people: 200
Televisions per 1,000 people: 68
Computers per 1,000 people: 6.6

Economy

Currency: Naira
Gross national income (GNI) in 2000: $32.7 billion U.S.
Real annual growth rate (1999–2000): 3.8%
GNI per capita (2000): $260 U.S.
Balance of payments (2000): $6,983 million U.S.
Goods exported:
Mostly: petroleum and petroleum products
Also: cocoa, rubber
Goods imported: Machinery, chemicals, transport equipment, manufactured goods, food, live animals
Trading partners: United States, United Kingdom, Spain, Germany, India

In 1992 elections for a new National Assembly, the Social Democrats won a majority in both legislative chambers.

However, in November 1992, Babangida announced that the change in government was being postponed from January 1993 to August 1993. In August 1993, Babangida resigned. His successor, Ernest Shonekan, was ousted in November by Defense Minister Sani Abacha, who proclaimed himself ruler. Abacha was challenged by Moshood Abiola, a millionaire businessman who had been the apparent winner of the June 1993 presidential elections, whose results Babangida had declared void.

In June 1994, Abiola declared himself the rightful head of the government. He was arrested and charged with treason. Unionized workers in the oil industry went on strike to demand political change but ended the strike in September without achieving that goal. The government suppressed human rights, censored the press, and removed several civilian and military officers from their posts. Abacha proclaimed that his regime had absolute power and that the courts had no jurisdiction over him. However, in 1999, civilian rule was restored, and a new constitution was adopted.

Land and Economy

The varied landscape of Nigeria forms ten different regions. In the far northwestern corner of the country lie the Sokoto Plains—an area of flat, low-lying land named for the Sokoto River. Along with several other rivers, the Sokoto floods the area in the rainy season. The floodwater deposits rich soil that allows Nigerians to farm the plains, but it can also destroy crops and homes.

In Nigeria's far northeast lies the Chad Basin, a region of short grasses and thinly scattered trees. Sandy ridges cross parts of the region, while other areas become swampy during the rainy season. Serious droughts can also occur in the Chad Basin.

The Northern High Plains cover almost 20 per cent of the country and lie about 2,500 feet (762 meters) above sea level. These vast, flat grasslands have only a few hills and granite ridges. Several rivers flow across the plains and create beautiful waterfalls as they tumble into deep gorges.

Within the Northern High Plains, near the center of Nigeria, lies the Jos Plateau. Cattle graze on the grasslands of the plateau, which rises more than 5,000 feet (1,500 meters) above sea level.

The Niger-Benue River Valley forms an arc through the center of Nigeria—the Niger River flows southeastward through the west-central section of the country to meet the Benue flowing from the east. The valley formed by the rivers has grasslands, forests of palms, and swamps, as well as rugged, rocky hills.

The Western Uplands are high grasslands dotted by granite hills. The Eastern Highlands consist of even higher plateaus and rocky hills and mountains.

The heavily forested Southwestern Plains slope down to the swamps and lagoons that line the coast of Nigeria. The Southeastern Lowlands are also covered with swamps and forested plains.

The Niger Delta, the southernmost region of the country, lies along the Gulf of Guinea. Where the Niger River flows into the sea, it deposits clay, mud, and sand. Lagoons, swamps, and mangrove trees cover the region, but the delta is also the site of an important natural resource that has helped change the country—petroleum.

Nigerian workers, *below,* stack sacks of peanuts ready for market. Nigeria is one of the world's major producers of peanuts.

A drilling platform sinks an oil well into the Niger Delta. Nigeria ranks as a leading exporter of petroleum, and oil accounts for more than 90 per cent of the total value of the country's exports.

The buildings of Lagos, *above,* reflect many architectural styles. The largest city, chief port, and commercial center of Nigeria, Lagos lies partly in the Southwestern Plains region and partly on four islands in the Gulf of Guinea.

A cattle herder tends his animals on the Jos Plateau in central Nigeria. In addition to the grasslands that provide pasture for dairy cattle, the plateau has important tin mines.

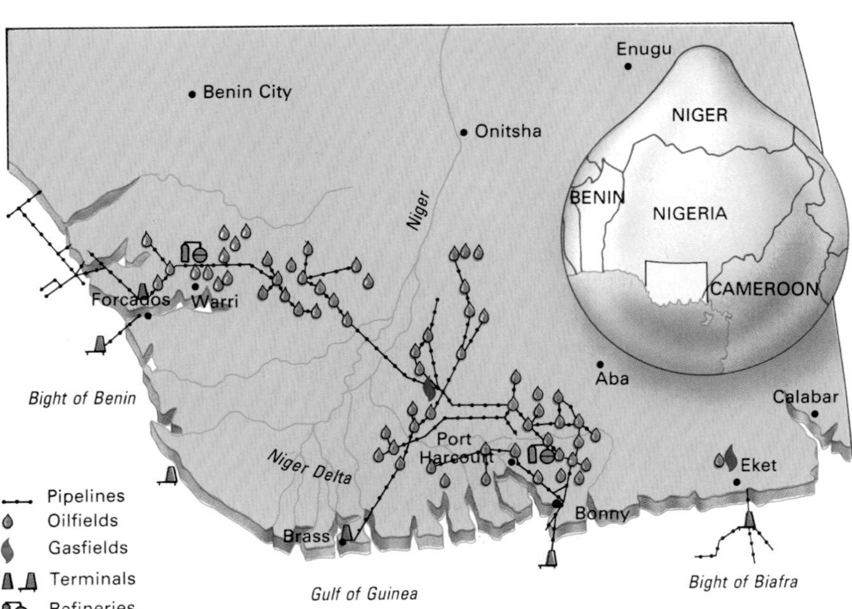

Most of Nigeria's oil and gas reserves lie beneath the Niger River delta and the Gulf of Guinea. Nigeria is a member of the Organization of Petroleum Exporting Countries (OPEC).

Nigeria is still a developing nation with an economy based largely on the land. Today, agriculture employs about two-thirds of all Nigerian workers but accounts for only about one-fifth of the country's economic production. In the 1960's, however, the oil industry began to be developed, and mining is now the fastest-growing part of the nation's economy.

Today, oil exports are the government's main source of income. Although foreign oil companies operate most of Nigeria's petroleum wells, they pay the government more than half their profits. The government has also established a national oil company to explore for and produce oil.

In addition to petroleum, Nigeria mines coal, gold, iron ore, lead, limestone, and zinc. The country also ranks as an important exporter of tin.

The government has used its new wealth to improve the nation's educational system, develop new industry, and modernize agriculture.

For example, farms in Nigeria average only about 2-1/2 acres (1 hectare), and traditionally most farmers have used old-fashioned equipment and methods. Today, the government sponsors programs to distribute new varieties of seeds, fertilizers, and insecticides.

Nigeria ranks among the world's leading producers of cacao, palm oil and palm kernels, peanuts, and rubber. Cotton is also grown. Important food crops include beans, cassava, corn, millet, rice, and yams. Nigerians raise livestock throughout the country, and coastal waters provide a bountiful catch of shrimp and other seafood.

Most businesses and industries in Nigeria are privately owned, but the government shares ownership of some enterprises. The country's factories produce a wide variety of goods, ranging from clothing and textiles to food products. Other Nigerian industries refine petroleum, process rubber, and produce steel.

People

With a population of more than 123 million, Nigeria has more people than any other country in Africa and ranks as one of the most populated nations in the world. And Nigeria's population is increasing by more than 2.5 per cent per year—a very high growth rate. In 1989, the government launched an educational program designed to limit family size.

Rural villages and crowded cities

About 85 per cent of Nigeria's people live in rural areas in homes made of grass, dried mud, or wood, with roofs of asbestos, metal, or thatch. Related families live in *compounds,* or clusters of these houses. A typical rural village consists of a group of such compounds.

Nigeria also has several large, crowded cities, including Lagos, Ibadan, and Ogbomosho. Well-to-do city dwellers live in modern houses or apartments, but many Nigerians live in squalid slums where mud

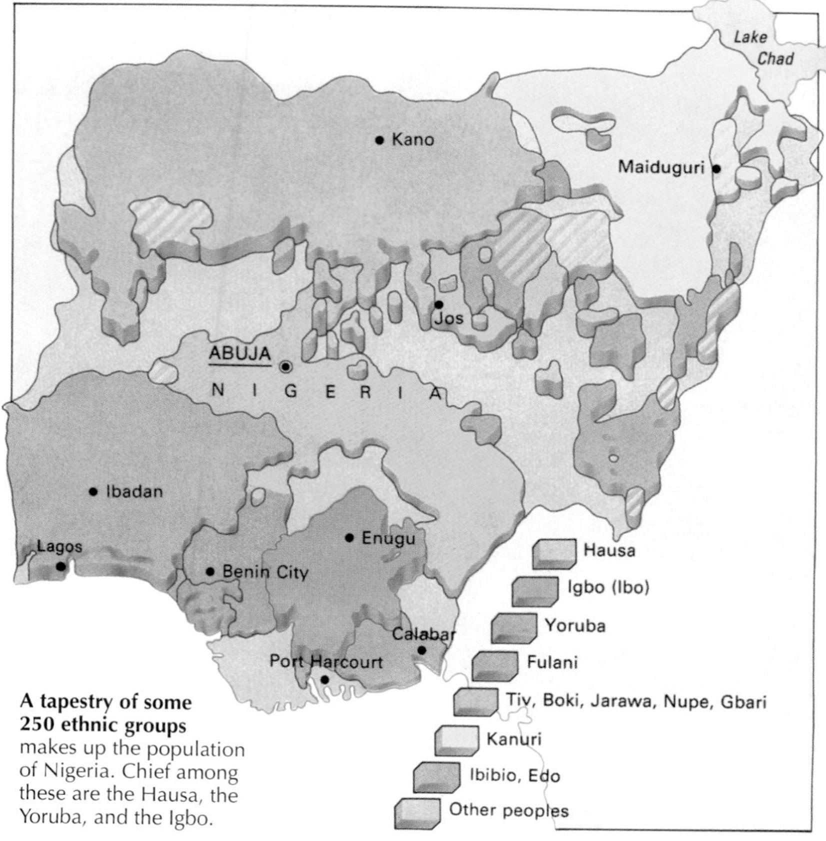

A tapestry of some 250 ethnic groups makes up the population of Nigeria. Chief among these are the Hausa, the Yoruba, and the Igbo.

A young herder of the Fulani ethnic group, *above,* wears a traditional head covering for protection against the hot sun.

At an outdoor market in Maiduguri in northeastern Nigeria, sleeping mats are offered for sale. This region is the homeland of the Kanuri, who trace their ancestry back to the ancient Muslim empire of Kanem.

Nigerian Muslims celebrate the end of Ramadan, the holy month of fasting in the Muslim year. About 50 per cent of Nigeria's people are Muslims, and they make up the majority of the population in the north.

Nigerian businessmen enjoy a game of golf, *below.* Like many city dwellers, who make up almost one-fifth of the population, they wear Western-style clothes.

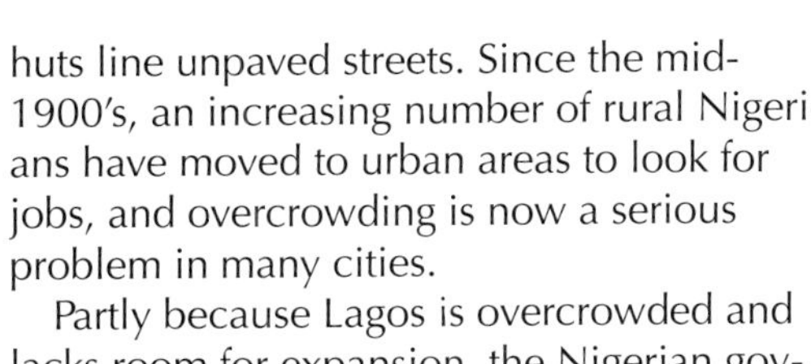

huts line unpaved streets. Since the mid-1900's, an increasing number of rural Nigerians have moved to urban areas to look for jobs, and overcrowding is now a serious problem in many cities.

Partly because Lagos is overcrowded and lacks room for expansion, the Nigerian government decided to move the country's capital to Abuja. Construction of the new capital was completed in 1992.

More than 250 ethnic groups

The people of Nigeria are as varied as its landscape. Although almost all Nigerians are black Africans, the nation's more than 250 ethnic groups speak different languages, and some follow different traditions.

The three largest groups are the Hausa, the Yoruba, and the Igbo. Together, these three groups account for about 70 per cent of the country's total population.

The Hausa people, who have inhabited the area for more than 1,000 years, live primarily in northern Nigeria. Most Hausa are farmers, but many also work as craftworkers or traders. The Hausa have become so intermixed with another group, the Fulani, that they are sometimes called the Hausa-Fulani.

The Yoruba live mainly in southwestern Nigeria. Many Yoruba people who live in cities go out to the surrounding countryside to farm the land.

The Igbo are the major ethnic group in southeastern Nigeria, but large numbers of Igbo have lived in other areas of the country since the time Nigeria was a British colony. The Igbo adopted Western ways more quickly than other Nigerian groups, and they were also more willing to travel away from their homes. For those reasons, the Igbo held important business and government positions under British rule.

Other leading ethnic groups include the Nupe and Tiv in central Nigeria; the Edo, Urhobo, and Itsekiri in the south-central section; the Ijo of the Niger Delta area; the Efik and Ibibio in the southeastern section; and the Kanuri of northeastern Nigeria.

The three most widely used languages in Nigeria are those of the largest ethnic groups—Hausa, Yoruba, and Igbo. Each ethnic group has its own distinct language and people use their ethnic language most of the time. However, many Nigerians also speak English, the nation's official language, which is taught in schools throughout the country. Nigerian Muslims use Arabic when taking part in religious activities.

Although most Nigerians are either Muslims or Christians, many Nigerians practice traditional African religions based on the worship of gods and spirits. Muslims make up the majority of the population in the north, and Christians live mainly in the south, but people throughout the country may combine Muslim or Christian religious practices with their traditional beliefs.

Most people in Nigeria wear traditional clothing, though some city dwellers wear Western-style dress. Traditional garments for men and women include long, loose robes made of white or brightly colored fabrics. Small, round caps are popular head coverings for men, while women often wear scarves or turbans.

Art and Culture

Nigeria is justly famous for the quality and variety of its art. Few people outside Africa knew anything about Nigerian art—or African art in general—until the 1900's, but it has since influenced artists throughout the world, including such masters as Spanish painter Pablo Picasso and British sculptor Henry Moore.

Magnificent sculpted heads show artistic styles typical of ancient Nigeria. A terra-cotta sculpture from the Nok civilization, *above*, has stylized facial features. The Ife people created more realistic carvings, *right*.

The Nok

The oldest known African sculptures are figures created about 500 B.C. by the Nok civilization of central Nigeria. The Nok people lived on the Jos Plateau, near the junction of the Niger and Benue rivers, until about A.D. 200.

Nok sculptured figures are admired for their high standards of production as well as for their artistic quality. The Nok sculptures are *terra-cotta* (clay) figures of animals and humans that range in size from 1 inch (2.5 centimeters) high to life size. The pieces that represent human heads have pierced ears and hollowed-out eyes.

The Nok art treasures were identified by British archaeologist Bernard Fagg, but scholars do not know what function the sculptures had in Nok society. Some experts believe that the sculpture of other west African peoples shows a definite Nok influence.

Ife

Little is known about life and culture in Nigeria during the 1,000-year period that followed the Nok civilization, but about A.D. 1000, villages in southern Nigeria began to merge and form city-states. One such community became the first of several great Yoruba kingdoms—Ife.

Historians believe Ife was the cradle of civilization of the Yoruba people. Superb terra-cotta and bronze sculptured heads were created in Ife in the 1200's. Although Ife never gained great military or political power, it was an important cultural center, and the kingdom had about 400 religious cults. The Yoruba worshiped many gods, including Oduduwa, believed to be the creator of the earth and ancestor of the Yoruba kings.

The Yoruba king of Ife, called the *oni*, was elected from a royal family. He supported his court by trading slaves and placing tolls on traded goods, such as the bronze used by Yoruba artists and other materials that were imported in large quantities from North Africa.

The Yoruba used the *lost-wax* process to make their splendid bronze statues. First, the sculptor made a wax model of the figure. The wax figure was then dipped in a kind of clay mixture and *fired* (baked until hard). As the figure hardened, the wax melted and drained out, leaving a hollow mold in the shape of the original figure. The Yoruba sculptor then poured liquid bronze into the mold to complete the process.

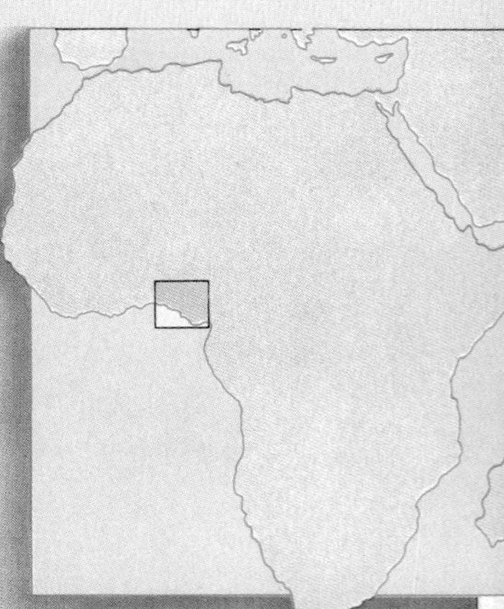

Nigeria's treasury of ancient art includes sculptures and carvings from the Nok culture and the Yoruba kingdom, which was centered in Ife. The Yoruba people later controlled Benin, which became a rich and powerful kingdom in the 1400's.

Benin

Over several hundred years, the Yoruba people spread out from Ife and founded or took over other territories. One such city-state, Benin, was already inhabited by Edo-speaking people when Ife took control of it. Benin eventually developed into the largest and most powerful state in the forest region of what is now Nigeria.

A Benin carving from the 1500's shows a struggle between two armed men, possibly Portuguese. By the time Benin became a flourishing kingdom, Europeans had arrived in Nigeria.

From the 1400's to the 1600's, the people of Benin produced sculptures that are now famous throughout the world. In addition to bronze, Benin sculptors worked with brass and ivory, fashioning exquisite ornaments and fine jewelry as well as figures, heads, and plaques.

Many of their works honored the king of Benin. This king, or *oba,* presided over a large court in his wooden palace, where he displayed his treasures of brass, bronze, and ivory works of art.

War with other states and revolts in states that Benin had conquered eventually led to decline. The ancient kingdom of Benin fell to the British in 1897.

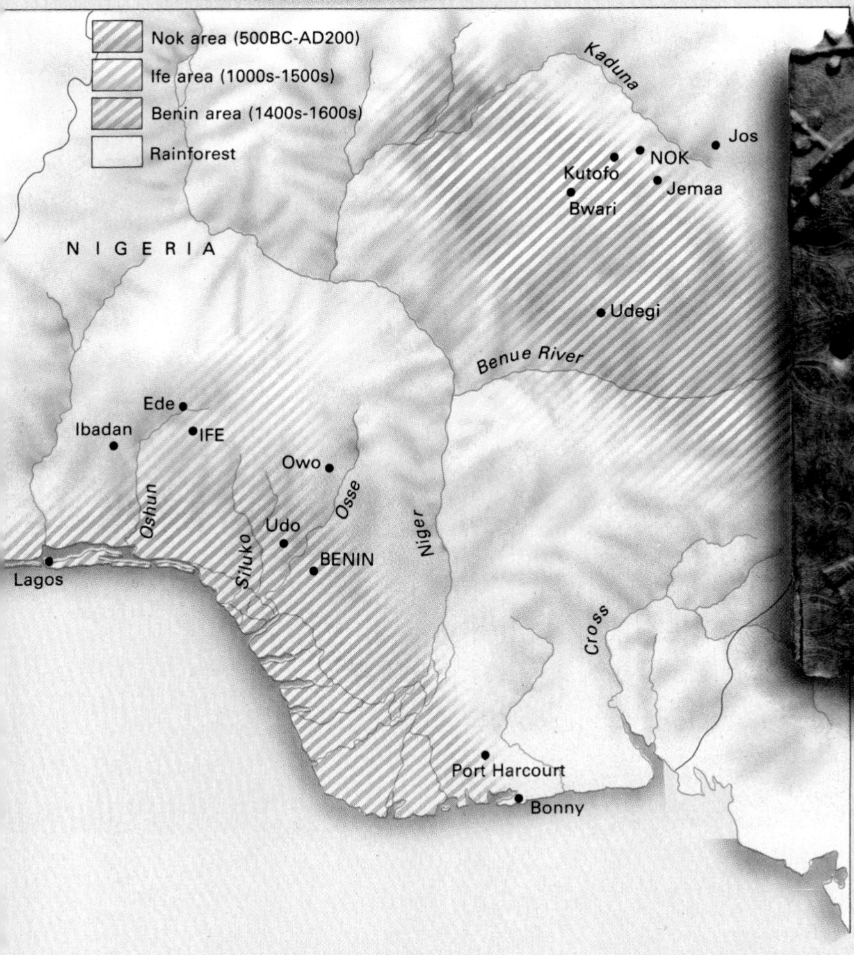

A bronze plaque, *below,* from the palace of the Benin *oba,* or king, depicts an acrobatic dance in honor of the god Ogun. Thousands of bronze plaques show scenes from life at the Benin court.

Nok area (500BC-AD200)
Ife area (1000s-1500s)
Benin area (1400s-1600s)
Rainforest
NIGERIA
Kaduna
Jos
NOK
Kutofo
Jemaa
Bwari
Udegi
Benue River
Ede
Ibadan
IFE
Owo
Oshun
Osse
Udo
Niger
Siluko
BENIN
Lagos
Cross
Port Harcourt
Bonny

Norway

Norway, also known as the *Land of the Midnight Sun,* is a long, narrow kingdom on the northwestern edge of the European continent. The country forms the western edge of the Scandinavian Peninsula and is bordered on the east by Sweden and in the far northeast by Finland and Russia. Norway's western shores lie along the North Atlantic Ocean.

Norway is noted for the hundreds of fiords that line its western coast. These narrow, steep-sided inlets, formed by ice and glaciers millions of years ago, make excellent harbors. Winds warmed by the sea keep these harbors free of ice all year long, even north of the Arctic Circle.

Most Norwegians live on or near the coast, partly because the inland regions are so much colder and partly because the country has relied on the sea for centuries. Since the time of the Vikings, the Norwegians have been a seafaring people. Norway began developing its shipping fleet during the 1600's and today the nation boasts one of the world's largest fishing and shipping industries.

The people of Norway have much in common with their Scandinavian neighbors, the Swedes and the Danes. Many are tall, with fair hair and blue eyes. Above the Arctic Circle, the Sami live in Lapland. Norway has a small population of slightly more than 4 million, and the Norwegian people enjoy a high standard of living.

Early settlements

People lived on the northern and western coasts of what is now Norway even before the Ice Age ended about 10,000 years ago, when most of the region was covered by thick sheets of ice. By 2000 B.C., the ice had melted, and Germanic tribes began to migrate to the region. They continued to arrive for hundreds of years after the time of Christ.

The tribes formed small communities led by local chiefs and kings, and in about 800 A.D., Viking sea raiders from these communities began a 300-year reign of terror on the northern seas. The Vikings attacked neighboring coastal regions, such as the British Isles, the Baltic states, northern France, and Ireland, sailing away with slaves and treasure.

About 900, much of present-day Norway was united under the country's first king, Harold I (Fairhair). However, full unification did not come until the early 1000's under King Olav II, who firmly established Christianity, which had been introduced to the Norwegian people by Olav I. Olav II was recognized as Norway's patron saint soon after his death in 1030.

In 1397, Queen Margaret, a Danish ruler, united Norway, Denmark, and Sweden in the Union of Kalmar. Norway remained under Danish rule until Sweden defeated Denmark in 1813 during the Napoleonic Wars. In the Treaty of Kiel, signed in 1814, Denmark gave Norway to Sweden.

The Norwegians did not recognize the Treaty of Kiel, and they elected an assembly to draw up a constitution for an independent Norway. However, Sweden refused to grant independence to Norway and attacked the country, quickly defeating it. The Norwegian parliament was then forced to accept Charles XIII of Sweden as ruler.

Independence from Sweden

Norway's merchant fleet was one of the largest in the world during the 1890's, but the Swedish foreign service handled Norway's shipping affairs in overseas trading centers. In May 1905, the Norwegian parliament passed a law creating its own foreign service, but the Swedish king vetoed it. On June 7, the Norwegian parliament ended the country's union with Sweden. In November, a Danish prince became King Haakon VII.

Norway remained neutral during World War I (1914–1918) and its economy expanded, but a postwar economic depression kept 25 to 30 per cent of all Norwegian workers unemployed. When World War II (1939–1945) broke out, Norway attempted to remain neutral once again, but German troops invaded the country in 1940 by attacking all its seaports at once. During this time, King Haakon VII fled to London and set up a government-in-exile.

After the Germans surrendered and the war ended, Norway rebuilt its fleets and industries with aid from the United States. By the 1950's, the Norwegian economy was thriving.

Norway Today

Norway is a constitutional monarchy, and the king or queen is held in great respect and affection by the people. However, Norway's monarch has limited political power, with the main duties of office including presiding over state occasions and appointing government officials on the advice of the Cabinet.

The government

The monarch also appoints the prime minister, who is usually the leader of the strongest party in parliament, as the head of the government. The prime minister appoints 17 members of the Cabinet—the Council of State—to act as ministers of the various government departments. Unlike the Cabinet system of Canada or the United Kingdom, a Cabinet member in Norway cannot also be a member of parliament. The *Storting* (parliament), Norway's lawmaking body, consists of 165 members elected to four-year terms.

A prosperous country with a relatively low unemployment rate, Norway has a well-developed economy, and its people enjoy a high standard of living. In 1994, Norwegians voted against joining the European Union (EU). Many voters felt Norway was strong enough economically to remain independent, and many opposed giving decision-making power to the EU's central organizations.

A shopkeeper at the local market in Bergen prepares a bouquet. Most Norwegians are descended from the Vikings, who settled the land about 1,000 years ago.

Almost all Norwegians can read and write, and the government provides the people with many welfare services. Because the population is considered too small, large families are encouraged by a yearly government allowance to each family for every youngster under the age of 16, beginning with the second child.

The National Insurance Act guarantees old-age pensions, job retraining, and aid for mothers, orphans, widows, widowers, and handicapped persons. All Norwegians are required to take part in this plan, which is paid for by the insured people, their employers, and the government.

About 25 per cent of Norway's people live in rural areas, and only six cities have populations over 50,000. Norwegian is the official language, with two forms—Bokmål and Nynorsk. Both forms are very similar to each other, and a person who speaks one form can easily understand the other. The two forms are gradually being combined into a single language called Samnorsk.

Way of life

Norwegians are outdoor sports enthusiasts, and recreation areas lie within short distances of all residential areas. Winter sports, such as skiing, ski-jumping, ice hockey, and

Fact Box

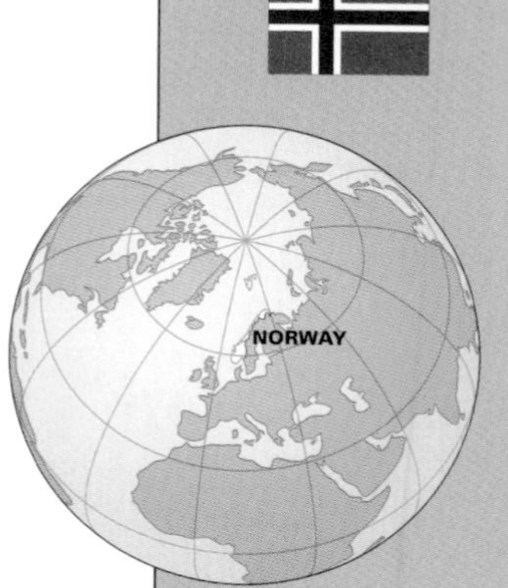

Country

Official name: Kongeriket Norge (Kingdom of Norway)
Capital: Oslo
Terrain: Glaciated; mostly high plateaus and rugged mountains broken by fertile valleys; small, scattered plains; coastline deeply indented by fjords; arctic tundra in north
Area: 125,182 sq. mi. (324,220 km²)
Climate: Temperate along coast, modified by North Atlantic Current; colder interior; rainy year around on west coast
Main rivers: Glåma, Lågen, Otra
Highest elevation: Galdhopiggeh, 8,100 ft. (2,469 m)
Lowest elevation: Norwegian Sea, sea level

Government

Form of government: Constitutional monarchy
Head of state: Monarch
Head of government: Prime minister
Administrative areas: 19 fylker (provinces)
Legislature: Storting (Parliament) with 165 members serving four-year terms
Court system: Hoyesterett (Supreme Court)
Armed forces: 31,000 troops

People

Estimated 2002 population: 4,505,000
Population growth: 0.5%
Population density: 30 persons per sq. mi. (12 per km²)
Population distribution: 74% urban, 26% rural
Life expectancy in years: Male: 76 Female: 82
Doctors per 1,000 people: 2.8
Percentage of age-appropriate population enrolled in the following educational levels: Primary: 102 Secondary: 121* Further: 65

Norway's parliament, called the *Storting,* has its headquarters in Oslo, the capital city, *above.* Oslo is also Norway's largest city and leading seaport.

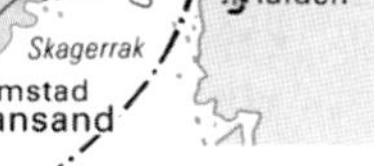

Norway is one of the northernmost countries of Europe. About one-third of its area lies north of the Arctic Circle and remains covered with a permanent layer of ice and snow. Hundreds of fiords along the coastline give Norway its distinctive shape.

Languages spoken:
- Norwegian (official)
- Sami
- Finnish

Religions:
- Evangelical Lutheran 86% (state church)
- other Protestant and Roman Catholic 3%
- none and unknown 10%

*Enrollment ratios compare the number of students enrolled to the population which, by age, should be enrolled. A ratio higher than 100 indicates that students older or younger than the typical age range are also enrolled.

TECHNOLOGY

Radios per 1,000 people: 915

Televisions per 1,000 people: 669

Computers per 1,000 people: 490.5

ECONOMY

Currency: Norwegian krone

Gross national income (GNI) in 2000: $155.1 billion U.S.

Real annual growth rate (1999–2000): 2.3%

GNI per capita (2000): $34,530 U.S.

Balance of payments (2000): $22,986 million U.S.

Goods exported: Petroleum and petroleum products, machinery and equipment, metals, chemicals, ships, fish

Goods imported: Machinery and equipment, chemicals, metals, foodstuffs

Trading partners: European Union, United States, Japan

ice skating, are very popular. Skiing, which may have started in Norway thousands of years ago as a means of traveling across snow-covered land, is the national sport. Summer sports include soccer, sailing, fishing, hiking, and swimming.

Norwegian law requires children from the ages of 7 to 16 to attend school. In addition, all Norwegian cities are required by law to have free public libraries.

A hardy, active people, the Norwegians usually eat four meals a day, and farm families eat five times a day. A typical breakfast includes cereal and open-faced sandwiches with cheese, jam, or marmalade, with goat cheese sandwiches being a particular favorite. Sandwiches are also served at lunch and at late-evening supper. Dinner is generally the only hot meal of the day and may include soup, meat or fish, potatoes, vegetables, and a dessert.

Environment

Norway owes much of its natural beauty to the North Atlantic Current, which is part of the Gulf Stream. Without the current's warming effect, Norway would have as little plant and animal life as Greenland, which lies at the same latitude. Sheep graze even in the country's northernmost regions, and the plentiful rainfall turns the landscape a vivid green in summer. Even as far north as the Lofoten Islands, 150 miles (240 kilometers) north of the Arctic Circle, January temperatures can be 45 Fahrenheit degrees (25 Celsius degrees) higher than the average for that latitude elsewhere.

The country does have barren and desolate areas, however—mostly in the inland regions within the Arctic Circle, where the warming effect of the North Atlantic Current is blocked by coastal mountains. The country's northern island territories—Svalbard, Jan Mayen Island, and Bear Island—are also barren, their mountainous landscapes carved by the glacier movements of the last Ice Age.

A peaceful scene in the Southeastern Lowlands, *below,* is typical of the landscape around Oslo, Norway's capital and largest city. This gently rolling landscape supports Norway's agricultural and forest industries.

Sunset bathes a fiord— one of the most distinctive features of the Norwegian landscape—in warm colors of pink and gold. The almost vertical sides of the fiord were carved by a mighty valley glacier during the last Ice Age.

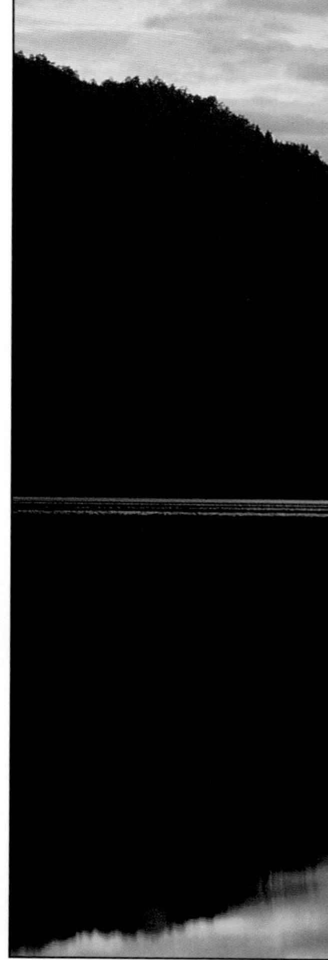

Mountains and lowlands

Norway has three main land regions: (1) the Mountainous Plateau, (2) the Southeastern Lowlands, and (3) the Trondheim Lowlands. Most of the country is a high, mountainous plateau covered largely by bare rock that has been smoothed and rounded by glaciers. The glaciers also formed many lakes and deep valleys throughout the countryside.

The jagged peaks of the Kjølen Mountains rise in the narrow northern part of Norway along the country's border with Sweden. In the southern part of the country, the Dovre Mountains extend in an east-west direction, while the Long Mountains rise to the south.

Norway's tallest mountain—Galdhøpiggen—lies in the Long Mountains, within the Jotunheimen range, also known as the *home of the giants*. The Hardanger Plateau, which slopes westward down the Long Mountains, is the largest highland plain in Europe. West of the Hardanger Plateau lies the 188-square-mile (487-square-kilometer) Jostedal Glacier—Europe's largest ice field outside Iceland.

Only about 20 per cent of Norway lies less than 500 feet (150 meters) above sea level. This area includes the Southeastern Lowlands and Trondheim Lowlands. The Southeastern Lowlands consist mostly of the middle and lower valleys of several rivers, including the Glåma. The Trondheim Lowlands—the lower ends of several wide, flat valleys—lie farther north, where the country grows narrower. These valleys make up one of the few areas of the country flat enough that railroad track may be laid there.

The warmest part of Norway during the summer, the lowlands are Norway's most densely populated area and have most of the country's few farming areas. Barley and potatoes are grown in the Trondheim Lowlands, and many dairy farms can be found in the region.

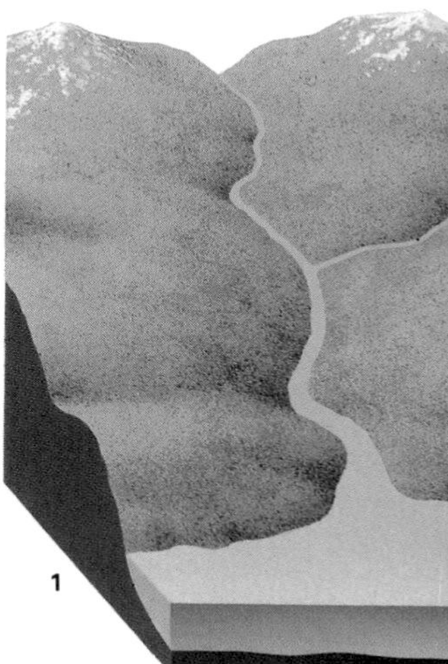

A church built during the 1100's nestles among the forested slopes of central Norway. Birch, pine, and spruce trees from this region provide timber for the country's lumber industry.

The white waters of the Stigfoss waterfall, *left,* crash down the steep sides of a valley. With its soaring mountains, icy glaciers, and spectacular waterfalls, Norway offers a wealth of dramatic scenery.

Geologists believe that the long, narrow, and winding inlets called *fiords* were formed by rivers flowing between the rugged slopes of Norway's mountainous plateau (1), and that the movement of the glaciers flowing in them carved the fiords during the Ice Age (2). After the Ice Age ended and the snow melted, the glaciers melted and the sea flowed into the ice-carved depressions (3). Most fiords have steep, rocky walls with thick woods and foaming, roaring waterfalls.

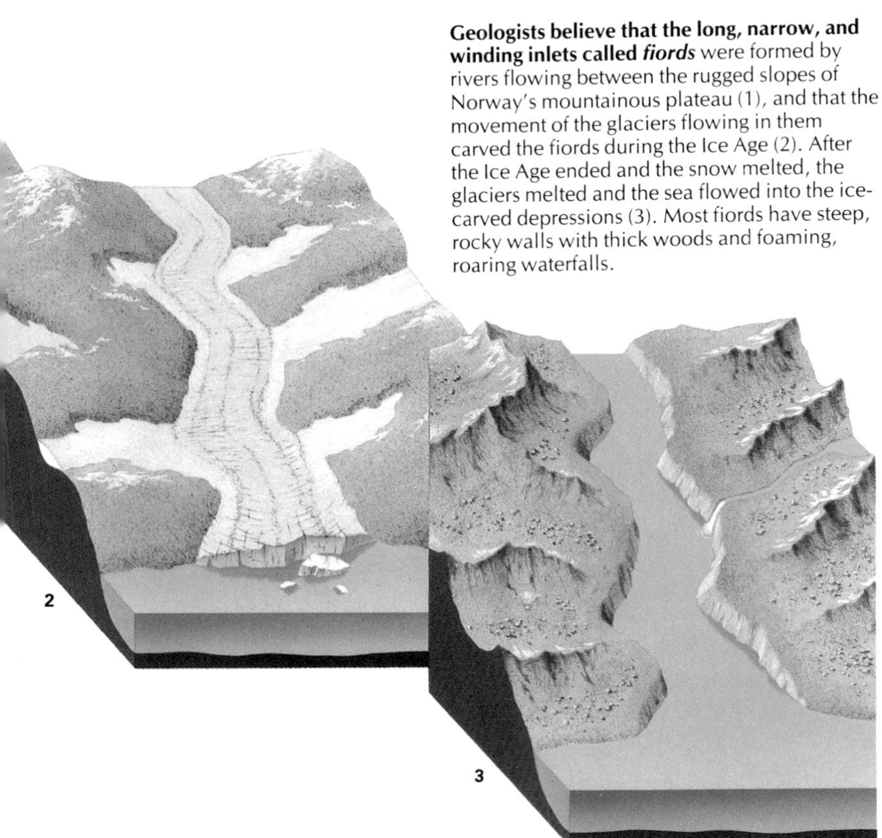

Coasts and islands

Norway has one of the world's most jagged coastlines. It is broken up by hundreds of fiords and peninsulas and fringed by about 150,000 islands and *skerries* (rocky reefs). Including all the fiords and peninsulas, the full length of the coast is about 13,267 miles (21,351 kilometers), which is about half the distance around the equator. Sogne Fiord, Norway's longest fiord, penetrates inland for 127 miles (204 kilometers).

The Lofoten and Vesterålen islands, situated off the northwestern coast, are Norway's largest offshore island groups, and the waters around them are filled with codfish. A swift and dangerous current known as the Maelstrom flows between two of the outer Lofoten Islands. A menace to sailors for hundreds of years, this current forms an immense whirlpool when the wind blows against it between high and low tide.

Economy

During the mid-1700's, industrialization began to spread throughout western Europe and the Northeastern United States. However, unlike Great Britain, Belgium, France, and other countries, Norway lacked coal to drive steam engines and make iron. Because Norway had to import its coal, manufacturing was very costly and growth was slow.

By 1900, however, the Norwegians had found a way to develop their own sources of inexpensive hydroelectricity to meet their power needs. In 1906, hydroelectric power enabled Norsk Hydro to become the first national company in the world to make nitrate fertilizers from atmospheric nitrogen. Soon, Norway's range of products greatly expanded, and the country began importing *bauxite* (aluminum ore) for the smelting of its aluminum.

Today, Norway is one of the wealthiest nations in the world in proportion to the number of people who live there. The country is one of the leading producers of aluminum and continues to import bauxite in order to refine it. In addition, petroleum and natural gas account for a large part of the national income. Government programs that promote investment and industry, as well as an increased demand for Norwegian goods and services, have helped fuel the rapid growth of Norway's economy.

The availability of cheap electricity has greatly benefited Norway's manufacturing industries. The nation's most important products include chemicals and chemical products, clothing, electrical machinery, furniture, petroleum products, processed foods, small ships, and such metals as aluminum and magnesium.

Mineral resources

Norway's oil and gas fields, which began to be worked in the 1970's, lie offshore in its territorial waters in the North Sea. Here, communities of workers live and work on immense rigs—often for months at a time.

During the mid-1980's, a drop in oil prices caused a temporary financial crisis for the oil industry, and, to a lesser extent, for the country as a whole. To solve the crisis, the oil companies reinvested oil revenues in other industries rather than oil. World oil prices rose again in the late 1980's.

Iron ore and *pyrite* (a compound of iron and sulfur) are also mined in Norway. Other minerals include ilmenite, lead, molybdenite, and zinc. Norway's only coal deposits lie in the northern island territory of Svalbard.

Fishing and forestry

The abundant stocks of fish in the waters of the North Sea and the Norwegian Sea have provided a livelihood for Norwegians for many centuries. The total catch of Norway's fishing fleet—which ranks among the largest and most efficient in the world—is about 2-3/4 million short tons (2.5 million metric tons) a year. Norwegian fishing crews bring in capelin, cod, haddock, herring, and mackerel.

The lumber industry has been an important part of Norway's economy for hundreds of years. The wood is used for building houses and making furniture throughout the country. Some timber is exported in the form of wood pulp and paper.

An oil-drilling rig awaits completion at the port of Stavanger in southwestern Norway, *right*. Along with other countries in northern Europe, Norway mines large amounts of mineral deposits beneath the North Sea.

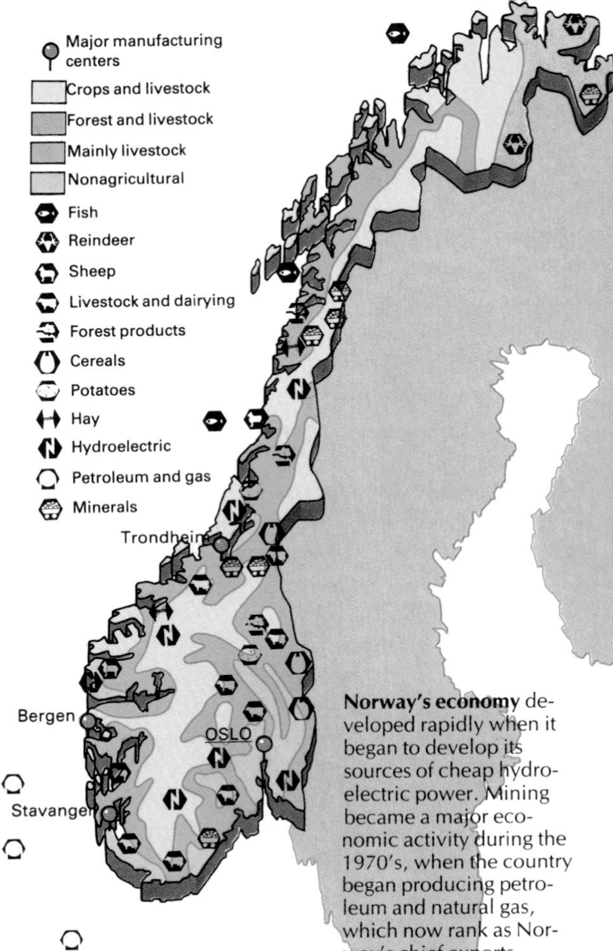

Norway's economy developed rapidly when it began to develop its sources of cheap hydroelectric power. Mining became a major economic activity during the 1970's, when the country began producing petroleum and natural gas, which now rank as Norway's chief exports.

Most crop production in Norway takes place on small strips of land in sheltered valleys or on flat land near the coast. About two-thirds of the farms cover 25 acres (10 hectares) or less, and most farms are used to grow livestock feed.

Factory ships process huge quantities of fish caught off the Norwegian coast. Since the 1960's, however, some kinds of fish, such as the cod found in the waters around the Lofoten Islands, have shown a reduction in numbers.

Norway once had a thriving whaling industry, but it declined sharply during the 1960's when large catches by Norway and other major whaling nations endangered many kinds of whales. In 1987, Norway joined an international *moratorium* (temporary halt) on commercial whaling.

Like its coastal waters, Norway's forests have also been a traditional source of income for its people. Timber has been an important export since the 1500's, and today much of it is used to produce wood pulp and paper. Government restrictions ensure that the cutting of timber never outstrips forest regrowth.

Although Norway has little suitable farmland, sizable crops of grains, potatoes, and vegetables, as well as hay and roots for livestock feed, are grown in the lowlands. During the 1980's, livestock production, especially sheep farming, increased in importance.

Norwegian Cities

Because Norway's mostly rugged, mountainous terrain has discouraged settlement in the more remote areas, most of the population is concentrated on or near the coasts. Many towns have grown up around fishing harbors, and only the cities of Bergen, Drammen, Kristiansand, Oslo, Stavanger, and Trondheim have more than 50,000 residents. Each town has a special charm all its own in this picturesque land where old Norwegian traditions mix with the sophisticated ways of modern life.

Oslo—old and new

In addition to being Norway's capital and largest city, Oslo is the nation's chief economic, industrial, and cultural center and one of its leading seaports. Situated on the southeast coast at the head of the great Oslo Fiord, the city has magnificent surroundings of hills, forests, and fiords.

Founded by King Harold Hårdråde about 1050, Oslo is a historic city. Fire destroyed the city in 1624, but the people rebuilt it northeast of Akershus Castle, which had been built on a rocky peninsula overlooking the fiord in 1299. Between 1624 and 1925, Oslo was called Christiana, in honor of King Christian IV of Denmark, which ruled Norway at the time.

By the mid-1800's, the city had grown into a major administrative, economic, and military center. Since then, the city has spread westward and eastward both inland and along the shores of the fiord. Today, with its shipping facilities, industry, and forest and agricultural resources, Oslo plays a major role in the nation's economy.

In spite of its growth and importance, Oslo is a clean and spacious city with an air of old-fashioned serenity. More than two-thirds of Oslo's metropolitan area consists of forests and lakes, and its people live in comfortable, modern apartment buildings. Attractive office buildings and modern stores stand next to carefully renovated historic buildings. Many parks and gardens add to the scenic beauty of the city.

Oslo's museums have carefully preserved many of Norway's most historic treasures, including many objects from the Viking period. Just outside the city, a museum at Bygdøy displays the ship used by Roald Amundsen as he sailed through the Northwest Passage between 1903 and 1906.

Reminders of the past also abound in Stavanger, in the extreme southwest region of Norway, where colorful wooden houses bring the past to vivid life. Today, however, Stavanger is more famous as the center of Norway's bustling oil industry. Many international corporations own large office blocks in the city, and much of Stavanger Fiord's landscape is dominated by drilling rigs.

Former capitals

Bergen, the second largest city in Norway, lies at the head of By Fiord and ranks as the chief seaport of western Norway. Seven mountains tower behind this busy port, which carries on a large trade in dried fish,

Bergen is Norway's second largest city and its chief seaport. The produce market lies on the north side of the harbor, along with many fine old stone warehouses.

The historic city of Oslo, *right,* is a leading seaport and manufacturing center. Major industries include shipbuilding and the production of chemicals, machinery, metals, paper, textiles, and wood products.

A magnificent bridge connecting the western part of the city of Tromsø with the mainland was built after World War II, when the previous one was destroyed. Tromsø, the largest town in northern Norway, lies on a small offshore island.

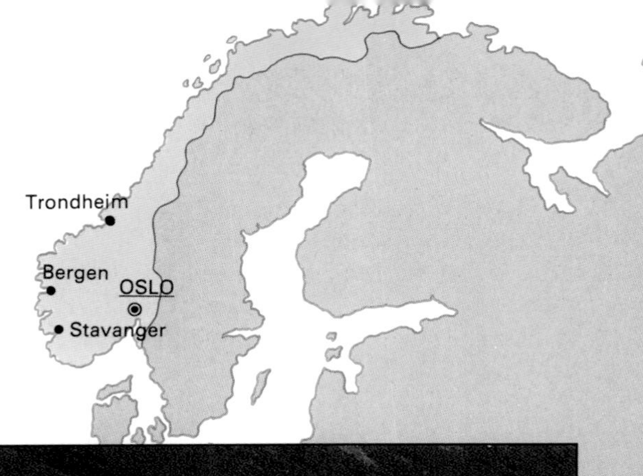

The busy commercial center of Stavanger is important to the economy of Norway because its strategic position on the southwest coast of Norway makes it an ideal base for Norwegian oil activities and interests in the North Sea.

Wooden warehouses perch on stilts above the water along the Nidelv River in Trondheim, Norway's third largest city. The city is surrounded by low hills, and the city center is almost entirely encircled by the Nidelv River.

herring, and machinery. The city was founded in 1070, and served as the capital until 1300.

From the 1300's to the 1500's, Bergen became a trading center of the Hanseatic League—a confederation of northern German cities. The old port area of Bryggen, as well as churches, the Bergenhus fortress, the old city hall, and the colorful flower and fish market, has been preserved from medieval times.

Farther north, but still only halfway up Norway's coastline, lies Trondheim, which also served as the capital during the Middle Ages. Its cathedral—built over the tomb of King Olav II during the mid-1100's to early 1300's—is the traditional site of Norway's coronations. The fortress of Kristiansten, dating from the 1600's, overlooks a medieval monastery on the island of Munkholm, which lies in Trondheim Fiord.

Svalbard

Lying in the Arctic Ocean about 700 miles (1,100 kilometers) from the North Pole, Svalbard is a group of islands that belong to Norway. The group consists of five large islands and many smaller ones. The main islands, in order of size, are Spitsbergen, North East Land, Edge Island, Barents Island, and Prince Charles Foreland.

Svalbard covers 23,958 square miles (62,050 square kilometers). It has a population of about 3,500. Mining companies, radio and weather stations, and a scientific research station provide jobs in Svalbard.

Svalbard's islands are the highest point of a submerged landmass that was once connected to Europe. The sharply folded rocks that make up their landscape date from more than 570 million years ago and include some of the oldest rocks in the world. On Spitsbergen, these rocks form rugged mountain chains. The sharp peaks rising from the icy ground led the Dutch explorer Willem Barents to name the island *Spitsbergen* (sharp mountains) when he arrived there in 1596.

Long before Barents landed on Spitsbergen, Svalbard was probably visited by Norse Vikings. Early Norwegian stories mention the island group, and in the Middle Ages, Norwegian kings claimed Svalbard.

Natural resources

During the 1600's, when many European nations began hunting whales, Dutch and English explorers reported that the Arctic waters were filled with whales. This news brought whalers to the Arctic from many countries, including Denmark, Great Britain, Germany, and the Netherlands. They found that bowhead whales were especially plentiful around Svalbard.

Svalbard thus became a major center of Arctic whaling, and Dutch and English whalers developed profitable whaling industries there. But by 1720, whalers had killed all the whales around Svalbard and moved on to other areas of the Arctic.

The Norwegians opened the first coal mines in Svalbard in the 1890's. Large-scale mining in Svalbard began in 1906, when John Munro Longyear, an American

A peaceful islet, *top*, along the western coast of Spitsbergen enjoys a summer day, while on Jan Mayen, a polar bear and cub pause in the snow.

European explorers first discovered Svalbard's coal deposits in 1610. Since then, deposits of phosphates, asbestos, and iron ore have also been found. Today, mining companies provide many jobs for Svalbard's 3,500 inhabitants.

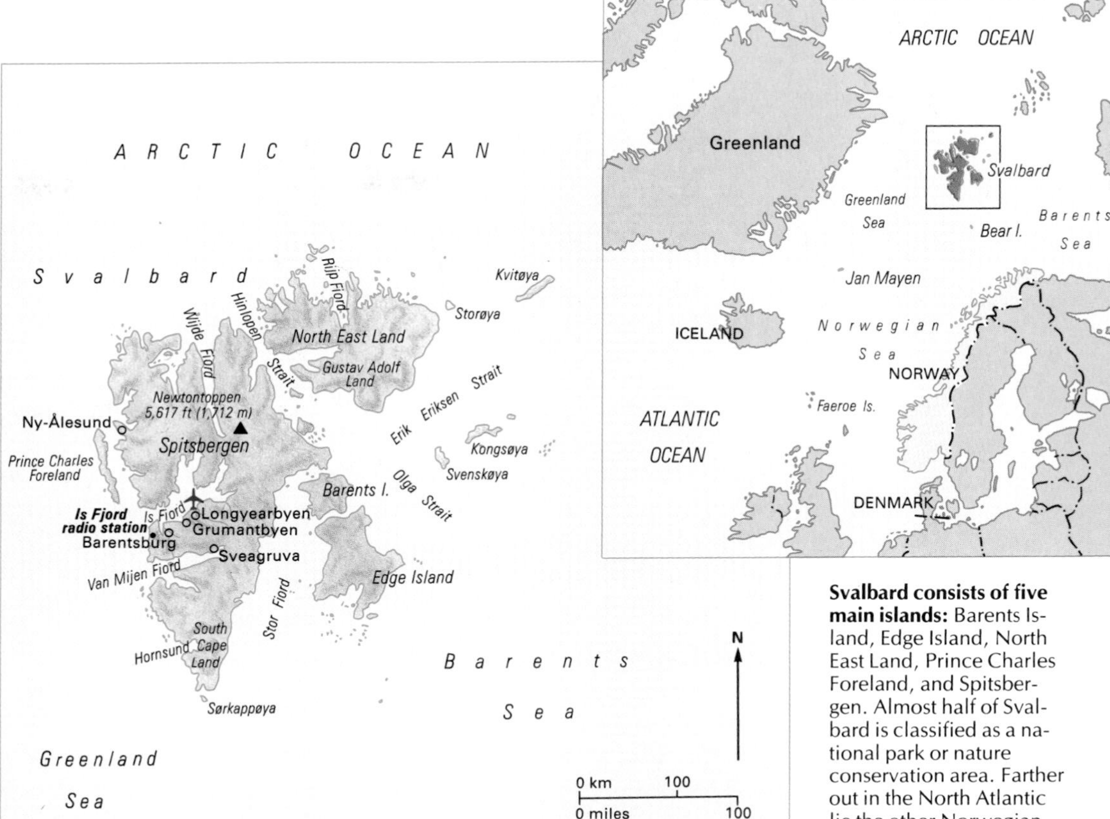

Svalbard consists of five main islands: Barents Island, Edge Island, North East Land, Prince Charles Foreland, and Spitsbergen. Almost half of Svalbard is classified as a national park or nature conservation area. Farther out in the North Atlantic lie the other Norwegian territories of Bear Island and Jan Mayen.

mining engineer, opened the first commercial mine. The growth of commercial mining led to a dispute over the ownership of the island group.

In 1920, the Svalbard Treaty officially recognized Norway's claim to Svalbard. The 38 other nations who signed the treaty have equal rights of access to Svalbard's natural resources.

Despite the area's harsh weather conditions, low taxes attract many people to Svalbard. About 750 of the 1,100 Norwegians who live in Svalbard work for the national mining company, and some 2,400 miners from former Soviet republics work in the Barentsburg and Pyramiden areas.

Svalbard's dramatic scenery and fascinating plant and animal life draw many visitors. The glistening, ice-covered landscape, pierced by deep blue fiords, has a tranquil beauty all its own. In spring, the tundra bursts into bloom, and millions of migratory birds return from the south to breed on the steep cliffs. Polar bears, arctic foxes, reindeer, northern fur seals, whales, and walruses add to the natural wonders of the Arctic landscape.

Bear Island and Jan Mayen

About midway between Svalbard and Norway, Bear Island, a Norwegian territory, occupies an area of about 69 square miles (179 square kilometers) in the Arctic Ocean. The cold, wet climate often cloaks the island in fog, and the staff of a Norwegian weather and radio station are its only inhabitants.

Between Greenland, Iceland, and Norway lies Jan Mayen, another island possession of Norway. Jan Mayen covers an area of 147 square miles (380 square kilometers). Discovered by the British explorer Henry Hudson in 1607, the island took its name from the Dutch captain Jan Jacobzoon May, who set up a whaling station there a few years later. Jan Mayen was formed by volcanic action and consists almost entirely of hard volcanic rock formations.

Oman

Oman is a small country on the southeastern corner of the Arabian Peninsula. It includes the tip of the mountainous Musandam Peninsula to the north, which is separated from the rest of Oman by the United Arab Emirates. From its position near the mouth of the Persian Gulf, Oman watches much of the world's oil pass on its way to nations around the globe.

Oman is one of the hottest countries in the world. Most Omani men wear white robes and turbans to protect themselves from the blazing sun. The women wear long, black outer dresses over colorful garments. Some wear black masks that cover most of the face, a practice common in Islamic countries. About 90 per cent of Omanis are Arabs, and almost all are Muslims. About 75 per cent follow Ibadi, a strict form of Islam.

The capital, Muscat, lies on the Gulf of Oman, just west of Matrah, the largest city. Many city people work for the oil industry or as government officials, laborers, merchants, or sailors, but nearly a third of Oman's people live in rural villages.

Al Batinah, a narrow coastal plain on the Gulf of Oman, is a fertile region where many Omanis work on date-palm plantations or fish for a living. Crews pull in large catches of fish from the gulf, especially sardines. Coastal villagers live in old wood and palm-thatched homes or in new concrete houses.

A rugged, steep mountain range called Al Hajar separates Al Batinah from Oman's vast, arid interior. The desert of Rub al Khali—the Empty Quarter—covers western Oman. In the interior, Omani villagers grow dates, fruits, and grain. These village farmers live in old mud and stone dwellings or new concrete houses.

Nomads also roam Oman's rural interior. They wander from place to place with their animals, living in tents and searching for food and water for their herds.

In a region called Dhofar in southwestern Oman, enough rain falls to allow tropical vegetation to grow. Farmers cultivate such fruits as bananas, coconuts, and limes, and many also raise cattle. Dhofar is famous for the frankincense trees that grow on a plateau just north of the Jabal al Qara, a mountain range that hugs the southwest coast.

Today, oil exports account for most of Oman's income. But Oman was an extremely poor country, with an economy based on farming and fishing, until 1964, when oil was discovered. Most Omanis still struggle to make a living, but oil money has been used to finance improvements.

The economy began to change in 1970 when Sultan Said bin Taimur, who was opposed to modernization, was overthrown

FACT BOX

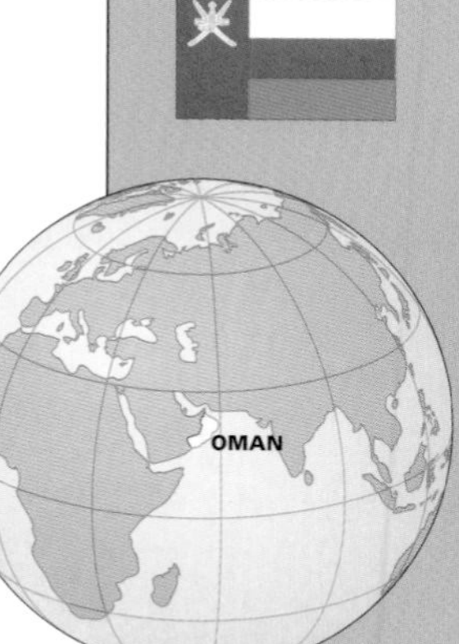

COUNTRY

Official name: Saltanat Uman (Sultanate of Oman)
Capital: Muscat
Terrain: Vast central desert plain, rugged mountains in north and south
Area: 82,031 sq. mi. (212,460 km²)
Climate: Dry desert; hot, humid along coast; hot, dry interior; strong southwest summer monsoon (May to September) in far south
Highest elevation: Jabal Shams, 9,957 ft. (3,035 m)
Lowest elevation: Arabian Sea, sea level

GOVERNMENT

Form of government: Monarchy
Head of state: Sultan and Prime Minister
Head of government: Sultan and Prime Minister
Administrative areas: 6 mintaqat (regions), 2 muhafazat (governorates)
Legislature: Majlis Oman consisting of the Majlis ad-Dawla (upper chamber) with 41 members and the Majlis ash-Shura (lower chamber) with 82 members
Court system: Supreme Court with non-Islamic judges; traditional Islamic judges and civil court system administered regionally
Armed forces: 43,500 troops

PEOPLE

Estimated 2002 population: 2,711,000
Population growth: 3.46%
Population density: 33 persons per sq. mi. (13 per km²)
Population distribution: 72% urban, 28% rural
Life expectancy in years:
Male: 70
Female: 74
Doctors per 1,000 people: 1.3
Percentage of age-appropriate population enrolled in the following educational levels:
Primary: 75
Secondary: 67
Further: N/A

A rural village in the dry, barren interior of Oman, *below,* is a cluster of flat-roofed mud and stone houses. Standing near many of these villages are the ruins of large stone fortresses dating from the Middle Ages. Arabs have lived in this region for thousands of years.

Oman, *right,* lies in an important position at the outlet of the Persian Gulf. The Gulf of Oman and the Arabian Sea border eastern Oman, providing the country with access to the ocean. Oman's northern tip lies on the strategic Strait of Hormuz—through which much of the world's oil is shipped.

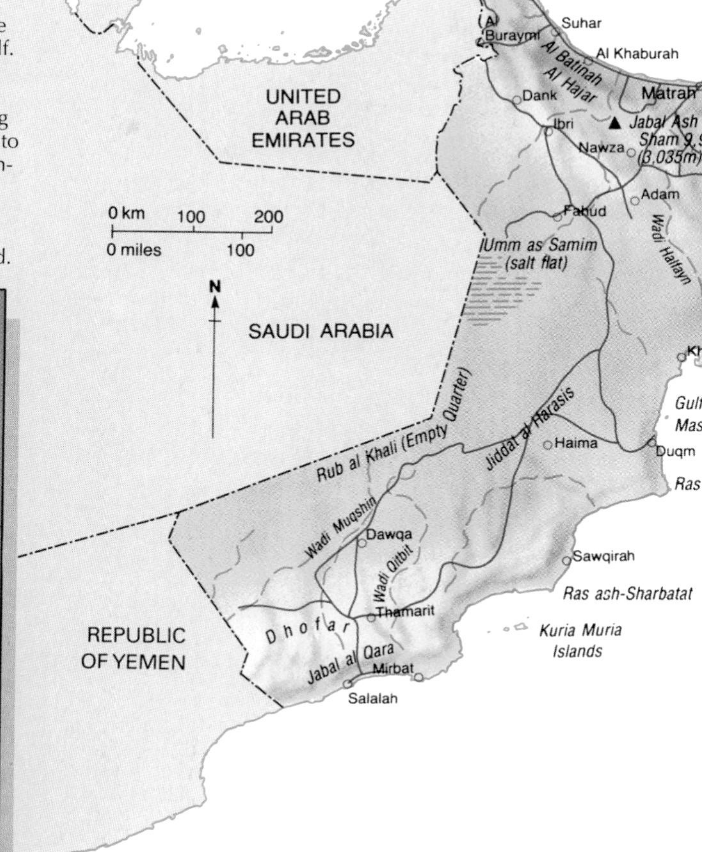

Languages spoken:
- Arabic (official)
- English
- Baluchi
- Urdu
- Indian dialects

Religions:
- Ibadhi Muslim 75%
- Sunni Muslim
- Shiah Muslim
- Hindu

Technology

Radios per 1,000 people: 621

Televisions per 1,000 people: 563

Computers per 1,000 people: 31.5

Economy

Currency: Omani rial

Gross domestic product (GDP) in 2001: $21.5 billion U.S.

Real annual growth rate (2001): 7.4%

GDP per capita (2001): $8,200 U.S.

Balance of payments (2000): $3,347 million U.S.

Goods exported: Petroleum, reexports, fish, metals, textiles

Goods imported: Machinery and transport equipment, manufactured goods, food, livestock, lubricants

Trading partners: Japan, United Arab Emirates, China, Thailand, United Kingdom

An Omani woman displays traditional Omani dress—a colorful inner robe covered with a long, black outer dress. In this strict Islamic society, many women also wear black veils.

by his son, Qaboos bin Said. As the new sultan, Qaboos developed the oil industry. With the oil income, he built roads, hospitals, and schools. He also helped farmers by promoting irrigation techniques and other modern methods. Omanis traditionally get their water from wells, some of which are fed by underground canals that were built in ancient times.

Sultan Qaboos is a member of the Al Bu Said family, which has ruled Oman since the 1740's. Since 1798, Oman and Great Britain have kept close ties. The British helped Qaboos's father put down a religious rebellion in 1959.

As ruler of Oman, the sultan appoints a 25-member cabinet to carry out the government's operations. Some of these cabinet members are princes of the sultan's royal family. A 55-member Consultative Assembly, also appointed by the sultan, advises him. Oman has no constitution, and political parties are not allowed.

The Pacific Islands

The Pacific Islands, or Oceania, is a group of about 20,000 to 30,000 islands scattered across the Pacific Ocean. Some islands cover thousands of square miles, while others are no more than tiny piles of rock or sand that barely rise above the water. Some Pacific Islands, particularly New Guinea and New Zealand, are also considered part of Australasia.

Not considered as among the Pacific Islands group are some islands near the mainlands of Asia, North America, and South America. For example, the islands that make up the nations of Indonesia, Japan, and the Philippines are considered part of Asia, and the Aleutians and the Galapagos are grouped with North America and South America, respectively. Australia, too, is outside the group because it is a continent.

Together, the Pacific Islands have an area of under 490,000 square miles (1,254,000 square kilometers)—less than the state of Alaska. New Guinea and the two main islands of New Zealand make up more than four-fifths of the total land area. About 12 million people live in the Pacific Islands. Only a few islands or island groups have large populations, while many have fewer than a hundred people and many others have none at all.

The Pacific Islands can be divided into three main areas: Melanesia, Micronesia, and Polynesia. These divisions are based on the geography of the islands and on the culture and ethnic background of the native peoples.

Melanesia is one of the three main areas in the Pacific Islands. Its name means *black islands* and is derived from the word *melanin*—a blackish or brownish pigment in the skin. The Melanesian people have large amounts of melanin in their skin, which makes their skin very dark. Melanesia includes New Guinea, the Solomon Islands, New Caledonia, and Vanuatu. Fiji is considered part of Melanesia because of its location, but its culture is much more like that of Polynesia. All the islands of Melanesia lie south of the equator.

Micronesia, whose name means *tiny islands,* is the second main area of the Pacific Islands. These islands lie north of Melanesia, and most of them also lie north of the equator. More than 2,000 islands make up Micronesia, mainly low-lying coral islands. Micronesia includes Nauru, Guam, the Caroline Islands, Mariana Islands, Marshall Islands, and Gilbert Islands.

Polynesia, whose name means *many islands,* is the third main area. Because of the long distances between its island groups, it covers the largest region in the South Pacific, from above the Tropic of Cancer to below the Tropic of Capricorn. Polynesia stretches 5,000 miles (8,000 kilometers) from Midway Island in the north to

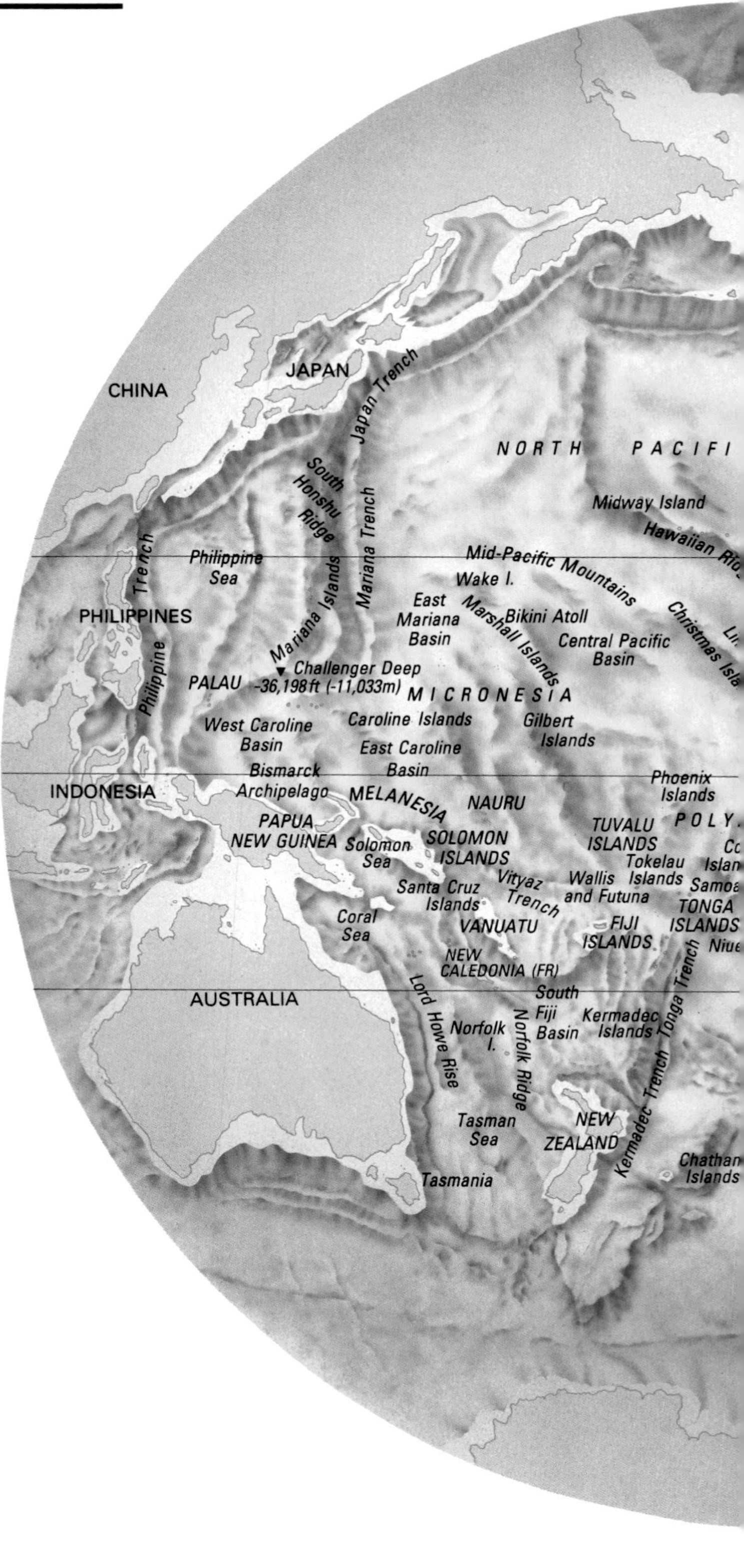

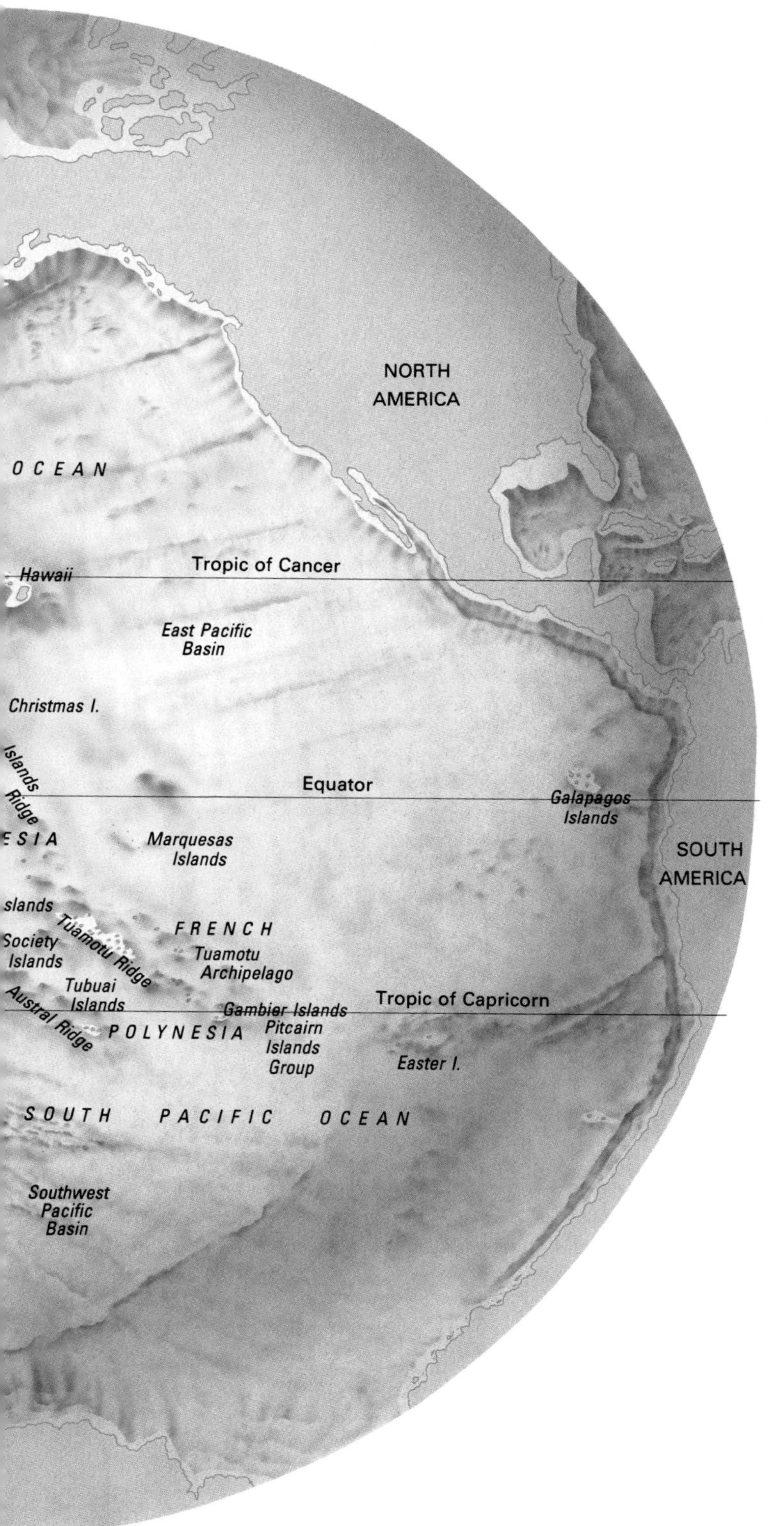

New Zealand in the south. The easternmost island in Polynesia, Easter Island, lies more than 4,000 miles (6,400 kilometers) east of New Zealand. Other members of this group include the Marquesas Islands, Society Islands, Cook Islands, Samoa, Tuvalu, Tonga, American Samoa, and the Hawaiian Islands, which, forming one of the United States, are distinct from the rest of the Pacific Islands.

Land and climate

The land and climate vary greatly among the Pacific Islands. Many of the islands, especially those in Polynesia, are noted for their sparkling white beaches, gentle ocean breezes, and swaying palm trees. Other islands, especially in Melanesia, have thick jungles and tall mountain peaks. Many lowland areas in these islands are extremely hot and humid, but snow covers the tallest mountain peaks throughout the year.

Economy

On most Pacific Islands, the people earn little or no money. Some islanders may earn a small income by selling coconuts, bananas, or sugar cane to export companies, but most live in villages, raise their own food, build their own houses, and make their own clothing. The people of New Zealand and Nauru are the exceptions because these islands have well-developed economies. New Zealand has thriving agricultural and manufacturing industries, and Nauru receives most of its income from mining operations.

The Pacific Islands have few mineral resources, except for valuable deposits of nickel on the island of New Caledonia, and copper, gold, and oil on New Guinea. New Caledonia also has some chromium and iron, and Fiji has small deposits of gold and manganese. Nauru has deposits of *phosphates,* chemical compounds used to make fertilizer.

Agriculture is the main industry of the Pacific Islands, and *copra* (the dried meat of coconut) is the most important agricultural product. Factories crush copra to produce coconut oil, which is used to make such products as margarine and soap. Many countries import coconut oil or copra from the Pacific Islands.

The tourist industry in the area has grown tremendously since the beginning of jet air travel in the 1950's. As growing numbers of tourists visit the islands, more airports, hotels, highways, shops, and restaurants have to be built. The Cook Islands, Fiji, and Tahiti encourage tourism and are working to construct these facilities, but some islanders fear that further growth of the tourist industry will destroy the natural charm and traditional ways of the Pacific.

People and History

Some scientists divide the people of the Pacific Islands into three races—Melanesian, Micronesian, and Polynesian. The Melanesians are the smallest in stature among the peoples of the Pacific and have the darkest skin. Micronesians are somewhat taller, with somewhat lighter skin than the Melanesians. Polynesians are the tallest of the Pacific peoples and have the lightest skin. Over the years, migrations between the islands and intermarriage between islanders and Europeans and Asians have produced islanders with mixed features. Nevertheless, racial differences are still apparent among people in the three major areas of the Pacific Islands.

The first settlers in the Pacific Islands probably came from Southeast Asia thousands of years ago. They sailed to the islands on rafts or dugout canoes and followed land bridges whenever possible. Over many centuries, people settled on the main islands of Melanesia and Micronesia. The main islands of Polynesia were settled later. With large expanses of ocean separating the islands, people in distant island groups had little or no contact.

Beginning in the early 1500's, European explorers began to visit the Pacific Islands. The most famous Pacific explorer of the 1700's was Captain James Cook of the British Royal Navy. His discoveries encouraged Protestants and Roman Catholics to establish missions throughout the area, and many island peoples who today are Christians are descendants of those converted during the 1800's. Many missionaries introduced genuine improvements to the islands, but others concentrated largely on doing away with native customs and traditions.

Traders searching for coconut oil, sandalwood, and other products came to the islands. Whaling vessels also stopped there. New settlers included many criminals and drifters, and lawlessness became a problem. Diseases brought by Europeans killed many islanders.

By the 1800's, France, Germany, Great Britain, Spain, and the United States were competing for control of the Pacific Islands, and each acquired several islands or island groups. After Spain's defeat in the Spanish-American War of 1898, Germany and the United States took over the Spanish possessions in Micronesia. By the early 1900's, Germany also held parts of Nauru, New Guinea, and Samoa. After Germany's defeat in World War I (1914–1918), control of its Pacific Islands was transferred to Japan, New Zealand, and Australia. Through all these changes of rule, the islanders had little or no voice in their government.

Japan increased its power in the Pacific after World War I. Finally, in December 1941, Japanese bombers attacked the U.S. naval base at Pearl Harbor, Hawaii, and opened the Pacific theater of World War II

The catamaran, a raftlike boat with two hulls, carried the people of the Pacific Islands on voyages between island groups. In 1774, Captain Cook mapped the region in Melanesia that he named the New Hebrides. The islands are now called Vanuatu.

The settlement of the Pacific Islands occurred thousands of years ago. The first inhabitants came from Asia and moved from island to island by raft and dugout canoe, using land bridges where possible. Melanesia and Micronesia, two of the three main cultural areas of the Pacific Islands, were settled first. Polynesia, the third cultural area, was settled last. A Polynesian people, the Maoris, arrived in New Zealand during the A.D. 900's. Europeans began exploring the Pacific Islands in the 1500's, following Magellan's voyage across the Pacific. By the late 1800's, France, Germany, Great Britain, Spain, and the United States were competing for control of the Pacific Islands. Japan increased its power in the Pacific after World War I. Since World War II, many island groups have gained their independence.

(1939–1945). By mid-1942, Japanese troops had captured islands as far east as the Gilberts and as far south as the Solomons. The United States then began to drive the Japanese off these islands. In September 1945, Japan surrendered, losing its huge Pacific empire.

After World War II, the United Nations decided that four areas in the Pacific should be governed as trust territories until they were ready for independence. Since 1962, several Pacific islands or island groups have become independent, and others have been working toward this goal.

Most Pacific islanders still live in small farming or fishing villages, and many live in the same kinds of houses, eat the same kinds of food, and wear the same kinds of clothing as their ancestors did. But these traditional ways of life are changing rapidly as an increasing number of people adopt Western customs and clothing. Many islanders have now left their villages to work in the area's few towns and cities. In these rapidly growing urban areas, houses look much like houses in Western countries, and many people wear Western-style clothing.

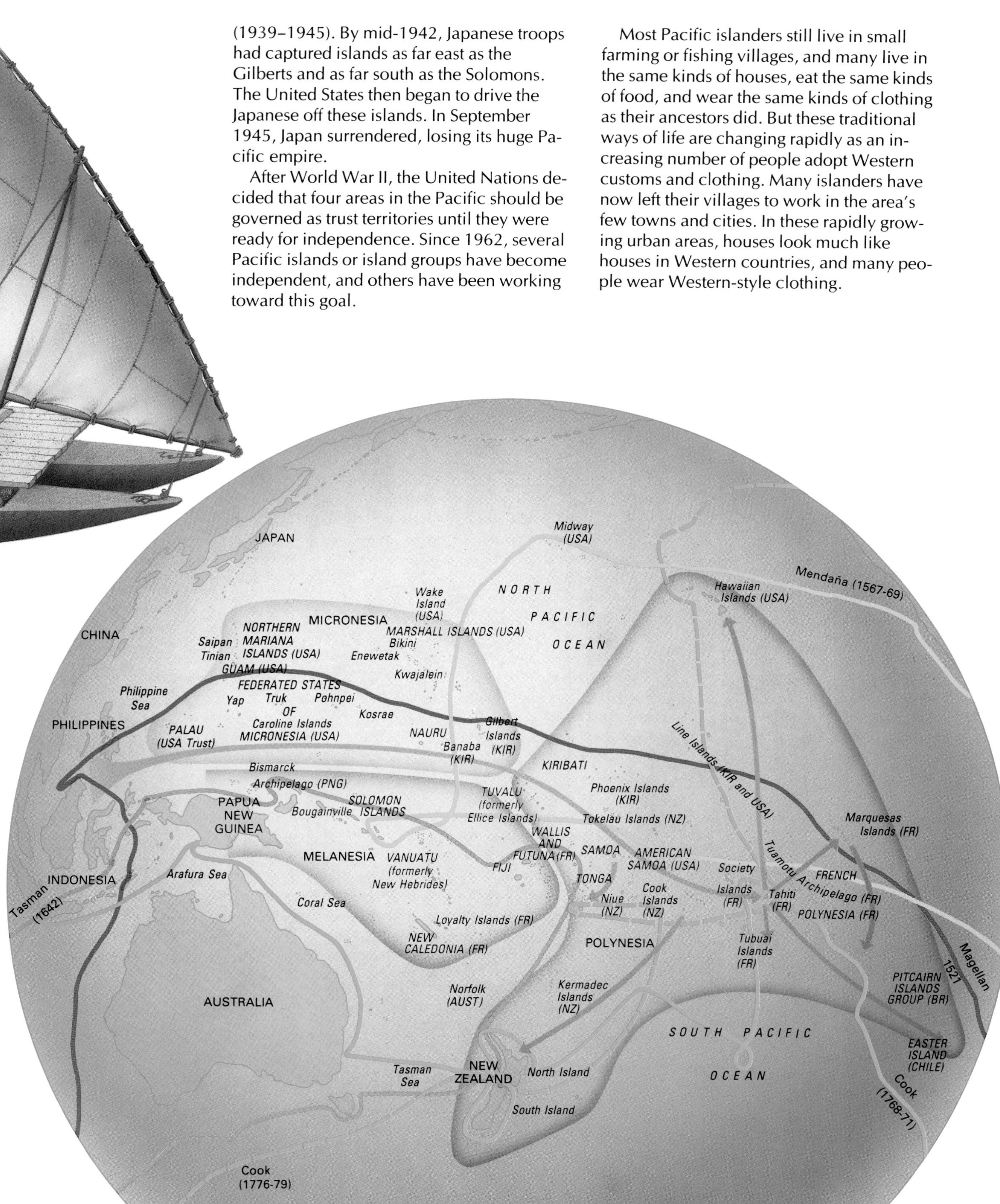

Pakistan

Pakistan is a Muslim nation in South Asia. It is bordered on the west by Iran and Afghanistan, on the north by China, and on the east by India. Its southern coast lies along the Arabian Sea. Pakistan is a land of soaring mountains, high plateaus, fertile plains, and hot, barren deserts. The Indus is Pakistan's major river.

The history of the region that is now Pakistan can be traced back about 4,500 years. However, it was not until 1947 that Pakistan became an independent nation. Since then, Pakistan has gone through many political and geographical changes. Numerous different cultural groups live in Pakistan, each with its own customs and language. These cultural differences have made it difficult for Pakistan to become a strong, unified nation.

Early history

The Indus River Valley in Pakistan is known as one of the cradles of civilization because of the important civilization that developed there about 2500 B.C. Ruins of that great culture's two cities, Harappa and Mohenjo-Daro, still survive today. These ruins show that it was a large, well-planned civilization. For unknown reasons, the Indus Valley civilization disappeared about 1700 B.C.

Throughout the following centuries, the Indus Valley was conquered by many different peoples. It was once part of the Achaemenid (Persian) Empire. Later, Alexander the Great conquered the region.

After the rise and fall of the Maurya Empire about 230 B.C., the Greeks ruled the Indus region. They were conquered by the Scythians from Afghanistan, who were replaced by the Parthians. The Kushan Empire succeeded the Parthians, and during the A.D. 300's, the region became part of the Gupta Empire. The Huns ruled the Indus in the mid-400's.

The coming of Islam

In 711, Arab Muslims sailed across the Arabian Sea, bringing the religion of Islam to the region. About 300 years later, Turkish Muslims established a Muslim kingdom in the Indus Valley. Later, the Delhi Sultanate, a Muslim empire, took over until Babar, a Muslim ruler from Afghanistan, established the Mogul Empire in 1526.

Beginning in the 1500's, the British East India Company, which already had a firm trading foothold in India, became even stronger in the region. Eventually, the company gained political power over much of India. When the British government took over the country in 1858, the region came to be known as *British India*.

An independent nation

In 1947, Britain gave in to the demands of the Indian people for independence. The country was divided into two separate nations according to its major religious groups. India was designated the Hindu state. The new state of Pakistan was made up of the two territories inhabited by Muslims—East Pakistan and West Pakistan. These territories were over 1,000 miles (1,600 kilometers) apart.

West Pakistan was made up of a mixture of the provinces of Sind, Baluchistan, the North-West Frontier, parts of Punjab, and a number of small principalities. The people of East Pakistan were mainly Bengalis. In contrast to their taller, lighter-skinned neighbors to the west, the Bengalis were dark-skinned people who spoke a different language.

Although the people of East Pakistan and West Pakistan shared the religion of Islam, important cultural differences, as well as a great distance, separated them. In 1971, civil war erupted between East and West Pakistan. On March 26, 1971, East Pakistan declared itself an independent nation called Bangladesh.

Pakistan Today

Since becoming an independent nation in 1947, Pakistan has been troubled by geographical disputes and political instability. Civil war has damaged its economy. The cultural differences between its many ethnic groups make it difficult to unite the people in solving the country's problems.

Civil war

On March 26, 1971, the civil war between East and West Pakistan intensified when East Pakistan declared itself the independent nation of Bangladesh. India joined Bangladesh in its fight against West Pakistan in December 1971. Only two weeks after India entered the war, Pakistan surrendered.

The war caused severe damage to Pakistan in many ways. Yahya Khan, the president who had tried to keep East and West Pakistan together, resigned. Pakistan lost about a seventh of its area and more than half its people. In addition, the nation's economy was badly disrupted.

Government

Zulfikar Ali Bhutto succeeded Yahya Khan as president of Pakistan. Under Bhutto's leadership, Pakistan adopted a new Constitution in 1973.

The Constitution established Islamic socialism as the nation's guiding principle and retained the structure of a federal republic. It provided for a parliamentary form of government, with a president serving as head of state. A prime minister is chief executive and leader of the majority party.

Each of Pakistan's four provinces consists of a variety of cultural groups. The Punjab in the northeast has the largest population. As a result, the Punjabis have controlled the government, economy, and armed forces of Pakistan through much of the nation's history.

Recent developments

When Pakistan adopted its new Constitution in 1973, Bhutto became prime minister and Chaudhri Fazal Elahi became president.

In 1977, when parliamentary elections resulted in a victory for Bhutto's party, the Pakistan People's Party (PPP), many people accused the party of election fraud. Violence once again broke out in Pakistan. Military officers led by General Mohammed Zia-ul-Haq removed Bhutto from office. Zia then suspended the Constitution and declared martial law. In 1978, Zia declared himself president after Elahi resigned. Bhutto was executed in 1979.

In August 1988, Zia was killed in an airplane crash. In November 1988, parliamentary elections were held. Benazir Bhutto, head of the PPP and daughter of Zulfikar Ali

Fact Box

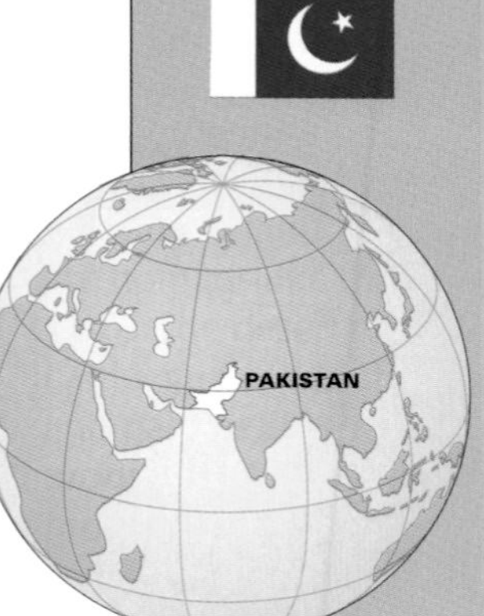

Country

Official name: Islamic Republic of Pakistan
Capital: Islamabad
Terrain: Flat Indus plain in east; mountains in north and northwest; Balochistan plateau in west
Area: 307,374 sq. mi. (796,095 km²)
Climate: Mostly hot, dry desert; temperate in northwest; arctic in north
Main rivers: Indus, Jhelum, Chenab
Highest elevation: K2 (Mt. Godwin-Austen), 28,250 ft. (8,611 m)
Lowest elevation: Indian Ocean, sea level

Government

Form of government: Federal republic
Head of state: President
Head of government: Chief executive
Administrative areas: 4 provinces, 1 territory, 1 capital territory
Legislature: Parliament was dissolved following a military takeover in October 1999
Court system: Supreme Court, Federal Islamic (Sharīa) Court
Armed forces: 587,000 troops

People

Estimated 2002 population: 144,135,000
Population growth: 2.17%
Population density: 469 persons per sq. mi. (181 per km²)
Population distribution: 67% rural, 33% urban
Life expectancy in years: Male: 60, Female: 62
Doctors per 1,000 people: 0.6
Percentage of age-appropriate population enrolled in the following educational levels: Primary: 86, Secondary: 37, Further: N/A
Languages spoken: Punjabi 48%, Sindhi 12%

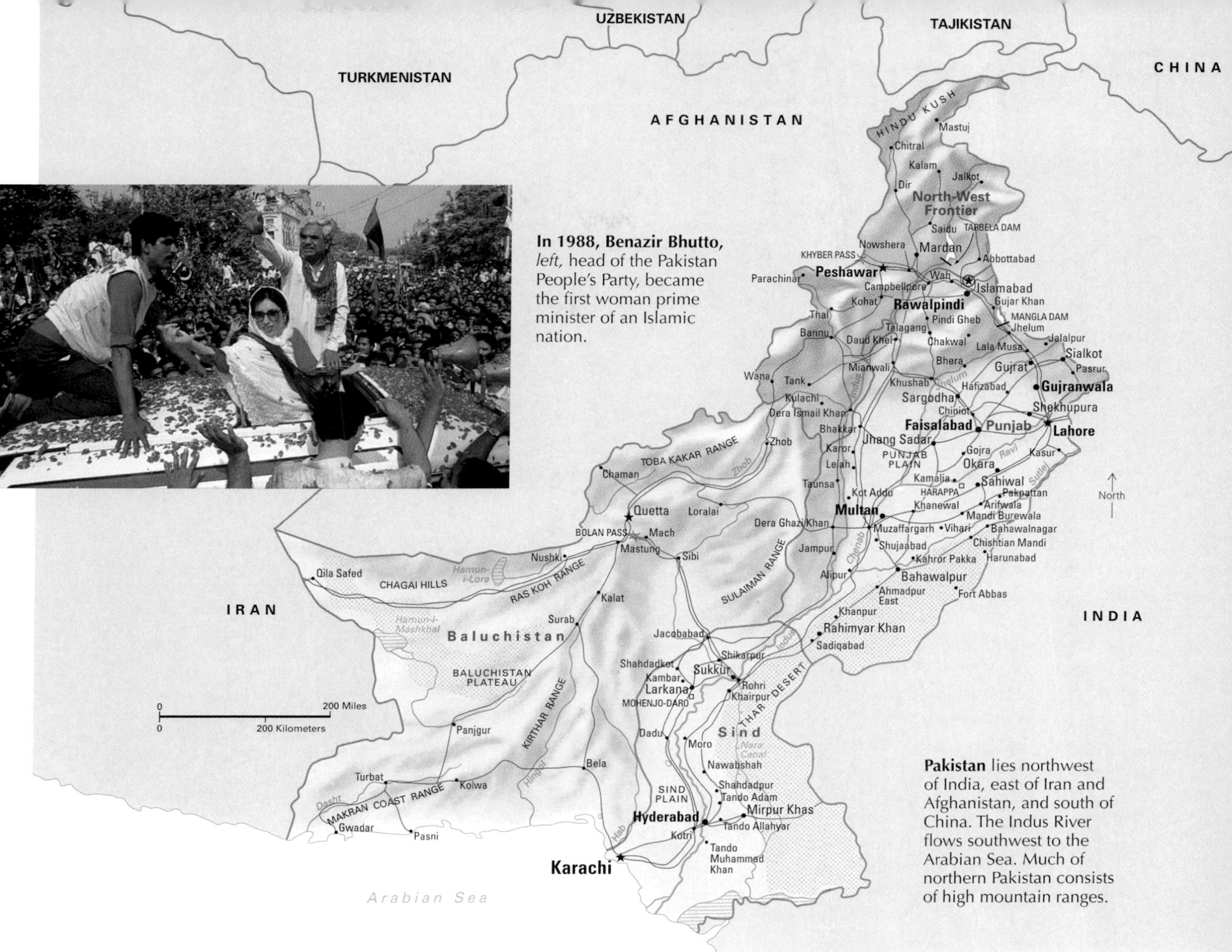

In 1988, Benazir Bhutto, *left,* head of the Pakistan People's Party, became the first woman prime minister of an Islamic nation.

Pakistan lies northwest of India, east of Iran and Afghanistan, and south of China. The Indus River flows southwest to the Arabian Sea. Much of northern Pakistan consists of high mountain ranges.

Siraiki (a Punjabi variant) 10%
Pashtu 8%
Urdu (official) 8%
Balochi 3%
Hindko 2%
Brahui 1%
English (official)
Burushaski

Religions:
Muslim 97% (Sunni 77%, Shiah 20%)
Christian
Hindu

Technology

Radios per 1,000 people: 105

Televisions per 1,000 people: 131

Computers per 1,000 people: 4.2

Economy

Currency: Pakistani rupee

Gross national income (GNI) in 2000: $61 billion U.S.

Real annual growth rate (1999–2000): 4.4%

GNI per capita (2000): $440 U.S.

Balance of payments (2000): -$2,208 million U.S.

Goods exported: Cotton, fabrics, yarn, rice, other agricultural products

Goods imported: Machinery, petroleum, petroleum products, chemicals, transportation equipment, edible oils, grains, pulses, flour

Trading partners: United States, Japan, Germany, Hong Kong, Malaysia, United Kingdom

Bhutto, became prime minister and head of the government.

In August 1990, Pakistan's president dismissed Bhutto's government. Nawaz Sharif of the Pakistan Muslim League became prime minister. In 1993 elections, Bhutto defeated Sharif and became prime minister once again. In 1996, following months of allegations of corruption, Pakistan's president again dismissed Bhutto's government.

In October 1999, General Pervez Musharraf led a military coup that overthrew Pakistan's democratically elected government. Musharraf dissolved the parliament, suspended the constitution, and declared himself the head of a transitional government. In a national referendum in April 2002, voters approved the extension of Musharraf's term as president for five years. In August 2002, Musharraf enacted sweeping constitutional changes that cemented his hold on power. He allowed parliamentary elections to be held in October 2002.

Environment

From its snowy peaks in the northern frontier to its southern shore on the Arabian Sea, Pakistan is a land of great geographical and climatic contrasts.

The country can be divided into four major regions: (1) the Northern and Western Highlands, (2) the Punjab and Sind plains, (3) the Baluchistan Plateau, and (4) the Thar Desert. Each region contains its own important land features.

The Northern and Western Highlands

Some of the most rugged mountains in the world cover northern and western Pakistan. The Karakoram Range stretches across Pakistan's northeast frontier. The Hindu Kush range extends across Pakistan's northwestern border. Travel through this area is difficult and dangerous.

The Karakoram Range is part of the Himalaya mountain system. It stretches across the northern part of Pakistan. The Karakoram contains the world's second highest peak, K2. It rises 28,250 feet (8,611 meters) above sea level.

The high valleys of the Karakoram Range are home to small, isolated communities. Each of these mountain communities has its own culture and language. About 3,000 Kalash people, for example, live in a border region near the town of Chitral. Unlike other Pakistanis, the Kalash never converted to Islam. They still worship their ancient gods.

Before Pakistan became an independent nation, the people of these mountain communities were much more politically and culturally independent. Now that the Karakoram Highway links Chitral with such communities as Swat and Dir, more trade and tourism has come to this area.

Mountain passes cut through the peaks of the Karakoram and the Hindu Kush at several points. One of the most famous is the Khyber Pass, which links Afghanistan and Pakistan.

These mountain regions have the coolest temperatures in Pakistan. Summer temperatures average about 75° F. (24° C), and winter temperatures often fall below freezing.

Boatmen in Sind navigate one of the many channels of the Indus River. These channels have been a major transportation system for centuries.

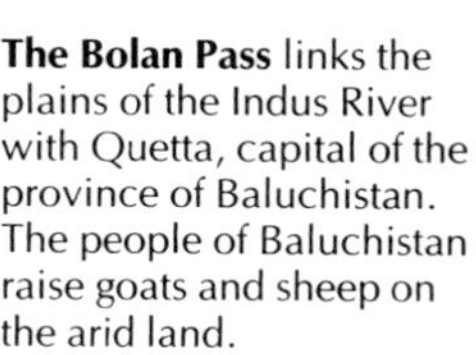

The Bolan Pass links the plains of the Indus River with Quetta, capital of the province of Baluchistan. The people of Baluchistan raise goats and sheep on the arid land.

A dense *deodar* forest blankets the hills behind the palace of the former ruler of Swat in North-West Frontier Province. The deodar is a durable cedar tree of the Himalaya.

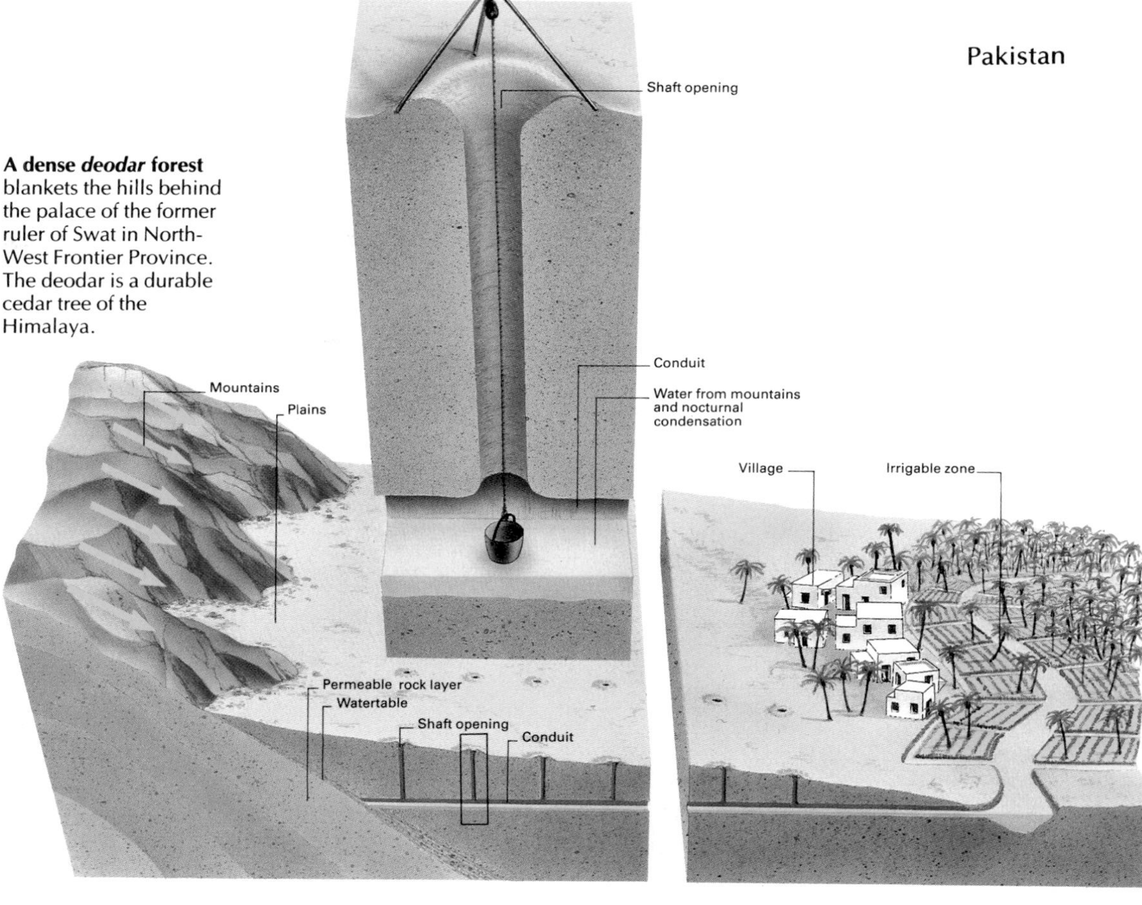

Qanats are underground channels for water used to irrigate farmland in areas that receive little or no rainfall. Farmers use these qanats to transport water over long distances without the risk of evaporation.

The Punjab and Sind plains

The Punjab and Sind plains cover most of eastern Pakistan. The Indus River flows through this region. Its land is called an *alluvial plain,* because it was created from soil deposits left by rivers.

The Indus and its four tributaries—the Chenab, Jhelum, Ravi, and Sutlej—water the Punjab in the north. These rivers meet in east-central Pakistan and flow together as the broadened Indus through the Sind Plain and southwest to the Arabian Sea.

The plains receive very little rainfall. The eastern part of the Punjab receives the most rain—more than 20 inches (51 centimeters) per year. Rain is brought by the moist summer *monsoon* (seasonal wind), which blows across Pakistan from July to September.

Due to extensive irrigation systems along the Indus and its tributaries, the Punjab and Sind plains have become major agricultural centers.

The Baluchistan Plateau

The Baluchistan Plateau lies in southwestern Pakistan. Because it is dry and rocky, plant life is sparse. The people who live in Baluchistan tend flocks of sheep and goats on the arid rangeland.

The Baluchistan Plateau is the driest area in Pakistan. It receives less than 5 inches (13 centimeters) of rain per year.

The Thar Desert

The Thar Desert is located in southeastern Pakistan. Although much of the desert is sandy wasteland, irrigation projects near the Indus River have made the land more suitable for farming.

People

When Pakistan became an independent nation in 1947, its population was about 30 million. Today, there are about 141 million people in Pakistan. This dramatic rise in population is due to the nation's high birth rate combined with a lowered death rate that has resulted from improved medical care.

However, Pakistan's death rate remains high by Western standards. About 12 per cent of infants born in Pakistan die in their first year, and about 25 per cent of Pakistani children die before they reach the age of 5. The major causes of death are poor hygiene and malnutrition, as well as lack of sanitation.

Overpopulation puts a heavy burden on Pakistan. At current rates of growth, the population of Pakistan could be about 175 million by the year 2010. Even with an increase in the amount of cultivated land, the country could not grow enough food to feed its people. In addition, demands for housing, health care, education, and electricity would be overwhelming.

In an effort to cope with overpopulation and its related problems, the Pakistani government's Population Welfare Division has developed programs that emphasize family-planning services and maternal and child health care.

Muslims rejoice at a religious festival in Peshawar. Most Pakistanis are Sunni Muslims and follow Islamic tradition in their everyday life.

Language and cultural groups

More than 50 per cent of Pakistan's population lives in the southeastern province of Punjab. As a result, Punjabis make up the largest cultural group in Pakistan. Although their language, Punjabi, is not Pakistan's official language, it is the principal language because the majority of the population speaks Punjabi.

The official language of Pakistan is Urdu, but less than 10 per cent of the population speak it as their primary language. Arabic remains the language of Islam, and English is the everyday language of the upper class.

The Sindhis, inhabitants of Sind province, make up the second largest population group. Their language is Sindhi, which has a rich literary tradition.

Pushtun tribes are also a large ethnic group. They live in the North-West Frontier Province and northern Baluchistan. Pushtuns speak Pashto, a language related to Persian.

The Baluchis are a group of tribes in the western province of Baluchistan. They live a nomadic life, raising herds of camels, cattle, goats, and sheep. They speak Baluchi, an Iranian language.

Religion

Islam shapes the social and religious life of Pakistanis. Even with their many different cultural groups, Pakistanis have a common ground in the religion of Islam. About 97 per cent of Pakistanis are Muslims. Most belong to the Sunni branch of the religion, but there is a small minority of Shiah Muslims as well.

A polo match is played on a dusty outdoor field. The game originated in Persia about 4,000 years ago. The modern version developed in the Punjab in 1862.

For most Pakistanis, religious duties are an important part of everyday life. These include praying five times a day, fasting during the holy month of Ramadan, and making a pilgrimage to Mecca. Midday prayers on Friday mark the Islamic holy day.

A Kalash girl wears the traditional headdress of her people—a cap of colored beads. The Kalash are a small community in the mountains of the Chitral region.

City and country life

More than two-thirds of Pakistan's people live in rural villages, farming the land or herding for a living. Islamic traditions guide the lives of the rural people. For example, women have far less social freedom than men. Most villagers live in clusters of two- or three-room houses made of clay or sun-dried mud bricks.

In the cities, most people are factory workers, shopkeepers, or craftworkers. They live in small houses in old, crowded neighborhoods. City workers follow the same Islamic customs as villagers. Only middle- and upper-class Pakistanis, some of whom have been educated in Europe and the United States, have adopted Western styles and ideas.

A snake-handler, *right,* performs in front of a crowd of Pushtuns at a country fair in the North-West Frontier Province.

Economy

Although industrial production has increased significantly since the country was created in 1947, Pakistan is still primarily an agricultural country. About half of Pakistan's workers are farmers who still use simple tools to till the land.

Foreign aid and investment have been very important in developing Pakistan's economy. The government has used these funds for a variety of development programs. Pakistani leaders have worked to modernize the country's farming methods and equipment. They have also expanded power facilities in the Indus Basin.

Agriculture

The Indus Valley in the Punjab province is Pakistan's main agricultural center. Wheat, cotton, rice, sugar cane, chickpeas, oilseeds, and fruits and vegetables are grown in the region's fertile soil. Most of these crops are used to feed the population.

An extensive irrigation network—the largest in the world—makes farming possible in the Punjab. This network of canals links the Jhelum, Chenab, and Ravi rivers and regulates their flow. Due to this system, otherwise barren land yields two crops per year.

The government encourages farmers to use fertilizers, pesticides, and new types of seeds. These new methods have increased their harvests. In 1981 and 1982, for the first time, Pakistani farmers grew enough wheat to feed the country's population and exported the surplus.

Even with the government's attempts to modernize farming methods, crop production is still limited by old-fashioned ways. Many farmers still use primitive tools and teams of oxen or buffalo to work the land.

Goats and sheep are raised in regions of Pakistan that are unsuitable for farming. Most of the wool from sheep is exported. Poultry farms are also common in most parts of the country.

Newly picked cotton is ready for transport to a processing plant. Cotton grown on the plains is the basis for Pakistan's textile industry.

Crops of barley, grapes, plums, and wheat are grown in the fertile valley of Hunza in the northern tip of Pakistan, *left*. Hunzukuts, many of whom live more than 90 years, believe their long lives are a result of the mineral-rich mountain water.

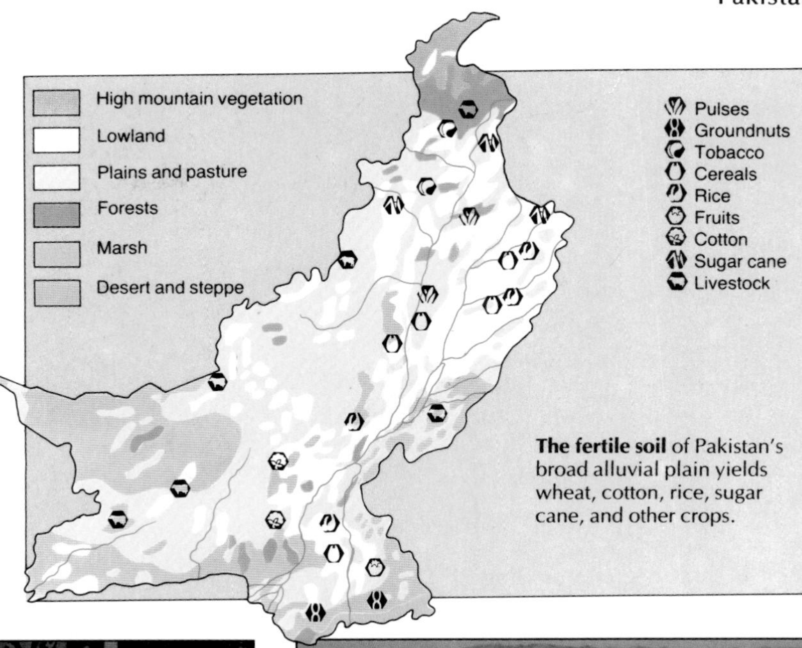

The fertile soil of Pakistan's broad alluvial plain yields wheat, cotton, rice, sugar cane, and other crops.

Pakistani craft workers are famous for their fine carpets. Pakistan is now the world's leading exporter of carpets.

Buffalo and oxen, still used as work animals on many Pakistani farms, go to market in Quetta, Baluchistan. They also provide meat, milk, and hides.

Industry

Industrial growth has been rather slow in Pakistan. When the country first became independent, it had few factories. Today, manufacturing industries employ about a seventh of the population.

Industry in Pakistan is limited by lack of money, natural resources, and technology. Exploration of the large natural gas fields that lie in central Pakistan has just recently begun. At present, the principal industries are textiles and food products.

The textile industry processes cotton grown on Pakistani farms. Yarn and fabrics are now among the country's leading exports. In addition to processing cotton, Pakistani mills also have begun to manufacture artificial silk and synthetic fibers. The food-products industry is based on the processing of flour, sugar, and other foods.

Pakistan is the world's leading exporter of carpets. The country has a rich tradition of carpet weaving, and Pakistani carpets are prized by collectors all over the world.

Cities of the Indus

About 4,500 years ago, in the valley of the Indus River, one of the world's first four civilizations was born. The people of the Indus Valley civilization built brick buildings, streets, drainage systems, and large warehouses to store grain. They created clay figures of humans and animals. They even had a writing system.

Less than 800 years later, this great civilization disappeared. Today, all that remains of these historic people are the ruins of their ancient cities, Mohenjo-Daro (also spelled Moen jo Daro) and Harappa. These ruins tell a remarkable story.

Discovery of a civilization

The ruins of the Indus Valley civilization lay undiscovered until the 1920's, when archaeologists found the remains buried in large mounds. The ruins showed that the Indus civilization covered an area about 1,000 miles (1,600 kilometers) long, extending from the Himalaya to the Indian Ocean.

At first, archaeologists dug mainly at the sites of Mohenjo-Daro on the Indus River and Harappa on the Ravi River, a tributary of the Indus. Later, several hundred smaller settlements were discovered.

An advanced culture

Despite a distance of 342 miles (550 kilometers) apart, Mohenjo-Daro and Harappa were quite similar. They show that a sophisticated culture planned each city very carefully.

The Indus people laid out their streets in a rectangular pattern. Some of the brick houses that lined these streets had elaborate courtyards. These dwellings had a private water supply. Drainage and sanitation systems have also been found.

The Indus people developed a form of writing that was engraved on small stone tablets used as seals. Unfortunately, scholars have so far been unable to translate this writing. As a result, the remains of the Indus Valley civilization leave many questions unanswered.

Archaeologists conclude that the people of the Indus Valley civilization were farmers and herders. The ruins show that the Indus people stored their grain in large warehouses. They probably traded goods with the people of Mesopotamia, central Asia, southern India, and Persia.

Indus art

Archaeologists have unearthed pots, pans, and other utensils made of copper, bronze, and silver in the Indus Valley. The Indus people apparently used some gold, but only for jewelry and decorations.

Many pieces of carved bone and ivory, like those used to decorate furniture, have also been found. From these pieces, scholars

Well-preserved stone steps, *above,* lead to the remains of brick dwellings at Mohenjo-Daro. Archaeologists uncovered the ruins of this ancient Indus city during the 1920's.

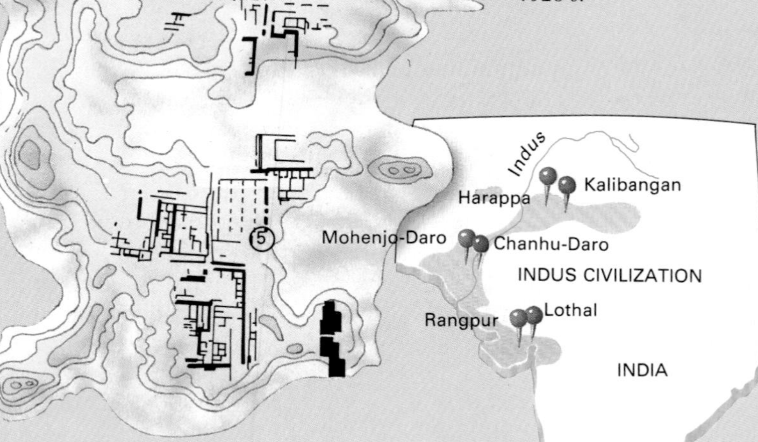

The remains of Mohenjo-Daro include the "Great Bath" (1), which may have been a place of worship as well as an area for washing. A Buddhist *stupa* (dome-shaped monument) (2), built centuries later, crowns the citadel (3), which also contains a grain warehouse (4). At the southern edge of the city stood a great pillared hall (5).

believe that making decorated furniture may have been an important craft.

Indus sculptors made clay, bronze, and stone figures of animals and human beings. These may have been used in magic ceremonies. Many of the characteristics of Indus sculpture appear later in Indian sculpture. These include an emphasis on harmonized forms and the contrast of linear rhythm with square and triangular shapes to produce movement.

A people lost to the ages

Scholars are unsure how the Indus Valley civilization began and how it ended. It is astonishing that such an advanced culture could arise from prehistoric farming communities. Why Mohenjo-Daro and Harappa were gradually abandoned is also a mystery.

There is evidence that a natural disaster, such as prolonged flooding, severely damaged the Indus region. Scientists have also noted changes in the courses of the rivers. If such a change left the Indus people without a reliable water supply, they may have become too weak to fight invaders.

Although the reason may never be known, the Indus Valley civilization disappeared by about 1700 B.C.

This statue of a woman, *far left,* was found at Mohenjo-Daro. Indus craft workers made many figures of animals and humans from clay, silver, and bronze.

The figure of a ram, *left,* is seen in the simple pottery toy that was no doubt enjoyed by a child of the Indus Valley civilization.

Palau

Palau lies about 500 miles (800 kilometers) east of the island of Mindanao in the Philippines. Palau, also spelled *Belau,* is part of the Caroline group of islands in the region of the Pacific referred to as Micronesia. Palau has a population of only 20,000 people. Peleliu, one of the southern islands in the group, has only about 610 people.

Land

The Palau group consists of a chain of islands surrounded by a coral reef. The islands extend about 100 miles (160 kilometers) from north to south and about 20 miles (32 kilometers) from east to west, and they have a land area of 177 square miles (459 square kilometers).

The northern islands are *volcanic islands,* made of lava built up from the ocean floor by eruptions of underwater volcanoes. Many trees, as well as tropical fruits and vegetables, grow on these fertile islands. The low, flat southern islands of the group are coral islands, consisting chiefly of upraised coral reefs, the limestone formations composed largely of the remains of tiny sea animals. Some of these islands are too rugged for people to live on.

History and people

Archaeological evidence suggests that the Palau Islands were one of the first island groups in Micronesia to be settled. Ancestors of the islanders probably arrived from Asia thousands of years ago. About two-thirds of the people of Palau live in Koror, the capital, and most work for government agencies. Most of the rest of Palau's people are farmers who live in rural villages. They grow only enough food for their families.

Palau belonged to Germany before World War I (1914–1918) and was turned over to Japan after the war. The Japanese used the islands as their headquarters for all Micronesia. They built roads and concrete piers, developed harbors, and brought in Japanese settlers. On Peleliu, the Japanese dug caves in the soft coral rock for use in defense. In 1935, Palau and other Japanese possessions among the Pacific islands were closed to foreigners.

In 1944, during World War II (1939–1945), U.S. forces drove the Japanese from the southern Palau islands. After the war ended, Japanese settlers in Palau were sent back to Japan. In 1947, the United Nations established the Trust Territory of the Pacific Islands,

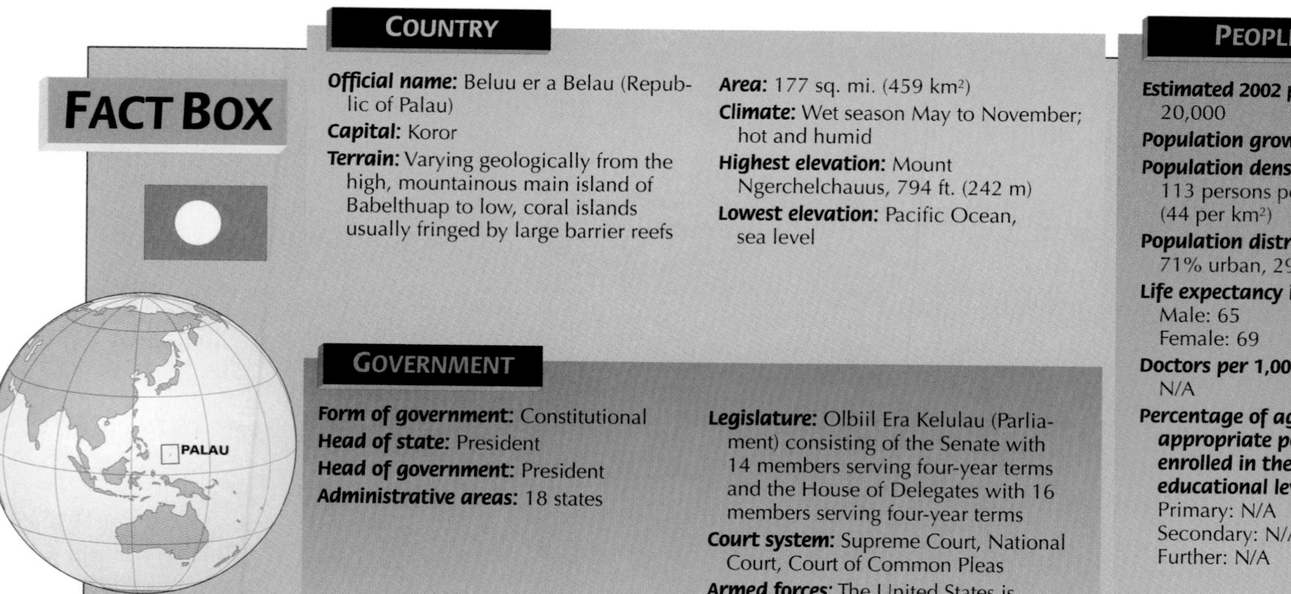

FACT BOX

COUNTRY

Official name: Beluu er a Belau (Republic of Palau)
Capital: Koror
Terrain: Varying geologically from the high, mountainous main island of Babelthuap to low, coral islands usually fringed by large barrier reefs
Area: 177 sq. mi. (459 km²)
Climate: Wet season May to November; hot and humid
Highest elevation: Mount Ngerchelchauus, 794 ft. (242 m)
Lowest elevation: Pacific Ocean, sea level

GOVERNMENT

Form of government: Constitutional
Head of state: President
Head of government: President
Administrative areas: 18 states
Legislature: Olbiil Era Kelulau (Parliament) consisting of the Senate with 14 members serving four-year terms and the House of Delegates with 16 members serving four-year terms
Court system: Supreme Court, National Court, Court of Common Pleas
Armed forces: The United States is responsible for Palau's defense

PEOPLE

Estimated 2002 population: 20,000
Population growth: 1.75%
Population density: 113 persons per sq. mi. (44 per km²)
Population distribution: 71% urban, 29% rural
Life expectancy in years:
Male: 65
Female: 69
Doctors per 1,000 people: N/A
Percentage of age-appropriate population enrolled in the following educational levels:
Primary: N/A
Secondary: N/A
Further: N/A

Palau, a chain of islands surrounded by a coral reef, lies about 500 miles (800 kilometers) east of the Philippines. Dense woods and sparkling beaches make Palau an attractive vacation spot.

under the administration of the United States. The trust territory consisted of about 2,100 islands and atolls in the western Pacific, including Palau.

In 1980, the United States agreed to grant the Caroline Islands a form of self-government called *free association.* The agreement divided the islands into two groups—the Palau Islands and the Federated States of Micronesia. In 1986, the Federated States became a self-governing political unit in free association with the United States. On Oct. 1, 1994, the Republic of Palau followed suit.

Under free association, residents of Palau may live and work in the United States. During the first 15 years of free association, Palau will receive more than $500 million in assistance from the United States. In return, the United States will continue to use the islands for military purposes and will defend Palau against attack.

A woodcarver, *above,* puts the finishing touches on a sign for a Palauan community organization. Such traditional crafts are an important part of Palauan culture.

Languages spoken:
English and Palauan (official in nearly all states)
Sonsorolese and English (official in Sonsoral)
Tobi and English (official in Tobi)
Angaur, Japanese, and English (official in Angaur)

Religions:
Christian
Modekngei 33%

TECHNOLOGY

Radios per 1,000 people: N/A
Televisions per 1,000 people: N/A
Computers per 1,000 people: N/A

ECONOMY

Currency: United States dollar
Gross domestic product (GDP) in 2001: $174 million U.S.
Real annual growth rate (2001): 1%
GDP per capita (2001): $9,000 U.S.
Balance of payments (2000): N/A
Goods exported: Trochus (type of shellfish), tuna, copra, handicrafts
Goods imported: Machinery and equipment, fuels
Trading partners: United States, Japan

Coconuts, *right,* yield a dried meat called *copra,* the chief export of Palau. In his right hand, this Palau islander holds a husked coconut seed—a ball of crisp, white, sweet-tasting meat covered by a tough, brown skin and a shell.

Panama

Panama is a small Central American country, but it has worldwide importance. The country lies on the narrow Isthmus of Panama, a strip of land connecting North America and South America, and separating the Atlantic and Pacific oceans. The Panama Canal cuts through the isthmus, linking the two oceans. Thousands of ships use the canal each year, making Panama so important to world shipping that it is often called the *Crossroads of the World.*

The canal cuts Panama into eastern and western sections. Almost all Panamanians live near the canal or west of it. Swamps and jungles cover much of the land east of the canal. Mountains in the interior and lowlands along the two coasts make up the three main regions of Panama.

The Central Highland is the mountainous interior. There, the Tabasará Mountains extend eastward from the Costa Rican border, decreasing in height until they are just low hills near the Panama Canal. The mountain valleys provide much good farmland. East of the canal, the San Blas Mountains and the Darién Mountains rise to about 6,000 feet (1,800 meters).

The narrow coastal lowlands lie along the Atlantic and Pacific coasts. The Atlantic coast is often called the Caribbean coast because it borders the part of the Atlantic called the

The Panama Canal cuts through the center of Panama. Built by the United States, it links the Atlantic and Pacific oceans. The canal is bordered on both sides by the Panama Canal Zone, a strip of land given to the United States in 1903 but returned to Panama in 1979.

FACT BOX

COUNTRY

Official name: Republica de Panama (Republic of Panama)
Capital: Panama City
Terrain: Interior mostly steep, rugged mountains and dissected, upland plains; coastal areas largely plains and rolling hills
Area: 30,193 sq. mi. (78,200 km²)
Climate: Tropical maritime; hot, humid, cloudy; prolonged, rainy season (May to January), short dry season (January to May)
Main river: Tuira
Highest elevation: Volcan de Chiriqui, 11,401 ft. (3,475 m)
Lowest elevation: Pacific Ocean, sea level

PANAMA

GOVERNMENT

Form of government: Constitutional democracy
Head of state: President
Head of government: President
Administrative areas: 9 provincias (provinces), 2 comarca (territories)
Legislature: Asamblea Legislativa (Legislative Assembly) with 72 members serving five-year terms
Court system: Corte Suprema de Justicia (Supreme Court of Justice), superior courts, courts of appeal
Armed forces: None

PEOPLE

Estimated 2002 population: 2,938,000
Population growth: 1.34%
Population density: 101 persons per sq. mi. (39 per km²)
Population distribution: 56% urban, 44% rural
Life expectancy in years:
Male: 73
Female: 78
Doctors per 1,000 people: 1.7
Percentage of age-appropriate population enrolled in the following educational levels:
Primary: 106*
Secondary: 69
Further: 32

Panama lies at the southern end of North America, the southernmost country on the Central American land bridge. This narrow country is 410 miles (660 kilometers) from west to east, with Costa Rica to the west, Colombia to the east, the Atlantic to the north, and the Pacific to the south.

Caribbean Sea. The western Pacific Lowland has much fertile farmland.

According to its Constitution, Panama is a republic. The people elect a president to a five-year term, and a Cabinet helps the president run the country. The president also appoints a governor to head each of Panama's nine provinces. The National Assembly makes the country's laws. Its members are also elected to five-year terms.

The government of Panama has not always followed its Constitution, however. At times, army officers have taken control of the government. In 1989, the United States invaded the country to arrest General Manuel Noriega, a military dictator who had removed one president from office and declared another presidential election invalid. Noriega surrendered to U.S. authorities in January 1990.

The United States has played a role in Panama's history in other ways. Panama was a province of Colombia until 1903, when the United States encouraged the people to revolt and form their own country. The United States then built the Panama Canal and established the Panama Canal Zone. Many Panamanians opposed the United States; some demonstrated and even rioted. In 1968, General Omar Torrijos Herrera became a dictator in Panama. Torrijos signed a treaty with the United States in 1977 that resulted in the transfer of the Canal Zone to Panama in 1979 and the transfer of the canal to Panama on Dec. 31, 1999.

In 1999, Mireya Moscoso became the first woman to be elected president of Panama.

Languages spoken:
Spanish (official)
English 14%

Religions:
Roman Catholic 85%
Protestant 15%

**Enrollment ratios compare the number of students enrolled to the population which, by age, should be enrolled. A ratio higher than 100 indicates that students older or younger than the typical age range are also enrolled.*

Technology

Radios per 1,000 people: 300

Televisions per 1,000 people: 194

Computers per 1,000 people: 37.0

Economy

Currency: Balboa

Gross national income (GNI) in 2000: $9.3 billion U.S.

Real annual growth rate (1999–2000): 2.7%

GNI per capita (2000): $3,260 U.S.

Balance of payments (2000): -$933 million U.S.

Goods exported: Bananas, shrimp, sugar, coffee

Goods imported: Capital goods, crude oil, foodstuffs, consumer goods, chemicals

Trading partners: United States, Sweden, Central America and Caribbean, Costa Rica, Japan

People and Economy

Panama has a racially mixed population of nearly 3 million people. The first inhabitants of what is now Panama were American Indians. In the 1500's, Spanish explorers became the first Europeans to arrive. Spanish settlers soon began to bring black Africans to Panama to work as slaves. Later, many more people of African descent came to Panama from Caribbean islands.

Through the years, these Indians, Europeans, and Africans intermarried. Today, about 70 per cent of Panamanians are *mestizos* (people of mixed Indian and European ancestry) or *mulattoes* (people of mixed African and European ancestry). Blacks and whites each make up 10 to 15 per cent of Panama's population; Indians make up about 6 per cent.

Spanish is Panama's official language, but many people speak English too. Some Indians speak their own Indian language in addition to Spanish.

Daily life

Most white Panamanians live near the Panama Canal, a bustling center of urban activity. A small group of Panamanians, most of them wealthy whites, are called the *elite*. The elite control the country's economic and political systems. The group includes landowners, doctors, lawyers, and political and military leaders whose families have had wealth for several generations. They take pride in their traditions and tend to avoid contact with less privileged Panamanians.

Many other Panamanians of European descent and many mestizos and mulattoes of the Panama Canal area are merchants, government officials, and office workers who belong to the middle class. Most Panamanians of African descent also live near the canal, but they are mainly poor laborers. As in many other countries, the Africans in Panama suffer from job discrimination.

Away from the canal, Panama is mainly a land of quiet rural areas—farms, tiny villages, and small towns. Most Panamanians who live away from the canal are farmers, and most farmers are mestizos or mulattoes. Many must struggle to produce even enough food for their own use.

The main Indian groups are the Chocó, the Cuna, and the Guaymí. Most Panamanian Indians live in rural areas and farm and fish for a living.

The economy

The Panama Canal is the most important single factor in the country's economy. Near the canal, workers are involved in business generated by the waterway—commerce, trade, and manufacturing.

The Panama Canal Commission, a U.S. government agency, collects tolls from ships that use the canal and pays the Panamanian government an annual fee as well as a percentage of the tolls. The canal also provides jobs for many Panamanians. Some workers operate or maintain the canal, and others work in stores or other businesses connected with the activity around the canal.

Commerce and trade flourish near the canal. Panama City and Colón are banking centers, and more than 300 import and export companies operate in Colón.

About two-thirds of Panama's manufacturing companies are located just west of the canal. Chief products are beer, cement,

Bananas contribute to Panama's export earnings, along with sugar and coffee. The country's fishing industry produces shrimp and anchovetta.

The Chocó Indians, *right,* live in the rural areas of Panama. Their ancestors were Caribbean Indians who lived in Central America and northern South America when the Spaniards arrived.

cigarettes, processed foods, and petroleum products.

Away from the canal, the economy is based on agriculture. More Panamanians work in agriculture than in any other activity—about a fourth of the nation's workers.

Most farmers work small plots of land using old-fashioned methods. They produce only *subsistence crops*—food for their own families. Rice is the main subsistence crop, followed by corn and beans.

Bananas, sugar cane, coffee, and tobacco are cash crops raised for export. They are grown mainly on large plantations owned by wealthy landowners.

A Cuna Indian woman, *below,* wears a bright and beautifully embroidered headscarf and a ring through her nose. The Cuna, or San Blas Indians, who live on the San Blas Islands off Panama's northern coast, are noted for their distinctive, colorful clothing and jewelry.

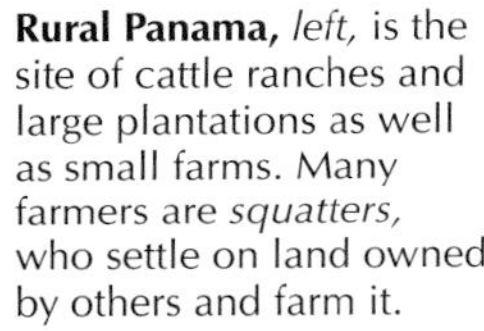

Rural Panama, *left,* is the site of cattle ranches and large plantations as well as small farms. Many farmers are *squatters,* who settle on land owned by others and farm it.

Fort San Lorenzo, near Portobelo, is now a playground for some Panamanian children, *below.* These young dancers are descended from blacks who came to Panama from Caribbean islands.

The Panama Canal

The Panama Canal is one of the world's greatest engineering achievements. The canal is a 50-3/4-mile (81.6-kilometer) artificial waterway that cuts across Central America to link the Atlantic and Pacific oceans. It enables about 12,000 ships each year to travel from one ocean to the other without sailing around South America, thus saving a voyage of more than 7,800 miles (12,600 kilometers).

Three sets of water-filled chambers called *locks* raise and lower ships from one level to another. The locks, which look like giant steps, were built in pairs so that ships can pass in both directions at the same time.

About 70 per cent of the ships that pass through the canal are sailing to or from U.S. ports. Ships from Canada and Japan also use the canal frequently.

People dreamed of a canal through Central America for hundreds of years. As early as 1517, the famed Spanish explorer, Vasco Nuñez de Balboa, who was then a colonial governor, saw the possibility of a canal connecting the Atlantic and Pacific oceans.

In the 1800's, Panama became a province of Colombia. During the 1849 California gold rush, many prospectors sailed from the East Coast of the United States to the Isthmus of Panama, crossed it on mule and on foot, then sailed to California. In 1850, Colombia allowed New York business executives to build the Panama Railroad across the isthmus.

At that time, a French company owned the rights to build a canal across Panama but failed in its attempt to build a sea-level canal. The rights and property were later offered for sale to the U.S. government.

In 1902, Congress gave President Theodore Roosevelt permission to accept the French offer if Colombia would give the United States permanent use of a canal zone. Colombia agreed, but held out for more money. The Panamanians, with the encouragement of France and the United States, revolted.

On November 3, 1903, Panama declared its independence from Colombia. About two weeks later, Panama and the United States signed a treaty giving the United States permanent, exclusive use and control of a canal zone 10 miles (16 kilometers) wide.

The greatest obstacle to building the canal was disease. The Isthmus of Panama was

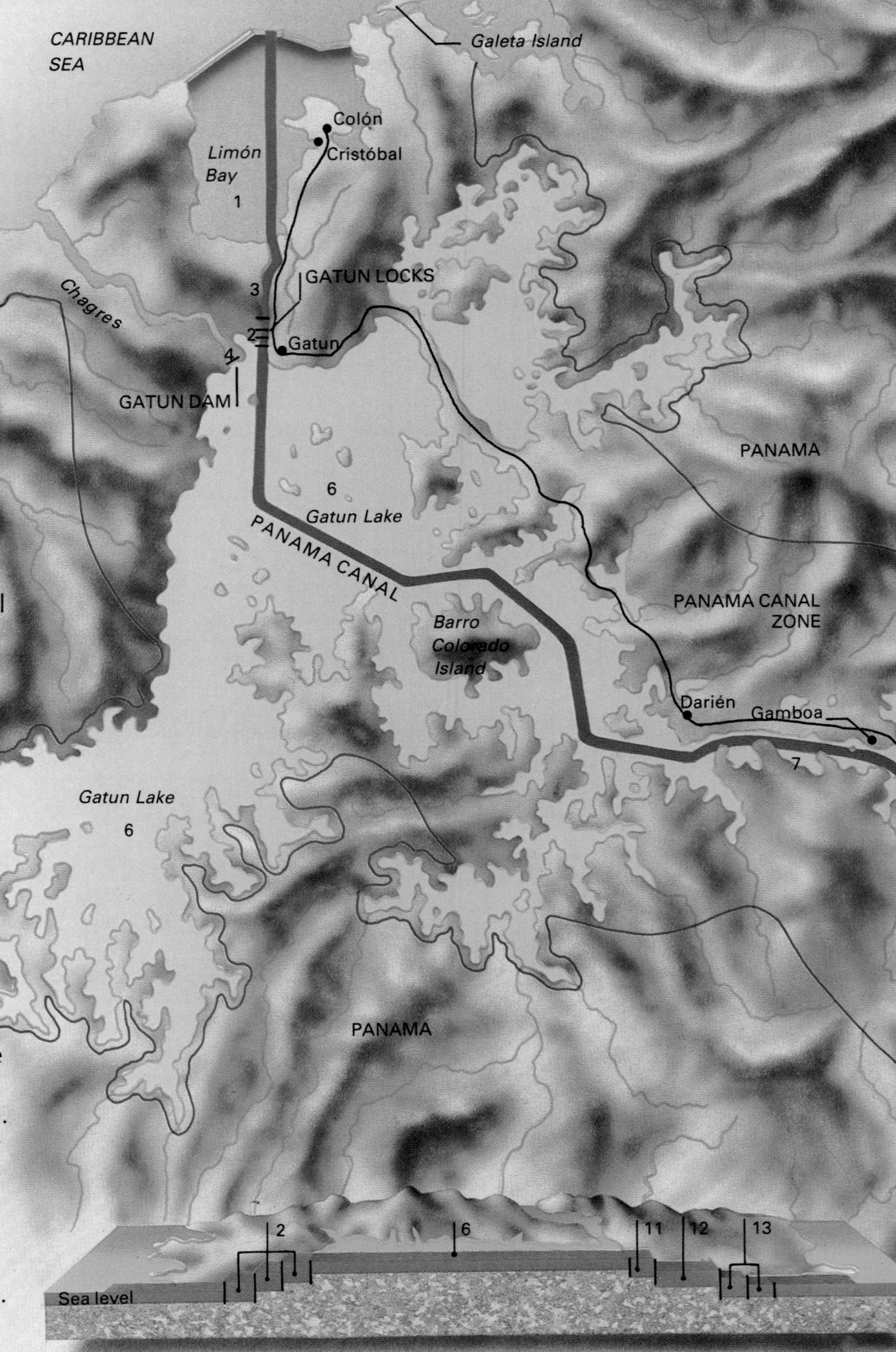

Traveling from the Atlantic to the Pacific through the Panama Canal, a ship first passes through Limón Bay (1) on the way to the Gatun Locks (2), which raise the ship in three stages about 85 feet (26 meters). To the west at this point lie the remains of the original French canal (3). Farther west lies the Gatun Dam (4) across the Chagres River (5), which creates Gatun Lake (6). The original course of the Chagres River serves as a deepwater channel for the ship through the shallow lake. The ship then sails through Gamboa Reach (7) at the entrance to the Gaillard Cut (8). To the northeast, the Madden Dam (9) provides hydroelectric power for the Canal Zone. The Gaillard Cut is named for the French engineer who planned the massive cut through 8 miles (13 kilometers) of hills. Even today, dredgers work constantly to keep this channel clear of earthslides. Along the Gaillard

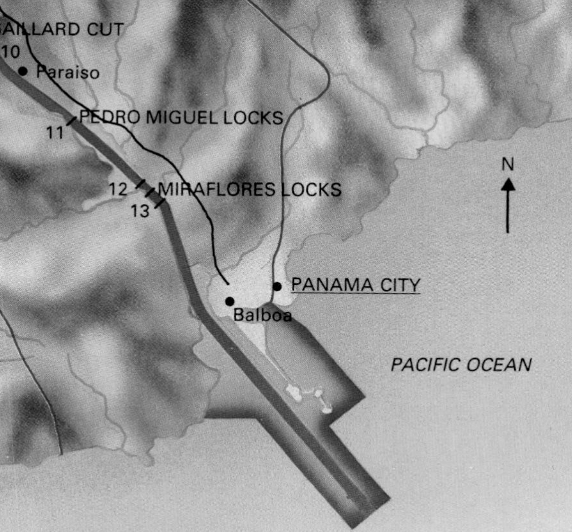

Cut, the ship also passes through the Empire Reach (10). The Pedro Miguel Locks (11) lower the ship 31 feet (9 meters) in one step to Miraflores Lake (12). The Miraflores Locks (13) then lower the ship in two steps to the level of the Pacific Ocean. The canal ends near Panama City.

The Panama Canal, *above,* can carry many oceangoing vessels, but not supertankers and naval supercarriers. Studies to widen the canal or build a new, sea-level canal are underway.

then one of the most disease-ridden places in the world. Colonel William C. Gorgas, an American physician, took charge of improving health conditions and launched a campaign to destroy the mosquitoes that carried malaria and yellow fever. The first two years of canal building were devoted largely to clearing the brush and draining the swamps where mosquitoes swarmed. Rats, which carried bubonic plague, were eliminated.

The actual construction of the canal included three major engineering feats: (1) the Gaillard Cut had to be made through hills, requiring the removal of millions of cubic yards of soil; (2) a dam had to be built across the Chagres River; and (3) locks had to be built to move ships between different water levels because engineers believed a canal with locks would be cheaper and faster to build than a sea-level canal.

At the height of the construction in 1913, more than 43,000 people worked on the canal. On Aug. 15, 1914, the *S.S. Ancon* became the first ship to travel through the new Panama Canal.

Papua New Guinea

Papua New Guinea is an independent nation in the Pacific Ocean just north of Australia. It consists of the eastern part of the island of New Guinea plus a chain of tropical islands that extends more than 1,000 miles (1,600 kilometers). Papua New Guinea shares New Guinea, the world's second largest island, with Papua, a province of Indonesia.

Papua New Guinea has a population of nearly 5 million. About 98 per cent of the people are Melanesian, a dark-skinned people with black, woolly hair. Other groups on the islands include people of Chinese, European, and Polynesian origin. Most of the people live in small rural villages. They farm the land and grow most of their own food.

About 40 per cent of the population live in valleys in the interior. These people were first discovered by Europeans in the 1930's, when a small number of Australians exploring for gold entered the highlands. People of the interior maintain many of their traditions, including the popular *sing-sings,* celebrations featuring exotic masks and costumes, body painting, music, and dance.

The people of Papua New Guinea speak more than 700 languages but manage to communicate with one another by using several widely understood languages. A little more than half of the people of Papua New Guinea have received any elementary education, and about 12 per cent have attended high school.

People lived in what is now Papua New Guinea at least 50,000 years ago. The earliest settlers probably migrated from the Asian mainland by way of the Malay Peninsula and Indonesia. In the early 1500's, Spanish and Portuguese explorers landed on the islands, and during the next 300 years the Dutch and English visited several of the islands.

In 1884, Germany took control of the northeastern part of the island, and the United Kingdom took the southeastern part. The United Kingdom gave its territory to Australia in 1905. After Germany's defeat in World War I (1914–1918), the League of Nations placed northeastern New Guinea under Australian rule, too. Australia granted Papua New Guinea control over its internal affairs in 1973, and in 1975 Papua New Guinea gained complete independence.

Bougainville Island declared itself independent in late 1975, but rejoined Papua New Guinea early in 1976. Since 1988, Bougainville rebels have been fighting to regain independence. Although a cease-fire was declared in 1998, unrest continues.

Papua New Guinea is now a parliamentary democracy. It is also a member of the Commonwealth of Nations, an association of

Fact Box

PAPUA NEW GUINEA

Country

Official name: Independent State of Papua New Guinea
Capital: Port Moresby
Terrain: Mostly mountains with coastal lowlands and rolling foothills
Area: 178,704 sq. mi. (462,840 km²)
Climate: Tropical; northwest monsoon (December to March), southeast monsoon (May to October); slight seasonal temperature variation
Main rivers: Fly, Puraru, Sepik
Highest elevation: Mount Wilhelm, 14,793 ft. (4,509 m)
Lowest elevation: Pacific Ocean, sea level

Government

Form of government: Parliamentary democracy
Head of state: British monarch, represented by governor general
Head of government: Prime minister
Administrative areas: 20 provinces
Legislature: National Parliament or House of Assembly with 109 members serving five-year terms
Court system: Supreme Court
Armed forces: 4,300 troops

People

Estimated 2002 population: 5,015,000
Population growth: 2.47%
Population density: 28 persons per sq. mi. (11 per km²)
Population distribution: 85% rural, 15% urban
Life expectancy in years:
Male: 61
Female: 65
Doctors per 1,000 people: 0.1
Percentage of age-appropriate population enrolled in the following educational levels:
Primary: 85
Secondary: 22
Further: 2
Languages spoken:
English 1% to 2%
pidgin English
Motu

Papua New Guinea occupies eastern New Guinea and includes a string of islands that lies farther east. The western half of the island belongs to Indonesia.

Pidgin English (Tok Pisin) and Police Motu, as well as English, are widely understood languages in Papua New Guinea. In addition, about 850 local languages are spoken.

Port Moresby, *far left,* lies on the hot, humid coast of southeastern New Guinea. The nation's capital has many modern buildings, but most people live in houses built on stilts.

715 indigenous languages

Religions:
indigenous beliefs 34%
Roman Catholic 22%
Lutheran 16%
Presbyterian
Methodist
London Missionary Society 8%
Anglican 5%
Evangelical Alliance 4%
Seventh-day Adventist 1%
other Protestant 10%

Technology

Radios per 1,000 people: 86

Televisions per 1,000 people: 17

Computers per 1,000 people: N/A

Economy

Currency: Kina

Gross national income (GNI) in 2000: $3.6 billion U.S.

Real annual growth rate (1999–2000): 0.3%

GNI per capita (2000): $700 U.S.

Balance of payments (2000): -$8 million U.S.

Goods exported: Oil, gold, copper ore, logs, palm oil, coffee, cocoa, crayfish and pawns

Goods imported: Machinery and transport equipment, manufactured goods, food, fuels, chemicals

Trading partners: Australia, Japan, Singapore, Germany

independent countries and other political units under British law and government.

As one of the independent members of the Commonwealth of Nations, Papua New Guinea recognizes the British monarch as head of the Commonwealth, and a governor general represents the British monarch on the islands. The monarch is mainly a symbol, however, with no real power to govern. The people elect a national legislature, which selects a prime minister to head the government. The government has made plans to modernize the country, but political unrest on some of the islands has interfered with those plans.

Port Moresby is the capital and largest city of Papua New Guinea. The city, which lies on a deep harbor on the southeastern coast of the island, is served by an international airport, and has a university and other educational institutions.

Land and Economy

Papua New Guinea lies only a few degrees south of the equator and a few degrees north of Australia. It has a total land area of 178,704 square miles (462,840 square kilometers). The eastern half of the island of New Guinea makes up most of the country. The rest of the country consists of the islands of the Bismarck Archipelago, Bougainville and Buka in the Solomon Islands chain, the D'Entrecasteaux Islands, the Louisiade Archipelago, the Trobriand Islands, and Woodlark Island.

The country has a hot, humid climate. Temperatures average from 75° F. to 82° F. (24° C to 28° C) in the lowlands and about 68° F. (20° C) in the highlands, with an average annual rainfall of about 80 inches (203 centimeters).

New Guinea's animals include crocodiles, tree kangaroos, and such snakes as the death adder, the Papuan black, and the taipan. The island also has many brilliantly colored birds and butterflies.

Volcanoes, rain forests, and coral

The country's larger islands, including New Guinea, New Britain, and Bougainville, have many high mountain ranges. These mountainous islands are located along the circum-Pacific belt, also called the *Ring of Fire,* which encircles the Pacific Ocean. Most of the world's volcanoes are found along this belt, and volcanoes are common on the northern coasts of these islands. Frequent, sometimes severe, earthquakes also occur on these islands.

Dense tropical rain forests cover about 80 per cent of the islands. Rain forests have more kinds of trees than any other area in the world and they are always green. In addition, about half the world's species of plants and animals live in tropical rain forests. Swamps cover much of the coastal land.

The country's outlying small islands are the tops of underwater mountains. Many of them are fringed with coral, a limestone formation molded in the sea by millions of tiny animals. When the animals die, they leave limestone "skeletons" that form the foundations of barriers and ridges in the sea called *coral reefs.* Some coral reefs protect harbors, but many endanger shipping.

The economy

New Guinea's economy is one of the least developed in the world. Most of the people in Papua New Guinea raise crops for a living. They grow most of their own food, including sweet potatoes, yams, and the potatolike root called cassava. They also produce products for sale, including cocoa, coconuts, coffee, palm oil, rubber, and tea.

Copper, the country's most valuable resource, accounts for about 60 per cent of the value of the nation's exports. Copper is mined on the island of Bougainville, the largest of the Solomon Islands. American, Australian, British, and other banking interests are helping develop one of the world's largest copper mines in Bougainville. Copper is also mined on the island of New Guinea near Papua New Guinea's border with Indonesia.

High mountain ranges cross New Guinea from east to west. Few people live on these rugged, forested slopes. Most of the island's people live in farming communities.

A government worker shows local farmers how to plant tree saplings that will renew the forests. When mature, the new trees will replace those that have been cut down to clear land for cultivation.

A New Guinean hunter, *right,* carries all his equipment with him to a festival. A member of another ethnic group has his face painted with vegetable dyes in preparation for a ceremony, *far right.*

New Guinea's coastal areas, *left,* consist mainly of swamps and clumps of mangroves. Off the coast lie coral reefs filled with colorful sea animals.

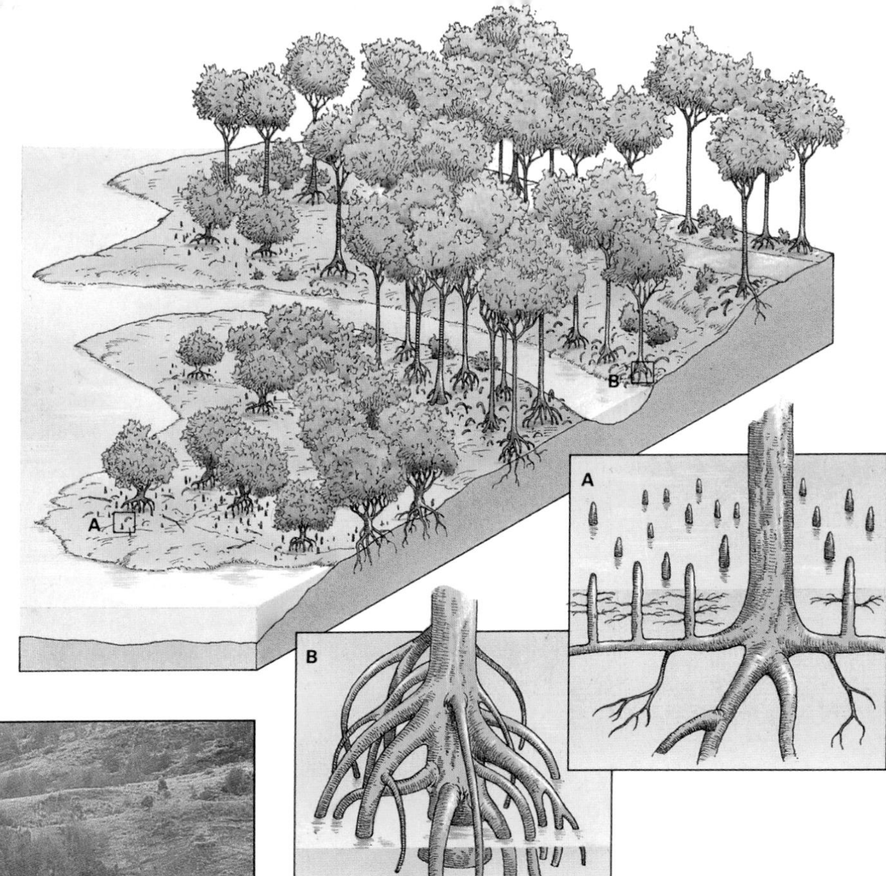

Mangroves grow along coasts in salty tropical waters. Mangroves colonize coastal areas by sending out pioneer roots (A) that trap mud. Thousands of stiltlike roots (B) anchor the trees. They also help build shorelines by catching and holding particles of dirt and sand.

Gold is another important natural resource, and Papua New Guinea ranked among the world's top 10 gold-producing countries in 1987. The islands also have sawmills that are used to process timber. Logs, sawed timber, plywood, veneers, and wood chips are exported to Australia, New Zealand, Asia, and Europe.

The country has about 10,000 miles (16,000 kilometers) of roads, but most of them are unpaved. The rugged terrain of Papua New Guinea has been an obstacle in its economic development. The dense forests, steep mountains, and swampy coasts make transportation difficult and expensive.

Paraguay

Paraguay is a small, landlocked country near the center of South America. It is surrounded by Argentina, Bolivia, and Brazil.

As a country rich in natural resources, including fertile soil, dense forests, and vast hydroelectric power potential, Paraguay has many opportunities for economic growth.

However, as a result of political instability and wars with neighboring nations, Paraguay is a poor country with a developing economy. Most Paraguayans belong to the lower class. About half the people are farmers, and most grow barely enough food for their families.

About 95 per cent of Paraguay's people are *mestizos*—people of mixed European and Indian ancestry. They are descendants of the Guaraní Indians, who intermarried with Spanish settlers. The Guaraní Indians lived in what is now Paraguay long before the first Spaniards arrived in the 1500's.

Early Spanish settlements

Spanish and Portuguese explorers first came to Paraguay in search of a shipping route westward across the continent to the gold and silver mines of Peru. In 1537, Juan de Ayolas traveled up the Paraná and Paraguay rivers to a point north of what is now the capital city of Asunción. Part of his expedition stayed behind to establish a settlement at Asunción, which became the seat of government for all of Spain's colonies in the southeastern part of South America.

The Guaraní offered little resistance to the Spaniards, and the territory became a Spanish colony in 1547. By 1588, Jesuit priests had arrived in Paraguay to convert the Guaraní to Roman Catholicism. The Jesuits organized mission settlements called *reducciones,* or *reductions,* where the Indians lived and worked, receiving food, clothing, and other goods in exchange for tending cattle and working in the fields.

By the 1730's, there were about 30 reducciones in Paraguay, with a total population of about 140,000—perhaps a third of the entire population of Paraguay. The reducciones, which had become quite prosperous as a result of their exports of cotton, tobacco, yerba maté, hides, and wood, also protected the Guaraní from Portuguese slave traders and Spanish colonists who wanted to use them for cheap labor.

A shopkeeper pauses for a refreshing cup of *yerba maté,* a favorite beverage of Paraguayans. Urban dwellers like this shopkeeper generally have a higher standard of living than the rural people because of educational and job opportunities. Medical services are also more readily available in the cities. Many city people work in government, business, or the professions, or as craft workers, unskilled laborers, or factory workers. About half the people in Paraguay live in cities and towns.

The success of the reducciones aroused the envy of the Spanish settlers, who complained to the Spanish king, Charles III. In 1767, King Charles expelled the Jesuits from Paraguay. Once the missionaries were gone, the reducciones were looted and later abandoned. The Indians who had lived on the reducciones either returned to their former way of life or went to work on the large colonial estates. In 1776, Paraguay became part of the Viceroyalty of La Plata, a large colony created by Spain out of its territories in southeastern South America.

This religious image dates from the late 1500's, when the Jesuits arrived in Paraguay to convert the Indians to Roman Catholicism. The Jesuits protected the Indians on huge estates called *reducciones* until King Charles III of Spain ordered the Jesuits to leave Paraguay.

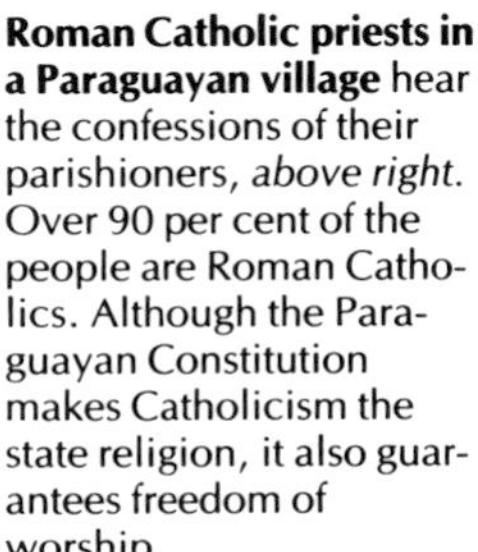

Roman Catholic priests in a Paraguayan village hear the confessions of their parishioners, *above right*. Over 90 per cent of the people are Roman Catholics. Although the Paraguayan Constitution makes Catholicism the state religion, it also guarantees freedom of worship.

A rural Paraguayan proudly wears a handwoven sash in his country's national colors during Independence Days, which are celebrated on May 14 and 15. Like most Paraguayans, he is a *mestizo* (a person of mixed white and Indian ancestry).

Independence and after

In 1811, Paraguay declared its independence from Spain. Since then, the country's history has been dominated by dictatorships or near-dictatorships. The first dictator was José Gaspar Rodríguez de Francia (known as *El Supremo*), who was chosen to serve as president by the new national assembly in 1814 and declared dictator for life two years later. Because Francia distrusted foreigners, he kept Paraguay isolated from the rest of the world.

After Francia's death in 1840, Carlos Antonio López ruled Paraguay as dictator. López reversed Francia's isolationist policies and encouraged trade with foreign nations. His son, Francisco Solano López, succeeded him after he died in 1862. Solano López provoked serious quarrels with Argentina, Brazil, and Uruguay. Hostilities eventually led to the War of the Triple Alliance in 1865—a conflict that left Paraguay in ruins when the war finally ended five years later.

Paraguay Today

In May 1989, Paraguay held its first free elections in 35 years. The people elected General Andrés Rodríguez Pedotti as president. Earlier that year, Rodríguez had led the overthrow of President Alfredo Stroessner, Paraguay's dictator since 1954. After Stroessner's fall from power, Paraguayans danced in the streets of Asunción, celebrating the end of what was perhaps the most brutal and corrupt dictatorship in Paraguay's history.

The rise of Stroessner

General Alfredo Stroessner served as commander in chief of Paraguay's armed forces. In 1954, he led a military overthrow of President Federico Chaves's government. Between 1954 and 1988, Stroessner was reelected seven times, but the elections were controlled by the police and military forces.

Paraguay's Constitution gives the president widespread powers, including the power to dissolve the national legislature. Stroessner used these constitutional powers, along with military and police power, to gain absolute control of the government.

Stroessner allowed little opposition to his rule, imprisoning some Paraguayans who criticized his policies and sending others into exile. Stroessner's secret police maintained an army of spies among the population who reported anybody who complained about the government, and ordinary people lived in constant fear of being turned in to the authorities by a jealous neighbor.

Stroessner brought political stability to Paraguay, but at the expense of civil and human rights. Because he was able to maintain a stable government, he attracted foreign aid and investment to Paraguay. Stroessner used the money to begin a broad program of economic development that included modernizing agriculture, building roads, and promoting industry, but in the end, his programs benefited only a small number of Paraguayans—mostly Stroessner himself, his associates, and the wealthy landowners.

Return to democracy

General Rodríguez's rise to power closely paralleled Stroessner's. Like Stroessner, Rodríguez was a military officer who seized control by overthrowing the government and holding elections before opposing political parties had a chance to form. Rodríguez was also a member of the Colorado Party, which had controlled the voting booths at all of Stroessner's reelections.

Even so, the 1989 elections were the first in 35 years that were not predetermined in favor of the Colorado Party. The majority of

FACT BOX

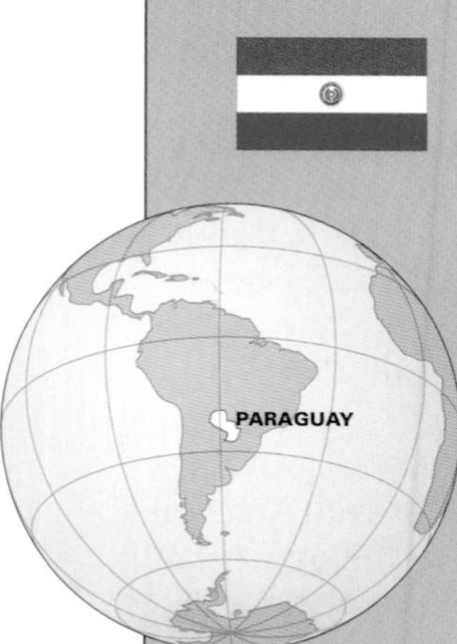

COUNTRY

Official name: Republica del Paraguay (Republic of Paraguay)
Capital: Asunción
Terrain: Grassy plains and wooded hills east of Rio Paraguay; Gran Chaco region west of Rio Paraguay mostly low, marshy plain near the river, and dry forest and thorny scrub elsewhere
Area: 157,047 sq. mi. (406,750 km²)
Climate: Subtropical to temperate; substantial rainfall in the eastern portions, becoming semiarid in the far west
Main rivers: Paraguay, Paraná, Tebicuary, Verde
Highest elevation: 2,231 ft. (680 m) near Villarrica
Lowest elevation: Junction of Rio Paraguay and Rio Paraná, 151 ft. (46 m)

GOVERNMENT

Form of government: Constitutional republic
Head of state: President
Head of government: President
Administrative areas: 17 departamentos (departments), 1 capital city
Legislature: Congreso (Congress) consisting of the Camara de Senadores (Chamber of Senators) with 45 members serving five-year terms and the Camara de Diputados (Chamber of Deputies) with 80 members serving five-year terms
Court system: Corte Suprema de Justicia (Supreme Court of Justice)
Armed forces: 20,200 troops

PEOPLE

Estimated 2002 population: 5,770,000
Population growth: 2.64%
Population density: 37 persons per sq. mi. (14 per km²)
Population distribution: 52% urban, 48% rural
Life expectancy in years:
Male: 71
Female: 76
Doctors per 1,000 people: 1.1
Percentage of age-appropriate population enrolled in the following educational levels:
Primary: 115*
Secondary: 51
Further: N/A
Languages spoken:
Spanish (official)
Guarani (spoken by most

BOLIVIA
BRAZIL
ARGENTINA
Bahia Negra
Fuerte Olimpo
Gran Chaco
Paraguay
Mariscal Estigarribia
Filadelfia
Puerto Casado
Apa
Pedro Juan Caballero
Verde
Pilcomayo
Concepción
Monte Lindo
San Pedro
Jejui
Aracanguy Mts.
Rosario
San Estanislao
Luque
ASUNCIÓN
San Lorenzo
Puerto Presidente Stroessner
Lambaré
Caaguazú
Itá
Villarrica
▲2,231 ft (680 m)
San Juan Bautista
Pilar
Encarnación
Paraná
0 km 200 400
0 miles 100 200

A small country near the center of South America, Paraguay is completely surrounded by Argentina, Bolivia, and Brazil. Despite its wealth of natural resources, it remains a developing country, with an economy based primarily in agriculture and forestry.

Paraguay's capital city of Asunción lies on the eastern bank of the Paraguay River, which flows into the Paraná River. These two rivers link Asunción with the Atlantic Ocean, about 1,000 miles (1,600 kilometers) by water to the south.

of rural population)

Religions:
Roman Catholic 90%
Mennonite
other Protestant

*Enrollment ratios compare the number of students enrolled to the population which, by age, should be enrolled. A ratio higher than 100 indicates that students older or younger than the typical age range are also enrolled.

Technology

Radios per 1,000 people: 182
Televisions per 1,000 people: 218
Computers per 1,000 people: 12.7

Economy

Currency: Guarani
Gross national income (GNI) in 2000: $7.9 billion U.S.
Real annual growth rate (1999–2000): -0.3%
GNI per capita (2000): $1,440 U.S.
Balance of payments (2000): -$299 million U.S.
Goods exported: Soybeans, feed, cotton, meat, edible oils
Goods imported: Road vehicles, consumer goods, tobacco, petroleum products, electrical machinery
Trading partners: Brazil, Argentina, European Union, United States

opposition votes went to the *Partido Liberal Radical Auténtico.* Rodríguez was elected president.

A new Constitution took effect in June 1992. Multiparty elections were held in May 1993. The Colorado Party candidate, Juan Carlos Wasmosy, was elected president. The Colorado Party also won most seats in the National Congress.

In 1999, Paraguay's vice president was assassinated. The National Congress blamed President Raul Cubas Grau in part for planning the assassination. Cubas resigned and fled the country. Senate President Luis Gonzalez Macchi then succeeded to the presidency of Paraguay.

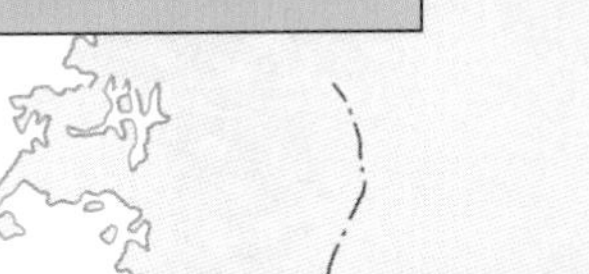

Land and Economy

Paraguay is divided by the Paraguay River into two major land regions. The Chaco, officially called Occidental Paraguay, stretches westward from the Paraguay River. It is a region of coarse grasses, scrub forests, thorny shrubs, and salt marshes. Eastern Paraguay, officially called Oriental Paraguay, lies east of the Paraguay River. A fertile region of rolling hills and thick forests, Eastern Paraguay is home to more than 95 per cent of the country's population.

The Chaco

A large region that occupies about three-fifths of Paraguay, the Chaco is part of the Gran Chaco that extends into Argentina and Bolivia. Covered with dry grass and sparsely dotted with quebracho trees and other hardwoods, the Chaco is a desolate, undeveloped region.

Paraguay fought for control of the Chaco in a war with Bolivia that began in 1932. Paraguay suffered many casualties during the war, but the fighting ended in a truce in 1935. A final settlement that gave Paraguay nearly all the disputed territory was reached in 1938.

Several slow-moving rivers flow through southern and eastern Chaco, including the Pilcomayo and the Verde. The Pilcomayo forms Paraguay's southwestern border with Argentina. Like other rivers in the Chaco, the Pilcomayo often overflows after heavy summer rains. Some rivers in the Chaco disappear during the dry winter season, forming salt marshes.

The underground water throughout much of the Chaco is too salty for drinking or irrigation, making the land unsuitable for farming. The quebracho trees that grow in the region are harvested for *tannin,* which is used in tanning hides.

Most of the Chaco is uninhabited. The few people who live in the Chaco include cattle ranchers in the south, a small group of German-speaking people of the Mennonite faith in the central part, and scattered tribes of Guaraní Indians in the most remote sections.

Eastern Paraguay

In contrast to the Chaco, Eastern Paraguay is the productive heartland of the country. Its rich soil yields such crops as *cassava* (a root vegetable), corn, cotton, rice, soybeans, sugar cane, and tobacco. The thickly forested Paraná Plateau occupies about a third of the region. Asunción, the nation's capital and largest city, lies in Eastern Paraguay.

Most of the people in Eastern Paraguay live in the southwestern part of the region where small towns and farming villages dot the countryside. Most rural Paraguayans live in *ranchos,* one-room houses with a dirt floor and walls made of reed, wood, or brick. A separate or attached shed serves as a kitchen. Few ranchos have indoor plumbing.

The setting sun shimmers in the waters of Lake Ypacaraí, which lies near the Paraguay River. Waterways are important transportation routes in Paraguay, and hydroelectric power plants on the Acaray and Paraná rivers provide plentiful electricity.

A mestizo woman sells oranges at a wayside stall, *below right.* Paraguayan mestizos, descended from Guaraní Indians who intermarried with Spaniards, still maintain many traditional Guaraní ways. Most Paraguayans speak both Guaraní and Spanish, but the Guaraní language is used in everyday conversation. The popular music of Paraguay also reflects the slow rhythm of traditional Guaraní music. The most famous Guaraní handicraft still practiced today is *ñandutí* lacemaking.

Farming and timber industries

Most Paraguayan farmers are *squatters* on public or private land. Rather than owning or even renting land, they farm small plots until the soil is no longer productive and then move on. Since the mid-1900's, the government has encouraged farmers to buy land in undeveloped areas, but only 20 per cent of the land that could be used for crop production is presently cultivated.

Today, about 75 per cent of the country's farmland remains in the hands of a few wealthy landowners. Several new large estates have been established since the 1950's—many of them German, Japanese, and Brazilian agricultural settlements.

Thick forests, which are valuable for the timber they produce, cover about half of Paraguay. Although the country's forests are one of its most valuable resources, the timber industry remains undeveloped because of the lack of roads and mechanized shipping facilities.

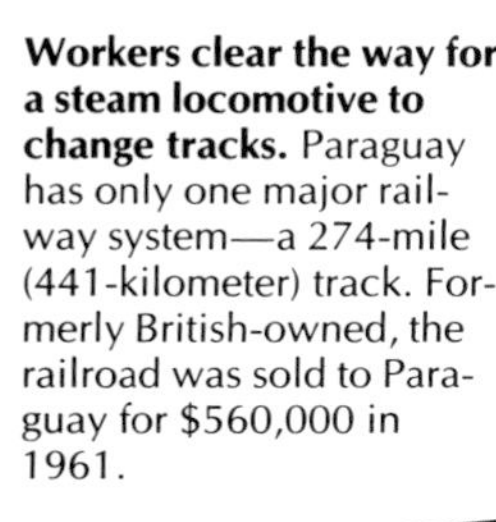

Workers clear the way for a steam locomotive to change tracks. Paraguay has only one major railway system—a 274-mile (441-kilometer) track. Formerly British-owned, the railroad was sold to Paraguay for $560,000 in 1961.

This shantytown, *below,* stands near the building that houses the national legislature in Asunción. Although Paraguay does not have the large urban slums typical of other Latin-American countries, some of the urban poor live in run-down shacks made from metal or wood scraps.

Peru

Surrounded by the rugged, sharply rising peaks of the Peruvian Andes, the famous "lost" city of Machu Picchu clings to a ridge 8,000 feet (2,400 meters) above sea level. An Inca refuge from the conquistadors' invading armies, Machu Picchu remained hidden from the outside world until it was discovered by Hiram Bingham in 1911. Today, as the cold mountain wind whistles through its stone ruins, Machu Picchu is a silent but awe-inspiring reminder of a once-mighty civilization cut down by invaders from half a world away.

While the Inca created the most famous of Peru's Indian civilizations, theirs was by no means the first. Scholars believe that Indians came from North America to settle in Peru about 12,000 years ago. The story of Peru, South America's third largest country, began in the small farming villages of these primitive tribes.

Peru's breathtaking scenery is a fitting backdrop for its long, eventful history. Its mountains are taller than Europe's Alps, its deserts are drier than Africa's Sahara, and its people and their story are no less dramatic.

Early civilizations

Peru's earliest people learned to farm, domesticated the llama, and were the first to cultivate the potato, which grew wild in the highlands. The Chavin Indians developed Peru's first known civilization, which reached its peak about 900 B.C. The Chavin spoke Akaro, which developed into the Aymara language, still spoken by a number of Peruvian Indians today.

Later, other groups, such as the Mochica, Tiahuanaco, and Chimu, developed civilizations in Peru. The Tiahuanaco settled near the cold, high shores of Lake Titicaca. Little is known of them except for the massive stone carvings, such as the *Puerta del Sol* (Doorway of the Sun), which they left behind. The remains of the Mochica, who settled in northern Peru, and the Nazca of the south contain secrets of their own.

The Mochica civilization flourished between about 200 B.C. and A.D. 600. The Mochica inhabited the almost rainless coastal strip of Peru but cultivated large areas

of farmland by developing irrigation techniques. They were also skillful builders, constructing huge stepped pyramids more than 100 feet (30 meters) high. The Nazca, who lived about the same time as the Mochica, etched huge geometrical and animal figures, visible only from the air, into the parched desert landscape.

The Chimu and Inca

The largest and most important pre-Incan civilization was that of the Chimu, who settled on the coastal plain near the present-day city of Trujillo. The Chimu settlements were among the largest urban areas of the time. The ruins of Chanchan, the capital city of the Chimu, still survive.

Scholars now believe that it was the Chimu who actually developed much of the political organization, irrigation techniques, and road-building skills for which the Inca became famous. The Inca conquered the Chimu in 1471, but they were no match for the devastating guns and horses of the conquistadors who came 61 years later.

The Spanish and independence

Spanish adventurer Francisco Pizarro was on a quest for fabled Incan treasures of gold and silver when he entered Peru about 1527. The riches he found then convinced him to return with about 180 men in 1532. With the aid of additional Spanish troops, he conquered most of Peru by the end of 1533. Soon after the conquest, the king of Spain appointed a *viceroy* (governor) to enforce Spanish laws and customs. Enslaving the Indians to work in the mines and on colonists' plantations, the Spanish made Peru one of their most profitable colonies. From time to time, Indians and *mestizos* (people of mixed Indian and Spanish ancestry) rebelled unsuccessfully.

Then, in the early 1800's, the heroes of Peru's wars of independence—José de San Martín, Simón Bolívar, and Antonio José de Sucre—freed Peru from Spanish rule. Today, though Peru suffers from economic problems and civil strife, the ruins of its ancient cultures stand as an eternal testament to its noble heritage.

Peru Today

Since its earliest days of independence, Peru has struggled with many political, economic, and social problems.

Social structure

Many of Peru's social problems stem from the strict class system established so long ago by its Spanish conquerors. Under this two-class system, a small group of whites—the upper class—controlled a huge population of Indians—the lower class. Some Spaniards and Indians married, and their descendants became known as *mestizos*. As the number of mestizos grew, they too became part of the lower class.

Although racial barriers are less rigid today, the great majority of Indians and most mestizos are still considered lower class. The small upper class of whites—about 10 per cent of Peru's population—control most of the nation's wealth.

Upper-class white families generally live in the expensive, fashionable sections of Lima, Peru's capital, and other large cities. They speak Spanish, wear modern clothing, and enjoy a varied diet of meat, fish, poultry, vegetables, and grains. During the 1900's, as the middle class grew, opportunities for education and better jobs opened up for many mestizos. However, many of Peru's Indians—a group that makes up about 46 per cent of the population—remain poor and uneducated. Their diet is meager, and they have little access to social services.

Struggle for equality

Until the 1920's, most of Peru's political parties favored the upper class. Then, in 1924, Víctor Raúl Haya de la Torre founded the *Alianza Popular Revolucionaria Americana* (American Popular Revolutionary Alliance, or APRA), a party that demanded equal rights for all Peruvians and public ownership of Peru's basic industries.

When Haya de la Torre lost the 1931 presidential election, APRA charged dishonesty in vote counting and staged violent antigovernment demonstrations. Quarrels with other political groups and continued violence led the government to outlaw APRA. The party participated in an election in 1945, but it was outlawed again during 1948. Although its legality was restored in 1956, APRA lost its popularity to Fernando Belaúnde Terry's Popular Action Party. Belaúnde was elected president in 1963 and worked for Indian rights.

In 1990, independent candidate Alberto Fujimori was elected president. Two years later, Fujimori suspended the Constitution and dissolved the legislature, which he claimed was corrupt. In September 1992, police arrested the leader of the Shining Path

Fact Box

Country

Official name: Republica del Peru (Republic of Peru)
Capital: Lima
Terrain: Western coastal plain (costa), high and rugged Andes in center (sierra), eastern lowland jungle of Amazon Basin (selva)
Area: 496,226 sq. mi. (1,285,220 km²)
Climate: Varies from tropical in east to dry desert in west; temperate to frigid in Andes
Main rivers: Amazon, Marañón, Ucayali
Highest elevation: Nevado Huascaran, 22,205 ft. (6,768 m)
Lowest elevation: Pacific Ocean, sea level

Government

Form of government: Constitutional republic
Head of state: President
Head of government: President
Administrative areas: 24 departamentos (departments), 1 provincia constitucional (constitutional province)
Legislature: Congresso Constituyente Democratico (Democratic Constituent Congress) with 120 members serving five-year terms
Court system: Corte Suprema de Justicia (Supreme Court of Justice)
Armed forces: 115,000 troops

People

Estimated 2002 population: 26,490,000
Population growth: 1.75%
Population density: 53 persons per sq. mi. (21 per km²)
Population distribution: 72% urban, 28% rural
Life expectancy in years: Male: 68; Female: 73
Doctors per 1,000 people: 0.9
Percentage of age-appropriate population enrolled in the following educational levels: Primary: 126*; Secondary: 81; Further: 29

The Plaza de Armas, a spacious central square in the Peruvian town of Arequipa, provides a comfortable spot for Indian women to work on their crafts. The Spaniards built many richly decorated buildings throughout Peru. Some have been destroyed by earthquakes and rebuilt in the traditional Spanish colonial style.

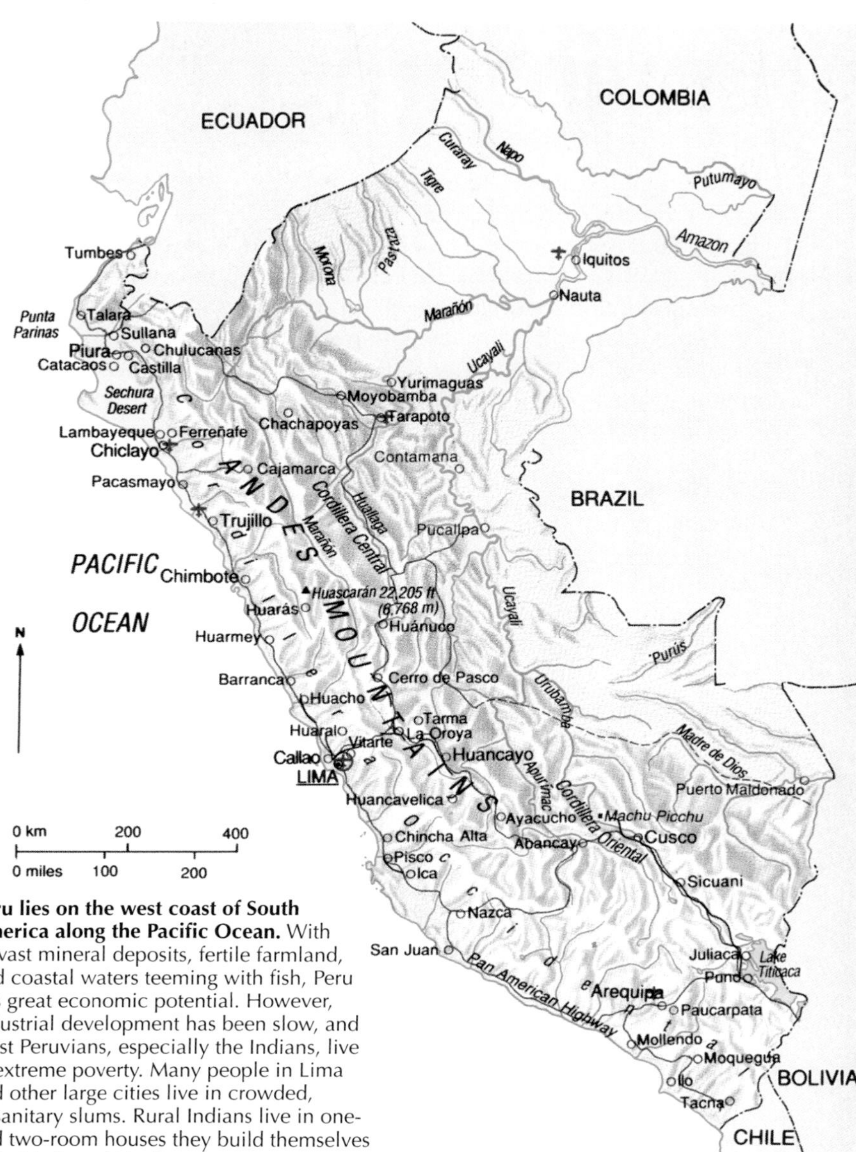

Peru lies on the west coast of South America along the Pacific Ocean. With its vast mineral deposits, fertile farmland, and coastal waters teeming with fish, Peru has great economic potential. However, industrial development has been slow, and most Peruvians, especially the Indians, live in extreme poverty. Many people in Lima and other large cities live in crowded, unsanitary slums. Rural Indians live in one- and two-room houses they build themselves with dried mud blocks.

Languages spoken:
Spanish (official)
Quechua (official)
Aymara

Religion:
Roman Catholic 90%

*Enrollment ratios compare the number of students enrolled to the population which, by age, should be enrolled. A ratio higher than 100 indicates that students older or younger than the typical age range are also enrolled.

Technology

Radios per 1,000 people: 273

Televisions per 1,000 people: 148

Computers per 1,000 people: 40.9

Economy

Currency: Nuevo sol

Gross national income (GNI) in 2000: $53.4 billion U.S.

Real annual growth rate (1999–2000): 3.1%

GNI per capita (2000): $2,080 U.S.

Balance of payments (2000): -$1,628 million U.S.

Goods exported: Fish and fish products, copper, zinc, gold, crude petroleum and by-products, lead, coffee, sugar, cotton

Goods imported: Machinery, transport equipment, foodstuffs, petroleum, iron and steel, chemicals, pharmaceuticals

Trading partners: United States, China, Colombia, Japan, Venezuela

guerrilla group, Abimael Guzmán Reynoso. He and 10 others were convicted of treason.

In 1993, Peruvians approved a new Constitution that allowed Fujimori to run for reelection in April 1995. He was reelected by a wide margin.

On December 17, 1996, the Tupac Amaru Revolutionary Movement (MRTA), a Marxist rebel group, seized the residence of the Japanese ambassador to Peru, taking 490 hostages. By spring of 1997, all but 72 hostages had been released. On April 22, 1997, Peruvian troops stormed the Japanese ambassador's residence and freed the hostages. All 14 rebels, 2 soldiers, and 1 captive were killed.

In 2000, after election scandals and revelations that his government was corrupt, Fujimori was declared "morally unfit" to be President by Congress. He then fled to Japan.

Environment

Peru is a land of great geographical contrasts. From the western coastal deserts to the cool central Andes and the humid eastern forests, the rugged landscape of Peru has had a profound influence on the life of its people. Peruvians in each of these very different regions have adapted their way of life to the unique characteristics of the land and climate around them.

The Pacific coast

Although nearly all of Peru's west coast along the Pacific Ocean is dry desert land, about 50 rivers flow down from the Andes Mountains and cross the region. The river water is used for irrigation, enabling farmers to grow crops in this otherwise barren land. Cotton and sugar cane are grown on these coastal farms.

The waters off the coast provide a rich catch for Peru's fishing industry, including anchovettas, sardines, tuna, and other ocean fish. The anchovettas and sardines are ground into fish meal and exported all over the world for use in livestock feed.

Peru's large cities and factories are also located in the coastal area. Lima, the capital and largest city, is the nation's major commercial, cultural, and industrial center. Lima is a bustling, modern city, with high-rise buildings lining the streets of its business district. The city's plants and factories produce beer, clothing, cotton and woolen fabrics, and fish meal.

While Lima's wealthy families live in spacious colonial mansions and luxurious suburban homes, the city's poor live in rundown public housing or crowded slums. About a third of the population lives in squatter communities known as *pueblos jóvenes* (young towns).

These new towns sprang up when former slumdwellers began to settle on public land outside the large cities. There, they built shacks made of cardboard, old metal, and other scrap materials. Because the so-called squatters paid no rent, some were able to save enough money to build a permanent house. To encourage these efforts, the government has supplied some new towns with running water and a sewerage system.

The Andes highlands

East of the coastal regions, the Andes Mountains rise sharply. The highland Indians make their homes in the plateaus and valleys between the soaring peaks. They work as farmers and herders, growing coffee on the lower eastern mountain slopes and herding llamas, alpacas, goats, and sheep in the higher valleys and on the Altiplano (plateau) surface.

These Indians live at elevations up to 15,000 feet (4,570 meters). Most of their houses have *adobe* (dried clay) walls and a roof made of grass thatch or handmade tile. Although the young people dress in modern clothing, many of the older Indians prefer the traditional garments of their ancestors. The men wear ponchos, leggings tied at the knee, and colorful caps with earflaps. The women wear layers of handwoven, brightly colored skirts and derby hats.

Highland Indians watch their herd of llamas outside their thatch-roofed house, *above*. These Indians live at elevations up to 15,000 feet (4,570 meters) above sea level. The Himalaya in Asia is the only other place on earth where people live at such high altitudes.

An Indian woman gathers potatoes in her woven basket. A native plant of South America, the potato was cultivated by the Inca Indians more than 400 years ago. From potatoes, the Inca made *chuño,* a light, floury substance that was used to make bread.

Squatter settlements spread out along the outskirts of Lima, *left.* Since the 1950's, large numbers of people have migrated from rural areas to the cities. By the 1980's, more than one-fourth of the entire population of Peru lived in the metropolitan area of Lima.

Carefully tended fields near Cusco extend to the Andean peaks. Once the heartland of the Inca empire, this region is now farmland where local people grow crops such as potatoes and corn. Many farm families produce barely enough to feed themselves.

The selva

Indians also make up the majority of the population in the selva, a region of forests and jungles in eastern Peru. The Indians of the selva belong to about 40 tribes and speak a variety of tribal languages. The houses in their scattered tribal villages are built of sticks or bamboo poles with a thatched roof of grass or palm leaves.

Most of the selva Indians grow a few crops, such as corn and *cassava* (a starchy root), but they hunt and fish for most of their food. The jungles provide a great variety of fish and small game, as well as several kinds of fruits and nuts.

An Indian of northeastern Peru's Amazon jungle, *left,* demonstrates his silent but deadly weapon—the poison blow dart. Using an age-old technique, he dips darts from his bark *quiver* (dart case) into the poison-filled gourd at his waist before loading them into his long blowgun.

Railroad Above the Clouds

"Wherever a llama can go, so can my railway!" These were the proud words of Henry Meiggs, the ambitious American engineer who laid the route for Peru's famous Central Railway in the late 1800's. Meiggs was sure that he could build a fast, direct rail link between Peru's huge upland mineral reserves and the port of Callao on the Pacific Ocean, which was a suburb of Lima.

Meiggs died in 1877, long before his project could be completed, and his dream of a railroad that would cross the Andes never quite came true. But although the track ends at Huancayo, Peru's Central Railway remains one of the great engineering marvels of all time.

The world's highest standard-gauge railroad, the Central Railway begins its journey at sea level and climbs to an incredible 15,844 feet (4,829 meters)—higher than Mont Blanc, the tallest mountain in the Alps.

For even the most adventurous traveler, a ride in the railway's yellow-and-orange cars can be a harrowing experience. During the 10-hour journey, passengers endure extremes of temperature—from Lima's summer heat and humidity to Huancayo's bitter cold. In the 1980's, the Shining Path's terrorist activities added a new element of danger to the ride. But the reward is a rare view of extraordinary scenery in this mountainous land.

The Central Railway's journey begins at Callao, but most passengers join the train in Lima at a station called *Desemparados* (The Forsaken Ones). The name seems appropriate to passengers waiting for a train that is often hours—even days—late. The train is scheduled to depart daily at 7:40 a.m., arriving at Huancayo in Peru's Altiplano mining region about 10 hours later. During its journey, the train crosses 59 bridges and goes through 66 tunnels.

The train pulls out of Desemparados past a vast shantytown crowding the banks of the Rímac River. Traveling eastward, the train crosses Peru's narrow, almost rainless coastal plain and passes through a small canyon—barely a cut in the rock—beyond Chosica. Then the train begins its remarkable climb,

A train passes through the Vilcanota Valley on the line that runs between Cusco in the Andean highlands and Puno on Lake Titicaca. Peru's railroads offer unforgettable views of the Andes Mountains.

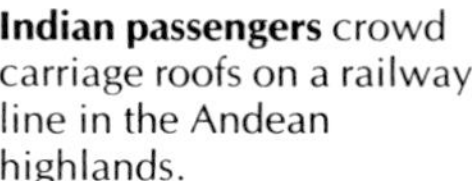

Indian passengers crowd carriage roofs on a railway line in the Andean highlands.

and high cliffs, often only a few feet from the carriage windows, dominate the view.

On its upward climb, the train seems to defy gravity. In some places, the rise is too steep to allow even zigzag bends. At these points, the train is driven along a ramp beyond the track, and then shifted to the next stretch of track.

By the time the train reaches Matucana, it has climbed to 7,842 feet (2,390 meters) above sea level. At this height, some passengers may begin to feel the effects of *soroche* (altitude sickness), such as dizziness, shortness of breath, or nausea. Attendants in white jackets are on hand to operate oxygen tanks for those who need help. Some passengers chew aspirin as they inhale the oxygen, while others rebuild their strength by taking glucose pills. Many Indians chew coca leaves, which may help keep them from feeling hungry or tired but do not nourish the body.

At Ticlio, the line forks. The main branch passes through the Galera Tunnel and then heads on to Huancayo. This branch reaches its highest altitude of 15,688 feet (4,782 meters) inside the Galera Tunnel. Another branch travels from Ticlio to the mining town of Mirococha. The highest point on the Central Railway is reached on a siding at 15,844 feet (4,829 meters) along this branch at La Cima.

Indian peddlers sell fruit, souvenirs, and handcrafted items to tourists riding the world's highest standard-gauge railroad.

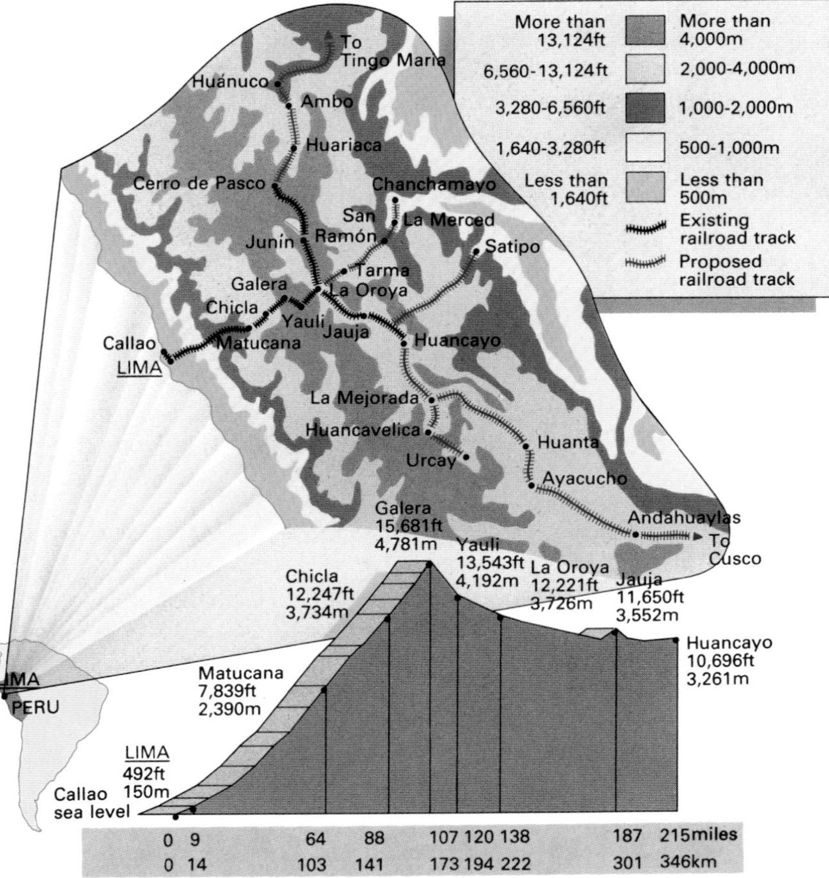

The world's highest standard-gauge railroad was built by Henry Meiggs, an American who fled to South America in the 1850's to escape his creditors. In the past, the railroad carried great quantities of gold, silver, lead, and mercury from the mountain mines to the port of Callao. Today, Peruvians ride the famous train up to Huancayo to enjoy the spectacular views and buy beautiful handcrafted items made by Quechua-speaking Indians.

The Inca

According to their legends, the Inca civilization began when the sun god created a brother and sister, Manco Capac and Mama Ocllo, and sent them to earth. The sun god gave Manco Capac and Mama Ocllo a staff of gold and told them to wander the land until the staff sank into the earth. The brother and sister walked and walked until the staff sank into the earth near where the city of Cusco, Peru, now stands. Cusco became the capital of the Inca empire.

Early history

Originally a tribe—or a group of tribes—that lived in the Cusco area, the Inca began to expand their rule over neighboring groups in about 1200. But it was not until 1438 that their emperor Pachacuti began to take over larger, more important regions south of Cusco.

By 1463, the Inca dominated almost all of what is now Peru. Pachacuti and his son Topa then turned their sights northward, and, by 1471, reached what is now Quito, in Ecuador. Topa's son, Huayna Capac, further expanded the Inca empire by taking over much of the region around present-day Guayaquil. He also marched north until he reached what is now the Colombian border. By the early 1500's, the Inca empire stretched along the west coast of South America for more than 2,500 miles (4,020 kilometers).

A Quechua Indian, *below,* displays her earrings, a reminder of the goldsmithing skills of her ancestors. Quechua, still spoken today, was the language of the Inca.

The massive walls of the Inca fortress Sacsahuaman, *top right,* contain some stones that are 16 feet (5 meters) long. Workers hauled the rock from quarries more than 35 miles (56 kilometers) away. Inca builders cut large stone blocks so precisely that they fit together perfectly without cement. Not even a knife blade can fit between them.

Irrigation canals at Tambomachay, Peru, *above,* still survive as evidence of the remarkable engineering skills of the Inca. To make irrigation easier in the highland regions, they cut terraces into the hillsides.

An advanced culture

Because the Inca did not develop a system of writing, historians have relied on other well-preserved archaeological remains to learn how they lived. The Inca were accomplished engineers and builders despite having no knowledge of the wheel. They constructed a network of elaborate footpath roads and suspension bridges connecting distant regions of their empire. The Inca were also skilled craft workers who created many fine articles from gold and silver.

The Inca were a deeply religious people. They believed nature was created by their most important god, Viracocha. The ruling family prayed chiefly to Inti, the sun god. The Inca also worshiped the earth and the sea as goddesses. They frequently held religious ceremonies in which crops and animals—and sometimes humans—were sacrificed to keep the good will of the gods.

A farming people, the Inca raised crops of corn, cotton, potatoes, an edible root called *oca,* and a grain known as *quinoa*. Those who worked the land lived in small houses made of adobe or built of stones set in mud. The nobles lived in spacious, richly decorated stone palaces.

March of the conquistadors

When the Inca emperor Huayna Capac died in about 1527, civil war broke out between rival groups following two of his sons, Atahualpa and Huáscar. Huáscar was the heir to the throne but Atahualpa had a large army. The fighting between the brothers' followers seriously weakened the empire. In

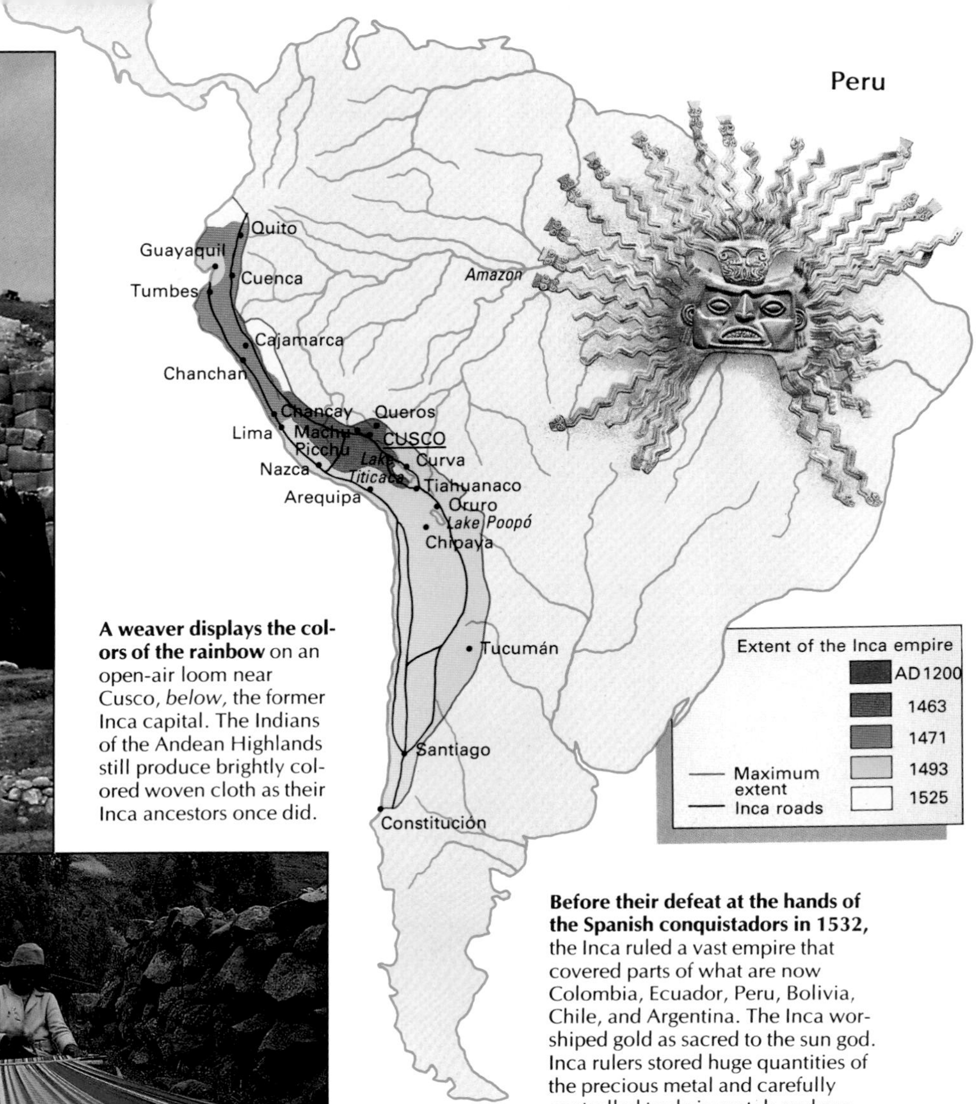

A weaver displays the colors of the rainbow on an open-air loom near Cusco, *below,* the former Inca capital. The Indians of the Andean Highlands still produce brightly colored woven cloth as their Inca ancestors once did.

Before their defeat at the hands of the Spanish conquistadors in 1532, the Inca ruled a vast empire that covered parts of what are now Colombia, Ecuador, Peru, Bolivia, Chile, and Argentina. The Inca worshiped gold as sacred to the sun god. Inca rulers stored huge quantities of the precious metal and carefully controlled trade in metals and precious stones. Gold objects were used by the families of Inca nobles, and gold figures were placed in many Inca graves.

Inca descendants celebrate the festival of the sun god with the Dance of the Condors. Most Indians have converted to the Roman Catholic faith brought by the Spaniards, but many also worship Inca gods.

1532, Atahualpa's army defeated and captured Huáscar. Meanwhile, the Spanish conquistador Francisco Pizarro marched into Inca territory with 167 men.

Pizarro and his men ambushed and captured Atahualpa in the city of Cajamarca, Peru. Although a ransom of a room filled with gold and a room filled twice with silver was paid for Atahualpa's return, Pizarro broke his word and executed his prisoner anyway. While the Spanish held Atahualpa prisoner, Atahualpa's army had executed Huáscar. The remaining Inca leaders retreated in shock and confusion and were quickly defeated by the Spaniards.

Lake Titicaca

Lake Titicaca, the world's highest navigable lake, lies on the border between Peru and Bolivia at an altitude of 12,507 feet (3,812 meters) above sea level. Shrouded in ancient Indian myth and mystery for thousands of years, the lake—resting high on a plateau in the central Andes—is unusual because of its size and high altitude.

Lake Titicaca is the result of water collecting on the plateau instead of flowing down from the mountains into the ocean. The water then flows from Lake Titicaca into Lake Poopó. Because the level of Lake Poopó has now fallen below its outlet, water usually can escape only through evaporation. When the water is high, it overflows into nearby swamplands.

In pre-Inca times, Lake Titicaca was the center of an important Indian civilization. Ruins of the ancient ceremonial center of Tiahuanaco stand 12 miles (20 kilometers) away. Lake Titicaca, which is about 110 miles (180 kilometers) long and about 45 miles (72 kilometers) wide, covers an area of some 3,200 square miles (8,300 square kilometers). Although ancient legends say that Lake Titicaca is bottomless, recent *sonar* (sound) measurements have found a maximum depth of 1,530 feet (466 meters).

From steamboats to reed boats

The first steamboat to cross Lake Titicaca was the *Yaravi,* a Scottish-built 200-ton steamer. In 1862, the *Yaravi* sailed from Scotland to the Peruvian coast, where it was completely dismantled. The ship's parts were then hauled up the rugged Andean terrain on the backs of mules. When the mules reached Puno, on the western shore of Lake Titicaca, the *Yaravi* was reassembled by Indian laborers.

Today, commercial ferryboats carry passengers and freight across the lake during the day, while smugglers operate in the dark of the night. Slipping past Bolivian Navy patrol boats, these smugglers carry meat, sugar, flour, and coca to Peru. They return to the Bolivian shore with clothes, radios, beer, and textiles.

An Aymara Indian, *right,* uses a pole to push his reed boat, known as a *totora,* through the water. He wears the traditional hat of his tribe—an ear-flapped, brightly colored woolen hat called a *gorro.* The slopes of the central Andes rise in the distance.

Modern steamships are now a common sight on the busy waters of Lake Titicaca, but for the Inca, the lake was a sacred place. They believed the sun god placed here Manco Capac and Mama Ocllo, the brother and sister he created to guide the Inca people.

Indian children chew on the soft cores of totora reeds, *above,* as if the reeds were sticks of candy. The totora reed, which the local Indians use to make their floating-island homes, is edible and forms an important part of the Indians' diet.

Sharing the waters of Lake Titicaca with these modern motorized boats are the Indians' *totoras*—small reed boats whose design dates from ancient times. In the mid-1940's, the totoras captured the interest of Norwegian ethnologist and author Thor Heyerdahl.

Heyerdahl asked the native totora builders in Suriqui, an island in the southern Titicaca region, to help him build a reed boat. He wanted to test his theory that the islands of Polynesia could have been settled by Indians from South America. In 1947, he sailed the balsa-wood raft he built, called the *Kon-Tiki,* from the coast of Peru to the Tuamotu Islands in eastern Polynesia to test his theory.

The Indians of the lake

Today, Aymara and Quechua Indians inhabit the shores of Lake Titicaca and the surrounding area. But centuries ago, a people called the Uru lived there. Larger Aymara tribes drove the Uru from their lands, and some Uru people fled the mainland to live on artificial islands on the lake. The Uru people have disappeared or merged with other tribes of the region, but some Indians still make their own floating-island homes by weaving totora reeds together into huge platforms.

These people eat potatoes, yucca, oca (a tuberous root), and a grain called quinoa—grown in soil taken from the lakeside and spread over the matted reeds. They also barbecue *cuy,* or guinea pigs.

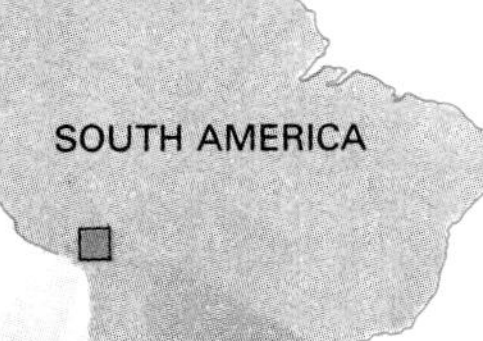

Lake Titicaca is located on the border between Peru and Bolivia. It is the highest navigable lake in the world.

***Totoras,* the small reed boats used by Indians in the Lake Titicaca region,** are made from totora reeds collected from the shallows of the lake. The green totora leaves are dried in the sun until they are free of moisture. The Indians then bundle them up and lash them together with grass to form the boat's hull. A mast with a reed sail completes the small craft. The dry reeds float easily on top of the water, but after a few months they become waterlogged and settle lower in the water. To keep their totoras "seaworthy," the Indians periodically dry their boats on shore and launch them again.

Philippines

The Philippines is an island country that lies off the Southeast Asian mainland in the Pacific Ocean. People live on only about 900 of the approximately 7,400 islands of the Philippines; fewer than half of these islands have names. Eleven islands make up more than 95 per cent of the country.

Thick tropical forests cover most of the Philippines, while narrow strips of lowland lie along the coasts. On most of the country's larger islands are volcanic mountains, many of them active. Violent earthquakes occur frequently on the islands. Another threat that nature poses to the area is that of typhoons, tropical storms that strike seasonally.

The people of the Philippines, called *Filipinos,* have a wide variety of languages, customs, and cultures. Their ancestors migrated from Indonesia and Malaysia thousands of years ago. Groups of these dark-haired, dark-skinned people formed small communities throughout the area, and each group developed its own culture.

Ferdinand Magellan, a Portuguese sea captain, led a Spanish expedition to the Philippines in 1521. He was looking for a western sea route from Europe to the Spice Islands, now part of Indonesia. Magellan remained in the Philippines for several weeks and converted many of the people to Christianity before he was killed in a battle between rival Filipino groups.

Another group of Spanish explorers followed in 1565, colonizing the Philippines and naming them after King Philip II of Spain. The Spaniards converted most Filipinos to Christianity, but some tribes kept their own religion. As Christianity spread through the islands, it worked as a unifying cultural force throughout the many scattered communities. Today, more Christians live in the Philippines than in any other Asian nation.

In 1898, as part of the treaty that ended the Spanish-American War, the United States paid Spain $20 million and took control of the Philippines. The United States ruled the islands until the Philippines became a self-governing commonwealth in 1935. During World War II (1939–1945), the Philippines had strategic importance and was the scene of extensive, heavy fighting. The Philippines became an independent nation on July 4, 1946, with a Constitution and economic system similar to those of the United States. Since independence, persistent economic inequalities, government corruption, interference with civilian rule by the military, and radical groups on both the right and left have presented the Philippines with its greatest challenges.

Philippines Today

In the 1990's, the Philippines tackled many political and economic problems. In 1996, the government signed a treaty with the Moro National Liberation Front (MNLF), the main Muslim guerrilla group that had sought an independent state. This treaty ended almost 25 years of civil war that had claimed tens of thousands of lives. However, another Muslim group, the Moro Island Liberation Front (MILF), continued to fight for a Muslim state in the southern Philippines. Philippine Communists still carried on their antigovernment activities, but violence waned toward the end of 1993. However, unemployment, poverty, and inflation also made life difficult for many Filipinos.

U.S. base disputes

Clark Air Base, a key U.S. military facility 10 miles (16 kilometers) from Mount Pinatubo, was buried under ash from volcanic eruptions in the early 1990's. As a result, the U.S. government decided to abandon the base. But it wanted to continue operations at Subic Bay Naval Station, the largest U.S. naval base abroad, 25 miles (40 kilometers) south of Pinatubo. On Aug. 27, 1991, the United States and the Philippines signed a treaty agreeing to extend the U.S. lease on the site for at least 10 years. But the Philippine Senate voted to reject the treaty because opposition to it was widespread. The United States withdrew from Subic Bay.

Government

The people elect the president and vice president to six-year terms. The Congress consists of a 24-member Senate and a 221-member House of Representatives. Fifty of the representatives are selected from lists drawn up by the political parties to ensure representation of women, ethnic minorities, and certain economic and occupational groups.

The Philippines is divided into 13 regions, each governed by a regional council. The regions are divided into 73 provinces, each province having a governor and other officials elected by the people. Each of the nation's 61 cities has an elected mayor. The country also has 1,400 *municipalities* (towns) and 42,000 *barrios* (villages), each governed by elected officials and councils.

FACT BOX

PHILIPPINES

COUNTRY

Official name: Republika ng Pilipinas (Republic of the Philippines)
Capital: Manila
Terrain: Mostly mountains with narrow to extensive coastal lowlands
Area: 115,831 sq. mi. (300,000 km²)
Climate: Tropical marine; northeast monsoon (November to April); southwest monsoon (May to October)
Main rivers: Agno, Pampanga, Magat, Cagayan, Agusan, Pulangi
Highest elevation: Mount Apo, 9,692 ft. (2,954 m)
Lowest elevation: Philippine Sea, sea level

GOVERNMENT

Form of government: Republic
Head of state: President
Head of government: President
Administrative areas: 73 provinces, 61 chartered cities
Legislature: Kongreso (Congress) consisting of the Senado (Senate) with 24 members serving six-year terms and the Kapulungan Ng Mga Kinatawan (House of Representatives) with 221 members serving three-year terms
Court system: Supreme Court
Armed forces: 110,000 troops

PEOPLE

Estimated 2002 population: 78,850,000
Population growth: 2.07%
Population density: 681 persons per sq. mi. (263 per km²)
Population distribution: 53% rural, 47% urban
Life expectancy in years:
Male: 65
Female: 70
Doctors per 1,000 people: 1.2
Percentage of age-appropriate population enrolled in the following educational levels:
Primary: 117*
Secondary: 78
Further: 35

Manila is the capital and largest city of the Philippines, as well as its banking, financial, and commercial center. Costly modern buildings stand in parts of Manila; however, the Philippines is still a poor nation, and Manila has many slums.

The Philippines, *right,* consists of more than 7,000 islands. The 11 largest make up more than 95 per cent of the country. Manila, the Philippine capital, is on Luzon, one of these islands. Luzon is also a rich agricultural and mining area. Only about 900 of the other islands are inhabited, and fewer than half even have names.

Languages spoken:
- Pilipino (official)
- English (official)

Religions:
- Roman Catholic 83%
- Protestant 9%
- Muslim 5%
- Buddhist

**Enrollment ratios compare the number of students enrolled to the population which, by age, should be enrolled. A ratio higher than 100 indicates that students older or younger than the typical age range are also enrolled.*

Technology

Radios per 1,000 people: 161
Televisions per 1,000 people: 144
Computers per 1,000 people: 19.3

Economy

Currency: Philippine peso
Gross national income (GNI) in 2000: $78.8 billion U.S.
Real annual growth rate (1999–2000): 4.0%
GNI per capita (2000): $1,040 U.S.
Balance of payments (2000): $9,081 million U.S.
Goods exported: Electronic equipment, machinery and transport equipment, garments, coconut products
Goods imported: Raw materials and intermediate goods, capital goods, consumer goods, fuels
Trading partners: United States, Japan, European Union, South Korea

Living standards

Economic conditions vary widely among the people of the Philippines. In rural areas, most farmland belongs to wealthy landowners, who hire laborers who live and work on their estates. In the cities, wealthy families live in large houses surrounded by walls. Government-built housing projects are common, but many poor urban people live in ramshackle shanties in sprawling slums.

About 95 per cent of Filipino adults can read and write. About half of all the country's workers make their living in agriculture, mining, or fishing, while 37 per cent are employed in service industries. About 13 per cent have jobs in manufacturing and construction.

Environment

The islands of the Philippines are covered largely with dense tropical rain forests. They extend 1,152 miles (1,854 kilometers) from north to south and 688 miles (1,107 kilometers) from east to west. They stretch across the South China Sea, which is part of the Pacific Ocean. The islands have many fine bays and harbors and several large lakes, but most of the rivers flow only in the rainy season, which lasts from June to February. Narrow strips of lowland lie along the coasts.

The Philippine islands lie in the *circum-Pacific belt*—one of the world's two major earthquake belts. Violent earthquakes occur frequently in this area. In addition, most of the world's volcanoes lie along this belt, which is also known as the *Ring of Fire*. In 1991, Mount Pinatubo, a volcano on Luzon, erupted many times, causing more than 550 deaths and destroying crops, homes, and other property. Off the coast of Mindanao lies the Philippine Trench, one of the deepest spots in all the oceans. It lies 34,578 feet (10,539 meters) below the surface of the Pacific, an ocean with an average depth of about 14,000 feet (4,270 meters).

A turquoise lake fills the crater of Taal Volcano south of Manila. The Philippines lie along the Ring of Fire, where volcanic eruptions occur frequently.

Climate

The Philippines has a hot, humid climate. During the hottest months, from March to May, temperatures may reach 100° F. (38° C). The weather cools off during the rainy season, but the temperature rarely falls below 70° F. (21° C). Rainfall in the Philippines averages 100 inches (250 centimeters) a year, with some areas receiving up to 180 inches (457 centimeters). Less rain falls on the lowlands than in the high mountain areas because the mountains block winds that carry rain-bearing clouds from the ocean.

About five typhoons strike the Philippines yearly. Between May and November, these storms, with winds of more than 74 miles (119 kilometers) per hour, howl down on the China Sea. Typhoons can rip banana groves to shreds and demolish buildings. Low islands have been completely swamped by the huge waves lashed up by these winds.

Wildlife

A wide variety of plants and animals lives in the Philippines. Banyan and palm trees flour-

A rocky islet, *left,* in the calm coastal waters of the Philippines has both wooded areas and secluded stretches of beach. The Philippine islands are peaks of an immense string of submerged volcanic mountain ranges.

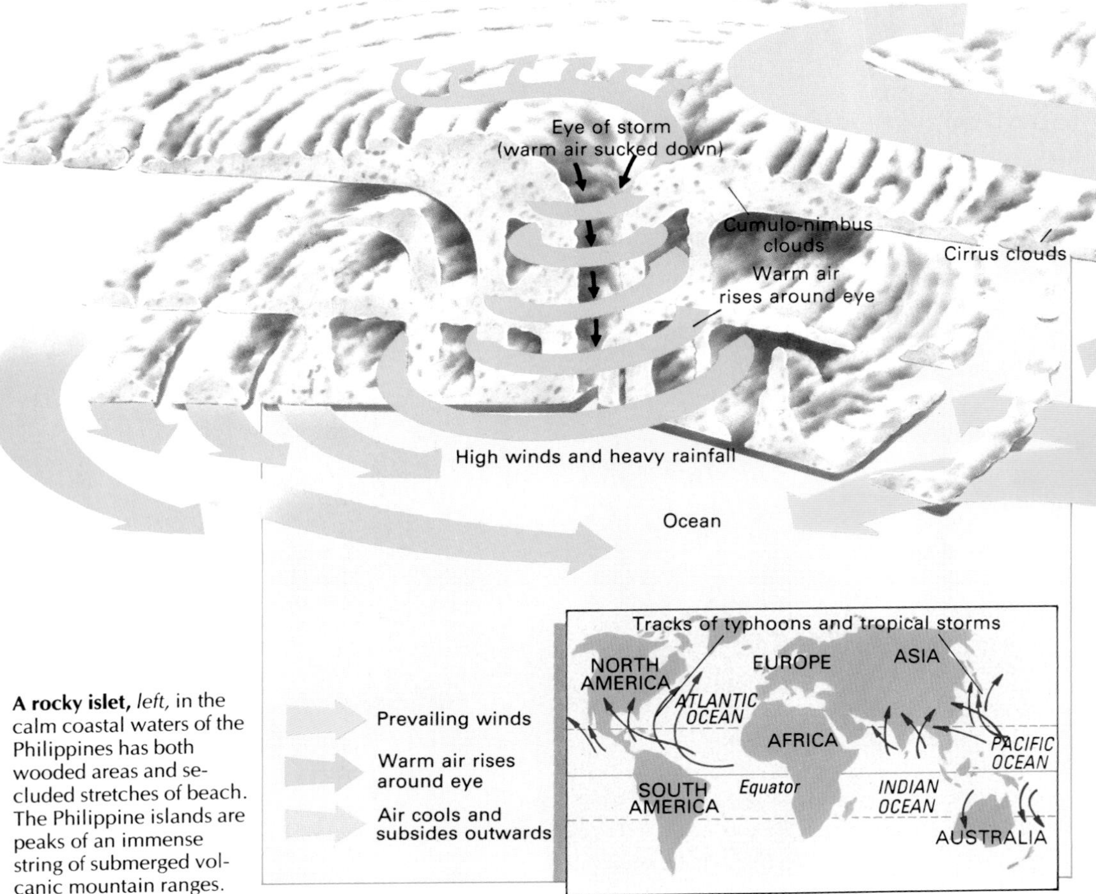

Typhoons—violent tropical storms that form in the western Pacific—often strike the Philippines. A typhoon is a low-pressure area in the atmosphere in which winds spiral inward. Near the center, or "eye," of the storm, wind speeds range from 74 miles (119 kilometers) per hour to 180 miles (290 kilometers) per hour. Lashing rains, violent thunder, and lightning usually accompany the winds. Typhoons measure from 200 to 300 miles (320 to 480 kilometers) across.

Fish pools, *left,* around Manila Bay provide milkfish, shrimp, and tilapia for domestic markets. Anchovies, sardines, and tuna thrive in the waters surrounding the islands.

ish in the forests, while thick groves of bamboo and about 9,000 kinds of flowering plants grow throughout the islands. Crocodiles, monkeys, snakes, and many species of tropical birds live in the Philippines. Tarsiers—small nocturnal mammals with large, owl-like eyes—are found only in the tropical rain forests of the Philippines and the East Indies.

Resources

The Philippine islands form three groups. The northern group consists of two large islands, Luzon and Mindoro. Luzon produces most of the nation's rice and tobacco, and has large deposits of copper, gold, and other minerals. Manila, the nation's capital, lies on Luzon's southwest coast.

The central group of islands, called the Visayas, consists of about 7,000 islands. Among them are Panay, Cebu, and Bohol, all densely populated islands with fertile agricultural land. Cebu, the most crowded island in the Philippines, produces corn, rice, sugar cane, tobacco, and coconuts. Its major city, also called Cebu, is a busy port.

The southern group consists of Mindanao and the Sulu Archipelago, a group of about 400 islands that extend south and west toward Borneo. Mindanao, at the southeastern end of the Philippines, has the country's highest mountains—including some active volcanoes. It is also one of the world's leading producers of abacá, a plant used in making rope.

People

The population of the Philippines reached about 65 million in 1992, and the number of people is increasing at a rate of more than 2 per cent per year. The world's average growth rate in the year 2000 was 1.3 per cent. By 2010, the Philippines' population is expected to reach almost 100 million.

In 2000, the population density in the Philippines was 701 persons per square mile (271 per square kilometer), far higher than the average population density in Asia, which is 221 persons per square mile (85 per square kilometer).

A blend of cultures

Anthropologists believe that a tribe of Negritos called the Aeta came to the islands from the Southeast Asian mainland more than 30,000 years ago. They were probably the first people to live in the Philippines.

About 3000 B.C., groups of Malays from Indonesia and Malaysia began to settle along the coasts of the islands. The Malays belong to the Asian geographical race, which includes the Chinese and the Japanese. Most Filipinos are descended from these Malays.

Chinese make up the second largest group in the Philippines, and smaller numbers of Americans, Europeans, Indians, and Japanese also live on the islands. All these groups have contributed to the Philippine culture, a blend of Asian and Western traditions. Philippine food, for example, is a mixture of American, Chinese, Malay, and Spanish dishes.

Languages

The Philippines has two official languages, Pilipino and English.

Pilipino is the national language, and it is a required subject in all elementary schools. Pilipino is a variation of Tagalog, the language of the people of the Manila area. More than 50 per cent of all the Philippine people speak Pilipino, and almost 75 per cent speak English.

English is widely used in commerce and government. In addition, about 70 native dialects, all based on Malay languages, are spoken in the Philippines.

A Moro man, *above,* of the Sulu Archipelago in the southern Philippines wears a smile. Strong-willed and fiercely independent, the members of this Muslim minority have risen up to demand political freedom for their people.

Filipino girls wear their best clothes to Mass. More than 80 per cent of Filipinos follow the Roman Catholic religion, which was introduced by the Spanish in the 1500's.

The carabao, the chief domestic animal in the Philippines, gets a holiday on May 14, Carabao Day. Farmers use the carabao, a type of water buffalo, to pull plows and haul loads.

A Filipino woman, *center,* enjoys her job as a security guard. A growing number of women fill such posts today.

An elaborate headdress symbolizes this elderly man's high position among his people. He belongs to one of the small tribal groups who live in the remote mountain areas. Cultural minorities make up about 10 per cent of the Philippine population.

Education

About 95 per cent of the Philippine people can read and write. The law requires children from 7 to 12 years old to attend school through at least the sixth grade. Teachers in public elementary schools conduct classes in the local dialect for the first two years and then introduce English and Pilipino. Most private schools, high schools, and universities use English.

Way of life

Most Filipinos wear Western clothing. On holidays and other special occasions, Philippine men may wear a *barong tagalog,* a beautifully embroidered shirt made of pineapple fiber, raw silk, or cotton, and women may wear a long, puff-sleeved dress called a *balintawak.*

Fifty-three per cent of the Philippine people live in rural areas, while 47 per cent live in the cities. About half the people live on Luzon, the largest island. Rural people farm for a living or work in the fishing, lumbering, and mining industries, while many people in the cities have jobs in factories.

The Philippine Constitution guarantees freedom of worship. About five-sixths of the people are Roman Catholics—a result of the Spanish colonization. The nation also has many Protestants, Muslims, and members of the Philippine Independent Church and the Philippine Church of Christ.

Most Filipinos have large families and maintain close relationships with family members, including elder relatives and distant cousins. Men generally hold positions of authority at home and in business, but many women work in professional fields and growing numbers of women work in factories.

Ethnic Diversity

The people of the Philippines make up a tapestry of ethnic communities. Ten per cent of the nation's population is made up of minority groups. Some of these groups live in rain forests or remote mountain provinces. Others live on the southern islands.

The government of the Philippines works with the nation's minority groups through an agency called PANAMIN. The agency takes a variety of approaches in working with these groups. In some cases, PANAMIN provides direct aid, while in others it helps preserve a group's culture and life style. The agency may work to draw a group into the mainstream of modern life. PANAMIN also collects crafts and artifacts of the country's ethnic groups and displays them in a museum in Pasay City, near Manila.

Some northern cultures

Negritos thought to have come from Southeast Asia more than 30,000 years ago were probably the first people to live in the Philippines. Today, Negritos live in small, isolated groups in various parts of the Philippines—in mountain jungles, along the shores of the northern provinces, and in the hills of Luzon.

Like African Pygmies, Negritos have dark skin and tightly curled brown hair, and stand less than 5 feet (150 centimeters) tall. Negritos have traditionally lived by hunting and by gathering plants and fruits. Today, the Negritos face cultural extinction.

The Ifugao, a mountain people of northern Luzon, were the architects of a spectacular series of rice terraces. These rice fields were built in the mountains 2,000 to 3,000 years ago and cover an area of 100 square miles (250 square kilometers). The Ifugao honor their ancestors and important spirits with worship, animal sacrifice, and magnificent sculptures.

Muslim cultures of the south

In the 1300's, some 200 years before Magellan landed in the Philippines, Muslim traders made contact with the southern islands of Mindanao and the Sulu Archipelago. They brought the Islamic faith with them, and it took a strong hold on the local people. The Spaniards who came later were unable

to convert these Muslims, or *Moros,* to Christianity.

Today, the Moros claim Mindanao and the Sulu Archipelago as their own holy land, and they seek political independence from the national government of the Philippines. Muslim uprisings have occurred on several islands, and political-cultural conflict continued into the 1990's.

The Moros are composed of several culturally distinct groups. The Tausug, one of the largest groups and the first community to convert to Islam, were notorious pirates and smugglers. Today, the Tausug's long, narrow

The Kalinga, a mountain people of northern Luzon, *below,* were once notorious headhunters. Today's Kalinga, including this man having his hair cut, are peaceful people. Their neighbors, the Ifugao, built the rice terraces of Banawe.

Stilt villages, perched above the waters of the Sulu Sea in the southern Philippines, are home to the Badjao peoples, also known as "sea gypsies." Many of these people are born in their boats and spend their entire lives on the water.

Southwestern Mindanao is home to the T'boli people, *right,* who number about 60,000. Villagers, such as this family, draw water from a well and live in long houses set apart from one another on high ground or along ridges.

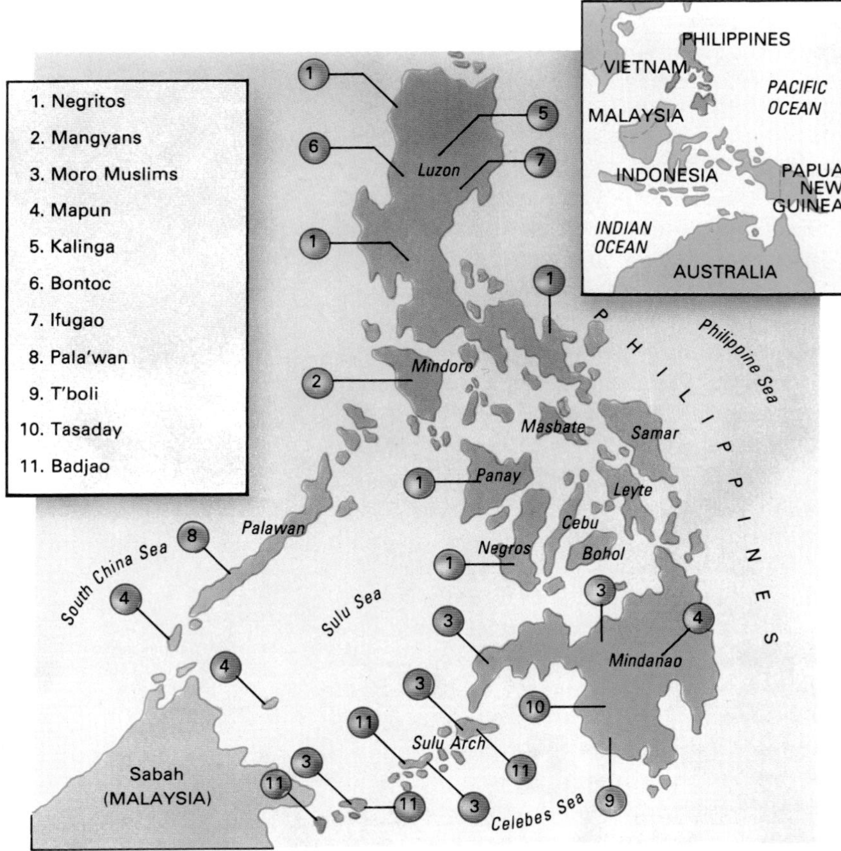

Ethnic minorities make up 10 per cent of the Philippines' population. Many of the groups live in the south of the country, especially on Mindanao, home to a large Muslim minority. Other ethnic groups, however, live in northern Luzon and in the island groups of the western Philippines.

PANAMIN, a government agency founded in 1967, helps ethnic groups through programs of direct aid, integration, and preservation.

This woman from northern Mindanao lives in an area with a mixed Muslim and Christian population.

motorboats make them masters of the trade between islands.

The Maranao, another Muslim group, live in isolation in northern Mindanao. Their major town, Marawi, is a center of Islamic learning.

The Badjao, a third Moro group, are seafarers who are born on their narrow-beamed wooden boats on the Sulu Sea. Some of the Badjao, who are sometimes called "sea gypsies," spend their entire lives on the water, traveling to land only to die.

Manila

The city of Manila became known as the *Pearl of the Orient* because of its beautiful setting and architecture. The city stretches along the east shore of Manila Bay on the island of Luzon. It covers a total area of about 15 square miles (38 square kilometers), and its metropolitan area covers 246 square miles (636 square kilometers). The capital and largest city of the Philippines, Manila also has the country's leading port and serves as its major cultural, social, educational, and commercial center. Parts of the city are luxurious and wealthy, while others are areas of extreme poverty and slums. The Manila metropolitan area is one of the largest in the world.

When the Spanish founded Manila in 1571, they enclosed their city with high walls and a wide moat to protect themselves from unfriendly Filipinos. This area, called Intramuros, or the Walled City, stands on the banks of the Pasig River. The Pasig cuts through the heart of modern-day Manila and forms part of the harbor on Manila Bay.

The walls of Intramuros and some of the churches, convents, monasteries, and public buildings still stand, despite heavy bombing during World War II (1939-1945). Among the old buildings is the impressive St. Augustine Church, built in 1599.

Fresh and dried fish await buyers in one of Manila's many markets. Anchovies, mackerel, sardines, and tuna are part of the daily catch in the waters around the Philippines.

Commercial hub

Manila is the banking, financial, and commercial center of the Philippines. It is also the headquarters of the Asian Development Bank, which lends money to promote economic growth in Asia. Manilan industries turn out a variety of goods, including textiles and clothing. Its processing plants produce beer, coconut oil, soap, and tobacco products.

In addition, Manila's superb harbor and location make it an important port on Pacific and Far East trade routes. Piers in Manila's harbor handle up to 12 large ships at one time.

Jeepneys, brightly decorated taxis, *below,* provide inexpensive transportation in cities throughout the Philippines. Made from World War II jeeps, these cabs carry 10 or more passengers.

Government center

Spain surrendered Manila to the United States in 1898 after the Spanish-American War. The American administration installed a modern water-supply system and electric lighting. Japanese forces seized Manila in

The city of Manila forms the heart of a metropolitan area that covers 246 square miles (636 square kilometers). The original business district of Manila lies along the north bank of the Pasig River.

January 1942, and few buildings remained standing when the Japanese finally surrendered the city to U.S. troops in 1945. However, the Filipinos began rebuilding almost immediately.

Manila became the national capital of the Philippines when independence was proclaimed on July 4, 1946. In 1948, the Philippine government made Quezon City the capital of the country. But Manila continued to serve as the seat of government, pending the completion of new government buildings in Quezon City. In 1976, however, the government again made Manila the country's official capital.

Cultural heart

The Luneta, one of Manila's spacious parks, overlooks Manila Bay from just outside Intramuros. A scenic boulevard runs along the bay from the Luneta past the graceful mansions and lovely hotels of Manila. It also passes through the poor areas of the city.

A large Chinatown draws visitors on the north bank of the Pasig River. Many tourists travel to Quiapo, also north of the river, to visit its colorful market and lively restaurants, shopping centers, and movie theaters. Thousands of people go to the Quiapo Church every Friday to worship at the shrine of the miraculous image of the Black Nazarene, which is thought to have healing powers. This life-sized image of Christ bearing the Cross was carved from black hardwood and brought from Mexico to Manila in the 1600's.

Manila has 17 universities. The oldest, the University of Santo Tomás, was founded in 1611. The city has a number of public libraries and museums, as well as a symphony orchestra and ballet and opera companies.

The crowded slums of Manila show the dark side of the capital city. In the Tondo section of northwest Manila, some 180,000 people live in 17,000 shanties, or shacks, such as these.

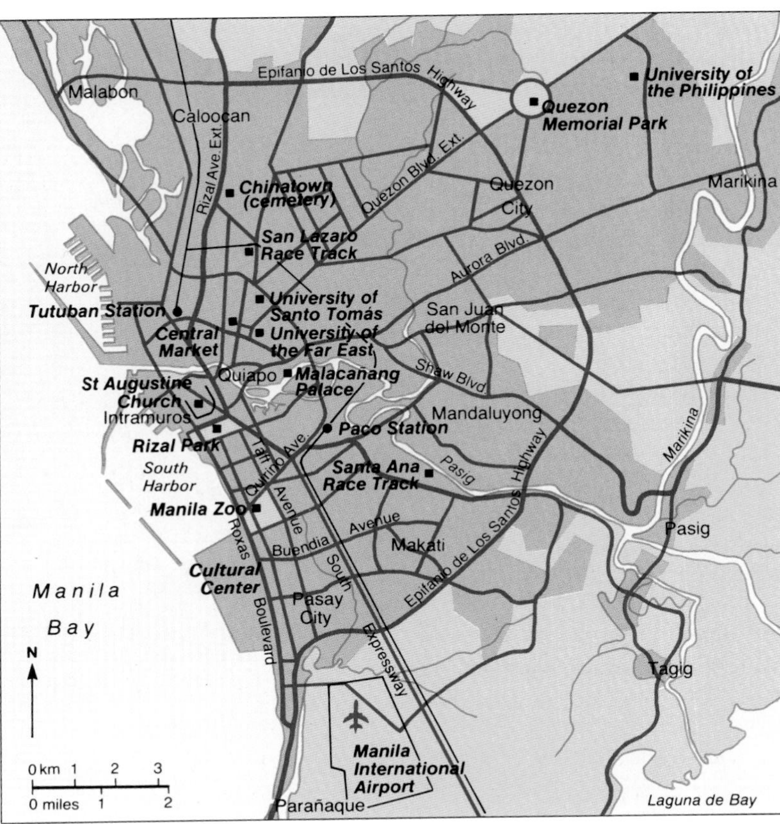

Manila, *right,* was once a Muslim settlement. The Spanish, however, laid the foundations of modern Manila in the Intramuros, or Walled City, in 1571. The construction of Intramuros was completed in 1739. It lies on the south bank of the Pasig River. North of the river lies the suburb of Quiapo with its many tourist attractions, and Malacañang, the home of the Philippine president. The University of Santo Tomás also lies north of the river.

Economy

The islands of the Philippines are rich in natural resources. Mineral deposits, fertile farmland, lush rain forests, and coastal waters teeming with fish have traditionally been the cornerstones of the nation's economy. Today, although agriculture and forestry still employ almost half of Philippine workers, manufacturing exceeds all other activities in product value.

Agriculture and forestry

Filipinos farm only about 35 per cent of the nation's land, but produce most of the food needed for the entire population. Many farmers rent their land and pay the owner part of their crop.

Farmers grow rice and corn on about two-thirds of the cultivated land. Rice is an essential crop because most Filipinos eat it at every meal. Other leading food crops include sweet potatoes and *cassava,* a starchy root. Bananas, coconuts, mangoes, pineapples, and sugar cane are raised for both local use and export.

Philippine farmers also raise a crop called abacá, or Manila hemp, used in making rope. Mindanao, the island at the southeastern end of the Philippines, is one of the world's leading producers of abacá. The leaves of this plant contain a fiber that has great natural resistance to water, sun, and wind. Abacá fiber is also used in the manufacture of paper products. The plant has become less important on the world market, however, since the development of strong synthetic fibers.

More than 3,000 kinds of trees grow in the forests that cover about half the land of the Philippines. About 90 per cent of the nation's timber comes from several related trees called Philippine mahoganies. Mangroves and pines also yield timber. Bamboo grows throughout the islands, and Filipinos use the stiff, hollow stems of this plant to build houses and make baskets, furniture, and other items.

Mining and fishing industries

Minerals contribute a large part of the Philippines' exports. Copper, found on Luzon,

A farm girl works at a wet, muddy, but essential job—transplanting rice. The rice fields of central Luzon produce more of this important food crop than any other area of the Philippines.

Fruits and vegetables make a tempting display in the market at Baguio in central Luzon. Fruit crops include bananas, coconuts, mangoes, pineapples, and sugar cane. Leading vegetable crops include cassava, corn, rice, and sweet potatoes.

Anchovies, one of the many types of fish found in Philippine coastal waters, are spread out to dry in the sun, *below.* Two other important fish, mackerel and tuna, are favorites in Philippine cooking.

Cargo and passenger ships use the docks of Manila, the Philippines' busiest port, *left.* The nation depends heavily on ships for local transportation and international trade.

Miners extract copper ore—the country's leading mineral—from underground mines. Many of these mines are located on Luzon. Other valuable mineral deposits include gold, nickel, and silver.

Cebu, Negros, and Samar, is the leading mineral. Large gold mines operate in northern Luzon, and the Phillippines ranked among the 10 leading gold-mining countries in 1992. The Phillippines also has deposits of coal, iron ore, limestone, manganese, nickel, silver, and zinc.

The waters surrounding the islands provide anchovies, mackerel, sardines, scad, tuna, and other fish. Crabs, shrimp, oysters, and sponges are found in the island waters.

Industry and economic development

The principal industries of the Philippines produce cement, chemicals, cigars, clothing, foods and beverages, refined metals and petroleum, sugar, textiles, and wood products. Many companies operate factories in *export-processing zones,* where businesses can import foreign goods without paying import taxes.

The country is a member of the Colombo Plan, which provides assistance for economic development to countries of South and Southeast Asia. The Philippines is also a member of the Association of Southeast Asian Nations (ASEAN), which promotes economic, cultural, and social cooperation among its members. The six member nations have agreed to share basic products during shortages and to gradually remove trade restrictions, especially taxes on imports.

Contributing to the Philippines' economic development is the nation's transportation system, one of the best in Asia. Despite the rugged terrain, roads cross the larger islands; railroads serve the largest island, Luzon; and a rapid transit rail system operates in the largest city, Manila. Ships and airplanes carry passengers and freight between islands; the leading ports are Manila, Cebu, and Davao. Manila also has a major international airport.

The nation has a well-developed communications industry, with several television networks and about 20 daily newspapers published in various languages.

History

In 1565, a group of Spanish explorers landed in the Philippines and claimed the islands for Spain. They divided the land among themselves, employing Filipinos as tenant farmers, laborers, and servants. Spanish priests converted most of the Filipinos to Roman Catholicism.

Spanish rule

Rebellion against Spanish rule first arose in the late 1800's. The great opposition leader from that period was José Rizal, a doctor who worked for reform until 1896, when the Spanish executed him.

Emilio Aguinaldo also led a movement for independence during that period. In 1896, he took part in an unsuccessful revolt against Spanish rule. Spain promised political reforms if Aguinaldo would end the revolt and leave the islands. Aguinaldo then sailed to Hong Kong, but the Spanish broke their promise and he returned in May 1898. The United States gained possession of the Philippines that year as part of a peace treaty with Spain.

U.S. rule

Aguinaldo claimed that the United States had promised to make the Philippines independent immediately. He declared the establishment of the Philippine Republic on Jan. 23, 1899, and his troops began fighting the U.S. occupation forces. The Americans captured Aguinaldo in March 1901, however, and the fighting soon ended.

In 1901, the United States set up a colonial government in the Philippines. Under American rule, the English language spread rapidly. American businesses invested heavily in the Philippines, and the nation's economy became dependent on the United States.

The United States began to allow Filipinos to hold government positions. In 1935, the

General Douglas MacArthur led U.S. troops as they liberated the Philippines from Japanese occupation during World War II. In this photo, MacArthur wades ashore on the island of Leyte.

c. 30,000 B.C. Negritos migrate to the Philippines.
c. 3,000 B.C. Malays migrate from Malaysia and Indonesia.
1100's Growth of Chinese influence.
1300's Muslim traders introduce Islam.
1521 Magellan lands in Philippines.
1565 Spanish explorers claim the Philippines for Spain.
1571 Spaniards begin construction of *Intramuros* (the Walled City) in Manila.
1600–47 Raids by Dutch fleet from East Indies.
1603 First of five rebellions by Chinese population.
1762–64 British occupy Manila.
1872 Spanish repression leads to Filipino national movement.
1896 José Rizal leads uprising against the Spanish and is executed.
1898 Spanish-American War; U.S. gains possession of Philippines.
1899 Emilio Aguinaldo declares the establishment of Philippine Republic.
1901 U.S. subdues nationalist forces and sets up colonial government.
1901–15 Rebellion of Muslim Moro peoples.
1935 U.S. grants commonwealth status to Philippines.
1941 Japanese troops invade Philippines.
1942–44 Japanese occupy country.
1944 MacArthur lands on Leyte with U.S. forces.
1946 Republic of Philippines established.
1947 U.S. leases military bases.
1949–54 Philippine army defeats Communist-led uprising.
1965 Ferdinand E. Marcos elected president.
1972 Marcos declares martial law.
1983 Benigno S. Aquino, Jr., assassinated.
1986 Protests force Marcos to resign; Corazon Aquino installed as president.
1989 Marcos dies.
1991 Mount Pinatubo volcano erupts. Clark Air Base closed.
1992 Fidel V. Ramos elected president. U.S. withdraws from Subic Bay.

Ferdinand Magellan
(1480?–1521)

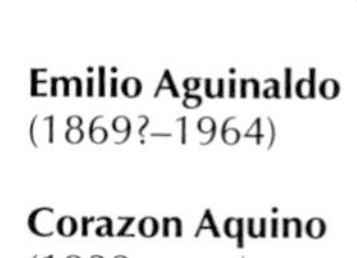

Emilio Aguinaldo
(1869?–1964)

Corazon Aquino
(1933–)

Migrating peoples from South Asia (to c. 500 BC)
Muslim traders and missionaries (1300s-1400s)
Voyage of Magellan 1521
Spanish conquest 1565
Trade routes (1600s-1700s)
Route of Manila Galleon
Muslim areas
Ruled by Spain 1571
Spanish colonial expansion
Cities

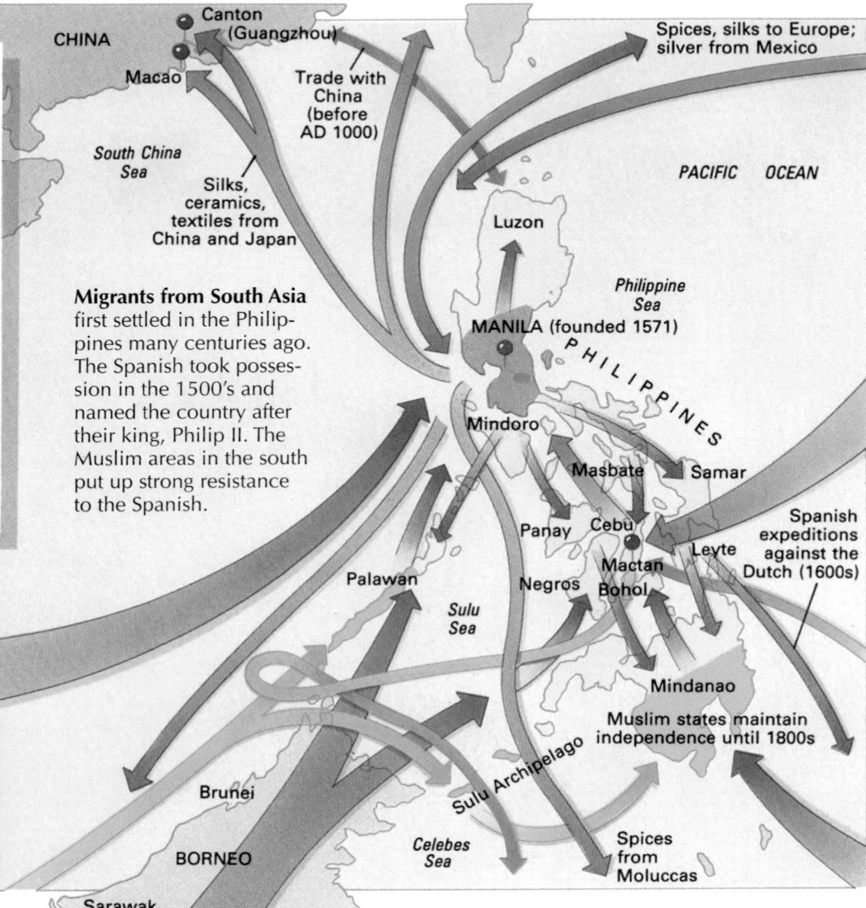

Migrants from South Asia first settled in the Philippines many centuries ago. The Spanish took possession in the 1500's and named the country after their king, Philip II. The Muslim areas in the south put up strong resistance to the Spanish.

Philippines became a commonwealth with an elected government and a Constitution similar to that of the United States.

The United States entered World War II (1939–1945) on Dec. 8, 1941, and on Dec. 10, Japanese troops invaded the Philippines. American and Philippine troops resisted the invasion until 1942, when most of the soldiers surrendered and were imprisoned. In October 1944, the United States sent fresh troops to the Philippines, defeating the Japanese several months later. The war hurt the Philippine economy and destroyed most of Manila.

Independence

The United States granted the Philippines complete independence on July 4, 1946. During the late 1940's, however, political problems and poverty caused widespread discontent among the Philippine people. The United States sent economic aid. The economy of the Philippines began to improve as industries built new plants and trade with other countries increased.

In 1965, Ferdinand E. Marcos became president, leading the country into almost 20 years of repression and government corruption. In 1986, protests and unrest forced Marcos to hold a presidential election. His chief opponent was Corazon Aquino.

The legislature ruled that Marcos won the election, but many Filipinos accused his party of election fraud. Widespread protests broke out, and Marcos lost key military support. He then left the country, and Aquino was sworn in as president. In 1999, the Marcos family agreed to pay $150 million to nearly 10,000 victims of human rights abuses under the Marcos administration.

Aquino promised many changes for the Philippines, but she failed to carry out her policies, partly due to seven coup attempts against her government.

In 1998, Joseph Estrada was elected president. In 2000, he was accused of corruption. He denied the charges. The House of Representatives voted to impeach him and the Senate took up the charges. Before a verdict was reached, Estrada lost the support of most politicians and stepped down. He was replaced by his vice president, Gloria Macapagal Arroyo.

Poland

Poland lies in central Europe and is bordered by the Czech Republic and Slovakia to the south and Germany to the west. To the east are several former Soviet republics, and to the north is the Baltic Sea. The country's central location has made it a crossroads for invading armies throughout its history, thereby resulting in many boundary changes.

Poland is named for the Polane, a Slavic tribe that lived more than 1,000 years ago in what is now Poland. The name *Polane* comes from a Slavic word meaning *plain* or field, a fitting name for this land of flat plains, gently rolling hills, and clear blue lakes.

A country with a long and varied history, Poland once ruled an empire that stretched across most of central Europe. The Polish empire reached its height during the 1500's, achieving important advances in its cultural, economic, and political development. However, after a long period of decline, Poland ceased to exist as a separate state in 1795 and was divided between Russia, Prussia, and Austria.

Poland came into existence again in 1918, after World War I (1914-1918), but Germany and the Soviet Union divided the country in half barely 20 years later, at the beginning of World War II (1939-1945). Once again, Poland disappeared from the face of Europe until a new country was formed at the end of World War II.

However, the new Poland was independent in name only. Its society and economy were entirely controlled by a Communist government that followed policies established by the Soviet Union. Not until the 1980's, when Poland was transformed from a one-party socialist system to a multiparty democracy, did the Poles regain a measure of their former freedom.

Even in the midst of continual political turmoil, the Poles have preserved their national identity, largely through their loyalty to the Roman Catholic Church. During the years between 1795 and 1918, when the Polish state did not exist, the people found themselves under pressure to be-

come either "Germanized" or "Russianized." The Germans were Protestant, and the Russians belonged to the Eastern Orthodox Church, so the Poles' Roman Catholic faith, which distinguished them from both, became the focus of their nationalism.

During the late 1940's and early 1950's, when Poland's leaders tried to destroy the influence of the Catholic Church, it proved to be a powerful spiritual force that helped unify the people. Today, about 95 per cent of the Polish people have been baptized in the Roman Catholic faith, and religious devotion goes hand in hand with patriotic fervor.

The Poles' national identity has also been preserved through the Polish language. During the 1800's, neither the Prussian nor the Russian authorities permitted the use of the Polish language in any educational institution. The Polish language survived as a means of communication between the people and was kept alive through songs, prayer books, and literary works.

While the return of democracy to Poland has resulted in a new flowering of Polish culture, Poland has produced many outstanding artists, musicians, and writers throughout its history. During the 1800's, when the Polish cultural identity was threatened by the Germans and the Russians, the paintings of Jan Matejko depicted scenes from Polish history, while the composer Frédéric Chopin wrote many works based on Polish dances. Leading Polish writers of the 1800's included the poet Adam Mickiewicz, the playwright Stanisław Wyspiański, and the novelist Henryk Sienkiewicz.

In the 1900's, many Poles have won fame in the graphic arts, especially in poster design, which has long been recognized in Poland as a sophisticated art form. The Poles have also distinguished themselves in the cinematic arts. Polish film directors, such as Andrzej Wajda, Krzysztof Zanussi, and Krzysztof Kieślowski, have produced many compelling works.

Poland Today

From 1947 until 1989, the government of Poland was controlled by the Communist Party. During the late 1940's, the Soviet Union gained increasing control over the Polish government. Most Poles opposed Communist rule, but the Communists used police power and other methods to crush resistance. They took control of industry, forced farmers to give up their land and work on collective farms, and conducted fierce antireligion campaigns.

During the 1950's and 1960's, many Poles expressed their discontent with government actions through strikes and riots. Beginning in the mid-1970's, high prices and shortages of food and consumer goods triggered more unrest. In the summer of 1980, as economic conditions worsened, workers in Gdańsk and other cities went on strike, demanding better pay, free trade unions, and political reforms. In November of that year, the strikers won recognition for Solidarity, a free trade union headed by Lech Walesa.

Meanwhile, the people continued to demand economic improvements and greater political freedom. In December 1981, General Wojciech Jaruzelski, the head of Poland's Communist Party, declared martial law and suspended Solidarity's activities. He also imprisoned Walesa and hundreds of other union leaders.

Walesa and some union leaders were released in October 1982, and martial law formally ended in July 1983. Although most political prisoners were freed in the next couple of years, the government continued to keep tight control over the people. In 1984, secret police officers kidnapped and murdered an outspoken pro-Solidarity priest, which led to further unrest.

In the late 1980's, the tide began to turn. Soviet leader Mikhail Gorbachev made it clear that the Soviet Union would no longer enforce its will on its Eastern European satellite countries. In 1989, after the Polish government reached an agreement with Solidarity that led to the legalization of the union and to changes in the structure of the government, a Senate was added to the parliament and a new office of the president was created.

In the freest elections in Poland to take place since World War II, non-Communist candidates were allowed to compete for all Senate seats and some seats in the lower house *(Sejm)*. Solidarity supporters took 99 of 100 Senate seats and gained a majority in the lower house. After the elections, the parliament elected Jaruzelski president, and Tadeusz Mazowiecki, a Solidarity leader, became the first non-Communist prime minister since World War II.

Fact Box

Country

Official name: Rzeczpospolita Polska (Republic of Poland)
Capital: Warsaw
Terrain: Mostly flat plain; mountains along southern border
Area: 120,728 sq. mi. (312,685 km²)
Climate: Temperate with cold, cloudy, moderately severe winters with frequent precipitation; mild summers with frequent showers and thunderstorms
Main rivers: Oder, Vistula, Warta
Highest elevation: Rysy, 8,199 ft. (2,499 m)
Lowest elevation: Raczki Elblaskie, 7 ft. (2 m) below sea level

Government

Form of government: Republic
Head of state: President
Head of government: Prime minister
Administrative areas: 16 wojewodztwa (provinces)
Legislature: Zgromadzenie Narodowe (National Assembly) consisting of the Sejm with 460 members serving four-year terms and the Senat (Senate) with 100 members serving four-year terms
Court system: Supreme Court, Constitutional Tribunal
Armed forces: 240,650 troops

People

Estimated 2002 population: 38,835,000
Population growth: -0.04%
Population density: 311 persons per sq. mi. (120 per km²)
Population distribution: 62% urban, 38% rural
Life expectancy in years: Male: 69, Female: 78
Doctors per 1,000 people: 2.3
Percentage of age-appropriate population enrolled in the following educational levels: Primary: 96, Secondary: 98, Further: 24

Once a part of the *Soviet bloc,* a group of nations led by the Soviet Union, Poland underwent dramatic political and economic changes in the late 1980's. The country saw the growth of Solidarity under the leadership of Lech Walesa, a former electrician at the Gdańsk shipyards who became president of Poland in late 1990. Today, Poland has adopted a multiparty democratic government and is in the process of changing from a planned socialist economy to a free market economy.

In 1990, the Communist Party was dissolved. Two social democratic parties were formed in its place.

Poland held its first direct presidential elections in December 1990. Lech Walesa received more than 75 per cent of the vote.

In January 1991, President Walesa selected Jan Krzysztof Bielecki as prime minister. Bielecki pledged to speed the pace of economic change in Poland, as the country faced the difficult transition from socialism to capitalism.

Poland held its first fully free parliamentary elections since World War II in October 1991. In the Senate, the Democratic Union, a party founded by former members of the Solidarity trade union, won the most seats with 21. In the Sejm, a total of 29 parties won representation.

Elections in 1993 gave Poland a left-wing coalition government. The election result reflected discontent over the increasing political power of the Catholic Church and economic difficulties.

Disagreements over the economy led to tension between the government and Walesa. Aleksander Kwasniewski, a former Communist, was elected president in 1995.

In 1997, Solidarity won the most seats in the parliamentary elections, and the country's new constitution went into effect. In 1999, Poland became a member of the North Atlantic Treaty Organization (NATO), a military alliance of Western nations.

A Roman Catholic priest hears confession in Częstochowa, Poland's holiest shrine. The vast majority of Poles are Roman Catholic, and the Catholic Church—a strong opponent of Communism—played a key role in the political upheavals of the 1980's.

Language spoken:
Polish

Religions:
Roman Catholic 95%
Eastern Orthodox
Protestant

Technology

Radios per 1,000 people: 523

Televisions per 1,000 people: 400

Computers per 1,000 people: 68.9

Economy

Currency: Zloty

Gross national income (GNI) in 2000: $161.8 billion U.S.

Real annual growth rate (1999–2000): 4.0%

GNI per capita (2000): $4,190 U.S.

Balance of payments (2000): -$9,997 million U.S.

Goods exported:
Mostly: manufactured goods and chemicals
Also: machinery and equipment, food and live animals, mineral fuels

Goods imported: Manufactured goods and chemicals, machinery and equipment, mineral fuels, food, and live animals

Trading partners: Germany, Italy, France, Russia

History

The first rulers of what is now Poland were members of the Piast family, beginning with Prince Mieszko I, who controlled most of the land along the Vistula and Oder rivers by the 900's. His son, Bolesław I, conquered parts of what are now the Czech Republic, Slovakia, eastern Germany, and the former Soviet Union and became the first king of Poland in 1025. After his death later that year, the country broke up into several sections, each ruled by a different noble.

A unified Poland

Poland was reunified in the early 1300's under Casimir the Great, the last Piast monarch. At the time of Casimir's death, Poland had a strong central government, a thriving economy, and a blossoming culture. In 1386, Queen Jadwiga of Poland married Władysław Jagiełło, the Grand Duke of Lithuania, and founded the Jagiellonian dynasty.

Poland prospered under the Jagiellonian dynasty and extended its boundaries to cover a large part of central and eastern Europe, including the Ukraine and other parts of what is now the former Soviet Union. After the mid-1500's, however, the monarchy began to lose power to the nobles, who dominated the national parliament. Poland lost much of its territory, and the decline of the empire continued into the 1700's.

In 1772, Austria, Prussia, and Russia took advantage of Poland's weakness and began to *partition* (divide) Polish territory among themselves. By 1795, after the third partition, the last remnants of Poland had disappeared.

In 1807, the French emperor Napoleon gained control of Prussian Poland and made it into a Polish state called the Grand Duchy of Warsaw. However, after Napoleon's final defeat in 1815, Poland was again divided among Austria, Prussia, and

Workers at the Lenin shipyard in Gdańsk went on strike in 1980, demanding higher pay, free trade unions, and political reforms. The action forced the Communist government to recognize Solidarity, an organization of free trade unions.

800's Slavic tribes united under Polane.
966 Prince Mieszko I converts to Christianity.
1025 Bolesław I is crowned the first king of Poland.
Mid-1100's Poland is divided into several sections.
1300's Poland is reunified.
1333-1370 Casimir the Great rules Poland.
1386 Jagiellonian dynasty is founded.
1493 The first national parliament of Poland is established.
1500's The Polish empire reaches the height of its powers.
1569 Poland and Lithuania are united under a single parliament.
1596 King Sigismund III moves the capital of Poland from Kraków to Warsaw.
1655 Poland loses most of its Baltic provinces to Sweden.
1772 Austria, Prussia, and Russia partition Poland.
1793 Prussia and Russia partition Poland.
1795 The third partition of Poland ends its existence as a separate state.
1815 Poland is divided among Austria, Prussia, and Russia.
1918 Poland becomes an independent republic.
1919 Poland regains territory from Germany under the Treaty of Versailles.
1920 Poland enters war with Russia over partition land.
1926 Józef Piłsudski overthrows democratic government.
1939 Germany invades Poland; Germany and the Soviet Union partition the country.
1944 Polish Committee of National Liberation is formed in Lublin.
1945 A Communist-dominated government is formed; Poland's present-day boundaries are established.
1955 Poland signs the Warsaw Pact, a treaty that held most Eastern European nations in a military command under tight Soviet control.
1956 Workers in Poznań and other cities stage antigovernment riots.
1970 Strikes and riots break out in Gdańsk and other cities.
1978 Polish Karol Cardinal Wojtyla becomes Pope John Paul II.
1980 The government recognizes Solidarity.
1981 General Wojciech Jaruzelski declares martial law and suspends Solidarity's activities.
1983 Solidarity leader Lech Walesa wins the Nobel Peace Prize.
1989 The government legalizes Solidarity; elections bring Solidarity-backed government to power.
1990 Poland's Communist Party is dissolved.
1991 Warsaw Pact is dissolved.

Thaddeus Kosciuszko (1746-1817) was a Polish patriot who fought for freedom in America and Poland.

Frédéric Chopin (1810?-1849), *far left,* was a great Polish composer.

Lech Walesa (1943-), became the leader of Poland's labor movement in 1980.

A painting of the Black Madonna of Częstochowa depicts the image revered by Poles since 1656.

Kraków, *left*, a city located in southern Poland, served as capital of the Polish kingdom from 1038 to 1596. This center of Polish culture is home to Jagiellonian University, founded in 1364 (reorganized during the Jagiellonian dynasty).

Russia, and a small, self-governing Kingdom of Poland was established under Russian control.

A new Polish state

After World War I (1914-1918), an independent Polish republic was formed. Under the Treaty of Versailles, Poland regained large amounts of territory from Germany, and the return of land in Pomerania, a region along the Baltic coast, gave Poland access to the sea. Poland's attempt to regain its territory to the east led to war with Russia in 1920. The 1921 Treaty of Riga gave Poland some of its prepartition land.

Although the 1921 Constitution allowed for a democracy, the Polish government suffered from political instability. In 1926, the weak democratic government gave way to dictatorship under Józef Piłsudski.

In August 1939, Germany and the Soviet Union signed a secret agreement to divide Poland among themselves. On September 1, Germany attacked Poland, and the Soviets invaded the country on September 17. The Poles were defeated within a month, after which Germany and the Soviet Union divided Poland. In 1941, Germany attacked the Soviet Union and seized all of Poland.

Poland lost its independence in 1795, when its powerful neighbors divided it up among themselves. Poland reclaimed its independence in 1918, but came under Communist control after World War II.

The rise of Communism

After the fall of Poland, a Polish government-in-exile was formed in Paris and later moved to London. In 1941, Polish Communists formed an exile center in the Soviet Union.

At the Yalta Conference of 1945, Allied leaders agreed to recognize the Polish Committee of National Liberation, which consisted almost entirely of Communists, as the provisional government of Poland if it was expanded to include representatives of the London government-in-exile. Agreements reached at the end of the war shifted Poland's borders westward, while the Soviet Union kept most of eastern Poland.

Environment

Much of Poland is covered by the Great European Plain—a vast expanse of flat countryside that stretches across Europe from France to the Ural Mountains. Majestic, snow-capped mountains rise in southern Poland, but the country lacks natural barriers on the east and west, a factor that has contributed to centuries of invasion by its neighbors.

Outside the flat central plain, Poland's landscape becomes as varied and spectacular as any in Europe. Deep river gorges pierce the southern mountain ranges, while the Białowieska Forest—the last tract of primeval woodland in Europe—covers 483 square miles (1,250 square kilometers) of Polish land in the northeast. Fir, pine, oak, hornbeam, lime, ash, and other species of trees, many of them over 130 feet (40 meters) tall and more than 500 years old, provide shade for the European bison who roam there.

The town of Elk lies in northeastern Poland, a forested region with thousands of lakes ranging in size from tiny woodland pools to large bodies of water. The lakes are surrounded by glacial debris deposited during the last ice age.

Land regions

Poland's seven land regions are the Coastal Lowlands, the Baltic Lakes Region, the Central Plains, the Polish Uplands, the Carpathian Forelands, the Sudetes Mountains, and the Western Carpathian Mountains.

The Coastal Lowlands extend in a narrow strip along the Baltic coast of northwestern Poland. Long stretches of sandy beaches and shifting dunes line much of the generally smooth coastline. About 12 square miles (32 square kilometers) of shifting sands in the village of Leba look so much like the deserts of North Africa that they were used in training troops for desert combat during World War II.

Most of northern Poland is covered by the Baltic Lakes region, a hilly, forested area dotted with small lakes. Lumbering is the most important economic activity in this region. *Peat bogs* (swamps made up of decayed plants) cover much of the land. Its scenic beauty makes it a popular vacation area for campers, hikers, and fishing enthusiasts.

South of the lake district and stretching across Poland, the Central Plains cover almost half the country. The plains are the country's major agricultural area and the site of some of Poland's most important cities, including Poznań, Warsaw, and Wrocław.

South of the Central Plains lie the Polish Uplands, a region of hills, low mountains, and plateaus. This densely populated area contains most of Poland's mineral wealth and much of its richest farmland.

South of the Polish Uplands, the land rises to the Carpathian Forelands, which lie within the branches of the Vistula and San rivers in southeastern Poland. With its fertile soil and important iron and steel industries, this region is one of the most densely populated areas in Poland.

Mountains and forests

The rounded peaks of the Sudetes Mountains—most of which are less than 5,000 feet (1,500 meters) high—border southwestern Poland. The Karkonosze Range,

Sandy beaches line Poland's Baltic coast. Major coastal cities include Gdańsk, Gdynia, and Szczecin. The Baltic coast has milder weather than the inland regions, while the mountain regions are cooler than the lowlands.

The soaring peaks of the Tatra Mountains, in southern Poland, are part of the Western Carpathian Mountains. Crystal-clear lakes, dark forests of pine and larch, and green meadows studded with rowan trees also characterize this region.

Small farming communities lie scattered across Poland's Central Plains, where farmers grow potatoes, rye, sugar beets, and other crops in spite of the poor, sandy soil. Near Warsaw, nature reserves protect elk, wolves, and wild boar.

whose highest peak, Snieżka, rises to 5,256 feet (1,602 meters), lies in the central part of the Sudetes. To the east and toward the Oder River, the range loses altitude, and the taller peaks give way to rounded mountains covered by forests. The valleys and foothills of the Sudetes are used for agriculture.

In Poland's southeastern corner, the Carpathian Forelands rise to the Western Carpathian Mountains, which consist of the Beskid and Tatra chains. Dense forests cover the rounded domes of the Beskids, and only a few peaks rise above the tree line. Bears, wildcats, and other animals live in these thickly forested mountains. The Tatra, a panorama of ancient craggy peaks, deep broad valleys, and numerous cascading waterfalls, rises beyond the Beskids. Rural towns and villages are nestled throughout the mountains in this part of Poland.

Warsaw

Warsaw is the capital and largest city of Poland, as well as the nation's center of culture, science, and industry. It is situated in east-central Poland along the banks of the Vistula River. Warsaw's Slasko-Dabrowski Bridge spans the river, dividing the city into the left bank and the right bank sections.

Early history

Warsaw traces its origins to a small Slavic settlement that existed as long ago as the 900's. In 1596, Warsaw became the capital of the Polish kingdom. Although Swedish invaders destroyed most of the city in 1656, Warsaw remained the capital until 1795, when Poland was divided between Austria, Prussia, and Russia.

Warsaw served as the capital of the Duchy of Warsaw, a state created by the French Emperor Napoleon, from 1807 to 1813. During the late 1800's, Russia controlled the city, while Germany took it over during the three years preceding Poland's independence in 1918.

The ravages of World War II

Warsaw was almost totally destroyed by the German army during World War II, and its people endured great suffering under the ruthless Nazi troops. The Germans took over the city in 1939, after a brutal, three-week siege.

During the German occupation, many of Warsaw's citizens were arrested and executed, while others were forced to leave the city. About 500,000 Jews were confined to a section called the *ghetto,* where many died of hunger and disease. Thousands of others were executed.

On August 1, 1944, the people of Warsaw revolted against the Germans. Although the Soviet army had by that time reached the outskirts of the city, they did not come to the aid of the Poles, who were forced to surrender to the Germans on October 3.

To punish the Poles for their uprising, the Germans destroyed what was left of Warsaw. More than 90 per cent of the city's factories were demolished, and 782 of its 957 historic buildings lay in ruins. By the end of the war, Warsaw had lost about 85 per cent of its population.

The towering Palace of Culture and Science, *above,* a gift from the Soviet Union in 1954, dwarfs the apartment and office blocks of modern Warsaw. The rapid growth of Warsaw's population after World War II resulted in severe housing shortages.

Rebuilding the city

But old Warsaw lived on in the hearts of its citizens. In a remarkable labor of love, the people of Warsaw set about restoring their city soon after the destruction, working from the original plan of the city, which had been hidden from the Germans during the war.

Brick by brick, Polish architects, historians, builders, and masons painstakingly incorporated the remaining fragments of ancient buildings and monuments into authentic reconstructions. Often, they used old photographs—and even paintings and sketches—to re-create the city's architectural treasures.

The project was completed with the reconstruction of the Royal Castle, in the center of Old Town, in 1981. Today, with its narrow, winding streets and cobbled marketplace, Old Town provides a rare glimpse into Warsaw's past. The Royal Castle is noted for the decorative paneling of its attic story. Similar attics, called *Warsaw lanterns,* crown many of the four- and

The Column of King Sigismund—one of Warsaw's most famous landmarks—stands in Zamkowy Square, in front of the Royal Castle. Built in 1644, the monument honors the king who moved the capital from Kraków to Warsaw.

five-story buildings surrounding Market Square *(Rynek)*.

Other famous landmarks rebuilt since World War II include the Cathedral of St. John and the ancient city walls, both dating from the 1300's. Today, these buildings and monuments from Warsaw's past, risen from the ashes, stand amid modern hospitals, schools, and government buildings. They are a moving reminder of the spirit and determination of the Polish people, whose national anthem is entitled "Jeszcze Polska nie Zginęła" ("Poland Has Not Yet Perished").

Warsaw's Market Square contains some of the city's most charming buildings as well as a number of elegant shops and cafes. Rebuilt after it was destroyed during World War II, the Market Square still displays an old-world charm.

A city of wide streets lined with modern stores and office buildings, Warsaw also boasts spacious parks and fine libraries, museums, and theaters, *map below*. Its opera house, one of the world's largest, was rebuilt from its ruins after World War II.

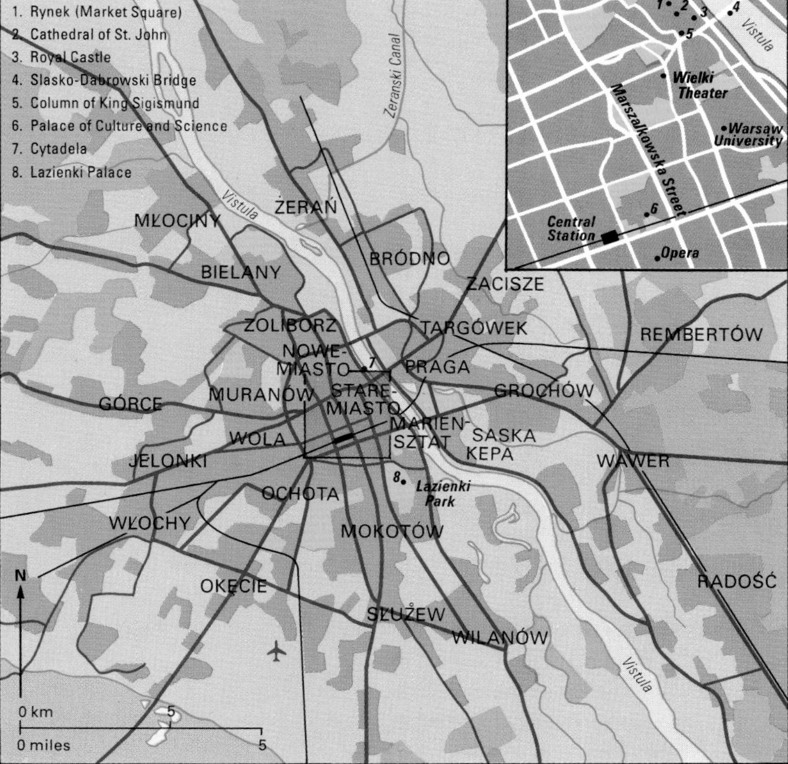

Economy

When the Communists took control of Poland after World War II, the nation's economy depended largely on agriculture. The Communists, however, worked to create an industrial economy. New industrial regions were established around Kraków, Warsaw, and other cities. Today Poland is one of the leading industrial nations of Eastern Europe. The nation's factories manufacture chemicals, food products, iron and steel, machinery, ships, and textiles. With its rich coal fields in the south, Poland also ranks among the leading coal-mining countries.

As part of the transformation from an agricultural to an industrial economy, Poland became a member of COMECON (Council for Mutual Economic Assistance), a now-defunct economic union that was made up of the Soviet Union and nine other countries. To meet its commitments to COMECON, Poland invested heavily in mining and the production of *capital goods,* such as machine tools and industrial equipment, and did not produce enough *consumer goods,* such as food and clothing. As a result, Poland had a lower standard of living than most other industrialized nations.

Food subsidies

In the early days of Communist rule, the government introduced massive subsidies on food in order to keep prices down and win popular support for their regime. However, what began as a temporary measure was difficult to stop, and the government faced ever-increasing expenditures. In addition, the artificially low prices gave farmers no incentive to increase production, so the subsidies eventually led to food shortages.

In the early 1970's, the Polish government tried to solve its problems by borrowing money from countries in the West. Huge loans enabled Poland to increase the production of consumer goods and to modernize industry. The government planned to repay the loans with the profits from increased exports. Unfortunately, the expected boom in exports never took place— due to increased prices for raw

Shipbuilding, one of Poland's major industries, takes place in the shipyards at Szczecin, on the Baltic Sea. Szczecin ranks as the nation's largest port, and also serves Czechoslovakia and Hungary.

Local farm produce draws shoppers to a rural market in northeast Poland, *above.* Under Communist rule, shortages of food and basic consumer goods forced Poles to economize.

Polish miners in a pit near Katowice in southern Poland work one of the world's richest coal fields. Poland also has deposits of copper, lead, silver, and zinc.

The majority of Polish farms consist of small family holdings. Many farmers resisted the Communist collectivization program, so about 80 per cent of Poland's farmland has been in private hands since the 1950's.

Poland's coal fields support heavy industry, but economic reforms have been designed to diversify the economy, *map right.* Today, industry employs about 34 per cent of all Polish workers, while about 29 per cent work in agriculture.

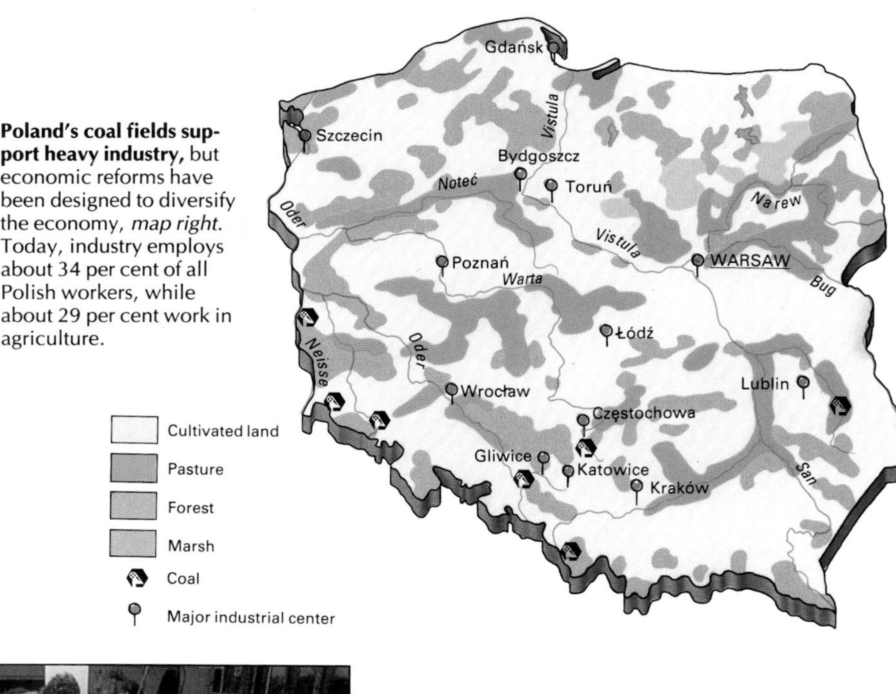

The owner of this clothing factory, *above,* represents a new generation of Polish business people. Although government austerity programs jolted the economy in 1990, they also paved the way for private enterprise and a free market economy.

materials and energy as well as a diminishing market—and Poland was unable to repay its loans.

Economic reform

When Poland's first non-Communist government since World War II took over in 1989, its new leaders prepared a radical plan to move the country from a centrally planned economy to a free market. International financial institutions, including the World Bank, viewed Poland's new economic plan as one of the most ambitious of its kind in Eastern Europe.

The new leaders encouraged the growth of private business and planned to transfer control of the nation's industries from the state to cooperatives or private individuals. By shifting the emphasis from heavy industry to light industry, the government also hoped to create jobs and attract foreign investors with Poland's low labor costs.

The plan included the removal of price controls as well as most subsidies. However, to prevent inflation, strict wage controls remained in effect. Under this austerity program, food became more readily available, but unemployment increased dramatically. The austerity program was expected to result in a 20 to 25 per cent loss in real wages for the average Polish worker.

In the early 1990's, many Poles simply could not afford to buy the consumer goods that they had been promised. The economy began to improve in the mid-1990's, however.

Portugal

The return of a fishing boat, laden with the day's catch, signals the end of another day in Mira, a small village on the west coast of central Portugal. A team of oxen hauls the small boat ashore. Days like this make up the lives of the hardy fishermen who brave the cold, rough waters of the Atlantic Ocean. In the time-honored fashion of their ancestors, the Portuguese often battle fierce elements to make their living from the sea.

Fishing—and farming—are a way of life for most Portuguese. Here, about two-thirds of the people still live in rural areas. About one-fifth of all adults cannot read and write.

Although Portugal remains a rural country, its cities—especially Lisbon and Porto—are growing rapidly. Each year, a large number of the nation's rural people move to urban areas to find jobs in industry or other city activities. Portugal's cities have buildings that are hundreds of years old as well as modern apartment and office buildings.

The Portuguese maintain close family ties. Often, two or more generations of a family live together in the same house. Men and women who move to cities from villages tend to keep in close touch with their relatives back home.

Portugal is one of the poorer countries in Europe, struggling to raise its people's standard of living. Fighting between political groups, along with periods of inflation and unemployment, have slowed progress.

In the 1400's and 1500's, Portugal was one of the mightiest nations in the world. The vast Portuguese Empire once ruled colonies in Africa, Asia, and South America. The discoveries of such famous Portuguese explorers as Bartolomeu Dias, Vasco da Gama, and Pedro Álvares Cabral began the Great Age of European Discovery.

During Portugal's Golden Age, from the 1400's to the 1600's, the arts flourished as painters and architects celebrated their country's achievements in their artistic masterpieces. All too soon, though, the Portuguese Empire declined. Held back by weak leadership, unstable governments, and a poor economy, Portugal has struggled to overcome its problems ever since.

Nevertheless, Portugal remains a beautiful country. Its natural charm is exemplified in its unspoiled coastline dotted with quaint fishing villages. Enhancing Portugal's beauty is the country's rich cultural heritage, which comes vividly to life in its folk music and dance, religious festivals, cuisine, and delightful customs.

Portugal Today

Modern Portugal came into being in 1974, when military leaders overthrew the dictatorship that had ruled the country since 1928. The revolution, known as the Armed Forces Movement, restored the rights of the people, abolished the secret police, and allowed the formation of political parties. Unfortunately, clashes between the new political parties led to further violence in 1974 and 1975, but for the most part, Portugal entered its new period of democracy with little trouble.

A new government

In 1976, Portugal adopted a new Constitution that guarantees such rights as freedom of speech, freedom of religion, and freedom of the press. Portugal is now a republic, with a parliament and a president elected by the voters. The prime minister is usually the head of the majority party in the parliament, which is known as the Assembly of the Republic.

Control of Portugal's government has changed hands many times since 1976. The main political parties have often banded together in *coalitions* that work together to win the majority of seats in the parliament, which would give them control of the government. In the late 1980's, the Social Democratic Party managed to gain a majority in the parliament without having to share power in a coalition.

The lack of cooperation between Portugal's political parties has been a continuing problem since the 1974 revolution. While the nation has experienced some economic growth since the 1960's, it still suffers from periodic problems of high unemployment and inflation. Nevertheless, in 1989, the growth of new industries led the World Bank and the International Monetary Fund (IMF) to rank Portugal 23rd among industrial nations.

War in the colonies

During the 1960's, the nation's economy was seriously weakened by costly wars in Portugal's African colonies. The wars started when rebels in the colonies of Angola, Mozambique, and Portuguese Guinea began armed resistance against their governments. Portugal sent troops to stop the rebellion, and thousands of people were killed on both sides of the struggle.

After the 1974 revolution, the provisional government ended Portuguese rule in the African colonies. In 1974, Portuguese Guinea was the first colony to gain its independence, becoming the nation of Guinea-Bissau. A year later, Angola, Cape Verde, Mozambique,

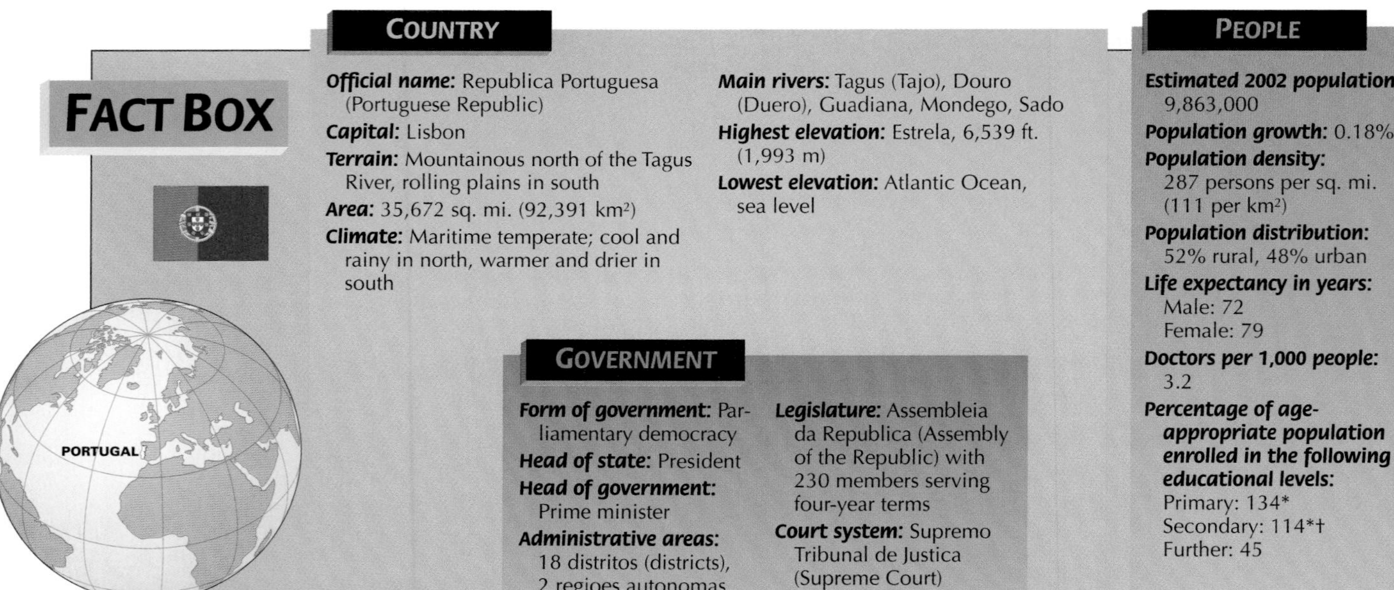

Fact Box

Country

Official name: Republica Portuguesa (Portuguese Republic)
Capital: Lisbon
Terrain: Mountainous north of the Tagus River, rolling plains in south
Area: 35,672 sq. mi. (92,391 km²)
Climate: Maritime temperate; cool and rainy in north, warmer and drier in south
Main rivers: Tagus (Tajo), Douro (Duero), Guadiana, Mondego, Sado
Highest elevation: Estrela, 6,539 ft. (1,993 m)
Lowest elevation: Atlantic Ocean, sea level

Government

Form of government: Parliamentary democracy
Head of state: President
Head of government: Prime minister
Administrative areas: 18 distritos (districts), 2 regioes autonomas (autonomous regions)
Legislature: Assembleia da Republica (Assembly of the Republic) with 230 members serving four-year terms
Court system: Supremo Tribunal de Justica (Supreme Court)
Armed forces: 49,700 troops

People

Estimated 2002 population: 9,863,000
Population growth: 0.18%
Population density: 287 persons per sq. mi. (111 per km²)
Population distribution: 52% rural, 48% urban
Life expectancy in years:
Male: 72
Female: 79
Doctors per 1,000 people: 3.2
Percentage of age-appropriate population enrolled in the following educational levels:
Primary: 134*
Secondary: 114*†
Further: 45

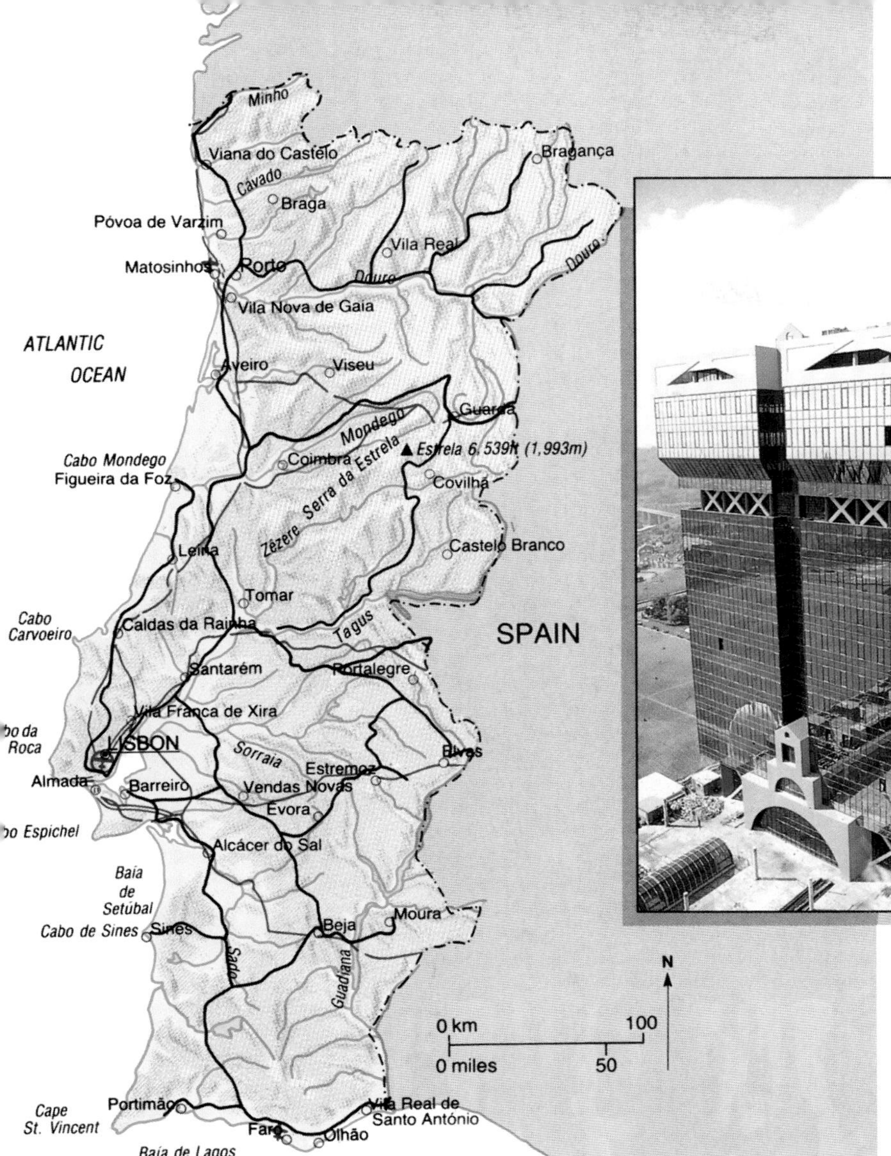

The nation of Portugal lies at the western edge of continental Europe. In addition to its mainland territory, which shares the Iberian Peninsula with Spain, Portugal includes the Azores and the Madeiras, two island groups in the Atlantic Ocean.

The new Amoreiras shopping and office complex is a dramatic addition to the skyline of Lisbon, Portugal's capital and largest city. Lisbon, which also serves as Portugal's economic and cultural center, lies at the mouth of the Tagus River near Portugal's southwest coast.

Language spoken:
Portuguese
Religions:
Roman Catholic 94%
Protestant

*Enrollment ratios compare the number of students enrolled to the population which, by age, should be enrolled. A ratio higher than 100 indicates that students older or younger than the typical age range are also enrolled.

†Includes training for the unemployed.

Technology

Radios per 1,000 people: 304
Televisions per 1,000 people: 630
Computers per 1,000 people: 299.3

Economy

Currency: Euro
Gross national income (GNI) in 2000: $111.3 billion U.S.
Real annual growth rate (1999–2000): 3.3%
GNI per capita (2000): $11,120 U.S.
Balance of payments (2000): -$11,012 million U.S.
Goods exported: Clothing and footwear, machinery, chemicals, cork and paper products, hides
Goods imported: Machinery and transport equipment, chemicals, petroleum, textiles, agricultural products
Trading partners: European Union, United States, Japan

and São Tomé and Príncipe became independent, and in 1976, Indonesia took over Portugal's colony of Portuguese Timor in the East Indies.

Portugal now rules only its mainland territory, along with the Azores and the Madeira Islands. Portugal had control of the tiny territory of Macao on China's southern coast, until 1999 when Macao passed back to Chinese control.

Looking to the future

Until the mid-1900's, Portugal's economy was based primarily on agriculture and fishing. Today, manufacturing is a growing element in the diversification of the economy, accounting for about 30 per cent of Portugal's economic production.

In 1986, Portugal joined the European Community, an economic organization of western European nations now known as the European Union (EU). By participating in the EU, Portugal's leaders hope to promote further economic growth and raise the country's standard of living.

Environment

Portugal is a small, narrow country situated on the western edge of the Iberian Peninsula. It extends 350 miles (563 kilometers) from north to south, but only 125 miles (201 kilometers) from east to west at its widest point. The Serra da Estrela mountain range, which cuts across the central part of the country, serves as a dividing line between northern Portugal and southern Portugal.

Coastal Plains

Portugal's broad Coastal Plains extend along its west coast. Numerous lagoons have formed where land meets water as the plains slope gently to the sea. Farmers grow rice in the flat river valleys of the plains, while corn is cultivated in the higher, drier areas. Lines of trees protect the fields against erosion by the wind.

In the southern Coastal Plains, large villages are set amid olive groves, vineyards, and cornfields. A wide depression near the mouth of the Tagus River has collected sediments from the sea and now provides very fertile land, yielding large crops of olives, rice, and wine grapes.

However, the land in this area is still sinking and is geologically unstable—a condition that sometimes causes earthquakes. Portugal's most serious earthquake occurred in 1755 and practically destroyed the city of Lisbon.

Northern Portugal

East of the Coastal Plains, northern Portugal consists of the mountains and plains of the Northern Tablelands. This region begins at the Minho River, which separates Portugal and Spain to the north, and extends to the Central Range, south of the Mondego River.

A continuation of Spain's Meseta, the Northern Tablelands consist mainly of plains broken up by mountain ranges. The Douro River cuts deeply into the land, forming a narrow, sunny valley. Grapes used in the production of Portugal's famous port wines are cultivated on steep slate terraces in the Douro Valley.

In the northeast, the high plateaus of the Northern Tablelands rise to heights of 1,640 to 2,460 feet (500 to 750 meters). The pla-

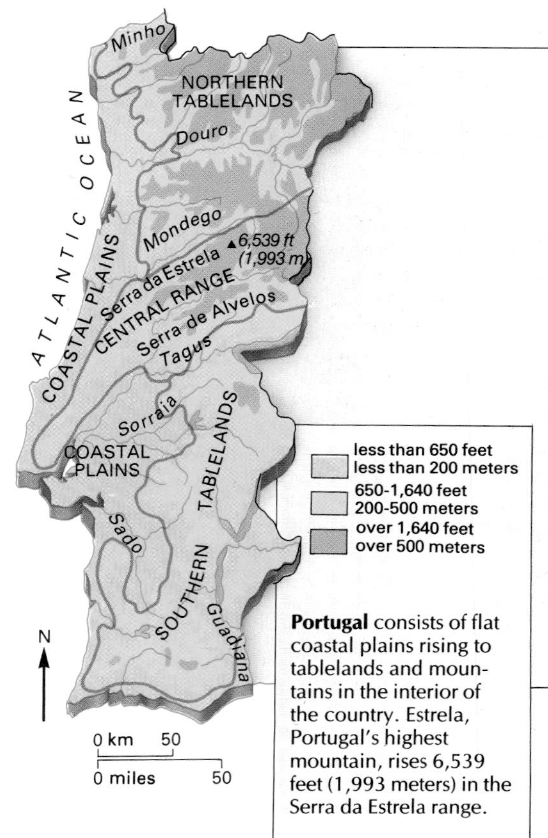

Portugal consists of flat coastal plains rising to tablelands and mountains in the interior of the country. Estrela, Portugal's highest mountain, rises 6,539 feet (1,993 meters) in the Serra da Estrela range.

The pine forests around Coimbra in northern Portugal yield resin, used in making turpentine, and lumber, used in making furniture. Cork bark is collected from the cork oak trees that grow in the southern and central regions.

Large farms surrounded by vast, rolling plains make up much of southern Portugal's landscape, *top*. Although larger, state-owned collective farms are more common in southern Portugal, most crop farms in this country are small, family-owned operations.

teaus are barren, desolate areas, with little vegetation. Closer to the west coast, small villages fringed by forests of beech and oak nestle in the meadows and fields.

South of the Douro River, the Northern Tablelands slope down to the plateau of Beira, a hilly region rising between 2,000 and 3,300 feet (600 and 1,000 meters). Beira is covered with olive groves and the Mediterranean shrub known as *maquis*.

Southern Portugal

The Serra da Estrela, the dividing line between northern and southern Portugal, is a region of bare granite uplands, formed during the Ice Age. The peaks of the Serra da Estrela, which rise more than 6,000 feet (1, 829 meters) above sea level, are snow-covered for several months each year.

South of the Serra da Estrela, the landscape consists of a series of wide plateaus covered by miles of wheat fields and pastureland. This gently hilly country develops into wide fields and bogs near the coast.

Farther south, the low plateaus merge with the barren, rounded hills of the High Algarve, a highland area. Farms in the Lower Algarve produce crops of almonds, carobs, figs, olives, and oranges, and cork oak trees.

A locomotive steams across the Douro River in northern Portugal, *above*. The Douro meets the Atlantic Ocean at the city of Porto. The river provides hydroelectric power, while the surrounding valley yields grapes for making port wine.

Bright sunshine, clear waters, and sandy beaches make the southern coast of Portugal a popular vacation spot. Temperatures are mild throughout the country, ranging from about 70° F. (21° C) in July to about 50° F. (10° C) in January.

People

Portugal has a population of about 10 million. About half of the country's people live in rural areas.

Most rural Portuguese live in small fishing or farm villages. Fishing villages line the country's coast. The people of these settlements have long relied on fishing for their livelihood. The men brave the rugged waters of the Atlantic Ocean in small boats to catch fish. The women and children do such chores as cleaning the fish and mending the nets.

Portuguese farmers raise a variety of crops, but they are best known for their fine grapes that are used to make wine. Wines from Portugal are enjoyed by people in many parts of the world. Some Portuguese winemakers still follow the colorful old custom of crushing the grapes with their bare feet.

Life in the capital

Lisbon, Portugal's capital, boasts one of Europe's most important natural harbors. Large shipments of Portuguese ceramics, cork, sardines, and tomato paste enter and leave the port of Lisbon every day. Just across the Tagus, one of Europe's major shipyards bustles with activity.

The largest city of Portugal, Lisbon is the nerve center of the nation. It has a long history, beginning more than 3,000 years ago. Ancient Greeks, Carthaginians, and Romans colonized Lisbon before the Moors seized it during the A.D. 700's. Later, in the 1100's, Christian forces led by King Afonso I reclaimed Lisbon.

The city became the official capital of Portugal in the late 1200's. It was in Lisbon that the great Portuguese explorers and adventurers planned their expeditions to the New World. Little remains of these early days because most of the city was destroyed on the morning of Nov. 1, 1755, by one of the worst earthquakes in history.

Within a few hours after the quake, huge tidal waves swept up the Tagus River from the Atlantic, flooding the city and drowning many of its inhabitants. Many more people were killed by the raging fires that followed. By the time it was all over, more than 60,000 people had died and two-thirds of Lisbon lay in ruins.

Portuguese architects soon planned a new city on top of the ruins. They introduced the wide, graceful boulevards, mosaic pavements, and symmetrical buildings that now give Lisbon its elegant character. Sadly, many of the buildings so masterfully constructed during this period were destroyed by fire during the summer of 1988.

Today, the city is a modern metropolis, complete with skyscrapers, an international airport, and a subway system. The people live in pleasant, pastel-colored houses and apartment buildings. Yet—even now—Lisbon retains an Old World quality in the cobbled streets and alleyways of *Alfama,* its oldest quarter.

Northern city dwellers

North of Lisbon in the central part of the country, the city of Coimbra is the site of one of the oldest universities in Europe. Along with its academic atmosphere, Coimbra keeps alive the folk tradition of *fado,* a popular form of Portuguese song accompanied by guitar.

An observation elevator in Lisbon, *right,* takes visitors high above the rooftops to view the city's sights. Downtown Lisbon, a low, flat district next to the harbor, is called the *Baixa.* About a fifth of Portugal's people live in the Lisbon area.

A fisherman at Nazaré, on Portugal's central Atlantic coast, repairs his nets. Traditionally a seafaring people, the Portuguese still brave the rough waters of the Atlantic Ocean in small boats. The catch includes cod, sardines, and many other kinds of fish.

Farther north, on the banks of the Douro River, lies Porto, Portugal's second largest city. From its ancient beginnings as a Roman trading community, Porto has grown to become the commercial and industrial center of northern Portugal. The city is also known for its role in processing and exporting Portugal's famous port wines.

About 50 miles (80 kilometers) north of Porto lies the city of Braga, often called *Portuguese Rome*. Braga's Holy Week procession is considered to be the finest in all of Portugal.

The face of a vineyard worker, *above,* weathered from many summers in the sun, displays the typical warmth and charm of the Portuguese people. Much of the population still lives in rural areas or small villages.

Workers gather to relax in Alfama, *below left,* after a long day's work. Formerly a Moorish town, Alfama is Lisbon's oldest quarter. *Alfama* is an Arabic word, as are many other words in the Portuguese language. Alfama's steep, narrow streets preserve the unique charm of the city's past.

A festive procession takes place during a harvest festival held every four years in the city of Tomar. The Roman Catholic religion plays an important role in the lives of the Portuguese. The shrine at Fátima, near Lisbon, is visited by thousands of pilgrims every year.

Economy

Although its economy has long been based on agriculture and fishing, Portugal has recently experienced a growth in industrialization. Manufacturing now accounts for about 30 per cent of the country's economic production, whereas agriculture and farming together account for 10 per cent. Service industries make up the remaining 60 per cent.

Portugal's entry into the European Community, now called the European Union, in 1986 provided a welcome boost to the nation's economy. Although Portugal is still one of the poorer nations in Europe, the future looks bright for its hard-working people. The tourist industry is enjoying steady growth, and some say that Portugal's tourist trade could someday equal Spain's.

Natural resources

Portugal has valuable natural resources, but for the most part, they remain undeveloped. Building stone, found throughout the country, has become Portugal's most important developed mineral resource.

The mountains of Portugal hold deposits of coal and copper, as well as wolframite, which is used in making tungsten. However, mining has not been well developed in Portugal.

Water is also one of Portugal's natural resources. Its rivers, particularly the Tagus and the Douro, provide valuable hydroelectric power for Portuguese factories and homes.

About a third of Portugal is covered by forests. Pine trees grow in northern Portugal, while cork oak trees thrive in the central and southern regions of the country. Cork is collected from the cork oak trees for use in making such products as bottle stoppers, bulletin boards, fishing floats, golf balls, and life jackets.

Industry and agriculture

The leading manufacturing activity of Portugal is textiles, with cotton fabric being the most important textile produced. Portuguese factories also produce cement, ceramics, cork products, shoes, and fertilizer.

Portugal's farmers raise a variety of crops, including almonds, corn, olives, potatoes, rice, tomatoes, and wheat. The most important agricultural product, however, is wine grapes.

The vineyards of the Douro Valley produce the grapes used in making port wine. Port is a *fortified wine* popular all over the world. Fortified wines have brandy or wine alcohol added to them, and they tend to be sweeter than most other wines. Portugal also makes a variety of red and white wines.

Portuguese farms are generally quite small and the farmers who own them often use old-fashioned methods and equipment. As a result, the farms are not as efficient as they could be, and production may be low. Since the 1974 revolution, the Portuguese government has set up large collective farms, mostly in the southern region of the country. These

The cork oak tree

Cork comes from the cork oak tree, which thrives in warm, sunny climates. Cork is a lightweight, spongy substance obtained from the bark of the tree. A cork tree must be about 20 years old before its bark is thick enough to be stripped, and then it can be stripped at intervals of about 8 to 10 years. The first layer removed is called *virgin bark*. Workers use a long-handled hatchet to cut long, oblong sections of bark from the top of the

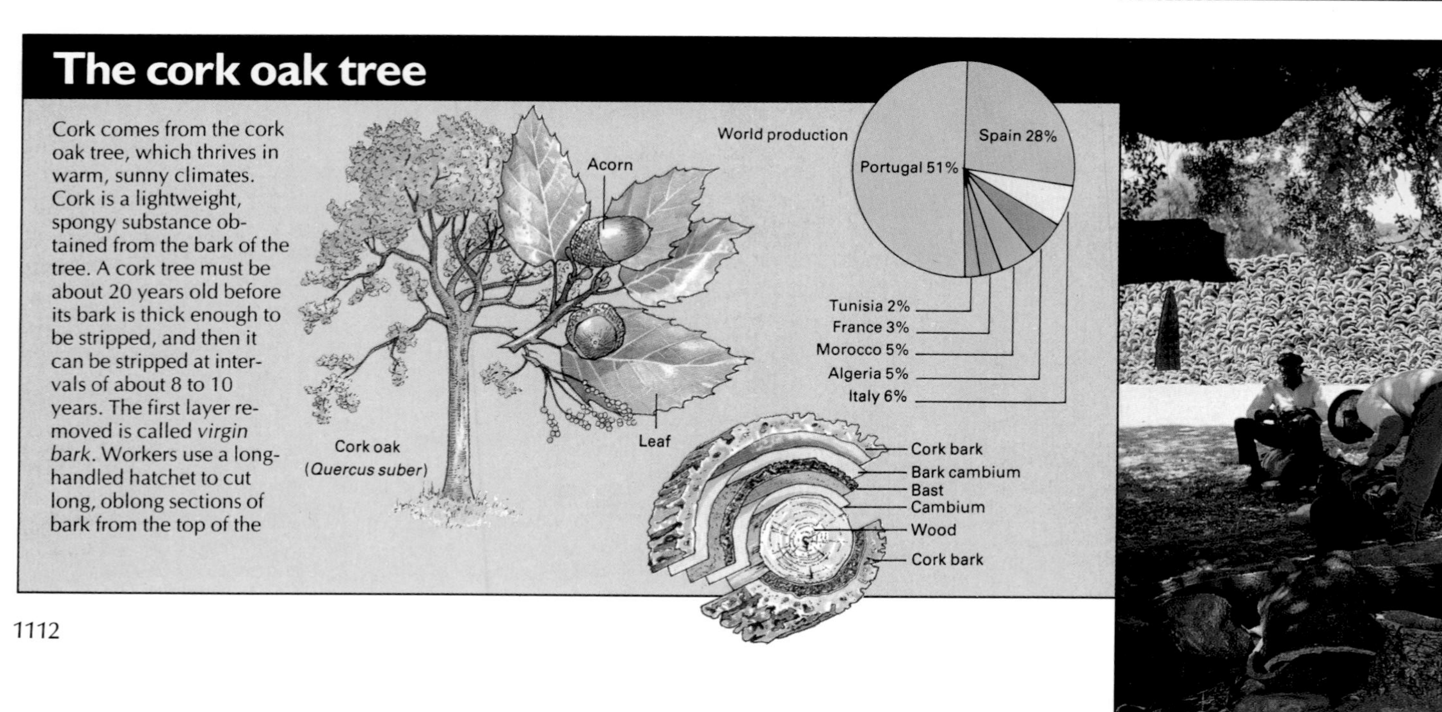

Barrels of wine are transported down the Douro River in picturesque boats displaying the names of wine merchants on their sails. These vessels are among the few surviving examples of *barcos rabelos*, the flat-bottomed boats used to carry port wine from the vineyards to the city of Porto for export. Every year on June 24, during the feast of *São Joao* (Saint John), the boats sail in a race on the river.

state-owned farms use up-to-date methods and modern equipment, which increase productivity. Properties are gradually being returned to private owners.

Fishing

Every day, Portuguese fishing crews set sail on the Bay of Biscay—and even far into the Atlantic Ocean—in search of deep-sea catches. Almost 300 deep-sea trawlers bring ashore about 390,000 short tons (350,000 metric tons) of fish and shellfish each year. Cod, sardines, and other kinds of fish make up the bulk of the haul.

Fishing crews check their nets after a day at sea, *above*. Many still use the traditional fishing boats of their ancestors. These boats are flat-bottomed, rising to a high, pointed bow and stern. Oxen are used to drag them out of the water, out of range of the pounding surf.

lowest branches to the bottom of the tree. These sections are boiled, scraped, straightened, and then dried in the sun. The cork is packed in bundles and graded for quality and thickness.

Portuguese tomatoes, noted for their delicious flavor, are sorted at a processing plant. In French cooking, dishes made with tomato sauce are often described as *à la Portugaise* (in the Portuguese style).

History

The recorded history of Portugal begins about 5,000 years ago, when a tribe called the Iberians occupied the area. Later, the Phoenicians, the Celts, the Greeks, and the Carthaginians invaded the peninsula.

After the Romans defeated the Carthaginians in 201 B.C., they claimed rights to the entire Iberian Peninsula, but it took them about 200 years to complete their conquest. The Romans named the Portuguese portion of their empire *Lusitania*. They called the city of Porto *Portus Cale*—the origin of Portugal's present name.

The Romans built cities and linked them with their system of roads. The use of Latin spread through the region, and Latin became the root of both the Portuguese and Spanish languages.

During the A.D. 400's, Germanic tribes swept across the Pyrenees to take over the country. In 711, Muslim armies from North Africa invaded the peninsula. They brought the Portuguese advanced concepts of architecture, improved roads and education, and new crops and farming methods such as irrigation in the dry south.

By the mid-1000's, the Christian forces of Iberia were gaining strength in their battle to drive out the Muslims. Meanwhile, King Alfonso VI, ruler of the Spanish Kingdom of Castile, named Henry of Burgundy the Count of Portugal. Henry was a French nobleman who had joined the Christians in their struggle against the Muslims.

Henry's son and successor, Afonso Henriques, won many battles against the Muslims. Afonso Henriques also broke away from Castile in 1143 and declared himself king of the independent kingdom of Portugal. By the mid-1200's, the Muslims were driven from Portugal. In 1297, Castile officially recognized Portugal's borders, which have remained almost unchanged ever since.

In 1385, Portugal and England signed the Treaty of Windsor. This political alliance is the oldest in Europe still in force.

The age of expansion

The Portuguese had long been a seafaring people. They were excellent sailors and knew a great deal about navigation and ship-building. Under the patronage of Prince Henry the

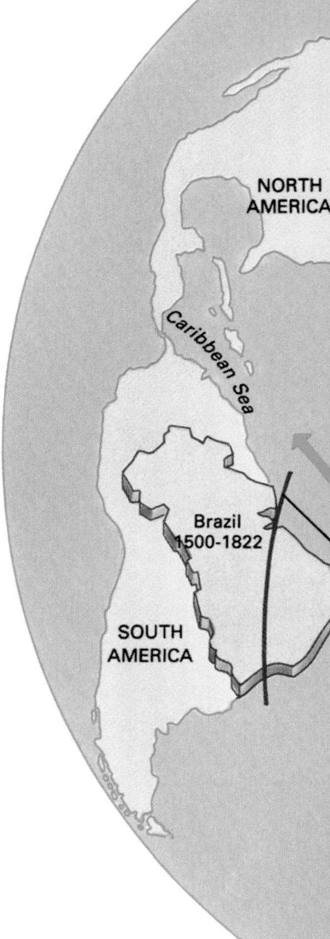

c. 3000 B.C. Iberian tribes inhabit what is now Portugal.
1000's B.C. Phoenicians from the eastern shore of the Mediterranean establish settlements on the Iberian Peninsula.
400's B.C. Carthaginians control much of the Iberian Peninsula.
201 B.C. Romans defeat Carthaginians and begin conquest and occupation of Iberian Peninsula.
c. 19 B.C. Rebellious local tribes finally brought under Roman rule.
A.D. 400's German tribes take over country.
711 The invasion of the Moors begins.
1096 Henry of Burgundy becomes Count of Portugal.
1143 Afonso Henriques establishes Portugal as an independent kingdom.
1212 Battle of Las Navas de Tolosa breaks Moorish power.
1297 Castile recognizes the boundaries of the Portuguese kingdom.
1385 Portugal enters into a political alliance with England.
1419 Prince Henry the Navigator launches the first Portuguese expedition to the West African coast.
1494 Treaty of Tordesillas divides the New World between Portugal and Spain.
1497–1498 Vasco da Gama sails around the Cape of Good Hope and on to India.
1500 Pedro Álvares Cabral claims Brazil for Portugal.
1580 Spain invades and conquers Portugal.
1640 Rebellion restores Portugal's independence.
1807 French forces under Napoleon I invade Portugal.
1822 Portugal loses its colony of Brazil.
1908 King Carlos I is assassinated.
1910 The monarchy is overthrown, and Portugal becomes a republic.
1914–1918 Portugal fights in World War I (1914–1918) on the side of the Allies.
1926 Army officers overthrow Portugal's civilian government.
1928–1970 António de Oliveira Salazar rules as dictator.
1960's African colonies revolt against Portuguese rule.
1974 Military officers overthrow the dictatorship.
1975 Almost all remaining Portuguese colonies are granted independence.
1976 Free elections are held.
1986 Portugal joins the European Community.
1999 Macao is returned to Chinese rule.

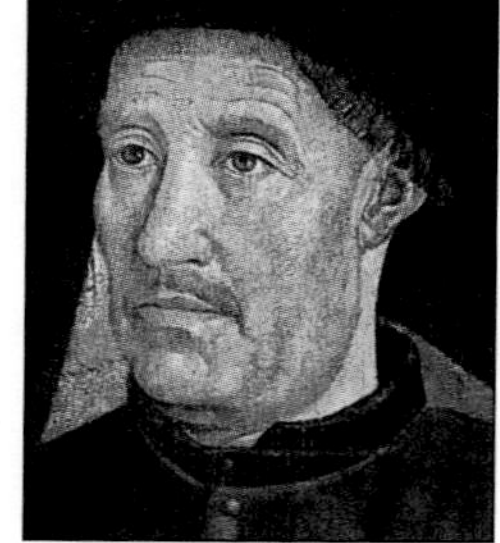

Prince Henry the Navigator (1394–1460), *left,* encouraged and sponsored explorations of the west African coast.

The Marquis of Pombal (1699–1781), *far left,* was prime minister of Portugal under King José I.

Mário Soares (1927–) opposed António de Oliveira Salazar's dictatorship during the 1960's.

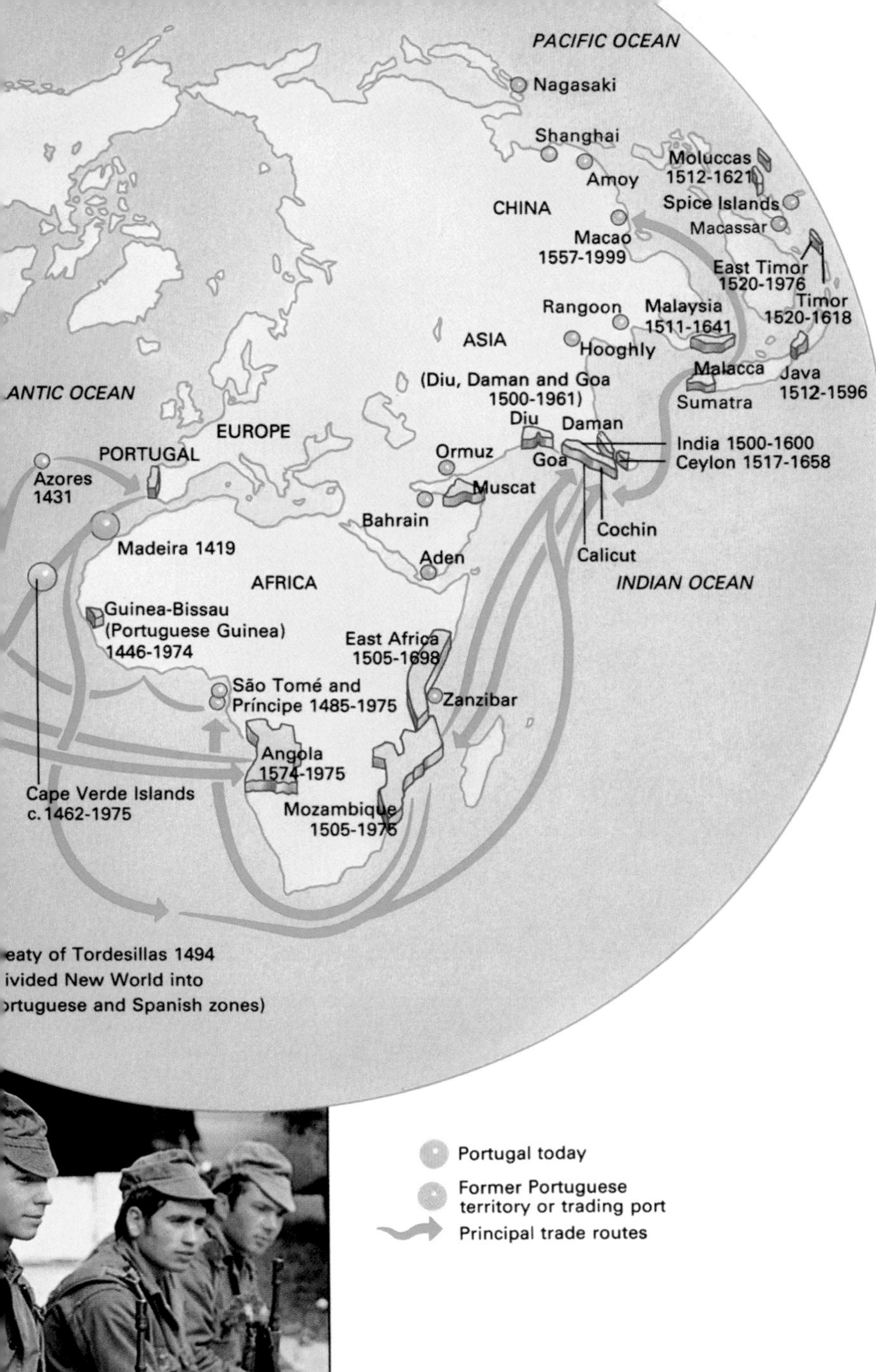

The rich and powerful Portuguese empire once spanned the globe. Its power and influence began to weaken in the late 1500's, but Portugal held on to much of its empire for more than 400 years. Between 1960 and 2000, however, Portugal lost all but two of its overseas territories—the Azores and the Madeiras.

Portuguese soldiers wear red carnations, the symbol of their country's 1974 revolution. Led by the military, the revolution brought a return to democracy after many years of dictatorship. In 1976, the country had its first free elections in more than 50 years.

Navigator, Portuguese sailors developed sailing skills that later helped Portuguese explorers span the globe and build a powerful empire.

Although Prince Henry never went on a sea voyage himself, he was very skillful at helping mapmakers, navigators, and explorers work together. He also built a famous navigation school at Sagres.

Prince Henry encouraged and sponsored many expeditions. Through his efforts, Portuguese explorers reached the Madeira Islands and the Azores. By the time Prince Henry died in 1460, the explorers had sailed along the west coast of Africa to Sierra Leone.

In 1497, Vasco da Gama took four ships on a daring voyage around Africa's Cape of Good Hope. By 1500, the Portuguese had reached the coasts of Africa, the Arabian and Malay peninsulas, the East Indies, and the Orient.

Years of decline

At its height, Portugal's empire stretched from Brazil to China. Resources from its colonies, including gold from Africa and diamonds from Brazil, brought great wealth to Portugal, but the small country found it too difficult to hold and manage such a vast empire. During the 1600's, England, the Netherlands, and France began to take over parts of the empire.

In 1580, Spain invaded Portugal and occupied the nation for 60 years, until Portuguese independence was restored in 1640. In 1807, Portugal was again invaded and conquered, this time by Napoleon's French armies. From 1808 to 1811, British forces helped the Portuguese drive out the French.

By the time Portugal's King John VI returned to the throne after the French occupation, a new political spirit had grown strong in Europe. Many Portuguese began demanding greater representation in their government, but for many years, little progress was made toward a republican government. Finally, in 1910, the monarchy was overthrown, and Portugal became a republic.

During the next 15 years, Portugal suffered through the political instability created by 45 different governments. In 1926, army officers overthrew the civilian governments. In 1928, they made António de Oliveira Salazar minister of finance. Within a few years, Salazar became dictator of Portugal.

Puerto Rico

Puerto Rico, a commonwealth of the United States, is a beautiful tropical island of the West Indies, about 1,000 miles (1,600 kilometers) southeast of Florida. The U.S. Congress is responsible for governing Puerto Rico, but the island has wide powers of self-rule.

Most U.S. federal laws apply to Puerto Rico as if it were a state. Voters elect a governor, who is the chief executive. The people also elect members of their two-house legislature.

The people

The people of Puerto Rico are U.S. citizens and can move to the mainland without immigration restrictions. However, when they live in Puerto Rico, they cannot vote in U.S. presidential elections and do not pay federal income taxes.

Puerto Rico is a crowded island with a population of more than 3 million. About two-thirds of the people live in urban areas. San Juan, the capital and largest city, has a metropolitan area of more than 1 million people.

Most Puerto Ricans are of Spanish descent and speak Spanish, though many Puerto Ricans also speak English. There are smaller numbers of Portuguese, Italian, French, and black Africans. Arawak Indians lived on the island before it was colonized by Spain, but nearly all were killed or died of disease. No full-blooded Indians remain on Puerto Rico, but some people have mixed Indian and Spanish ancestry.

The economy

More than 1-1/2 million tourists visit Puerto Rico every year. They are attracted by its balmy climate. Average temperatures range from 73° to 80° F. (23° to 27° C), and sea breezes make the temperature especially comfortable.

The climate attracts not only tourists but also businesses. Manufacturing is the single most valuable industry. About 140,000 Puerto Ricans work in factories that produce chemicals, machinery, food products, scientific instruments, and clothing. Many factories were set up under Operation Bootstrap, a government program that helped businesses find locations, finance construction, and train workers.

Puerto Rican men enjoy a game of dominoes, *below,* at a local meeting place.

The foothills of Puerto Rico are carpeted with dry grass, *right.* The *Cordillera Central* (Central Mountain Range) runs east and west across the island.

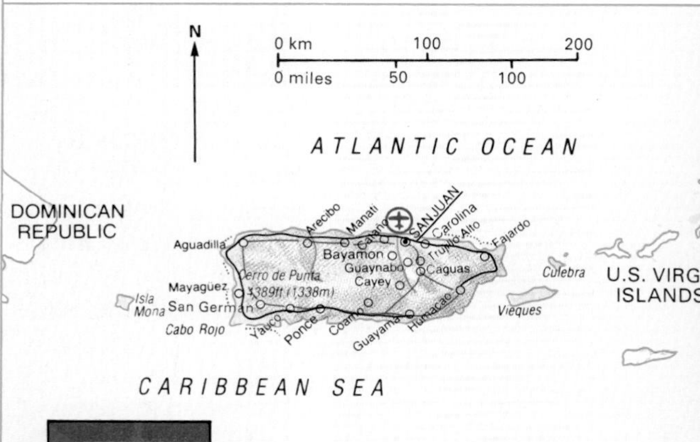

Puerto Rico is the smallest and easternmost island in the Greater Antilles. Covering an area of 3,515 sq. mi. (9,103 km^2), Puerto Rico includes many smaller islands; the largest are Vieques, Mona, and Culebra. The highest elevation is at Cerro de Punta, 4,389 ft. (1,338 m) high in the central mountains. The lowest elevation is sea level at the coast.

Coconut palms rise from the sand on the Puerto Rican coast, *above*. Tourists—most of them from the U.S.—are attracted by these beautiful beaches and the balmy climate. Tourists spend about $900 million every year in shops, hotels, and restaurants.

The climate also allows Puerto Ricans to grow tropical crops. In addition to sugar cane and coffee—the leading crops—farmers grow avocados, bananas, citrus fruits, coconuts, pineapples, plantains, and tobacco. Milk, poultry, and eggs are Puerto Rico's most valuable farm products. The island has increased its production of livestock to help feed its growing city population.

More than 70 per cent of Puerto Rico's workers have service jobs. The government employs more people than any other economic activity in a variety of services, including education, medical care, and defense.

History

The economy and government of Puerto Rico are unusual in the West Indies because of the island's history. Christopher Columbus landed in Puerto Rico in 1493. Spaniards, led by Juan Ponce de León, established the first European settlement in 1508. For more than 300 years, the island colony grew slowly, through hurricanes, plagues, and attacks by the Carib Indians and the Dutch, English, and French. By the late 1800's, Puerto Ricans had been given a large amount of local rule by Spain.

When the Spanish-American War began in 1898, U.S. forces landed in Puerto Rico. Spain surrendered the island to the United States when it lost the war.

A civil government was established for Puerto Rico in 1900, and in 1917 Puerto Ricans were made U.S. citizens.

In the early 1940's, a program called Operation Bootstrap began to improve living conditions on the island. In 1947, Puerto Ricans elected their first governor. The Puerto Rican people and Congress approved a constitution for the island, and on July 25, 1952, Puerto Rico became a self-governing commonwealth of the United States.

El Moro Fortress commands the coast near San Juan. Built by Spain in 1539, the fort is a reminder of Puerto Rico's colonial past.

Qatar

The small Arab country of Qatar sits on a peninsula that juts from eastern Arabia into the Persian Gulf. Most of the peninsula is a hot, stony desert, where summer temperatures rise above 120° F. (49° C) and annual rainfall is rarely more than 4 inches (10 centimeters). Barren salt flats cover the southern portion of the peninsula. For thousands of years, the people of Qatar made their living by tending camel herds, fishing, or diving for pearls in the gulf. In 1939, however, oil was discovered in western Qatar. World War II (1939–1945) delayed oil production for about 10 years, but since the 1950's, oil profits have made Qatar a rapidly developing nation.

The oil industry has also created many new jobs, and, as a result, thousands of people have moved to Qatar from other countries. From 1950 to 1990, the population of Qatar grew 20 times larger. Today, only about 40 per cent of Qatar's people are Arabs.

Most of Qatar's people live in or near Doha, the capital city, in modern houses and apartments. The majority work in Doha or other cities or in the oil fields. Some Qataris wear Western clothing, but most prefer traditional Arab robes. While Arabic is the official language, many business executives and government officials speak English when they are dealing with people from other countries.

In the mid-1970's, the Qatar government took over the petroleum industry from a foreign-owned company. The export of petroleum and petroleum products provides 95 per cent of the nation's income, and Qatar ranks among the world's richest nations in terms of average income per person.

The government has used its oil profits to develop the nation. The government provides free health care, free housing for needy people, and free education, including special schools where adults learn to read and write. The number of schools in Qatar rose from just 1 in 1952 to about 160 in 1990.

But the government has also encouraged manufacturing, fishing, and farming so that Qatar will not be entirely dependent on oil income in the future. In addition to petroleum wells and refineries, the government owns and operates a fishing fleet, flour mills, and plants that produce cement, fertilizers, petrochemicals, plastics, and steel. Fertilizers are now an important export in addition to petroleum.

Fact Box

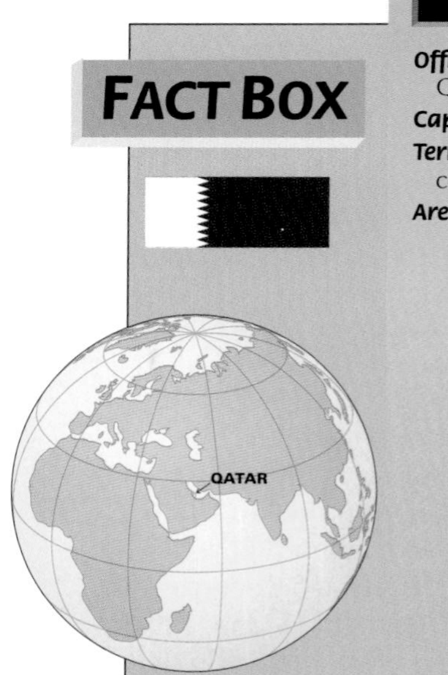

Country

Official name: Dawlat Qatar (State of Qatar)
Capital: Doha
Terrain: Mostly flat and barren desert covered with loose sand and gravel
Area: 4,416 sq. mi. (11,437 km²)
Climate: Desert; hot, dry; humid and sultry in summer
Highest elevation: Tuwayyir al Hamir, 338 ft. (103 m)
Lowest elevation: Persian Gulf, sea level

Government

Form of government: Traditional monarchy
Head of state: Emir
Head of government: Prime minister
Administrative areas: 9 baladiyat (municipalities)
Legislature: Majlis al-Shura (Advisory Council) with 35 members serving four-year terms
Court system: Court of Appeal
Armed forces: 11,800 troops

People

Estimated 2002 population: 617,000
Population growth: 3.35%
Population density: 145 persons per sq. mi. (56 per km²)
Population distribution: 91% urban, 9% rural
Life expectancy in years:
Male: 70
Female: 75
Doctors per 1,000 people: N/A
Percentage of age-appropriate population enrolled in the following educational levels:
Primary: N/A
Secondary: N/A
Further: N/A

The government has also dug wells to make farming possible in otherwise uncultivated areas, as well as distributed free seeds and insecticides. Qatar now produces enough vegetables for its people, though it still imports much of its meat and other food. Seawater is distilled to provide fresh drinking water.

The government of Qatar is an *emirate,* ruled by a leader called an *emir.* The emir is a member of the al-Thani family, whose chiefs, or *sheiks,* became leaders of tribes in Qatar during the 1800s. The al-Thani family has ruled Qatar ever since.

In 1916, Qatar became a British protectorate, but it gained complete independence in 1971. In 1972, Khalifa bin Hamad al-Thani became emir after peacefully overthrowing his cousin, Emir Ahmad bin Ali al-Thani. Khalifa bin Hamad al-Thani was in turn overthrown by his son in 1995.

The emir appoints an 18-member Council of Ministers to help run the government. An advisory council, made up of 35 ministers appointed to serve four-year terms, also aids the emir. The government of Qatar allows no political parties.

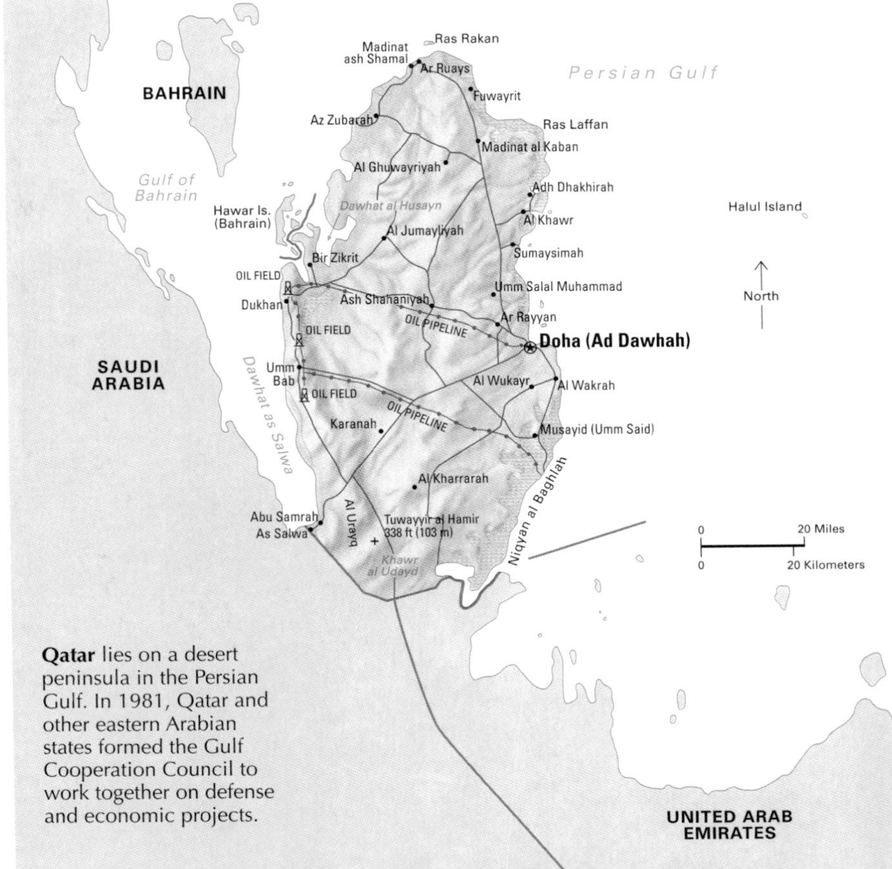

Qatar lies on a desert peninsula in the Persian Gulf. In 1981, Qatar and other eastern Arabian states formed the Gulf Cooperation Council to work together on defense and economic projects.

Languages spoken:
Arabic (official)
English (common second language)

Religion:
Muslim 95%

Technology

Radios per 1,000 people: N/A

Televisions per 1,000 people: N/A

Computers per 1,000 people: N/A

Economy

Currency: Qatari riyal

Gross domestic product (GDP) in 2001: $16.3 billion U.S.

Real annual growth rate (2001): 5.6%

GDP per capita (2000): $21,200 U.S.

Balance of payments (2001): N/A

Goods exported:
Mostly: petroleum products
Also: fertilizers, steel

Goods imported: Machinery and transport equipment, food, chemicals

Trading partners: Japan, United Kingdom, France, Singapore, South Korea

Hawks trained to hunt small game are sold in the market at Doha. Falconry, once the "sport of kings," has been practiced in the Middle East for more than 3,000 years.

Foreign technicians, *above,* staff the control room of Qatar's oil refinery at Umm Said, which opened in 1984.

Reunion

About 400 miles (640 kilometers) east of Madagascar, in the waters of the Indian Ocean, lies the island of Reunion.

Like Mauritius, its neighbor to the east, Reunion is a volcanic island. It was formed when *magma,* or melted rock, rose from beneath the ocean floor, broke through the surface, and piled up enough to rise above the level of the water. Reunion now covers a total area of 970 square miles (2,512 square kilometers).

The interior of the island is made up of volcanic mountains with tropical rain forests scattered throughout. Reunion's highest point, Piton des Neiges, towers 10,069 feet (3,069 meters) above the forests. An active volcano, Piton de la Fournaise, stands in the southeast part of the island.

Reunion generally has a tropical climate, but temperatures are cooler at higher elevations. Rainfall also varies, from as much as 140 inches (350 centimeters) per year on the east coast, to only half that amount on the northern coast.

Portuguese sailors discovered the island in the early 1500's. It was uninhabited at the time and remained so for about 100 years. Then in 1642, the French took possession of the island and named it Bourbon. The French first used the island as a colony for prisoners. In 1665, the French East India Company, a trading firm, set up an outpost there, and the colony prospered in the coffee trade. Later, colonists used the island as a stopping-off place on the way to Mauritius. Reunion received its present name in 1848.

Since 1946, Reunion has been an overseas department of France. It is one of the few remaining possessions of France's colonial empire. The people of the island have a voice in their government, however. They elect 36 members to a governing council.

The people of Reunion are largely French and African, and the total population of the island is about 515,800. About 20 per cent of the people live in the capital city of Saint-Denis. Smaller towns dot the island, mainly along the shore, and a coastal road rings the entire island. A university operates in Saint-Denis.

Tourism has become increasingly important to the economy of Reunion. The

Twisting roads wind between fields of sugar cane on the green hillsides of eastern Reunion. Sugar cane is an important cash crop on the island, accounting for most of its earnings from exports.

A vanilla worker, *above,* sorts the valuable pods. Reunion produces much of the world's supply of vanilla, which is used as a flavoring.

Workers on a banana plantation carry their produce in a traditional way—atop their heads—along a lane shaded by tall palm trees. Many kinds of crops thrive on the island of Reunion.

Streams of lava, *right,* from one of Reunion's volcanoes provide a spectacular sight for tourists, who watch from the safety of dried lava beds. Tourism is becoming more important to the island's economy.

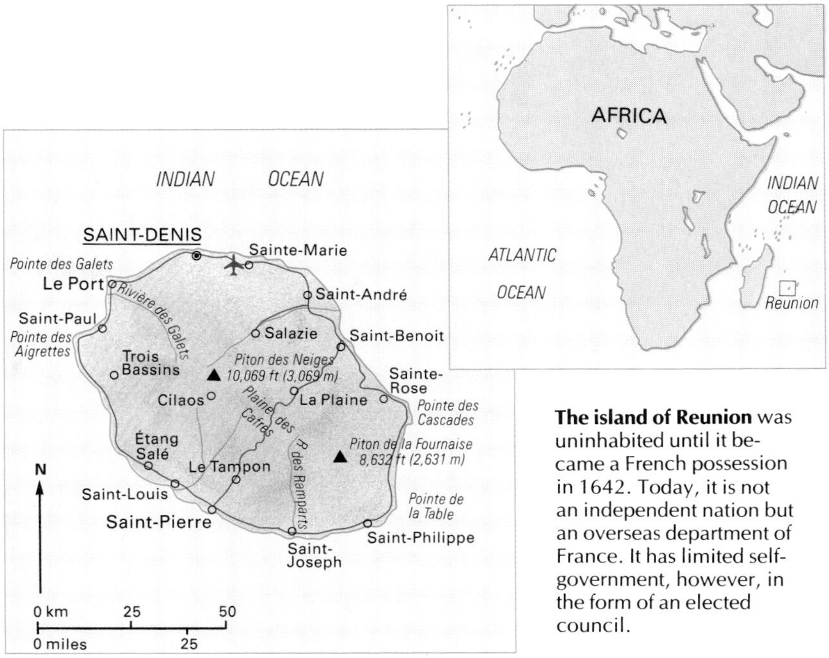

The island of Reunion was uninhabited until it became a French possession in 1642. Today, it is not an independent nation but an overseas department of France. It has limited self-government, however, in the form of an elected council.

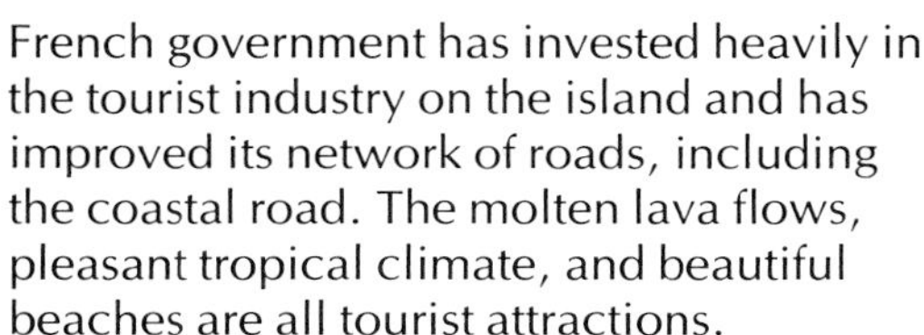

Saint-Denis, the capital of Reunion, *above,* overlooks the blue waters of the Indian Ocean. Situated on the northern coast of the island, the town is home to about 20 per cent of the island's population. Saint-Denis was founded by the French and is still quite French in character. It has many attractive buildings in the colonial style of the 1700's and 1800's, as well as spacious squares and wide avenues.

French government has invested heavily in the tourist industry on the island and has improved its network of roads, including the coastal road. The molten lava flows, pleasant tropical climate, and beautiful beaches are all tourist attractions.

Many of the people of Reunion, however, are farmers. The island's most important agricultural products are corn, perfume oils, sugar cane, tea, tobacco, and vanilla.

Reunion produces much of the world's supply of vanilla from orchids that grow on the island. These climbing orchids grow on a vine that attaches itself to trees. The plant produces pods, or beans, that are gathered when they are yellow-green in color, then dried, or cured. This process shrinks the pod and changes its color to a rich, chocolate-brown color. This curing process also gives the vanilla bean its familiar flavor and aroma.

Reunion's tropical flowers are also the source of the perfumes produced on the island. Fragrant plants have tiny sacs that make and store the substances that give them their pleasant scent. Workers on Reunion extract these substances— called *essential oils*— from flower petals as well as other parts of plants to make perfumes and colognes.

Romania

Romania lies west of Moldova, south of Ukraine, and north of the Balkan Peninsula in eastern Europe. The country was a monarchy from 1881 until the end of World War II (1939–1945). In 1947, it became a Soviet satellite with a Communist government controlled by the U.S.S.R. During the 1950's, Romanian leaders began to oppose Soviet intervention, and they insisted that Romania be allowed to make its own foreign policy.

Nicolae Ceausescu, who had served as general secretary and leader of the Romanian Communist Party since 1965, became head of state in 1968, and he continued Romania's efforts to free itself from Soviet control. During this time, Romania entered a period of rapid industrial expansion, financed by Western credit and the exploitation of the country's labor force.

In an attempt to solve an economic crisis that arose in the early 1980's, the Romanian government declared that it would pay back all its foreign debts. To meet its payments, Romania dramatically increased its exports while decreasing its imports, which resulted in serious shortages of food and consumer goods for the Romanian people. Meanwhile, Ceausescu's luxurious lifestyle stood in dramatic contrast to the poverty of the people.

The Romanian people suffered in other ways under the Ceausescu regime. A report issued by the worldwide human rights organization Amnesty International in July 1987 condemned the government's restrictions on the lives of the Romanian people.

In March 1988, Ceausescu began a controversial program of "rural urbanization." The plan called for the destruction of about 8,000 Romanian villages. The villagers were then to be resettled into multistory housing complexes, which would form part of the new agro-industrial centers. Ceausescu's plan brought both national and international criticism.

The economic hardships, the human-rights abuses, and the rural-urbanization plan helped bring down Ceausescu's Communist regime in December 1989. The revolutionaries seized control of the radio and television stations and formed the National Salvation Front (NSF).

During the revolution, Ceausescu and his wife were caught near Tîrgovişte as they were trying to escape. They were later executed, after being tried and convicted of various charges, including mass murder, corruption, and the destruction of the Romanian economy.

Multiparty presidential and legislative elections held in May 1990 gave the NSF

Fact Box

Country

Official name: Romania
Capital: Bucharest
Terrain: Central Transylvanian Basin is separated from the Plain of Moldavia on the east by the Carpathian Mountains and separated from the Walachian Plain on the south by the Transylvanian Alps
Area: 91,699 sq. mi. (237,500 km²)
Climate: Temperate; cold, cloudy winters with frequent snow and fog; sunny summers with frequent showers and thunderstorms
Main rivers: Argeş, Danube, Ialomiţa, Jiu, Olteţ, Prut, Siretul
Highest elevation: Moldoveanu, 8,343 ft. (2,543 m)
Lowest elevation: Black Sea, sea level

Government

Form of government: Republic
Head of state: President
Head of government: Prime minister
Administrative areas: 40 judete (counties), 1 municipiu (municipality)
Legislature: Parlament (Parliament) consisting of the Senat (Senate) with 143 members serving four-year terms and the Adunarea Deputatilor (Chamber of Deputies) with 343 members serving four-year terms
Court system: Supreme Court of Justice
Armed forces: 207,000 troops

People

Estimated 2002 population: 22,171,000
Population growth: -0.21%
Population density: 241 persons per sq. mi. (93 per km²)
Population distribution: 55% urban, 45% rural
Life expectancy in years:
Male: 66
Female: 74
Doctors per 1,000 people: 1.8
Percentage of age-appropriate population enrolled in the following educational levels:
Primary: 103*
Secondary: 80
Further: N/A
Languages spoken:
Romanian
Hungarian
German

An agricultural country before the Communists gained control, Romania has always been one of Europe's least developed nations. As a result of the industrialization program of the 1960's, industry has now surpassed agriculture in economic importance.

A flower vendor serves a customer along a quiet street in Bucharest, Romania's capital and largest city as well as its chief commercial and cultural center. Parts of the city are patterned somewhat after Paris and feature wide boulevards.

Religions:
Romanian Orthodox 70%
Roman Catholic 6%
Protestant 6%
unaffiliated 18%

*Enrollment ratios compare the number of students enrolled to the population which, by age, should be enrolled. A ratio higher than 100 indicates that students older or younger than the typical age range are also enrolled.

Technology

Radios per 1,000 people: 334
Televisions per 1,000 people: 381
Computers per 1,000 people: 31.9

Economy

Currency: Leu
Gross national income (GNI) in 2000: $37.4 billion U.S.
Real annual growth rate (1999–2000): 1.6%
GNI per capita (2000): $1,670 U.S.
Balance of payments (2000): -$1,359 million U.S.
Goods exported: Textiles and footwear, metals and metal products, machinery and equipment, minerals and fuels
Goods imported: Machinery and equipment, fuels and minerals, chemicals, textiles, and footwear
Trading partners: Italy, Germany, France

an overwhelming victory. Ion Iliescu, leader of the NSF, became president.

In mid-1990, pro- and anti-government demonstrators clashed in Bucharest, injuring hundreds. In late 1991, following strikes and riots by miners, the NSF government resigned. It was replaced by a coalition dominated by the NSF.

In general elections held in September 1992, the Democratic National Salvation Front (DNSF), a leftist group that had split from the NSF earlier in the year, won the majority of the seats in the legislature.

Romania's economy worsened. The country's national debt expanded and it attracted little foreign investment. In 1994, wages fell and 11 per cent of workers were jobless. Romania joined the Partnership for Peace, a program of cooperation with the North Atlantic Treaty Organization (NATO), in January 1994. In 1996, Romania elected its first non-Communist government since the fall of the Ceausescus in 1989.

Environment

Lying deep in the heart of eastern Europe, Romania is bordered to the north by Ukraine, to the east by Moldova, to the west by Hungary and Serbia and Montenegro, and to the south by Bulgaria. The Black Sea lies along the country's southeast coast for 130 miles (209 kilometers), and the Danube River flows through Romania for about 900 miles (1,400 kilometers).

Romania has a landscape of striking contrasts. The mountain region of the northern and central part of the country features breathtaking scenery, hiking trails, and many ski and vacation resorts, with numerous tiny lakes adding a special touch of beauty. Picturesque villages lie scattered across the vast fertile farmlands surrounding the mountains, while sandy beaches line the sunny coast of the Black Sea.

Romania's many important natural resources include fertile cropland, rich pastureland, forests, and valuable mineral deposits in the mountains and plateaus. The country's six land regions are Transylvania, Bukovina, Moldavia, Walachia, Banat, and Dobruja.

Transylvania

Transylvania, the largest and most diverse of Romania's land regions, includes most of the country's mountains, the Transylvanian Plateau, and the northwestern plain. Beautiful towns, churches, villages, and farms are set among its highlands and broad valleys. Farmers grow corn, grapes and other fruits, potatoes, sugar beets, and wheat in the fertile soil of the plains and plateaus.

The great arc of the Carpathian Mountain System encircles the Transylvanian Plateau. The Moldavian, or Eastern, Carpathians extend from the northern border to the center of the country, while the Transylvanian Alps, or Southern Carpathians, stretch westward from the Moldavian range. The Bihor Mountains and other ranges make up the Western Carpathians.

The Carpathians are neither very high nor steep, and the many passes cut through them enable tourists to explore the mountains and to observe foxes, lynx, badgers, wolves, and even bears in their natural habitat. Hikers enjoy following tracks over the peaks and cliffs and through gorges, dense forests, and mountain meadows.

Today, Transylvania may be best known as the home of Count Dracula—the wicked nobleman in the famous vampire story. Northeast of Transylvania in the Moldavian Carpathian Mountains lies the thickly forested region of Bukovina.

"Dracula's Castle," the stronghold of the cruel prince from Walachia who inspired the legend, stands high atop a mountain in the Transylvanian Alps in south-central Romania. The character of Dracula is based on Vlad Tepes, a prince who committed hundreds of savage murders in the 1400's and executed many of his enemies by driving a sharpened pole through their bodies. The novel *Dracula* (1897), by the English author Bram Stoker, made the legend internationally famous.

Houses and farm buildings are clustered in a valley in the Transylvanian Alps, *right*. Mount Moldoveanu, Romania's highest mountain, is located in the Transylvanian Alps.

Plains and plateaus

In the regions of Moldavia, Walachia, and Banat, the land descends from mountains near Transylvania, to hills, and then to plains that provide Romania's best farmland. Moldavia forms part of the Russian steppes, but the original steppe vegetation

has disappeared with crop cultivation. The city of Bucharest, Romania's chief industrial center, is located in Walachia.

Dobruja, a small plain between the northern course of the Danube River and the Black Sea, is home to an abundance of wildlife, including 300 species of birds. Sturgeon, the source of caviar, are also found in the waters of the Danube where the river empties into the Black Sea.

Fishing crews sail downriver at the Mouths of the Danube. Near the city of Galaţi, the Danube breaks up into a three-pronged delta consisting of rivers, islands, lakes, ponds, and streams. Wildlife in the region is now threatened by pollution.

Herds of cattle are watered in a stream in Walachia, *far left.* Livestock accounts for about two-fifths of the value of Romania's agricultural products, and crops account for about three-fifths.

On the Moldavian plain, women in traditional dress stack hay to dry in the sun. Farmers grow barley, beets, corn, grapes, and sunflowers in Moldavia's fertile soil.

People

The Romanians are the only people in eastern Europe who trace their ancestry and language back to the Romans. Today, 85 per cent of the people in Romania are descended from the Dacians and Romans and from tribes such as the Goths, Huns, and Slavs.

Early migrations

The Dacians lived in what is now Romania before the Romans arrived. By the 300's B.C., they were farming the land, mining gold and iron ore from the mountains, and trading with neighboring peoples. In A.D. 106, the Romans, led by Emperor Trajan, conquered the Dacians and made the region a province of the Roman Empire. Roman soldiers occupied Dacia and Roman colonists settled there. The Dacians intermarried with the Romans and adopted their customs and the Latin language. The region, which had previously been called *Dacia*, became known as *Romania*.

Barbarians arriving from the east and north during the 200's forced the Romans to abandon the province. From the late 200's to the 1100's, a series of invaders swept through Romania, including Bulgars, Goths, Huns, Magyars, Slavs, and Tatars. Like the Romans, these groups—especially the Slavs—also intermarried with the Romanians.

The Romanian language, which developed from Latin, is not at all like other languages in eastern Europe. Romanian most closely resembles French, Italian, Portuguese, and Spanish— languages that also developed from Latin.

Minority groups

Romania's largest minority group is the Hungarians, who make up about 8 per cent of the population and live mostly in Transylvania. The region in which the ethnic Hungarians now live consists of territory taken from Hungary after World War II (1939-1945).

In the late 1980's, the Romanian government was severely criticized for not adequately recognizing the ethnic and cultural rights of the Hungarians living in Romania. The government also encouraged the Hungarian minority to blend in with the Romanian culture.

Religious worship, *top,* was suppressed during the period of Communist rule in Romania. However, many people continued to attend church services and celebrate religious festivals. Most Romanians belong to the Romanian Orthodox Church, an Eastern Orthodox church.

Rural Romanians, *above,* often celebrate weddings, christenings, and religious holidays by wearing colorful costumes.

Thousands of ethnic Hungarians would like to leave Romania and resettle in Hungary, and the fall of the Ceausescu regime prompted a new exodus across the border. In March 1990, several people died in clashes between ethnic Hungarians and Romanian nationalists in Tîrgu Mures.

Ethnic Germans make up about 2 per cent of Romania's population. In 1919,

Everyday life in Romania contrasts sharply with life in Western Europe. For example, less than 1 per cent of the people own a car, and only 15 per cent own a television set. City dwellers also face a serious housing shortage.

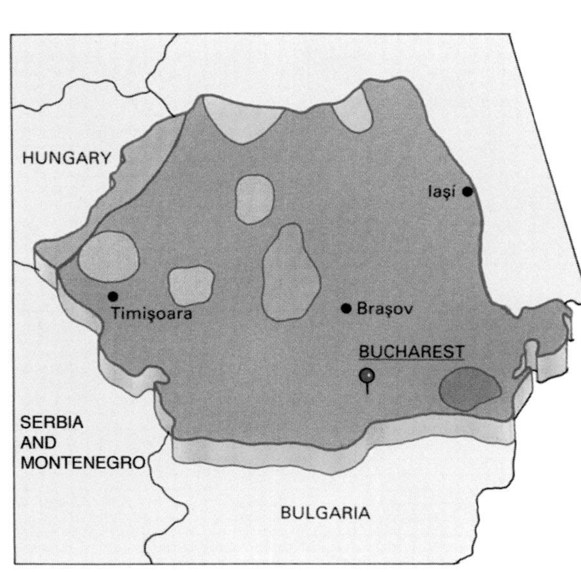

After Romanians, Hungarians are the largest ethnic group in Romania. Germans, Ukrainians, and Turks also contribute to the country's population.

A fisherman propels his flat-bottomed boat through the dense reeds in Romania's delta region, *left*. About half of Romania's people live in rural areas, but an increasing number of people are moving to the cities to take jobs in industry.

In addition to people of German origin, *below*, and ethnic Hungarians, who are the largest minority group, Romania is also home to Gypsies, Jews, Turks, and Ukrainians. Schools provide lessons in Hungarian and German as well as in Romanian.

German settlers in Transylvania and part of Banat agreed to join the new Romanian state, which promised them many rights and freedoms. After World War II, however, many ethnic Germans fled or were expelled from Romania.

Their departure, along with Romania's poor economic conditions, left many German settlements in a state of decay. The big country estates are falling into disrepair, the soil remains untilled, and the churches are locked up and boarded.

Given the conditions in Romania, there has been little to persuade minorities to stay in the country. About half of the 200,000 Germans living there have now applied for permission to move to Germany.

Romanians have one of the lowest living standards in Europe. Although almost all Romanian workers earn enough to pay for basic needs, few can afford luxury items. Rapid population growth has caused a housing shortage in the cities, and most city people live in crowded apartments.

Russia

From the gently rolling European Plain to the vast Siberian wilderness, and from the soaring Ural Mountains to the depths of Lake Baikal, the huge country of Russia spreads across the two continents of Europe and Asia. It is a nation whose long and tumultuous history has shaped world affairs as few others have.

The historical roots of the Russian people date from the early migrations of the Slavs, who had established settlements in what is now the European part of Russia and who became known as the Eastern Slavs. About 988, Grand Prince Vladimir I, the ruler of the Eastern Slavs, converted to Christianity, and most people under his rule became Christians.

As Russia expanded its territory and absorbed other nationality groups, its rulers forced the conquered peoples to adopt Orthodox Christianity and the Russian language. These rulers were known as *czars* (emperors), and they created a centralized state that had complete power over every aspect of Russian life.

Under the czars, the country was largely cut off from the industrial progress made in Western Europe in the 1800's, and most of its people remained poor, uneducated peasants. Despite their difficult life, the peasants loved their country, which they called "Mother Russia."

In 1917, the *Bolsheviks* (later called *Communists*) drove the last czar, Nicholas II, from power in what is now known as the October Revolution. In 1922, the Communist leaders, who had taken over the Russian government, formed the Union of Soviet Socialist Republics (U.S.S.R.), made up of four union republics, of which Russia was the largest and most powerful. The first republic formed after the Bolshevik Revolution, Russia became the Russian Soviet Federative Socialist Republic (R.S.F.S.R.). By 1940, 12 other republics had joined—or were forcibly annexed to—the Soviet Union, making it the largest and most powerful Communist country in the world.

After the establishment of the Soviet Union, the Russians continued to dominate other nationality groups throughout the union republics. Soldiers, bureaucrats, and teachers carried out "Russification" programs, and in the 1930's, as workers moved to non-Russian republics during Joseph Stalin's industrialization program, Russian influence spread even wider.

After the Soviet Union was dissolved in December 1991, Russia, now an independent nation, and its president, Boris Yeltsin, played a leading role in the formation of the new Commonwealth of Independent States, an association of independent countries that were formerly republics of the Soviet Union.

Russia Today

The Russian republic was the first republic organized after Russian workers overthrew the czarist government in 1917. More than 70 years later, it became the center of protests that led to an attempted government coup. This coup—which helped bring an end to Communist rule and the dissolution of the Soviet Union—promised a new beginning for the Russian people.

When the Communists first took over the country, Russia's people were poor and uneducated. The Communists, who wanted to make the Soviet Union—including Russia—a modern, powerful state, expanded the economy under a series of plans emphasizing industrialization.

As a result, the Soviet Union became the world's largest centrally planned economy. The Soviet government owned most of the nation's banks, factories, land, mines, and transportation systems. It also planned and controlled the production, distribution, and pricing of almost all goods.

However, the focus on heavy manufacturing that made the Soviet Union a leading industrial giant caused frequent shortages of consumer goods. As a result, improvements in living conditions came more slowly, and there were often shortages of food and other basic household necessities. In addition, the Communists placed serious restrictions on people's basic freedoms. Those who opposed government policies were often expelled from their homes, sent to prison labor camps or mental hospitals, or executed.

In 1985, Mikhail S. Gorbachev became the leader of the Soviet Union and instituted many reforms. His policy of openness, became known as *glasnost*.

Meanwhile, popular movements in Russia and the other republics of the Soviet Union threatened the unity of the nation. Gorbachev called for a new treaty that would grant the republics a large amount of independence.

On Aug. 19, 1991—the day before the treaty was to be signed—conservative Communist officials attempted to overthrow Gorbachev's government. Boris N. Yeltsin, president of the Russian republic, led a popular uprising against the coup, which collapsed after two days.

On December 17, 1991, Yeltsin and Gorbachev agreed to dissolve the Soviet Union and replace it with the Commonwealth of Independent States (CIS), a new association of former Soviet republics.

In 1992 and early 1993, economic and political problems troubled Russia. The 1992 inflation rate added up to 2,000 per

FACT BOX

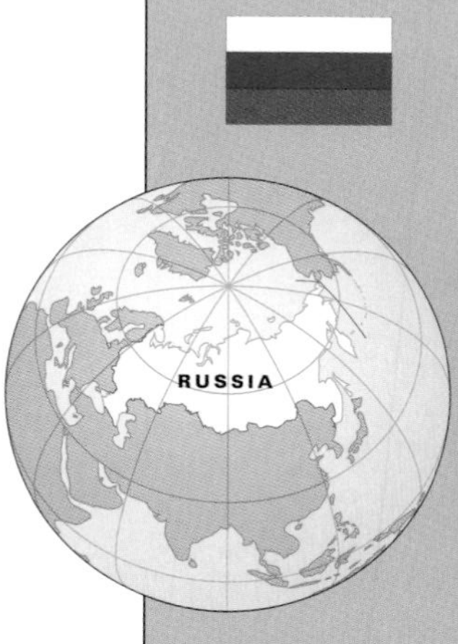

COUNTRY

Official name: Rossiyskaya Federatsiya (Russian Federation)
Capital: Moscow
Terrain: Broad plain with low hills west of Urals; vast coniferous forest and tundra in Siberia; uplands and mountains along southern border regions
Area: 6,592,772 sq. mi. (17,075,200 km²)
Climate: Ranges from steppes in the south through humid continental in much of European Russia; subarctic in Siberia to tundra climate in the polar north; winters vary from cool along Black Sea coast to frigid in Siberia; summers vary from warm in the steppes to cool along Arctic coast
Main rivers: Lena, Ob, Volga
Highest elevation: Mt. Elbrus, 18,510 ft. (5,642 m)
Lowest elevation: Caspian Sea, 92 ft. (28 m) below sea level

GOVERNMENT

Form of government: Republic
Head of state: President
Head of government: Prime Minister
Administrative areas: 49 oblastey (oblasts), 21 respublik (republics), 10 avtonomnykh okrugov (autonomous okrugs), 6 krayev (krays), 2 federal cities, 1 avtonomnaya oblast (autonomous oblast)
Legislature: Federalnoye Sobraniye (Federal Assembly) consisting of the Sovet Federatsii (Federation Council) with 178 members serving four-year terms and the Gosudarstvennaya Duma (State Duma) with 450 members serving four-year terms
Court system: Constitutional Court, Supreme Court, Superior Court of Arbitration
Armed forces: 1,004,100 troops

PEOPLE

Estimated 2002 population: 146,376,000
Population growth: -0.38%
Population density: 22 persons per sq. mi. (9 per km²)
Population distribution: 73% urban, 27% rural
Life expectancy in years:
Male: 62
Female: 73
Doctors per 1,000 people: 4.2
Percentage of age-appropriate population enrolled in the following educational levels:
Primary: 107*
Secondary: N/A
Further: 41

Russia is the world's largest country in area and is almost twice the size of the second largest country, Canada. Russia extends from the Arctic Ocean south to the Black Sea and from the Baltic Sea east to the Pacific Ocean.

cent, and in early 1993 it rose by 10 per cent a week.

In September 1993, Yeltsin dissolved the Congress, which voted to impeach him and remained barricaded within the parliament building. On Oct. 2 and 3, supporters of the Congress battled with police. On Oct. 4, troops loyal to Yeltsin attacked the parliament building and arrested opposition leaders. In all, 142 people died.

Inflation stabilized in 1994, falling from about 20 per cent monthly in January to 6 per cent monthly in August. Unemployment and violent crime continued to rise.

In December 1994, Russian troops invaded the autonomous republic of Chechnya to put down a separatist movement. The Russians claimed victory but the Chechens fiercely resisted. Fighting continued until 1996, when an uncertain cease-fire was negotiated.

In 1999, Islamic militants attempted to unite Chechnya and the neighboring republic of Dagestan. Russia invaded Chechnya to defeat the rebellion, which heavily damaged Chechnya's cities and killed many civilians. Many nations protested Russia's handling of the conflict.

Despite political turmoil and ill health, Yeltsin won reelection as president in 1996. On the last day of 1999, Yeltsin resigned and appointed Vladimir Putin, Russia's prime minister, as acting president. In presidential elections in March 2000, Russians voted overwhelmingly for Putin.

Language spoken: Russian

Religions: Russian Orthodox, Muslim

**Enrollment ratios compare the number of students enrolled to the population which, by age, should be enrolled. A ratio higher than 100 indicates that students older or younger than the typical age range are also enrolled.*

Economy

Currency: Ruble

Gross national income (GNI) in 2000: $241 billion U.S.

Real annual growth rate (1999–2000): 8.3%

GNI per capita (2000): $1,660 U.S.

Balance of payments (2000): $41,846 million U.S.

Goods exported: Petroleum and petroleum products, natural gas, wood and wood products, metals, chemicals

Goods imported: Machinery and equipment, consumer goods, medicines, meat, grain, sugar, semifinished metal products

Trading partners: Germany, Ukraine, Belarus, United States

Technology

Radios per 1,000 people: 418

Televisions per 1,000 people: 421

Computers per 1,000 people: 42.9

Early History

The history of Russia began many centuries ago, when the broad steppes of the southern region formed a natural corridor for migrating peoples. By the A.D. 800's, Slavic groups had built many towns in what is now the European part of Russia and Ukraine. The first state they founded was called Kiev Rus, and the city of Kiev became its capital.

According to the *Primary Chronicle,* the earliest written Russian history, a group of Vikings called the *Varangian Russes* captured Kiev in 882. By the 900's, the other Russian *principalities* (regions ruled by a prince) recognized Kiev's importance as a cultural and commercial center.

During the 1200's, *Tatar* (Mongol) armies swept across Russia from the east, destroying one town after another, and in 1240, when the Mongols destroyed Kiev, Russia became part of the Mongol Empire. Under Mongol control, Russia was cut off from the influence and new ideas of the Renaissance—an important cultural movement that dramatically changed Western Europe and later its overseas colonies.

The first czar

During the early 1300's, the Mongols grew weak and the small northeast principality of Moscow became rich and powerful. By 1480 its leader, Ivan III, had made the final break from Mongol control, and in 1547, Ivan IV (Ivan the Terrible) became the first ruler to be crowned czar. A crafty and cruel leader who passed a series of laws that bound the peasants to the land as *serfs*—making them part of the landowner's property—Ivan the Terrible also laid the foundation for the growth of Russia. Under his rule, Russian forces crossed the Ural Mountains to conquer western Siberia and also took control of the region along the Volga River.

After Ivan's death in 1584, Russia was torn by civil war, foreign invasion, and political confusion until 1613, when an assembly of nobles and citizens elected

The Trinity Monastery of St. Sergius at Sergiyev Posad, northeast of Moscow, served as a treasury of Russian art and literature for centuries.

A.D. 800's Slavic groups settle in what is now the European part of Russia and Ukraine. Eastern Slavs establish the state of Kiev Rus.
c. 988 Grand Prince Vladimir I converts to Christianity.
1237 Batu, grandson of Genghis Khan, leads Mongol troops into Russia.
1240 Mongols destroy Kiev; Russia becomes part of the Mongol Empire.
c. 1318 Prince Yuri of Moscow is appointed the Russian grand prince.
1380 Grand Prince Dmitri defeats a Mongol force in the Battle of Kulikovo.
Late 1400's Moscow becomes the most powerful Russian city.
1480 Ivan III breaks Mongol control over Russia.
1547 Ivan IV (Ivan the Terrible) becomes the first ruler to be crowned czar.
1554 Russian forces conquer western Siberia.
1556 Ivan IV defeats Astrakhan.
1604-1613 Russia is torn by civil war, invasion, and political confusion during the Time of Troubles.
1613 Michael Romanov becomes czar.
1600's Russia extends control to Ukraine and Siberia.
1682-1725 Peter I (Peter the Great) reigns as czar.
1703 Peter the Great founds St. Petersburg.
1709 Russia defeats Sweden in the Great Northern War.
1762-1796 Empress Catherine II (Catherine the Great) rules Russia.
1773-1774 Russian troops crush a peasant revolt.
Late 1700's Russia gains parts of Poland, the Crimea, and other Turkish lands.
1812 Napoleon leads French army to Moscow, but is forced to retreat.
1825 Government troops crush the Decembrist uprising.
1853-1856 Russia fights the Ottoman Empire in the Crimean War and is defeated.
1861 Alexander II frees the serfs.
1904-1905 Japan defeats Russia in the Russo-Japanese War.
1905 A revolution in January forces Nicholas II to establish a parliament; a general strike in October paralyzes the country.
1914-1917 Russia fights Germany and Austria-Hungary in World War I.

Ivan the Terrible (1530-1584), crafty and cruel, forced the Russian people to accept the total power of the czar.

Peter the Great (1672-1725), *far left,* is famous for introducing Western customs and institutions to Russia.

Catherine the Great (1729-1796) became empress of Russia in 1762 and greatly expanded the country's frontiers.

In 1905, thousands of unarmed workers marched to the czar's Winter Palace in St. Petersburg to demand political and social reforms. Government troops fired into the crowd, killing or wounding hundreds of people.

The expansion of the Russian Empire

1360

1360-1524

1524-1689

1689-1917

MOSCOW

Michael Romanov czar. His descendants ruled Russia for three centuries.

Under the leadership of Czar Peter I (Peter the Great), who ruled from 1682 to 1725, Russia came to be a major European power. Peter expanded Russian territory to the Baltic Sea and introduced many Western ways to the nation. His successors, including Empress Catherine II (Catherine the Great), continued to promote Western culture and ideas in Russia— lavish parties took place at the czar's palace, the arts were encouraged, and many new schools were established. But the great majority of the Russian people continued to live in extreme poverty, and the landowners kept tight control over the serfs.

Harsh rule continued in Russia until Alexander II, who reigned from 1855 to 1881, introduced major reforms. In 1861, Alexander freed the serfs, distributed land among the peasants, and established forms of self-government in the towns and villages. However, many young Russians felt that Alexander's new policies did not go far enough, and after a revolutionary tried to kill Alexander in 1866, the czar began to weaken his reforms. He was killed by a terrorist bomb in 1881, and his son, Alexander III, began a program of harsh rule.

The coming of revolution

In 1894, Nicholas II became Russia's last czar. When a series of bad harvests caused widespread starvation, discontent grew among the rising middle class and workers in the cities, and various political organizations emerged. After an economic depression began in 1899, student protests, peasant revolts, and worker strikes increased. But, other than making a few constitutional reforms— such as forming a Duma (parliament)— the czar and his officials refused to give up power.

During World War I (1914-1918), the Russian economy could not support both the fight against Germany and the people at home, and severe shortages of food, fuel, and housing occurred throughout the nation. In March 1917, the Russian people revolted, and when soldiers called in to halt the uprising sided with strikers and demonstrators, the days of the Russian czars were ended forever.

Modern History

By March 9, 1917, about 200,000 Russian workers were demonstrating in Petrograd (now St. Petersburg), then the capital of Russia. In the midst of the riots and strikes, which became known as the February Revolution, the Duma established a *provisional* (temporary) democratic government, and a new Soviet of Workers' and Soldiers' Deputies was formed in Petrograd in March. Nicholas II, who had lost all political support, gave up the throne on March 15.

The October Revolution

Neither the provisional government nor the Soviet of Workers' and Soldiers' Deputies was powerful enough to rule on its own. In late 1917, the *Bolshevik* (majority) wing of the Russian Social Democratic Labor Party, under the leadership of Vladimir I. Lenin and Leon Trotsky, seized power and formed a new Russian government. They spread Bolshevik rule through the local *soviets* (councils).

The new government soon faced a civil war against antirevolutionary forces aided by troops from France, Great Britain, Japan, the United States, and other countries opposed to the Bolsheviks' Communist policies. The civil war between the *Reds* (the Bolsheviks, renamed the Russian Communist Party) and the *Whites* (the anti-Communist forces) lasted from 1918 to 1920, when the Reds defeated the poorly organized Whites.

By 1921, seven years of war, revolution, civil war, and invasion had exhausted Russia and severely disrupted its economy. In an effort to deal with the growing discontent and new uprisings, the government introduced the New Economic Policy (NEP), which permitted small industries and the retail trade to operate on their own.

In 1922, the new Russian Republic became one of the four founding republics of the Union of Soviet Socialist Republics (U.S.S.R.). It was the U.S.S.R.'s largest and most powerful republic.

The rise of Stalin

By the mid-1920's, as a result of Lenin's New Economic Policy, all the nation's fac-

Cheering Muscovites display the red, white, and blue banner of the Russian republic after the failure of a coup in August 1991.

In June 1941, German troops invaded the Soviet Union, penetrating deep into the Ukraine, Byelorussia, and the Baltic States, *map far right.* By late 1941, the Germans came close to Moscow before retreating. In the north, their siege of Leningrad (now St. Petersburg) lasted until they were driven back in January 1944. After World War II (1939-1945), the nations of Eastern Europe freed from German control by the Soviets became satellite Communist nations, *map below.*

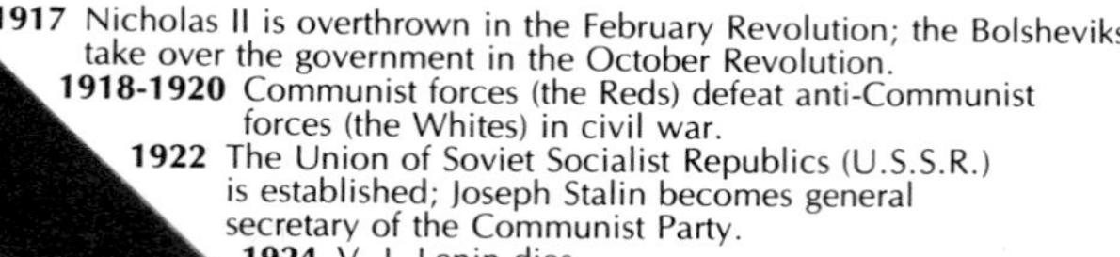

1917 Nicholas II is overthrown in the February Revolution; the Bolsheviks take over the government in the October Revolution.
1918-1920 Communist forces (the Reds) defeat anti-Communist forces (the Whites) in civil war.
1922 The Union of Soviet Socialist Republics (U.S.S.R.) is established; Joseph Stalin becomes general secretary of the Communist Party.
1924 V. I. Lenin dies.
1928 The First Five-Year Plan begins.
1929 Stalin defeats his political rivals and becomes dictator of the U.S.S.R.
Mid-1930's Millions of Soviet citizens are imprisoned or executed during the Great Purge.
1941 German forces invade the Soviet Union during World War II.
1942-1943 Soviet troops prevent the Nazis from capturing Stalingrad.
1945 The Soviets' capture of Berlin leads to a German surrender.
Late 1940's The Soviet Union gains control in Eastern Europe by setting up satellite states with Communist governments. The Iron Curtain falls and the Cold War develops.
1953 Stalin dies; Nikita Khrushchev becomes head of the Communist Party.
1957 Soviet scientists launch the satellite *Sputnik 1.*
1961 Yuri Gagarin becomes the first person to orbit the earth.
1961 China breaks off relations with the U.S.S.R.
1962 The Cuban missile crisis occurs.
1964 Khrushchev is overthrown and replaced by Leonid I. Brezhnev as head of the Communist Party.
1982 Brezhnev dies. Yuri V. Andropov becomes Communist Party head.
1984 Andropov dies. Konstantin U. Chernenko replaces Andropov.
1985 Chernenko dies. Mikhail S. Gorbachev becomes head of the Communist Party and announces a policy of *glasnost* (openness) and *perestroika* (restructuring).
1990 Gorbachev is awarded the Nobel Peace Prize.
1991 Conservative Communist officials fail in their attempt to overthrow the central government. Gorbachev resigns from the Communist Party, and all party activities are suspended. The Baltic States gain independence from the Soviet Union. Ten of the 12 remaining republics declare their independence. In December, the Soviet Union is dissolved, and Russia becomes a member of the new Commonwealth of Independent States (CIS).
1992 Russia ends decades-old subsidies that had kept the price of most basic goods and services beneath the cost of producing and providing them.

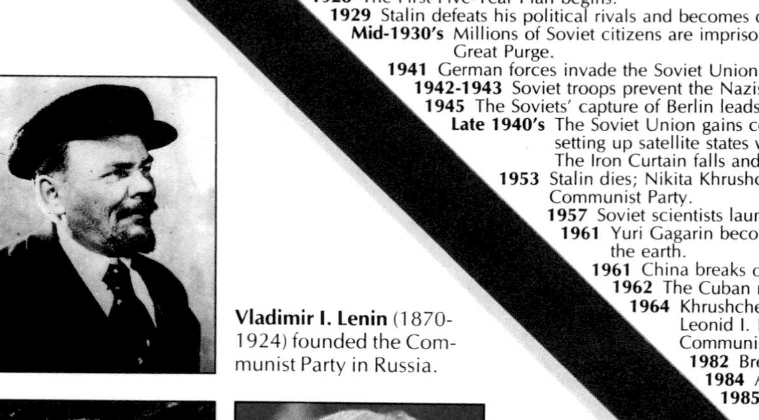

Vladimir I. Lenin (1870-1924) founded the Communist Party in Russia.

Joseph Stalin (1879-1953), *far left,* was dictator of the Soviet Union from 1929 to 1953.

Mikhail S. Gorbachev (1931-) was the last leader of the Soviet Union before it was dissolved in December 1991.

A study in the Winter Palace at Petrograd (now St. Petersburg), which served as the headquarters of the provisional government in 1917, stands in shambles after it was stormed by armed workers and Bolsheviks during the October Revolution.

Soviet soldiers advance through the ruins of Stalingrad (now Volgograd), *middle left,* during the struggle against German forces in the winter of 1942-1943. After five months of bitter fighting, the Germans surrendered.

At the Yalta Conference in February 1945, key Allied leaders met to address the major problems in a postwar Europe. *Left to right:* Winston Churchill, Franklin D. Roosevelt, and Joseph Stalin.

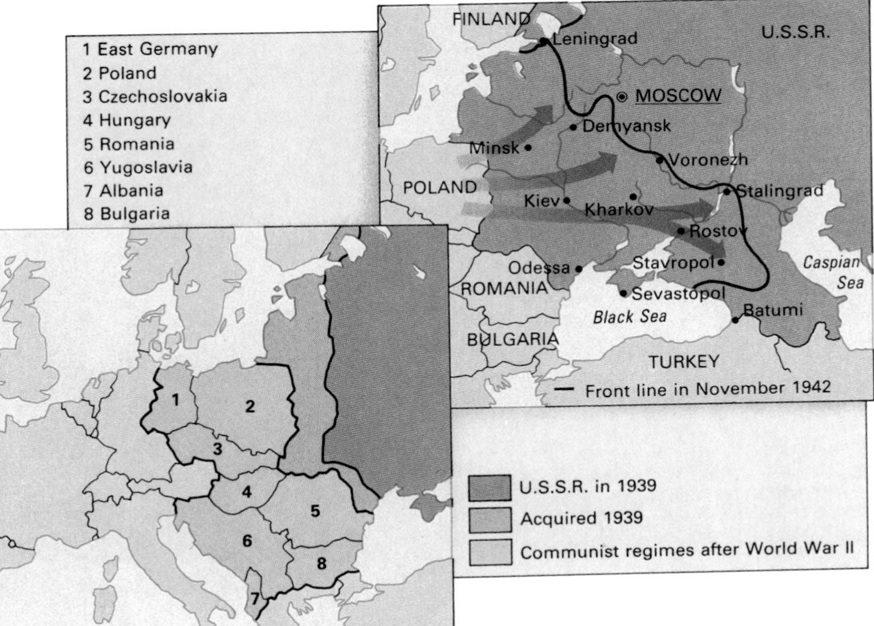

tories and other means of production were operating again. Lenin died in 1924, and Joseph Stalin, who had become general secretary of the Communist Party's Central Committee, began his rise to supreme power. By 1929, Stalin had become dictator of the Soviet Union.

Under Stalin's First Five-Year Plan, farmers were forced to give most of their products to the government at low prices. But the farmers, resisting Stalin's orders, destroyed much of their livestock and crops. This action caused widespread starvation, and Stalin sent several million peasant families to prison labor camps in Siberia and Soviet Central Asia.

During the 1930's, Stalin began a program of terror called the Great Purge, in which his secret police arrested anyone and everyone suspected of being a threat to his power. Up to 20 million people may have been killed during this period.

During World War II (1939-1945), following the German invasion of the U.S.S.R., the Soviet Union became a partner of the Allies. After World War II, Stalin gradually cut off almost all contact between the U.S.S.R. and Western nations.

Post-Stalin

Soviet relations with the West did not improve until after Stalin's death in 1953. His successor, Nikita Khrushchev, announced a policy of "peaceful coexistence" and eased some restrictions on communication, trade, and travel. Khrushchev was replaced by Leonid I. Brezhnev, who also pursued a policy of friendlier relations with the West. He was succeeded by Yuri V. Andropov, who was later replaced by Konstantin U. Chernenko. Mikhail S. Gorbachev came to power in 1985. Under him, the Soviet Union changed rapidly, then dissolved. In December 1991, the world recognized Russia as an independent nation led by Boris N. Yeltsin.

Russian Way of Life

When the Communists took over the Russian government in 1917, they hoped to create a classless society—one with neither rich people nor poor people—by taking control of the economy, the educational system, and the cultural life of the people. However, the Communists failed to achieve that goal. Under the Soviet system, certain privileged groups enjoyed special rights, while the vast majority of Soviet citizens had a generally lower standard of living than people in the United States and Western Europe. In addition, they suffered great restrictions on their personal freedom.

In the past, people who criticized the country's political system were severely punished, or even killed. During the 1930's—the years of Stalin's Great Purge—the government's secret police arrested millions of Soviet citizens suspected of anti-Communist views or activities. These people were either shot or sent to labor camps in Siberia.

A new openness

In the late 1980's, however, Mikhail Gorbachev's policy of glasnost led to greater freedom for the Soviet people. The government relaxed its control of newspapers, radio, and television. Greater religious freedom was permitted, and a wave of cultural activity swept across the country. After the Communist Party fell from power in 1991, party officials and other privileged groups lost their special rights.

Although glasnost and the suspension of the Communist Party created a new spirit of openness in the U.S.S.R., many serious problems have remained in the independent state of Russia. Most of the people live in urban areas, and cities are very crowded. Millions of families live in small, plain, crowded apartments, and housing shortages frequently force many families to share apartments.

In addition to the lack of housing, the Russian people are plagued with frequent shortages of food and other consumer

After they rose to power in 1917, the Communists— who believe there is no God—destroyed many churches and persecuted religious leaders. But many people continued to worship in private. In 1990, the government ended all religious restrictions.

A St. Petersburg couple examine a bulletin board advertising apartments available. Most apartments are very small and cramped.

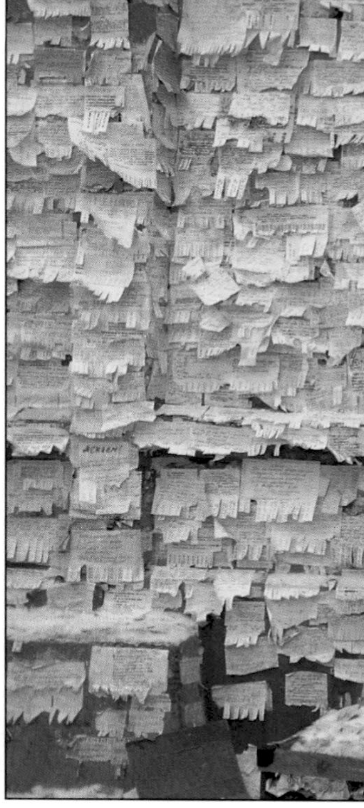

A huge display of wild mushrooms is spread out in a stall at Moscow's private market. Russian people often sell food collected in the wild or grown on small, private plots.

In the wake of the unsuccessful coup of August 1991 and the downfall of the Communist Party, Russian youths jeer at the fallen statue of the founder of the KGB.

goods. Shoppers must often go from store to store in search of meat and clothing, often finding little to buy. For imported goods, they may have to stand in line for hours. And the little that is available is now costing as much as three to four times what it had cost under a Communist economy.

Most Russian women have full-time jobs and choose from a wide variety of careers. However, they are also responsible for all household duties, such as cooking, cleaning, child care, and grocery shopping. The lack of time-saving appliances and the long lines at grocery stores mean that most women spend much time away from their children. The resulting pressure has taken its toll on family life in Russia, and alcoholism and divorce are on the rise.

Living conditions are much worse in rural areas, where people live in small log huts or in community barracks. These buildings often have no plumbing, running water, or gas for heating and cooking, and some do not have electricity. Shopping is even more difficult in rural areas because there are fewer stores. The quality of education is also far below that of the cities.

Ballet dancers perform to enthusiastic audiences at the Kirov Theater in St. Petersburg and the Bolshoi Theater in Moscow. Tickets to the ballet are difficult for ordinary citizens to obtain, but most Russian families enjoy a visit to one of the country's museums, such as St. Petersburg's Hermitage, *above*.

Russian education

In addition to their goal of creating a classless society, the Communists also intended to build the country into a major industrial power. At the time, however, Russia was largely a country of poor, uneducated peasants. To train the large numbers of workers needed in an industrial society, the Communists quickly began establishing educational programs throughout the country.

Today, Russia boasts a highly developed educational system. Nearly all the nation's citizens can read and write, and Russian achievements in science and technology are among the highest in the world. All Russian students know that education is the surest road to success in their country, and those who perform well are rewarded with high-paying careers.

The Volga River

Flowing for about 2,193 miles (3,530 kilometers) through the heart of Russia, the mighty Volga River ranks as the longest river in Europe. From the earliest days of Slavic settlement, the Volga has served as an important trade and communications route.

Ever since Viking sailors navigated the river, trading furs and slaves for silver and silks from Asia, many key events in Russian history have taken place along its shores. The beauty and significance of *Matushka Volga* (Mother Volga) have long been celebrated in the country's music and literature.

A major waterway

The Volga River rises in the Valai Hills, between Moscow and St. Petersburg, at an elevation of only about 748 feet (228 meters) above sea level. It first flows eastward, passing to the north of Moscow, and then southwest after passing the city of Kazan. South of Volgograd, the river turns southeast before discharging its waters into the Caspian Sea through a 100-mile (160-kilometer) delta. At the Caspian Sea, the Volga is 92 feet (28 meters) below sea level.

With its many tributaries, the Volga forms a major river system that drains an area of about 525,000 square miles (1,360,000 square kilometers). Farmers grow wheat and other crops in this fertile river valley, which is also rich in petroleum, natural gas, salt, and potash. The delta region and the Caspian Sea provide one of the world's great fishing grounds.

The river begins to freeze at the end of November, and in some areas, the ice does not clear until April. When it is not frozen, the Volga, including many of its tributaries, is navigable for almost its entire length. Canal networks, such as the Volga-Don Canal in the south, link the river with the Baltic, White, and Black seas, and its tributaries carry timber to the Volga from as far away as the Urals. The Volga carries a large amount of the river traffic in Russia, including steamships that transport passengers as well as freight.

Pleasant beaches line the banks of the slow-moving Volga and provide recreational areas for vacationers. However, the rising levels of water pollution now discourage bathers. Official figures from the Volga-Caspian region suggest that 918 million cubic feet (26 million cubic meters) of mainly untreated sewage and liquid waste are discharged into the Volga every year.

Don

The Volga River winds through Russia on its way to the Caspian Sea. The Volga River Basin is a center of Russian agriculture, industry, and commerce; some of the country's most important manufacturing cities, such as Volgograd and Nizhny Novgorod, stand on its banks. Nine major hydroelectric power stations and several large artificial lakes formed by dams also lie along the Volga.

Tsimlyansk Reservoir

Sea of Azov

Black Sea

The Volga begins in the forested countryside and flows through Tver, *left,* the first major city on its banks. Later, the river is swelled by its many tributaries, including the Oka, the Kama, the Vetluga, and the Sura rivers.

Along the banks of the Volga, the city of Volgograd, once known as Stalingrad, was the site of an important Soviet victory during World War II. Today, the city is a major industrial center and an important stop for traffic on the river.

Pollution problems

In its journey to the Caspian Sea, the Volga passes through some of the most densely populated areas of Russia. Unfortunately, the intensive development of manufacturing, mining, petroleum, and modern agricultural production in the river basin has created serious pollution problems.

Industrial and agricultural activity uses huge amounts of river water, much of which is discharged back into the river. In addition, numerous dams slow the river's flow, reducing its natural ability to purify itself.

Dams also prevent the sturgeon from migrating to its normal spawning ground. The eggs, or *roe,* of these large, freshwater fish are known as *caviar,* one of the region's most famous and valuable food products. To solve the migrating problem, authorities have set up artificial hatcheries, where they produce sturgeon to stock the river.

Moscow

The largest city in Europe and the third largest city in the world, Moscow is the capital of Russia. Moscow lies in the western part of Russia, about 400 miles (640 kilometers) southeast of St. Petersburg. More than 8,775,000 people live in this great city.

From the air, Moscow looks like a huge wheel, with boulevards extending from the center like spokes. Circular roads cross the boulevards, forming inner and outer rims. It is a city of extraordinary cultural spectacles, fascinating historical sights, and breathtaking architecture. From the famous Bolshoi Ballet, whose dancers are considered by many to be the most skilled and graceful in the world, to the huge GUM department store, Moscow dazzles visitors with its many sights and sounds.

An old Russian proverb states, "Above Russia there is only Moscow; above Moscow, only the Kremlin; and above the Kremlin, only God." Many Russian citizens dream of living in this historic city, but the severe shortage of housing means that no one may live there without official permission from the government.

Early history

Moscow was founded in 1147 by Yuri Dolgoruki, a prince of the region. Lying along the banks of the Moscow River, the town grew wealthy and prosperous as a trading center. Then, during the 1200's, the Tatars (Mongols) conquered the area. The Tatars, who were primarily interested in maintaining their power and collecting taxes from the conquered Russian principalities, began to allow the grand prince of Moscow to collect the taxes for them. Ivan I, the prince of Moscow, kept some of the tax money and used it to buy land and expand his territory. As Moscow grew stronger and richer, the Tatars' power grew weaker, and in the late 1400's, Moscow threw off Tatar control.

The city grew rapidly in the 1600's and became the home of the czars. Even after Peter the Great built a new capital at St. Petersburg, Moscow remained an important center of culture, industry, and trade. In 1812, French armies led by Napoleon reached Moscow, but a mysterious fire—believed by some to have been set by the

Muscovite shoppers throng GUM, the largest department store in Russia. This shopping complex, which stands on the site of a historic market, displays goods from all over the country, from clothing to caviar.

Graceful street lanterns tower above the crowded Arbat, *right,* a Moscow street long famous as a gathering place for writers and artists. Before the days of glasnost, the Arbat was a refuge for intellectuals who disagreed with government policies.

Russians themselves—destroyed most of the city.

In 1918, the Bolsheviks moved the capital back to Moscow, and the city was once again the nation's political center. In 1991, Moscow became the center of protests that helped end the coup attempted by conservative Communist officials.

A center for industry and culture

Moscow is the most important industrial city in Russia. Its factories produce a wide variety of products, including automobiles, buses and trucks, chemicals, electrical machinery, measuring instruments, steel, and textiles.

The city's many important educational and cultural institutions include the Lenin State Library, which has one of the largest collections of books and manuscripts in the world. More than 30,000 students attend classes at Moscow State University, whose 37-story science building dominates the city's skyline.

Perhaps the most impressive of Moscow's buildings is the Kremlin, the fortified enclosure within the city. With its many gilded domes, its tapered gate towers, and the contrast between its forbidding walls and the beauty of its interior, it offers one of the most breathtaking sights in the world.

Moscow spreads in rings outward from its historic center along the banks of the Moscow River. This huge metropolis is the focal center of the nation's transportation network, with 11 railways meeting at 9 terminal stations, 13 main highways, and 4 airports. More than 5 million passengers a day travel on the Metro, Moscow's subway system, which has 93 miles (150 kilometers) of track and more than 70 stations, all beautifully maintained and decorated with chandeliers and statues.

The walls of the Kremlin tower over Red Square in the heart of Moscow, *above left.* The Kremlin is a massive fortress housing museums, magnificent palaces, and cathedrals. Its triangular enclosure extends almost 1-1/2 miles (2.4 kilometers) around. The Kremlin's present walls have stood since the late 1400's.

A Moscow street vendor in a fur cap sells tulips. Private enterprise began to flourish in Moscow in the late 1980's as a result of President Gorbachev's policy of perestroika.

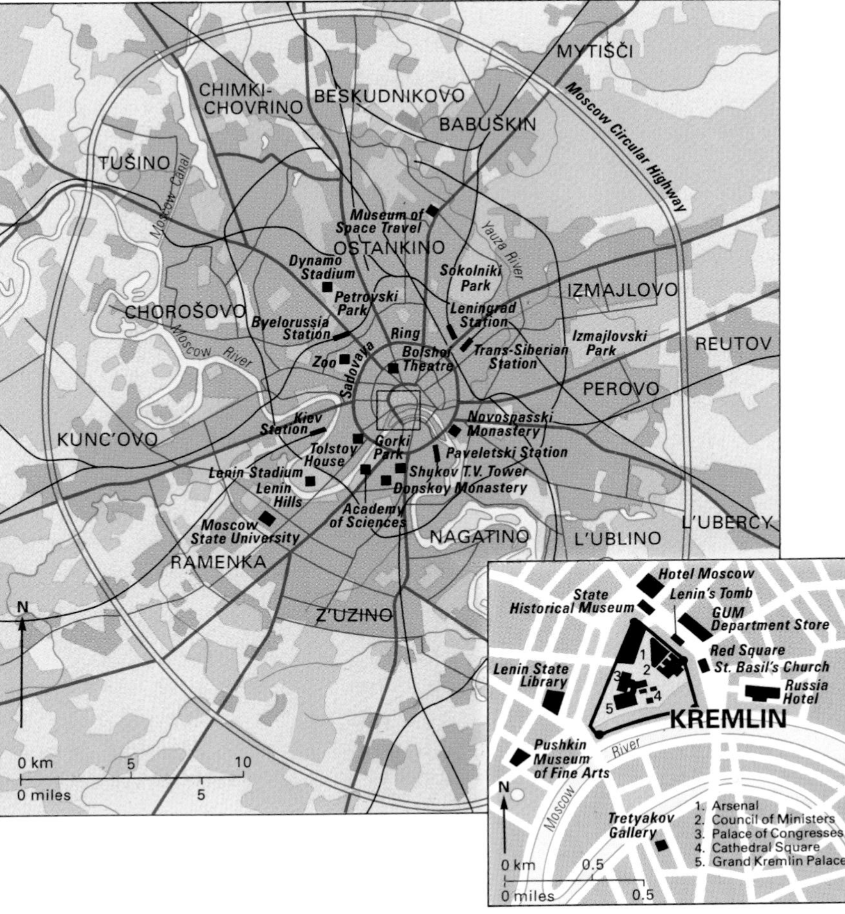

St. Petersburg

St. Petersburg, the second largest city in Russia, lies in the northwestern part of the country, at the eastern end of the Gulf of Finland. A major port and one of the world's leading cultural and industrial centers, St. Petersburg is a magnificent city of luxurious palaces, handsome public buildings, fine museums and theaters, and wide public squares resembling those of the great Western European cities.

From 1924 until 1991, the city had been known as *Leningrad*—after the Communist leader Vladimir I. Lenin. In 1991, however, as Communist influence declined in the country, Leningrad's citizens voted in a nonbinding referendum to restore the city's original name of St. Petersburg. In September 1991, the Soviet government officially approved the change.

Russia's "window to the west"

St. Petersburg was founded in 1703 by Peter the Great as St. Petersburg. Peter the Great, the first Russian czar to visit Western Europe, was impressed by what he saw there, and he returned from his travels determined to bring Western culture and technology to Russia. He promptly ordered the building of a "window to the West"—a city that would serve as a showcase for his efforts to westernize Russian life.

The site he selected—a marshy lowland where the Neva River empties into the Gulf of Finland—was less than ideal. The ground, which consisted entirely of silt, was subject to flooding, and the region also lacked the necessary building supplies of stone and timber. However, Peter saw that the area would provide good river links to the interior if it had a canal system.

Forced laborers, including prisoners of war, were brought in from across the empire to drain the marshes and dig the canals, and French and Italian architects were hired to design and erect buildings and churches. Then Peter forbade the building of stone houses elsewhere in Russia, saying that all the nation's stonemasons were needed in the new city.

The results were astonishing. Where once there was a vast, deserted swampland, there stood a dazzling city whose beauty rivaled that of Paris, London, and Vienna. The city boasted some of the finest examples of baroque and neoclassical architecture in the world. Wide boulevards, known as *prospekts,* had been built along the canals, and splendid palaces outside the city, such as Pavlovsk, Petrodvorets, and Pushkin, became the summer residences for the Russian imperial family.

Peter moved the nation's capital from Moscow to St. Petersburg in 1712, and the new capital soon became the intellectual and social center of the Russian Empire. Many of the greatest Russian writers of the 1800's lived and worked in St. Petersburg, and even today, its residents are proud of their city's cosmopolitan atmosphere and Western outlook.

War and revolution

Over the years, St. Petersburg has served as a backdrop for many of the great events in Russian history. When Russia went to war against Germany at the outbreak of World War I, the city's name was changed

Petrodvorets Palace, located on the outskirts of St. Petersburg and once the summer residence of the Russian czars, was restored to its former splendor after being almost completely destroyed during World War II.

The golden dome of the Cathedral of St. Isaac of Dalmatia, *right,* along with the golden spire of the Admiralty Building and the blue-and-white Hermitage Museum, grace the St. Petersburg skyline. In the distance stand the city's factories.

A single shot from the cruiser *Aurora* opened the October Revolution of 1917, when the Bolsheviks seized power in what was then Petrograd. Moored in the Neva River, the ship now serves as a museum. St. Petersburg's other museums include the Hermitage Museum, world famous for its magnificent works of art.

from St. Petersburg to Petrograd, to avoid the German ending of *burg*. After the February Revolution of 1917, the beautiful Winter Palace in the center of the city became the headquarters of the provisional government.

Only a few months later, the Bolsheviks seized Petrograd during the October Revolution, and they moved the capital back to Moscow in 1918. When Lenin died in 1924, Petrograd was renamed Leningrad. In 1934, Sergey Kirov, a prominent Soviet leader, was assassinated in the city—an event that triggered Stalin's Great Purge.

During World War II, the Germans laid siege to the city from September 1941 to January 1944. About a million people died during the siege, mostly from starvation, and much of Peter the Great's dazzling city was laid in ruins. After the war, however, many beautiful and historic buildings were lovingly restored and rebuilt, and St. Petersburg is once again the spectacular city it was in imperial times.

The afternoon sun casts a golden light over St. Petersburg's elegant Griboyedov Canal, *left*. Graceful old apartment buildings line boulevards called *prospekts*.

St. Petersburg, the first Russian city built in the Western European style, is home to many world-renowned cultural institutions, such as the Russian Museum, which has a large collection of Russian art, and the Kirov Theater, which presents ballet and opera. The Rimsky-Korsakov Conservatory of Music, established in 1862, is the nation's oldest music school, and St. Petersburg's Choreographic School has trained such famous ballet dancers as Vaslav Nijinsky, Rudolf Nureyev, and Anna Pavlova.

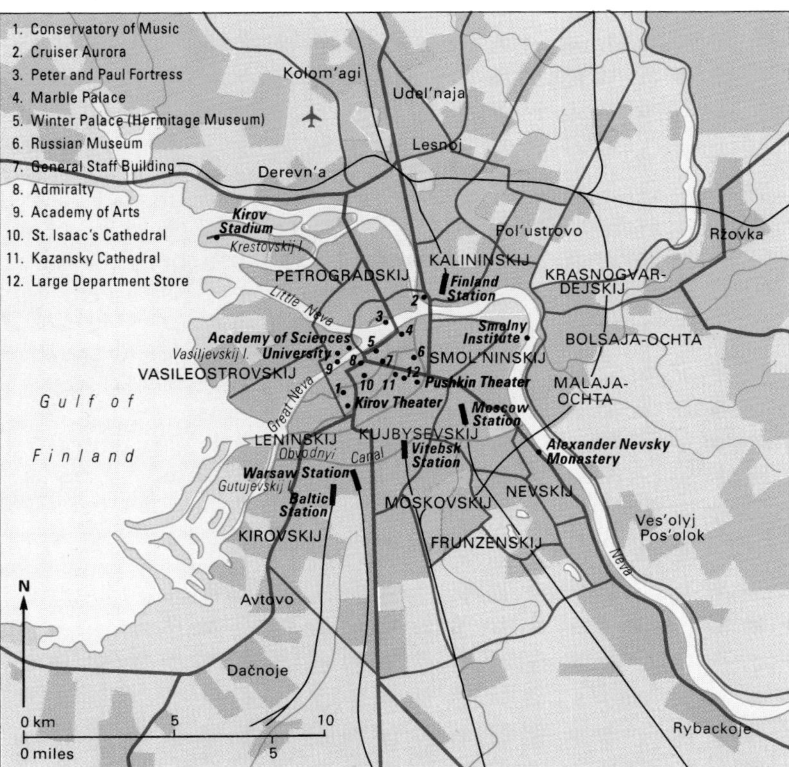

Siberia

A vast, thinly populated region in northern Asia, Siberia covers some 4,929,000 square miles (12,766,000 square kilometers). Bounded by the Ural Mountains to the west, the Pacific Ocean to the east, the Arctic Ocean to the north, and China and North Korea to the south, Siberia is part of Russia. The historical area of Siberia is divided into three economic regions—West Siberia, East Siberia, and the Far East.

The region's abundant natural resources make Siberia extremely valuable to the Russian economy. Oil fields along the Ob River produce a large percentage of the nation's oil, and much of its coal comes from deposits in the Kuznetsk Basin. Siberian forests provide large supplies of timber. In addition, the region has extensive natural gas reserves near the Arctic Circle and around Yakutsk.

Russian rulers once banished millions of criminals and political prisoners to the huge, frozen wilderness of Siberia. Today, its abundant natural resources have made it an important region for mining, logging, oil and gas production, and hydroelectric power. Siberian manufacturing is centered mainly in the Kuznetsk Basin.

Environment

The *tundra*—a cold, dry region where no trees can grow—lies along Siberia's Arctic coasts. The only vegetation consists of mosses, lichens, grasses, low shrubs, and grasslike plants called *sedges*. Few people live in the tundra, and arctic foxes, lemmings, and reindeer roam freely.

South of the tundra, the evergreen forests of the *taiga* stretch from the Urals all the way to the Pacific. The taiga's wildlife includes ermines, lynxes, red foxes, and sables. The *steppes* (grasslands), in the extreme southwest, contain the region's richest farmland.

Siberia's temperatures are among the coldest on earth, and the region's harsh climate has always been a barrier to settlement. Eastern Siberian winters are longer, colder, and drier than winters in the western regions, with January temperatures averaging a bitter −30° F. (−35° C). Along the Pacific coast, the winters are wet and stormy. Siberian summers are brief, with average July temperatures below 75° F. (24° C), and the growing season is short—from 90 to 150 days. In most of eastern Siberia, the ground remains frozen for many months of the year.

Land regions

Siberia's three main land regions are the West Siberian Plain, the Central Siberian Plateau, and the East Siberian Highlands. Extending from the Ural Mountains to the Yenisey River, the West Siberian Plain ranks as the world's largest flat region. Its landscape is broken only by a few *moraine* hills formed from glacial deposits. Because the land is so flat, rain water drainage is poor, and the area is covered with swamps and marshes.

The Central Siberian Plateau lies between the Yenisey and Lena rivers. Because the plateau is cut by deep river valleys, it often appears mountainous—particularly in the north and west, where the rivers have carved steep canyons through thick layers of volcanic rock.

The East Siberian Highlands consist of a series of mountain ranges between the Lena River and the Pacific coast. In the north, the Verkhoyansk Range and the Cherskiy Range form a huge crescent that rises 10,000 feet (3,350 meters) in some areas.

In the northeast, the Anadyr Range and the Koryak Mountains make up the spine of the Kamchatka Peninsula. This peninsula has about 25 active volcanoes, including Klyuchevskaya, the highest point in Siberia at 15,584 feet (4,750 meters). Along the Chinese border to the south, the Yablonovyy and Stanovoy ranges form a rugged highland region that reaches to the Pacific Ocean.

Lake Baikal

Lake Baikal, the world's deepest lake, lies on the southern edge of the Central Siberian Plateau. Although the lake is 395 miles (636 kilometers) long and 49 miles (79 kilometers) wide, its surface is frozen from January to May. The large volume of water in Lake Baikal affects the weather in the area surrounding it. The area nearest the lake is several degrees warmer in winter, and cooler in summer, than places farther away from the moderating influence of the lake.

The Indigirka River, in northeast Siberia, *left,* winds through a landscape of evergreen forests and bogs typical of the taiga. Most of the trees in this region are needleleaf evergreens. Hydroelectric dams on Siberia's rivers provide a small portion of Russia's electric power.

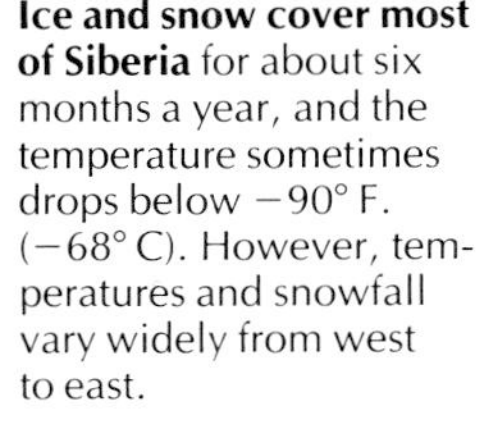

Ice and snow cover most of Siberia for about six months a year, and the temperature sometimes drops below −90° F. (−68° C). However, temperatures and snowfall vary widely from west to east.

A worker repairs a pylon at the Ust-Ilmsk hydroelectric station, *top,* near the outlet of the Bratsk Reservoir, west of Lake Baikal. Development of Siberia's huge mineral and energy resources has been a priority for the Russian government.

People of Siberia

Although Siberia covers about 75 per cent of Russia, only about 22 per cent of the Russian people live there. The region's harsh weather, poor soil, and rugged terrain have long discouraged settlers, and even today Siberia has an average population density of only 6 persons per square mile (2 persons per square kilometer).

Early settlement

A group of Asian nomads called Tatars, led by the Mongol conqueror Genghis Khan, invaded the southern steppes of Siberia in the 1200's and drove the region's original inhabitants into the northern forests. In the late 1500's, the Tatars in southwestern Siberia were conquered by a band of Russian Cossacks.

Gradually, the influence of the Russians spread eastward into the forests. Russian fur traders reached the Pacific coast about 1630, and the settlement of Okhotsk was founded in 1649. By 1700, Russia controlled nearly all of Siberia.

Many of the early Russian settlers were drawn by the profits to be made in trapping the numerous fur-bearing animals of the Siberian forests—particularly sables. Many others migrated to Siberia in hopes of escaping religious persecution and the miserable social and economic conditions in the overcrowded farmlands of European Russia.

Soon the Russian czars began using the Siberian forests as a place of exile for political opponents. After Russia became part of the Soviet Union, Joseph Stalin followed the same policy in the 1930's, banishing millions of Soviet citizens to labor camps in the Siberian wilderness.

Many political exiles were forced to work as laborers in Siberian mines, factories, and construction projects. During World War II (1939-1945), Siberia's population grew as the Soviet government moved hundreds of factories and thousands of workers east of the Urals to protect them from invading German armies. When Stalin died in 1953, the use of forced labor in Siberia ended.

These Buryat women on a collective farm near Ulan-Ude represent one of Siberia's major native groups. The Buryats are descendants of the Mongols and live in their own autonomous republic east of Lake Baikal.

Snow blankets a village near Lake Baikal, *right,* but life for the villagers goes on as usual. Only about 30 per cent of the Siberian people live in rural areas, building simple log houses in the expansive wilderness.

Siberians today

Most present-day Siberians are Russian, and many are descendants of settlers and fur traders who arrived in the 1600's. However, many people whose ancestors were the original inhabitants of Siberia still maintain their old territories and way of life.

The Buryats, a group of North Mongolians, and the Yakuts, who live in eastern Siberia, have their own autonomous republics. About 1,500 Eskimos live on the northeastern tip of Siberia and make their living by herding reindeer, hunting walruses and other animals, and selling carvings and other handicrafts. The Evenki hunt and herd reindeer in the central and eastern Siberian tundra and taiga.

About 70 per cent of Siberia's people live in cities, where they are crowded into small apartments. Many people in rural

Watermelon offered for sale in a market in Irkutsk is imported from warmer regions. Siberian crops consist mostly of barley, oats, and wheat, grown on the southern steppes during the short summer growing season.

High wages lure workers like these Mongolians to Siberia, *left,* but living conditions can be both harsh and tedious. Most of the profits from Siberian products flow west, leaving little behind for developing the area or establishing cultural activities for the people.

Robes and furs protect a Khanty mother and her child from the cold. Most of the Khanty people, also known as Ostyaks, live in the Ob River Basin.

areas live in simple, but more spacious, log houses. Novosibirsk, the largest city in Siberia, has a population of about 1-1/2 million. Other Siberian cities with more than 500,000 people include Omsk, Krasnoyarsk, Vladivostok, Irkutsk, Barnaul, Khabarovsk, Novokuznetsk, and Kemerovo.

Living standards in Siberia are lower than elsewhere in Russia, and many Siberians complain of boredom and a lack of cultural activities. In addition, working conditions in the bitter cold of Siberia are often extremely difficult.

In an effort to attract workers to Siberia, the Russian government has offered high salaries and long vacations, but many people stay only a few years. However, others accept the hardships more readily, knowing that social and professional advancement come more quickly in Siberia than elsewhere in Russia.

The Trans-Siberian Railroad

Just after 10 o'clock every morning, a train known as *Rossiya No. 2* leaves Moscow's Yaroslavl Station for Vladivostok, a port on Russia's Pacific coast. In its seven-day journey across the great Siberian wilderness, the train travels more than 5,000 miles (8,000 kilometers) and crosses seven time zones. Known as the Trans-Siberian Express, it travels along the same route as the original Trans-Siberian Railroad line—the longest railroad in the world.

Construction of the Trans-Siberian Railroad in the early 1900's encouraged the development of trade and industry in Siberia. In the Russo-Japanese War (1904–1905), and during World Wars I and II, the railroad was a valuable asset, providing transportation for troops and supplies across the vast landscape.

Building the railroad

The Trans-Siberian Railroad was the first railroad built across Siberia, a vast region that covers most of the Asian part of Russia. Before the railroad was constructed, the only route across Siberia was a trail of mud and dust in the summer and snow in the winter, traveled by few people except convicts, bandits, and political exiles.

After approving the construction of the great railroad, Czar Alexander III added "Most August Founder of the Great Siberian Railway" to his many titles. Begun in 1891 and finished in 1916, the Trans-Siberian Railroad was built in several sections. The section in eastern Siberia, between Vladivostok and Khabarovsk, was completed about 1897. By 1904, a continuous railroad stretched from Vladivostok across China and Siberia to the Ural Mountains.

However, the Russians wanted a route that did not cross China, so in 1916 they completed a line north of China from Khabarovsk to Kuenga—the last link in a continuous railroad on Russian soil. Since the 1920's, the Trans-Siberian has been joined to other railroads in neighboring republics that once comprised the Soviet Union, and the Trans-Siberian route is now part of the rail network that links this vast territory spanning Europe and Asia.

Prisoners and laborers

In the early years of building the railroad, migrant farmers and peasant settlers provided most of the labor. As construction progressed and more workers were needed, the Railway Committee began using thousands of convicts, social misfits, and political prisoners who had been banished to Siberia. These prisoners earned a reduced sentence in return for their labors.

The work was very difficult, and conditions were both harsh and hazardous. The engineers lacked heavy machinery, and workers had only wooden shovels to break through the frozen ground. Winters were bitterly cold, and during the summer, flies and mosquitoes from the swamps were a constant torment. The railroad workers also had to battle disease, bandits, and even the Amur tiger.

All aboard

The 1914 edition of *Baedeker's Guide to Russia* advised travelers on the Trans-Siberian Railroad ". . . to carry a revolver in Manchuria and on trips away from the railway." While today's passengers no longer need to bring a gun, the accommodations on the Trans-Siberian Express are less than luxurious by Western standards.

Boarding the train, passengers are greeted by a *provodnik*—an attendant whose many duties include making sure passengers are not left behind during stopovers; tending the *samovar* (a coal stove used to heat water for tea); and scraping ice off the steps of the train. Each car in the first-class section has a toilet and washbasin, but washing up can be an awkward experience due to the small size of the area and the constant movement of the train. And all first- and second-class passengers must make up their own berths.

Whistling past a small community in the *taiga*, *below,* a region of vast evergreen forests, the Trans-Siberian Express gives passengers an ever-changing view of life on Russia's vast frontier. For foreign travelers, the train's final stop is the Pacific port of Nakhodka.

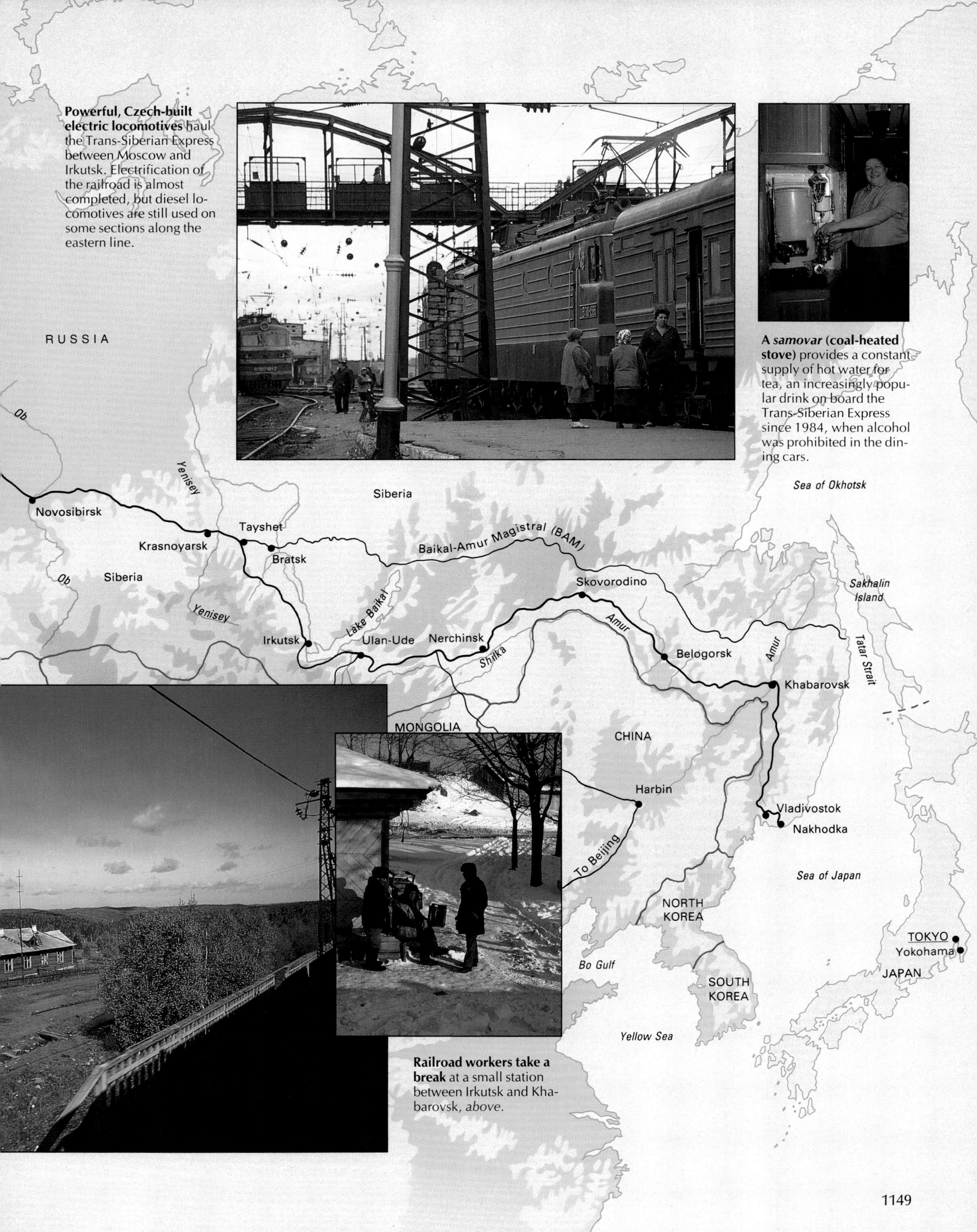

Powerful, Czech-built electric locomotives haul the Trans-Siberian Express between Moscow and Irkutsk. Electrification of the railroad is almost completed, but diesel locomotives are still used on some sections along the eastern line.

A *samovar* **(coal-heated stove)** provides a constant supply of hot water for tea, an increasingly popular drink on board the Trans-Siberian Express since 1984, when alcohol was prohibited in the dining cars.

Railroad workers take a break at a small station between Irkutsk and Khabarovsk, *above*.

Rwanda

Rwanda, a small country in east-central Africa, is one of the most crowded countries on the continent, with an average of 711 persons per square mile (274 persons per square kilometer). Because it has little industry and more people than its small land area can support, Rwanda is also one of Africa's poorest countries.

People and economy

Most Rwandese are farmers, but many can grow only enough food to feed their families. Their food crops include bananas, beans, cassava, sorghum, and sweet potatoes. Some farmers also raise cattle. Before civil war broke out in 1994 the Rwanda government was working toward economic progress in the country. Production of some goods had increased, but Rwanda has few manufacturing industries and no railroads.

About five-sixths of Rwanda's people belong to the Hutu ethnic group. Some Hutu work in urban areas, but many have left Rwanda to seek work in other countries.

About one-sixth of the Rwandese people belong to the Tutsi ethnic group and work in business or government agencies. Pygmies make up less than 1 per cent of the people.

FACT BOX

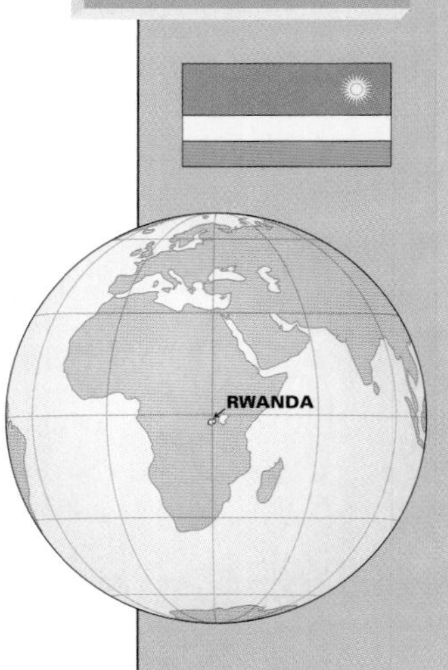

COUNTRY

Official name: Republika y'u Rwanda (Rwandese Republic)
Capital: Kigali
Terrain: Mostly grassy uplands and hills; relief is mountainous with altitude declining from west to east
Area: 10,169 sq. mi. (26,338 km²)
Climate: Temperate; two rainy seasons (February to April, November to January); mild in mountains with frost and snow possible
Main rivers: Rusizi, Kagera, Akanyaru, Nyabarongo, Mwago
Highest elevation: Volcan Karisimbi, 14,826 ft. (4,519 m)
Lowest elevation: Rusizi River, 3,117 ft. (950 m)

GOVERNMENT

Form of government: Republic
Head of state: President
Head of government: Prime minister
Administrative areas: 12 prefectures
Legislature: Assemblee Nationale de Transition (Transitional National Assembly) with 70 members
Court system: Constitutional Court
Armed forces: 37,000 to 47,000 troops

PEOPLE

Estimated 2002 population: 8,063,000
Population growth: 1.14%
Population density: 793 persons per sq. mi. (306 per km²)
Population distribution: 95% rural, 5% urban
Life expectancy in years:
Male: 39
Female: 40
Doctors per 1,000 people: Less than 0.05
Percentage of age-appropriate population enrolled in the following educational levels:
Primary: 114*
Secondary: 9
Further: 1

*Enrollment ratios compare the number of students enrolled to the population which, by age, should be enrolled. A ratio higher than 100 indicates that students older or younger than the typical age range are also enrolled

History and government

Hutu farmers and Pygmy hunters were the first known inhabitants of what is now Rwanda. About 600 years ago, the Tutsi invaded from the north and took control.

Germany conquered the area that is now Rwanda and Burundi—the country to the south—in 1897. Belgium later took control of the region, called Ruanda-Urundi.

The death of the region's king, Mwami Mutara III, in 1959 led to violence. The Hutu rebelled against the Tutsi, and about 150,000 people died. Another 150,000 Tutsi fled. The Hutu then gained control of the government and economy.

In 1961, the people of Ruanda-Urundi voted to make their country a republic, and Ruanda-Urundi became two independent nations—Rwanda and Burundi—on July 1, 1962. Gregoire Kayibanda was elected Rwanda's first president.

Military officers led by Major General Juvenal Habyarimana overthrew Kayibanda's government in 1973, but Habyarimana gradually put civilians back into government positions. Habyarimana was elected president in 1978 and again in 1983.

In April 1994, a suspicious plane crash in which the presidents of Rwanda and Burundi were killed prompted the Hutu-controlled military to kill an estimated 200,000 to 500,000 Rwandans, mostly Tutsi. In July, the rebel Rwandan Patriotic Front proclaimed victory in the civil war.

Fearing rebel reprisals, up to 2 million Hutus streamed across the Rwandan border to Congo (Kinshasa). The exodus triggered a massive humanitarian crisis. In April 1995, the Rwandan government closed all refugee camps in the country and transported refugees home. About 2,000 people were killed when refugees in the Kibeho camp in southwest Rwanda resisted its closure.

In 1998, 22 people were found guilty of organizing and leading the 1994 massacres and were executed.

Acres of crops surround the farm buildings on a palm oil plantation, *far left.* Palm oil is not as important to Rwanda's economy as coffee, which is the nation's chief export.

A colorful headdress is worn by a young woman of the Hutu, an ethnic group that was dominated by the minority Tutsi until 1959.

Languages spoken:
Kinyarwanda (official)
universal Bantu vernacular
French (official)
English (official)
Kiswahili (Swahili)

Religions:
Roman Catholic 65%
Protestant 9%
Muslim 1%
indigenous beliefs

Technology

Radios per 1,000 people: 76

Televisions per 1,000 people: 0

Computers per 1,000 people: N/A

Economy

Currency: Rwandan franc

Gross national income (GNI) in 2000: $1.9 billion U.S.

Real annual growth rate (1999–2000): 5.6%

GNI per capita (2000): $230 U.S.

Balance of payments (2000): -$7 million U.S.

Goods exported: Coffee, tea, hides, tin ore

Goods imported: Foodstuffs, machinery and equipment, steel, petroleum products, cement and construction material

Trading partners: Kenya, Brazil, Germany, Belgium, Tanzania, United States

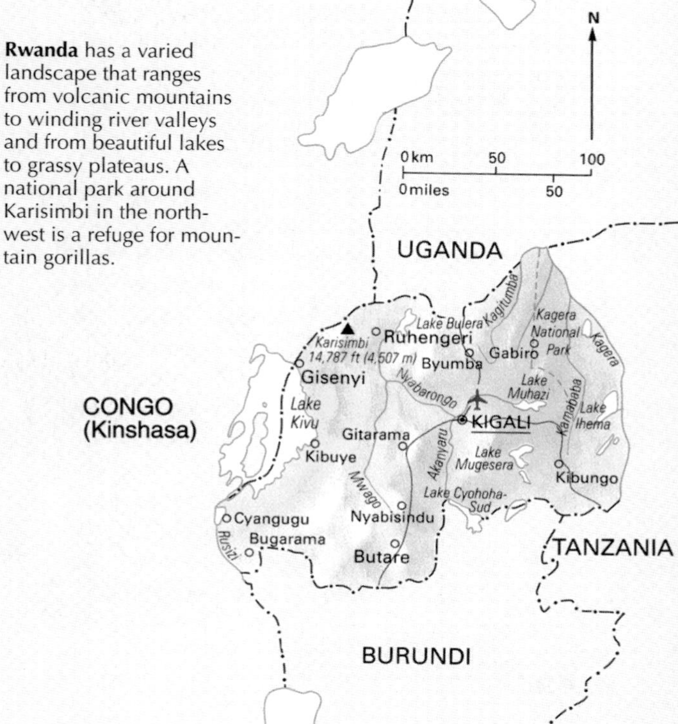

Rwanda has a varied landscape that ranges from volcanic mountains to winding river valleys and from beautiful lakes to grassy plateaus. A national park around Karisimbi in the northwest is a refuge for mountain gorillas.